THE PRISONER LEAPS

PREFACE

THIS is an account of day-to-day life and Christian service in Java, based on diaries written in the heat of the type of warfare which is here described. No liberties have been taken with either facts or characters, except that the names of towns and villages (apart from a few large towns) have been altered, and Javanese people who figure in the book have been given fictitious names. In almost all cases, however, these names are genuinely Javanese, and the reader may find it a useful guide to pronunciation to know that the penultimate syllable should always bear the emphasis. It has been felt best to retain the freshness of the original record even at the cost of an occasional mixture of past and present tenses.

Since a considerable number of people are mentioned in this book and since information about them is not presented systematically but emerges piecemeal as the tale proceeds, I give on pp. 351–352 a list of the Javanese men and women who are actually named, in the order in which they appear. Each is briefly identified and his place of residence indicated. The wives of many of the men play an important role in the story, but they are not separately listed, nor is there any mention of Chinese, nor of Javanese people not distinctly named, although all had their part to play in the unfolding of the drama. The end is not yet and this book has been completed as we are about to look these many friends in the face once more.

DAVID BENTLEY-TAYLOR

DAVID BENTLEY-TAYLOR

THE PRISONER
LEAPS

A Diary of Missionary Life in Java

Jesus shall reign where'er the sun
Doth his successive journeys run;
His kingdom stretch from shore to shore,
Till moons shall wax and wane no more.

Blessings abound where'er He reigns;
The prisoner leaps to lose his chains,
The weary find eternal rest,
And all the sons of want are blest.
                                    ISAAC WATTS

LONDON
CHINA INLAND MISSION
Overseas Missionary Fellowship
AGENTS: LUTTERWORTH PRESS

© China Inland Mission
First printed January 1961

Made in Great Britain

Published by the China Inland Mission,
Newington Green, London, N.16,
and printed by The Camelot Press Ltd.,
London and Southampton

Trade Agents: The Lutterworth Press,
4 Bouverie Street, London, E.C.4

CONTENTS

CHAPTER I

TREASURE IN PRISON

RUFUS took his turn peering through the little square hole in the door of the cell. On the concrete pavement just outside two sentries were playing cards, their guns propped against the wall. The roof projected over them and gave shelter from the rain which had hemmed them in close to their prisoners for the whole afternoon. There were just two tiny cells to guard, each containing eight men. The walls were thick, the only airholes were three-inch slits, nine feet above the ground; both doors were padlocked, and they held the keys and the guns. So it was boring work, with cards and smoking the only diversions.

The unhappy little building was cordoned off by barbed wire, rather to keep the curious at bay than to prevent the prisoners escaping, for not one of them contemplated such folly. Inside the wire the dusty earth was now unprofitable mud, awaiting to-morrow's blazing sunshine to turn it hard and bare again. Beyond the wire, lorries crashed heedlessly through potholes in the road, from which cascades of water fell into the deep ditches which were already swirling torrents heading madly for the stream below the mosque. The weather had driven most people indoors, but now and then a lonely cyclist raced past, his soaking shirt and trousers clinging to his limbs.

Across the road Rufus could see a house standing back among enveloping trees. It gave him a transitory, nostalgic pleasure to catch glimpses of home-life over there. He saw a woman open a door, carry a chair in from the verandah, and shut the door again. Suddenly it seemed to him wonderful to be able to do such glorious things, to possess a chair, to be free to open and shut doors, to move from one room to another. At that moment he would have given all he possessed for such sublime privileges and marvelled that he had not appreciated them more in all the years when he had had them. A little girl came out, her baby brother strapped on to her back. There were pots of flowers standing on the verandah and he caught glimpses of the child moving behind them, trying in vain to keep her in view and see what she was doing. He had children of his own.

It was a weary day in November 1944 and Java was enduring her third year of occupation by the Japanese Army. When they first came storming in, landing unopposed off the tranquil Java Sea on to the low-lying, teeming farmlands of the north coast, it had made little difference to Rufus' life. Although there was not much fighting the invaders soon showed that they were men to be feared and obeyed without question. Their strong, stocky soldiers with ever-threatening bayonets did horrible deeds which froze the blood. Tens of thousands suffered agonies at the hands of the men of the north, before whom the gentle Javanese could not stand; tens of millions, who knew all about it, quailed but did not suffer to the same extent in their own persons, and one of these was Rufus. His home was far away on the south coast and it was some time before any Japanese even reached the district. When they did arrive, the sheer mass of humanity grappling with the rich and co-operative soil was the best protection to any individual. And so it came about that Rufus, though living in the midst of danger and uncertainty, daily plagued by distress of mind, was yet able to continue his normal life and work right into the third year of enemy occupation.

He was a pastor of the East Java Church. Soon after the invasion all Dutchmen were rounded up and interned. There were very large numbers of them, for Java, the heart of the Netherlands East Indies, had been under their control for over three centuries. And that was why Rufus had been educated in Dutch, though from infancy the language of his heart had been his own Javanese. Dutch missionaries had gone into the camps together with their fellow-nationals, and so at a stroke the care of all Christian churches fell to such as Rufus, men of the land who had been trained for the ministry. At a time like that it had not been easy to preach, to advise, to shepherd the flock, to know what could with impunity be done and said and what must be carefully avoided. It was wiser not to make yourself prominent in case the new rulers noticed you, and yet the churches needed leadership and Rufus knew that the hand of God was upon him and that he could not shirk the responsibilities of the hour. Happily he was by nature inconspicuous, an ordinary man, ordinary in appearance and in abilities, not obviously dangerous or significant, just a Javanese of the Javanese. And so he passed quietly on his way, living in a village far removed from any city, happy in his own family with wife and children, busy day by day visiting the sick and elderly, taking church services on Sundays, baptising, marrying, burying—until suddenly he was plucked away.

The summons had seemed innocuous enough. Everybody had had to register themselves with the new authorities and Rufus was no stranger to long queues of timid people standing all day in sun and rain, tramping back home disconsolate at night and reassembling for the same unprofitable vigil early the next morning, till at last they reached a room and a desk and were thankful if they emerged without blow or wound. And so he had gone without any particular forebodings. After a wait of only two hours he had been called in and his identity checked. Then all his belongings were taken from him, his clothes removed except for shirt and trousers, and he had been escorted across to the cell in which he had been ever since.

Three weeks had passed since that dismal hour and he wondered whether his wife knew that he was alive. His deepest bitterness was the thought of what she would be suffering at his disappearance. That was one reason why he liked to take his turn regularly at the tiny square hole in the door: passers-by on the road almost always looked over at the cells and although only his eyes, nose, and mouth were visible he hoped that someone might recognise him and carry the news home fifty miles away. In fact, although he knew it not, this had already happened. Nearly all Javanese pastors were being arrested at that time so that Christians everywhere had an eye for prisoners and were quick to get news back where it was most needed.

Rufus yielded his place at the door and sat down again on the floor of the cell, leaning his back against the wall. There were no seats of any kind, just the walls and the floor and dim light reflected through the high slits. It was chilly after the heavy rain outside, for none of them had many clothes. Now and then they got cigarettes by permission of the guards, who were Javanese like themselves. Down the road there was a woman who cooked for prisoners and sent the food along in baskets by her daughter, rice and a little vegetable, not much, but enough to stave off real hunger.

Darkness succeeded the rain. Traffic ceased on the road outside. The guards were changed and the new ones, on duty for the night, peered through the hole in the cell doors, shining a torch in to count the prisoners. Rufus and his companions covered almost all available floor space as they slept; being countrymen they were accustomed to taking their rest in their working clothes and without the luxuries of mattress or sheets.

Soon after dawn there was a clicking of rifle breeches on the road outside the wire. The prisoners rose to their feet as the key turned in the lock and the door swung open, letting in a flood of light and air. Rufus stepped out quickly, glad to seize every moment of respite. Sixteen men formed up in two lines inside the wire; two guards were there with them and across the road four others stood with rifles at the ready. The wire gate was opened and the procession shuffled off down the road to have their daily bath in the stream beside the mosque. The guards, uniformed and booted, were all round them; the prisoners, barefoot and subdued, meandered along as slowly as seemed wise. When they reached the stream the guards stood on the road and the bridge while the men took off their clothes and went into the water, squatting down in it, splashing it over themselves, and rubbing their bodies. The sun shone powerfully down through the coconut palms; men and women trudging to market scarcely seemed to notice the accustomed sight; farmers working in the fields did not look up; children going to school clutched their satchels and chattered their own affairs. For Rufus it was always the best moment in the day, the nearest approach to freedom and a normal life; at home they had no other bathroom but the nearest stream, so he was just doing what he always did.

After five minutes the men came out of the water, pulled on their two garments apiece, lined up again and started the two hundred yards' stroll back to the cells. As they did so they passed a group of Japanese soldiers off duty, laughing and ragging at the roadside. Paying no attention to the file of prisoners, one of the men backed away from his fellows in their fun and bumped into Rufus; he immediately swung round and lashed out at him with his heavy boot. Rufus took the kick just below the right knee. Involuntarily he let out a scream of pain and fear, as he lurched among his fellows, but the file moved on, the soldier paid no further attention to him, and a moment later they were back at the cells. Again the guards stood across the road with their rifles. The prisoners passed through the wire. One man entered each cell with a broom, swept it out, put the broom against the outer wall, and then the rest filed in, the two guards inside the wire closed and locked the doors, pocketed the keys, and settled down to cards once more. Rufus lay on the floor of his cell nursing his leg while the others sympathised with him. He tried to find a more comfortable position in which to lie, but there was none to be had. It was swelling already and very painful. There was nothing to do but bear it. Now even the daily walk to the stream would be a nightmare. He lost his desire to stand at the hole in the door and just lay in hopelessness and uncertainty. But this he knew, that God was with him. He was in that cell because he was a Christian minister and for no other reason; he might have repudiated his faith when it was so dangerous to confess it, but he had not done so. Therefore the invaders regarded him as associated with the Dutch, for they considered Christianity to be the religion of the Dutch and of their other European enemies. So his misery was for Christ's sake and Christ would not desert him.

But he was tempted to wonder if Christ had not in fact done so when still more evil days arrived. He had been moved to a larger prison and one day his name resounded down the bleak, stone corridor. The door was unlocked, but not for bathing. He limped down between his escorts, and when he limped back at night he

had been through the bitterest experience of his life—beaten, off
and on, for seven hours. The next day came the same call, "Rufus,
Rufus", and the same unrelieved horror. Nor was that the end.
But after five days he knew that the end was very near. So far as
he could think at all he believed that his hour had come and that the
Lord was about to dispense with his feeble efforts upon earth and
remove him to heaven. He was not sorry either, only grieved
beyond words to think of his wife and his children, grieved to tears
and agony of mind, yet not to fury, for he was not a man given
to fury.

But that fatal call was not repeated. High over Hiroshima a plane
was circling, and Rufus was one of the countless millions whose
lives were saved by that much-maligned atomic bomb. There was
a slight easing in the gaol in Java and beatings ceased. He had not
yet recovered from his vicious ordeal when he found himself
dazed with joy mounting the steps on to a verandah, his own
verandah, seeing the door open and a woman come rushing out,
his own wife. And behind her came a little girl with her baby
brother on her back, his own children. And so he was not deserted
after all.

But neither did he live happily ever afterwards. For a while he
continued the same steady round of worthy work which had been
his before the war. He visited, he preached, he baptised, he married,
and he buried, but the total effect of his labours was not particularly
impressive. He was generally liked by the churches he served, for
he had a way of endearing himself to people, but he did not cause
any radical changes for the better. His sermons were always read
from full manuscript, for that was how he had been taught to deliver
them; he devoted much time to their preparation, yet they came
out as essays, orthodox and Biblical in their way, but not very
striking and above all not gripping or transforming in their effect.
At times his comparative ineffectiveness worried him for he
remembered the triumphant crusade of the early Church recorded
in the Acts of the Apostles, but such heights seemed beyond his
reach. And middle-age was coming on. Worst of all, as their family
increased, his wife became more hard-worked than ever and she
seemed to have less interest in his work than of old; it was not so

much something she shared and supported as something she tolerated because there was no other course open to her.

And then the unbelievable happened. He had been transferred to a new district and a new church, but from the moment of his arrival there was deep-seated trouble and division among the Christians for whom he was responsible. Some welcomed him with eagerness, but others repudiated him altogether and it seemed impossible to bring the two groups together. He tried to do it, but while his friendships deepened so did the animosities. In the end his opponents prevailed, his actions were misrepresented, and eventually he was handed over to the police by his own congregation as a malefactor.

Once more he was on the wrong side of that little square hole in the door. Once more he heard the click of breeches and suffered the ignominy of being marched under armed guard to his daily bath. But this time there was an underlying bitterness which he now realised had been absent before. His first imprisonment had been part of the national enslavement to the Japanese, it had been shared by many others, it had been directly occasioned by his profession as a Christian minister, by his loyalty to Christ. But the second was personal; no one else shared his predicament; in the whole history of Christianity in Java he could not recollect hearing of any other pastor who had been put in prison by his congregation. He wondered if it was partly due to his own mishandling of the situation. And his wife, instead of being whole-heartedly with him, rather blamed him this time. "When you come out," she had said, "let's do something else in life. I've had enough of the church. It has twice led to you being in prison and me having to look after the family alone." In his heart he knew that her attitude was wrong, that what she was saying was the very temptation which he must resist, and yet he could not blame her for feeling like that. What she said was true, and moreover twice a week she had to walk ten miles each way to bring him food. This long journey was a sore trial to her, but for his sake she did it faithfully, even though she knew that not all the food she carried would get past the guards. His name had been taken off the roll of ministers; he was getting no salary; and one of the children was sick. This made a bus, a taxi, or a cart

out of the question, she simply had to walk. They could not
see each other alone and, while he looked forward immensely
to their meetings, they were always brief and unsatisfactory;
she was invariably tired, and news of the children was often
not good. Furthermore he was shut up with real criminals
this time. His companions were not farmers who had had
the misfortune to come to the notice of the Japanese military,
but law-breakers apprehended by their own Javanese police,
robbers, would-be murderers, evil and godless men without
exception.

Living with such people day by day made Rufus realise afresh
how fortunate he had himself been. Sitting on the floor of the cell
he had plenty of time to think back to his home and his parents.
He had been born in a Christian village, not a Muslim village turned
Christian, but an entirely new community consisting only of those
who acknowledged Christ, established by migration of believers in
the nineteenth century. The village was close to the sea but separated from it by a steep ridge of jungle-covered mountain so forbidding that he had not often been to the shore. And that was
partly because the village, though well above sea-level, was itself
on another shore, the shore of a huge swamp, a great mountain-girt
lake at high altitude, so shallow that you could wade in most parts
of it, and thus it came to be covered with houses and villages built
on stilts above the water. Between the jungle crag and the city
swamp, on a narrow rib of land, he had been born in a humble
house under the waving palms. His father, who was the village
schoolmaster, had him baptised at once and from childhood he
heard Bible stories; he had never known any faith but the Protestant
Christian faith. His environment had been Christian from the very
first, and when his father died before he himself reached manhood
the family and all their friends had been comforted by the knowledge that this good man, teacher of boys and servant of Christ, was
with the Lord for ever where the righteous shine like the stars in the
kingdom of their Father. Then came the long struggle when he and
his mother had spent themselves to bring up the younger children,
followed by his successful application to enter the ministry of the
East Java Church, the years at a seminary, ordination, marriage, and

a succession of pastorates. Broken only by the nightmare of his imprisonment under the Japanese it had all been a steady story of noble development. He had not gone astray nor fallen into sin. He had stood for God, for Christ, for His Church, and for righteousness, just as his father had done. It was a fine inheritance and as he looked around in the cell he was not in the least ashamed of it. He did not envy these poor men reared in another religion, acknowledging God but living devoid of the power of God, lost in this world's darkness, the slaves of sin, as ruined in their own hearts as in their family lives. He was genuinely thankful to God that his own lot had been cast in a Christian village which had given him not only good and wholesome things but a purified heart and a happy home.

None the less this tremendous difference in upbringing and background from these unfortunates who were yet his own people and his own race made him feel awkward in their presence. Of course he had met plenty of non-Christians before, but he had never been compelled to live with them week after week like this. As he listened to their conversation and came to know the level of their lives he felt profoundly sorry for their predicament. He began to feel that he ought to be able to say something to them. Though they were not members of his congregation, not officially his pastoral responsibility, yet daily proximity laid upon him a sense that he had a duty to help them. As a fellow-prisoner and a pastor without salary there was no material aid he could offer. The help he saw they needed was not of that order at all. These men were bad inside, it was their hearts that were dark, and hence of course their deeds were dark too. It was help in the inner man they needed. And it was help in the inner man that he knew he was supposed to be able to give. But he was not too sure how to approach them or what to say. His own wave-length was the Christian village wave-length, but now he was far from any such atmosphere. Here in prison was no neat village church, no bell tolling to service, no familiar hymnbook, no knowledge of the life of Christ or the stories of the Old Testament. How was he even to begin to get near the hearts of men whose plight he could see but had never experienced? What was it they really needed? What was it he ought to be giving

them? He was sure he should know the answer, yet he was equally
sure that it was beyond him.

Day by day in the cell his meditations ran this way. The same
thoughts went chasing through his head in the daily strolls to the
stream. Gradually the answer took clear shape in his mind. What
these men needed was Christ, Christ Himself. There was plenty of
religion in the land. What they needed was not more religion, not
even a superior religion, but power to subdue their own evil hearts
and to order their lives according to the will of God. And yet
even power was not quite the right word, not personal enough
—yes, that was it, they needed a person, a superior Person,
none other than Christ. It was Jesus Christ that he ought to be
giving them. That was the essence of his calling as a Christian
minister.

The thrill of this discovery, this rediscovery of something previously known and acknowledged in a vague and indistinct way,
transformed his prison cell. He began to see that there was purpose
behind God's strange ways with him. He even started to enjoy the
barren floor and the cheerless nights. This was his school, the school
to which God had sent him so that he might learn the gospel anew.
He said nothing as yet, because he wanted to think it all out more
clearly. After a decade in the ministry the doctrines of Christianity
were not strange to him. He had never denied them, only in some
indefinable way, connected with his own very familiarity with
them from childhood, he had not strongly felt them nor vividly
enjoyed them. The forgiveness of sins, for instance, had been a truth
he could never properly explain. For him it was a valid idea, but
blurred, and even years of theological study had not really enlightened him. But sitting in the darkness of the cell while others slept,
divorced from his New Testament but remembering many of its
sayings, he needed no instructor other than the Holy Spirit to
connect the forgiveness of sins with the death of Christ upon the
cross. "Because He died I can be forgiven", he said, half aloud, and
then peering across the outlines of his companions he stretched his
hand towards them and added over and over again, "and so can
they, for He loved them too."

The cell had been his school and now it became his pulpit. He

never really knew whether any of those unfortunate men turned
from their sin to Christ because of what he said, but he himself
derived immense benefit and encouragement from speaking to
them. The effort crystallised his new convictions. And he at once
observed that although his congregation was in this case unable to
avoid him, yet there was something in them which responded to
his message and welcomed it. They did not need to tell him in
words that their hearts were hungry for comfort and hope. The
news that there was a Saviour aroused their interest. Nor did they
rebel openly against the name of Jesus. It was a surprise to him to
notice the welcome his words had, even from these men who were
not the best specimens of Javanese society. It struck him that if
people of this sort were not inclined to repudiate the gospel then it
was probable that the mass of more respectable and honest folk
might be ready to receive it too.

And then release came. It was as though God decided he could be
graduated now. But this time he went home with more misgivings
than in 1945, for he remembered his wife's frame of mind and the
ignominy and distress through which she had passed. He had prayed
often for her and he believed there was a possibility that her attitude
would soften now that he was free again. The moment he met her
he felt in his heart that it was so. At first he said nothing about the
things that he had learnt in prison, till one night when the children
were asleep they had a long talk about the future. His health was not
good, two of the children were ailing, and he had neither work nor
salary, but they agreed together that they would trust the Lord to
see them through and that, even though the Christian ministry
seemed closed to them at the moment, they would not turn to
another way of life. While he recuperated a friend allowed them to
live in a tiny bamboo shack beside his own house. They were still
in the same village where the congregation had handed him over
to the police, but time and adversity had won them much sympathy. The feeling that Rufus had been unjustly accused and dis-
gracefully maligned grew to a general conviction. When the rice
harvest was reaped so many people set aside sheaves for him that
half the shack was filled with grain. Others brought vegetables; his
host told him to help himself to the fruit trees; and so there passed

a quiet year, during which he was not fit for active life, but at the end of which he and his family stood high in the esteem of the community. He was reinstated on the roll of the ministers of his church, and invited to go as pastor to the Christian village of Karangan, on the Indian Ocean.

CHAPTER 2

THE WAY TO JAVA

1956. April 28th. The sun has shone all day upon the Bay of Biscay —calm, studded with ships to east and west—and gone down as we reached Cape Finisterre. Being alone I have felt rather an oddity. Accommodation on board is meagre, just the bar and one small lounge. There are a hundred and fifty tourist passengers and my first impression is that there are not many Christians among them, although I noticed a girl in Salvation Army uniform when we were boarding at Southampton. I plunged at once into the study of the Indonesian language.

I am sharing a cabin with one Simpson, bound for Penang, who tells me that he has been led astray in the bar by old friends and has been fast asleep ever since. At tea I found myself alongside an Arabian police officer. He explained to me that in London he had found the problem of eating meat rather difficult, since animals were not killed facing Mecca, nor with utterance of the name of God, nor with any certainty that the blood had not flowed back into the body. Coming across me later on deck he said confidentially, "Is there any command in the Bible not to eat pork?" Punctuating my answer with two games of table tennis, I endeavoured to relate Leviticus 11:7, "The swine is unclean to you", to 1 Timothy 4:4-5, "Every creature of God is good, and nothing to be refused, if it be received with thanksgiving, for it is sanctified by the word of God and prayer." His notion was that all religions are basically the same and since Islam and Judaism prohibit pork it is probable that Christianity does the same. Although the Muslim fast month began on April 11th he has postponed observing it till he gets back to Arabia. He admitted that he had not kept the five times of prayer regularly in England either, but told me that he had just rebuked an Egyptian for drinking on board the ship. He is a very charming, cultured, sparkling man. I alluded to Christ and said that Christianity addressed itself to the heart and the heart's sinfulness.

Sunday, *April 29th*. Early in the morning, while I was walking up and down the deck reading the New Testament, I came across the Arabian again and showed him some verses in Mark 7, "There is nothing from without a man that entering into him can defile him, but those things which come out of him, those are they that defile the man. . . . For from within, out of the heart of men, proceed evil thoughts. . . ." Although there was no one else around he was very nervous at looking into a Bible in public.

There was a packed attendance at the ship's service but it seemed to me that the Captain felt embarrassed and out of place in conducting it. Although I had been singularly unsuccessful in finding anyone else among the passengers who seemed likely to stand with me, with the possible exception of the rather elusive Salvation Army girl, I decided to approach the purser and ask if a Sunday evening service could be arranged on deck. Lined up behind several others who wished to speak to him, I overheard the lady in front of me make precisely the same request for an evening service. She proved to be one of a party of four women missionaries bound for Africa. They were very pleased to have a man to support them and we decided to run a Sunday School as well as an evening service. Almost fifty children came to the Sunday School, which we divided into classes. I myself addressed twenty-five who were over seven years old and from that moment found myself delightfully known and welcomed by all the children on board. Fifteen people came to the evening service on the tourist deck, several of them Indians, while another ten listened from a discreet distance. I preached on the text, "This is a faithful saying and worthy of all acceptation that Christ Jesus came into the world to save sinners." It did me good to utter the gospel, to feel that the Christian colours had been displayed and that those not ashamed to confess the name of Christ had begun to find one another. We agreed to hold a fellowship meeting each evening.

Seeing a man wearing a clerical collar I invited him to our evening meeting. "No, I shall not be coming," he said pleasantly, explaining that he was a Roman Catholic priest. "What firm are you in?" he added. I told him that I was a missionary, but he made no comment. And the sea gave us one of its glorious displays as at sunset we reached Cape St Vincent. Like a track runner rounding a bend our Captain skimmed past only a few hundred yards from the rocks, so that the lighthouse keeper switched on his beam as if to warn us clear. Most magnificent is the rampart Portugal presents to the Atlantic breakers. As far as the eye could see in both directions sheer cliffs rose hundreds of feet from the waves in serried array. At the foot of the lighthouse a cross stood out vividly on the whitewashed wall, a church on one side of it and a convent-like fortress on the other. Beyond the cape its twin, Sagres Point, home of Henry the Navigator, stood equally grim and magnificent in the now slightly oriental light.

Trafalgar passed in the night, but I was on deck alone to enjoy Tarifa, the southern tip of Europe, where the Muslims crossed in A.D. 710. Africa was in sight and the Pillars of Hercules, Gibraltar and Mount Ares. We anchored in that perfect Bay of Algeciras where the hills of Andalusia stand respectfully back from the Rock, as if acknowledging it to be one of the wonders of the world.

"People like to kiss my hand," said the Arabian, a descendant of the prophet Muhammad. "I try to stop them but they explain that it is not me personally they are honouring." An Indian chemist, homeward bound from Chicago, hailed me, under the impression that I was an American. He asked what business was taking me to Java and then said impudently, "I see, you preach, but don't practise, eh?" He thought the West stood more in need of religion than the East. I maintained that both alike needed Christ. In the dining-room I sit at a table with an Irish scientist and an Indian lawyer and today the fourth and vacant seat was taken by Marigold, an English girl, who apparently observed that I was travelling alone. "Do you spend your time maintaining converts or making them?" she asked when she learnt that I was a missionary. The scientist suggested to me that the Reformation was due to Henry VIII desiring a divorce; although in general a very intelligent man he is grossly ignorant where Christianity is concerned.

May 1st. The Mediterranean, free from that strong Atlantic swell, welcomed us with perfect calm and idyllic sunshine, while the Captain has done his utmost to make the journey a sightseeing cruise. He took the liner so close to Algiers that we could hear men whistling at us from the shore and for hours since I have sat on deck inspecting these delightful Algerian mountains at closest possible range—towns and villages, farms and castles, rivers coming out to wrap the ship in their muddy embrace, terraced fields climbing the slopes beside the sea and the valleys in between the ranges. No wonder the Romans liked North Africa. We are nearing Augustine's diocese now. "Never knew there was no land in these parts before," said the deck steward. At night, when the children were all in bed, we held in the ship's nursery the first of our Christian fellowship meetings. I was in the chair amidst eight noble ladies.

May 2nd. It turned rough off Tunisia and for twenty-four hours a roaring wind has pushed us along and heavy seas rolled us about. In the Bay of Tunis we passed close under Zembra Island, an astonishing slab of rock not unlike Gibraltar, rising sheer to perhaps 800 feet. Forbidding Cape Bon followed, where Rommel's Afrika Corps surrendered.

At tea a grey-haired Czech from Chile joined me. I had observed him on Sunday night listening to me at a respectful distance. He introduced himself as a merchant on his way to India but confessed that he was primarily seeking spiritual truth. A rubber planter from Malaya sat with us and listened in silence to all that followed. Stimulated by the fact that there seems to be no other man on board to give supporting fire I spoke as firmly as possible about sin and salvation and said that Christ alone could satisfy the human heart. He found this rather intolerant and suggested that Krishna would do equally well, Christ being only one of many manifestations of God. Shortly afterwards two turbaned Sikhs from the Punjab drew their chairs up to mine. They had just spent six months in my home town in England, but their English was very limited and they had difficulty in understanding what I tried to say about the Lord. It is hard to assess the value of these encounters, yet what can one do but shoot at each target which presents itself and then pray? Any number of people are most friendly and initiate conversation with me. Each evening I play violent games of deck tennis with men in the police in Malaya.

Late in the day we came to Gozo and Malta, bleak and dusty. Then came Valetta and the Grand Harbour, switching on its lights. The weather was very rough and I thought of St Paul's ship wrecked so long ago on this treeless coast. Crossing the deck became an adventure; piles of plates went smash; deck-chairs careered against the rails; books tumbled to the floor in the cabin. Four Indians, members of the Mar Thoma Church, came to our evening fellowship meeting. "Don't you dance?" asked another Indian as we struggled to climb the stairs against the roll, but his capacity for listening to my answer proved very limited. Wine spilt in the lounge. A blazing planet shone calmly down upon the heaving ship. A short, stout man crashed to the deck before me, purple in the face, but he recovered in a few minutes, saying that his cigarette smoke had choked him. "A whole gale" was the Captain's description of what had struck us as we rolled through 21 degrees. "What happens if she fails to right herself?" an elderly lady asked him. I was one of a group invited to his cabin before supper. I found him an attractive character, free and easy, though he was careful to give me not the slightest opportunity to allude to the gospel all evening. Since I am not much good at talk of wines, cigarettes, and perfumes, and had to keep refusing cocktails, champagne, sherry and liqueurs, I fear I was hardly his idea of a good guest. It has been difficult to rest well these nights rolling on the deep. We are eight days out and about 3000 miles from home.

May 4th. This evening an Anglican missionary, a priestly kind of man, drew me aside and confided that he felt unhappy about coming any more to the fellowship meeting. "I belong to the strictest sect of the Church of England," he said. Although not yet ordained he aims to become a monk. We leant over the rail and chatted for half an hour and I asked him when he had found Christ as his personal Saviour. "I never have," he replied. He seemed glad to talk and so I spoke to him quite freely about the necessity for a personal relationship to Christ. He said he could not attend the meetings because "I am bound by the Thirty-Nine Articles". Since he held a Prayer Book in his hands I asked him to show me the

Articles which bound him. Into this trap he fell headlong and we read together several of the admirable statements of evangelical truth contained in the Articles, none of which gave any support to what he was maintaining. He became harassed and repeatedly apologised that he could not share in our simple meetings, admitting that it was too bad and he really ought to be able to do so. Perhaps I was wrong to corner him as much as I did, but the statement he had made suggested to me that he had never properly thought out his position. There were fourteen of us at the meeting in the nursery that night, including the four Indian men of the Mar Thoma Church. One of them, a doctor and a very forceful character, kept on quoting the Bible and speaking about the Lord Jesus Christ, which got him into difficulties with the two pastors of his own church, who had come up from playing cards to join us. By 10 p.m. the sea was dead calm off the Nile Delta, and I paraded the deck in the cool of the night with the Arabian, who gave me a most interesting account of part of his homeland, especially the problem of Indians getting all the best jobs and of English officials whose knowledge of Arabic was not good enough for them to enter into the feelings of the local people.

May 5th. We reached Port Said at dawn and I joined a conducted tour of the city, whose size and beauty surprised me. The railway station makes most of its kind in England look like slums. We visited a magnificent mosque made of stone from Upper Egypt; it contained a 310-light chandelier from Czechoslovakia, enormous Persian carpets, a wide green frieze of texts from the Koran, and a small annex at the end furthest from Mecca for the women. We were also taken to the Roman Catholic Church of Mary, Queen of the World, an equally impressive building; it was all Mary, Mary, Mary, with the figure of Christ in a side-chapel. We passed through the Suez Canal at night, each ship with its headlights on. At sunset I watched a turbaned member of our crew standing alone on deck gazing out over the unprofitable Plain of Pelusium as he went through his prayers and prostrations. He got the direction of Mecca a bit wrong and was headed more towards Jerusalem.

May 6th. At dawn we were in the Gulf of Suez and our admirable Captain took us very close to the desolate mountains and islands

on the western shore. As we debouched into the Red Sea proper
we ran under the jagged peaks of Shadwan Island, scorched and
fruitless, its broad watercourses devoid of the slightest trickle, the
incarnation of unprofitable sterility. And on the other side we saw,
as clearly as one is ever likely to from the sea, the equally forbidding
peaks of Sinai.

Hot sun and cool bathing competed with the Sunday School;
but twenty-five children came and there were as many adults
eavesdropping. At the evening service on the tourist deck the
congregation numbered twenty and we induced one of the Mar
Thoma pastors to take it. He used the liturgy diffidently but
preached firmly, though in a rather stiff manner about God's great
act in Christ and our response to it.

May 7th. And then another missionary suddenly appeared among
the tourist passengers. I can only suppose that excessive shyness has
enabled him to remain concealed for ten days. We have also discovered two Baptist ladies in the first class. With these reinforcements our nightly meeting rose to an attendance of twenty. One
of the Mar Thoma pastors gave an excellent account of his most
ancient church.

May 8th. The darkness of night and heat-haze by day blotted
out the southern end of the Red Sea and we slipped through the
Strait of Bab-el-Mandib—the Gate of Affliction—without seeing
land until we reached the fierce mountains surrounding the huge
refinery at Little Aden and anchored for a few hours at Tawahi.
I got a taxi and drove for six miles to one of Aden's hospitals where
the head male nurse took me round the wards filled with 400 men
and women from Aden Colony and Protectorate, the Yemen, and
Saudi Arabia. Then Dr Fawdry drove me out of Aden across the
long sandspit to the oasis of Sheikh Othman, all scorched and dried
under five hours' rain per year. In the oasis camels stood parked
like cars and the oldest part of the town is a forbidding village on a
mound with bleak outer walls and tiny high windows. Back in
Aden we passed a dreadful mass of squalid mat sheds, four feet
high, swarming with humanity like flies on a refuse heap. They
were pilgrims from further east, Mecca-bound. To the passing
stranger the waterless heat of Aden seemed awful—boys and men

fast asleep on pavements and steps, grim houses, crowded alleys, no
women visible save the very old, and all this set amidst towering,
merciless, pinnacles of rock. But I freely admit that the passing
stranger is not well placed to arrive at a proper understanding of
anything. At Aden I lost my Arabian friend and several missionaries
disembarked en route to Africa.

May 11th. Unruffled seas, negligible wind, and stuffy cabins have
shrouded the ship's company in inertia and boredom since leaving
Aden. At night there are whist drives—men's first prize a bottle of
whisky, ladies' first prize a bottle of gin—notwithstanding, the
Christian fellowship continues each evening. I stroll through the
bar to get and to return the key of the nursery, a large Bible
under one arm, and am regarded (I think) as the unofficial padre, the
others being "your flock". Anyway they have asked me to be a
judge of the fancy dresses at the Gala tonight.

It is the nearest I have been to attending a dance for many years.
Marigold, having repeatedly failed to get a rise out of me, most
graciously and humbly enquired whether I would be offended if she
transferred to another table for the occasion. I joined an Englishman
who, in answer to my enquiries, explained that he was not married
and that he preferred to hire a wife when he needed one. The ship
was handsomely decorated and the Captain made a speech. Later I
sat on the dias with the Indian lawyer, an Irish belle, and a Chinese
lady to judge the very excellent fancy dress parade. The learned
lawyer was quite hopeless at it and in the end all three of them just
copied my result card.

May 12th. My cabin companion, Mr Simpson, has been in a deep
sleep all day as an aftermath of the Gala. I sat beside him studying
Indonesian. Towards sunset we met in the wide spaces of the
Arabian Sea another liner westward bound. Both ships hove to and
a lifeboat transferred to us a couple of stowaways from Bombay.
Everyone lined the rails in the afterglow, with Venus and the crescent
moon as additional spectators. Then both ships uttered long blasts
of greeting and returned each other to the vast and lonely sea. Our
final Christian fellowship meeting was led by the Salvation Army
girl, who told us about the manifold activities of the Army, but it
transpired that one of the Mar Thoma pastors knew more about the

THE WAY TO JAVA

movement than she did, for he had married a Salvationist and was an enthusiast for their work.

May 13th. This was our third Sunday at sea and as usual I was arrested by children on deck at 8 a.m. and told them a Bible story. When I had finished a boy of eight suddenly said, "I asked Jesus into my heart last night." But in the main the company is fully occupied with drinking, flirting, and sleeping; interest in anything more serious has sagged with the heat. I am now more isolated than I was, for the long, gay evenings have knit people into pairs and groups. We had a good Sunday School in spite of rather a hostile atmosphere. The Salvation Army girl led it excellently and a gracious Mar Thoma schoolmaster told bravely the story of Christ walking on the water. The shy missionary, who seems to live in his cabin, spoke at the evening service on deck. Since we are due in Penang next Sunday and since all those who have in any way shared in Christian witness except myself disembark tomorrow at Bombay, this presumably closes organised testimony for Christ on this ship. It was a stiflingly hot day but as soon as the sun dropped into the sea a cool breeze sprang up and everyone revived. On deck I encountered a Malayan Chinese with an Italian girl and they gave me the chance to speak to them about the Lord, which I was specially glad to do as these two have behaved in a particularly unedifying manner throughout the voyage. After dark a faint glimmer of light appeared on the horizon, straight ahead, growing gradually into a long, low, luminous cloud, and changing at last into Bombay, the Gateway of India.

Back on board after some hours ashore I found that my situation had not exactly improved. At meals I am now alone with Marigold. She is a dignified and refined person in a way, but dresses with the maximum daring, fraternises solely with men, and makes no contact with other women. I have often been able to speak to her about Christ. Then in my cabin I am shut in with Mr Simpson, to whom I have in eighteen days never had the chance to say one word about the gospel. Tonight I was working at the cabin table when he came in and although it was only 7 p.m. went to bed saying, "I'm rather drunk." As he lay there he apologised profusely for his behaviour and thanked me for never having thrust religion at him. His enunciation was indistinct; he was jovial and forgetful. "You are a missionary," he said, "and I'm afraid we belong to different worlds." He was so far gone that I encouraged him to sleep. Soon afterwards two of his friends, who were anxious about him, came into the cabin, but one of them was in a similar condition, soggy with liquor. I was a little apprehensive that they might become violent, so I followed them into the bar and sat with them for some time. "It's a matter of different professions," they said, which I denied, explaining that Christ is able to save anyone who turns to Him from sin and evil. Simpson is the kind of man who sits all day in the bar with pals, sipping beer. "Oh, I've got a conscience," he says each time he sees me now. I have tried to urge all three of them not to drink again tonight, as I feel the devil would be glad enough to brew up something still more unpleasant.

May 15th. Happily Simpson's "conscience" kept him on orange-ade. At night I sat in the bar with his friends again and they were kind enough to stand me a soft drink while I talked with them again about "the way of righteousness". A Sinhalese grandmother came over to my table to ask whether it was true, as the Mar Thoma pastors had suggested to her, that the Lord was only being cynical when He said, "Make to yourselves friends of the mammon of unrighteousness."

May 19th. We paused briefly at Colombo which was all set to celebrate the 2500th anniversary of the Buddha's enlightenment. Most of the available space on board is monopolised by revelry, dancing, drinking, whist drives, racing, the tote, and the cinema, so I have pressed ahead with the study of Indonesian. Each morning six children meet me on deck at 8 a.m. for a Bible story, but there are no members of the Christian fellowship meetings left now. At breakfast time we entered Indonesian waters and for eight hours Sumatra was in sight. There is a cluster of beautiful, mountainous islands off its northern tip, leaving a channel a few miles broad in between. However, the Captain took us within three hundred yards of the mainland so that we could clearly see the wide plain at the mouth of the Atjeh River and Kotaradja, second city of North Sumatra. The whole region is jumbled and tumbled about into a vast, untamed mystery, shrouded in jungle and cloud. And thence

we headed across the placid sea towards the glorious island of
Penang.

May 20th. Sunday, and a day of pure delight for me, free from
drinking and folly. To my surprise I was met by a man whose
business it is to attend to Penang's water supply, a devoted servant
of Christ. He took me at once to the morning service at the American Southern Baptist Mission and thence to lunch at a Chinese
Christian home where I had stayed in years gone by. It was a heart-
warming experience to be among believers again. At 5.30 p.m. I
preached in the Chinese Methodist Church to about 150 people and
again at 8.30 p.m. in a lovely flat into which thirty persons of all
persuasions were packed. This was indeed a great day, bringing
with the beauty of Penang the ways of Malaya so familiar to us
from our former residence there, the warmth of Chinese Christians, and the opportunity of giving to others messages from the
Word of God. I met one missionary who told me that in his
school he had almost all the Indian Muslim boys living in Penang.
"Do they ever become Christians?" I asked. "Oh no," he replied,
"but I hope they may become better Muslims."

May 21st. All day we have meandered down the Straits of
Malacca, the sea motionless, Malayan mountains riveting the eye,
and night has fallen with the Cape Rachata light blinking at us
and Malacca straight ahead. A myriad shoals and sandbars on the
Sumatran side force traffic over towards Malacca; the water is very
shallow all the way and the navigable channel only a few miles
wide.

May 22nd. I rose at 4 a.m. and stood alone on deck to watch the
lights of Pontian, where we used to live. Then we came to Kukup
Island and the end of the mainland of Asia at last. Ahead the glow
of Singapore anticipated the sunrise and a powerful searchlight
scoured the Strait of Johore.

I had hoped to have several days in Singapore but the first news
that greeted me was that I was sailing again in 24 hours for Java.
This brief period was entirely filled with interviews at the headquarters of the China Inland Mission, though I stole time to walk
across the Singapore River and up to the statue of Sir Stamford
Raffles, "to whose foresight and genius Singapore owes its existence

and prosperity". Headquarters looked very lovely next day in the morning sunlight. There is an attractive lightness, airiness, cleanness, newness, and tastefulness about the premises, not a little enhanced by the majestic beauty of the trees in the Botanical Gardens across the road. We sailed at 6.30 p.m. just as hundreds of ships added their lights to the growing illuminations of Singapore's waterfront and the towers of the city stood out against the evening sky. We went eastwards at first and then turned south, entering Indonesia by the Riau Strait between Batam Island and Bintan Island, but at 9.30 p.m. we stopped with engine trouble and anchored back in the entrance to the strait for the whole night. From this improvised anchorage, right in the main fairway and only five miles off the south-eastern tip of Malaya, we made a second start next morning and so I had my desire of sailing through the rugged Riau Islands in broad daylight. Just now we are eight miles off the southern shore of Bintan, low and green above a green sea, with misty uplands rising inland and island after island tailing off to the south, some just boldly wooded tufts, others with considerable ridges and ranges. Near at hand, athwart the channel, lies Pangkit Island with mangrove swamps at the water's edge varied by dazzling beaches under the palm trees, beneath whose shade nestle the homes of the islanders, from which they sally forth to their fish traps to spend the night on flimsy platforms twenty feet above the water. Heavier forest covers most of the island, whose luxuriant vegetation gives it an uninhabited appearance, which is no doubt quite misleading. On the west we are at the moment very close to Karas Island and precisely the same description applies to it. There is all that and nothing but that to be seen, and it certainly looks as though it is "always afternoon". Night fell as we crossed the equator with the full moon right ahead, Venus behind, on the east the Great Bear upside down, on the west the Southern Cross. In this little ship the only saloon passengers beside myself are an Indian couple, who eat alone, so at meals I am at the Captain's left hand among the officers. I have a three-berth cabin to myself and the cool lounge, narrow but spanning the whole ship, is virtually my private study.

May 24th. We have been all day on an unruffled sea between the

Lingga Archipelago and Karimata Island off the coast of Borneo. The Captain is a good talker and a good listener. He likes verbal sparring, so it has not been hard to commend the truth. He was mightily surprised when I dubbed drunkenness a sin, since he has often indulged in it. He considers life very easy—"you just drift along." We sit and drink together before all meals, but our drinks are different. Tonight he produced a Chinese compradore and so I spoke Mandarin for the first time for twelve months, the Captain listening in amused ignorance. But the compradore had a serious question. If he became a Roman Catholic could he perform the traditional duties for his parents when they died? From this text we moved to the evangel and I was at once struck with the fact that he was easier to attack closely than the Captain.

May 25th. The second officer also is a Roman Catholic. Drawing correct deductions from my geographical enquiries, he roused me at 4 a.m. to examine the outlines of Serutu (1600 feet) and Karimata (3100 feet) as we glided past them at eight miles' range. The temperature at that hour on the open bridge was delightful and while the wind dealt with my sleepiness he took me up on a chance remark of mine that "man is born unto trouble". In spite of a mother ludicrously jealous of his wife he agreed with the Captain that "life is very easy". We talked up there till Karimata was a blur on the horizon and low hills ahead tried to cheat us into thinking they were another lonely island instead of the south-west corner of the vast land of Borneo. Since both the Captain and the Chinese compradore plunge into questions at the very sight of me we are having a gay time, and it is I who have to leaven the conversation with mundane matters. The Captain has attained corruption with joviality. He twinkles his eyes and wonders how he can best shock me. Like a fly buzzing round and round a light he is unable to keep off spiritual matters. He has special information about hell—it has changed since the Yanks got there and is now well stocked with refrigerators, bars, and girls. The compradore asked me why Christ allowed Himself to be crucified, so I spent half an hour explaining it to him as we watched great shoals of fish breaking the surface of the sea alongside us every few minutes. During lunch, when we were about a hundred miles from land, I was amazed to see a tiny bird, not four inches long, come hopping into the saloon. There seemed to be no seagulls in these waters, but suddenly we saw a hawk. Before long it caught the little bird and circled the ship holding it in its mouth, but it came too close and one of the crew accomplished the feat of seizing it and dashing it down on deck. Shortly after I noticed a curious fish about eight inches long and very thin. It bounced on the water but it did not seem to be a flying fish. At the third bounce it reared itself at right angles to the surface of the sea while still moving forwards fast, its tail just tipping the water for about six yards. Then it took two more bounces on its tummy before performing another erect, acrobatic surge. This ritual it repeated several times.

May 27th. On waking I beheld Madura Island, a long low shore looking as jungle-bound as the Riau Islands, although in this case I well know that it is the home of two million people. Hundreds of Madurese fishing boats and picturesque ocean-going junks cluttered up the Madura Strait as we nosed slowly to our anchorage in Surabaja harbour. Chinese Christians met me with two large cars and thanks to their skilful aid we were soon feasting and rejoicing in Mrs Tan's capacious home. Many others dropped in and after the strenuous battles of the long voyage it was cheering to be received so joyfully by oriental believers and I basked in the sheer goodness of Christian fellowship once more. Then a big Chevrolet was at the door and we were piloted through miles of congested streets out into the teeming countryside of Java and whisked away to what I will call "the city" where I was in time to slip into the back of the Chinese Christian church, for it was a Sunday afternoon, and join three hundred people in singing the praises of Christ, who redeems from all evil. Then I passed to a suburban Chinese home where sixty teenagers were assembled for a Sunday night sing-song. Later I strolled alone through the city. Unless I am mistaken there is a greater sense of peacefulness, of assurance and maturity. The Bible College, where I am back in my old room, looks magnificent with new trees and shrubs grown up around the buildings, staff, students, and children looking fresh and clean, and everything taste-fully arranged. Thus, though separated by the width of the world from my wife and children, I was reminded at the very outset of this new period of service in Java how deep and strong is the work of the Spirit of God in the hearts of large numbers of Chinese Christians who have found in Jesus Christ their Saviour and Master.

CHAPTER 3

THE ROAD TO SABRANG

THE day that Rufus and his family moved to Karangan marked an entirely new start in life for him, and he knew it. It was perfectly obvious to him that the years of uncertainty, the tentative years, were passed. Rich years lay ahead. The shack they had lived in was pulled down as soon as they got away and the ground sown with tapioca. It seemed symbolic of the closing of an era in his life.

They were quite a large party boarding the bus—himself, Mrs Rufus, the five children, six bulky packages tied up with string, and a youth named Budi who had come from Karangan to help them with the move. Rufus was attracted to Budi from the first; he liked his massive frame, his cheery face and his willing service; from that hour he took him as his friend and servant, treating him as though he were his own son.

The first stage of their trip took them up a steep hill off the plain into rolling hills where rice yielded to rubber and sugar gave way to coffee. But still no land was wasted and far away on either side, where no motorable road went, houses, farms, and plantations blanketed the mountains. The unsurfaced road deteriorated as they moved southwards until at a village in a sheltered hollow it came to an end altogether. They all dismounted and Rufus hired two carriers to help with the luggage. Mrs Rufus carried the youngest child on her back and Budi shouldered the other children in turns when they got tired of walking. The path twisted through the uplands for half an hour and then came out on top of a ridge from which it dropped sheer down into the Karangan valley, now seen for the first time. Far below lay the Indian Ocean, two headlands protruding into it with islands off-shore. Between them a crescent of golden sand curved for a mile, otherwise there was no beach, only jungle-covered crags tumbling confusedly into the water. Inland from the sand was a broad strip of jungle and behind that several miles of green rice, ready for harvesting, waving in the breeze. Inland again from the rice lay the village itself, a wide residential area half-hidden in palm trees, which continued to the foot of the steep hill from whose summit they surveyed the glorious scene. To right and left lofty ridges of jungle dropped steadily towards the ocean and thus the Karangan valley was shut in from the rest of the world on all four sides: on the north the steep hill, on east and west the jungle ridges, and on the south the strip of jungle and the sea. It took two hours to get down to the houses.

Karangan was a place no man ever passed through, for it led to nowhere, a world away from the world, cut off by nature from the normal haunts of mankind, but home to two thousand souls, and a Christian village. If it had not been a Christian village it would not have been a village at all. Until seventy years ago few had penetrated these formidable mountains. In the rich northern plains and the fantastically productive central volcanic belt the Javanese people multiplied into tens of millions in times gone by, but it was not till the early nineteenth century that people began to find their way from Islam to Christ. When they did so, they were in an unenviable position, acknowledging Jesus in a Muslim world. And so they sought escape from it, desiring liberty to read the Scriptures, to meet together in the name of Christ, to sing His praises, to take marriage vows of lifelong faithfulness to one another, to bring their children to baptism, and to bury their dead not facing Mecca. And so they resorted to a time-honoured but often neglected method of Christian life and work. They emigrated. But since they were farmers and their own country provided in its Southern Mountains a hinterland unexplored and unsettled, it was there they went. Small bands of men led the way through the hills to the sea, felled the jungle with prodigious labour, erected their humble shelters, sent for their families, hacked out ricefields, levelled, irrigated, planted, reaped, built substantial houses, laid out gardens and roads, spanned their streams with bridges, dedicated their churches —and there they have remained as Christian villages until this day. Such was the origin of Karangan.

The path down to the floor of the valley was painfully steep and

Rufus was thankful for the assistance of Budi in carrying the smaller children. Monkeys sprang chattering away into the trees as the little cavalcade passed by. Often they stood aside to yield the path to climbers bound for the outside world above, mostly women bowing low under great piles of firewood strapped to their backs. The men they met were toiling up under carrying poles from the ends of which swung baskets loaded heavy with sparkling, granite-like, blocks of stone to sharpen the knives of the northern cities. Half-way down they came to a house on a tiny plateau and were thankful to rest on the benches under low-sweeping eaves. Water was boiling on the fire and a woman served them steaming black coffee, the grains swimming so thickly on the surface that you had to blow them back every time you took a sip. It was some years since any of them had walked a country path like this, so their feet and legs were sore with the strain of descending, searching always for a safe footing. The sun was hot and they rested for half an hour before going on down. Rufus realised that once settled into Karangan his wife and children were not likely to come out again very often. At last they reached the palms, forded a stream on rocky boulders, and came to level ground. The path became a wide road, soft and grassy, a road that had never known the wheel of a car. In fact one of the first things that struck Rufus was the quietness of Karangan. Here were thousands of people but no factory, no police, no car, no noise, no electricity, no running water save the three rivers coursing through the village. Neither was there any formal street or shopping centre. Each house stood back by itself in its own garden at the end of its own drive. Countless palms, countless fruit trees, countless bamboo clumps, flowers and foliage of every hue, hid the houses from one another and scattered the community far and wide over the gentle foothills just above the levelled ricelands. You could walk two miles in any direction and still be in the village. On either side of the rice its outskirts trickled right down to the jungle fringe blocking off the sea.

As soon as they reached the houses under the palms they were stopped by people running out of their homes to greet them. The news spread that the pastor had come, with wife and children. Right down the avenue of trees ahead of them Rufus could see knots of people standing at their gates in patient curiosity. Their hands were shaken hundreds of times. They were invited in to high, cool rooms, adorned with fronds and flowers, family photographs and Bible scenes, where they were again refreshed with coffee. It soon became impossible to accept all the invitations and Rufus concentrated on keeping the party moving slowly through the village, dallying long enough with each welcoming group not to give offence. Mrs Rufus was the hardest one to move because the women crowded round her, introducing one another, squatting down for a better look at the children, all eager to entertain her and get her into their homes. The carriers went on ahead to the house they were to occupy. Budi too, seeing how tired the children were getting, ferried them one by one into his own home where his wife took charge of them till Mrs Rufus could win her way through. It was late afternoon before the whole family were gathered at last under the roof that was to be their own for five years, but Mrs Budi already had supper cooked. Sleep enwrapped the children and to Rufus and his wife came the thrill of feeling that they were wanted and loved even before they were properly known.

It was true that the family did not often climb out of the Karangan valley. Even Rufus himself went for months without seeing any other human settlement, for he found a big task awaiting him. Most of the people, though Christian in name, had only a very limited knowledge of the gospel and the Bible. Even allowing for a good many children among the population, it had been a surprise to find only eighty people attending church. So for five years he toiled to teach and to preach Jesus Christ and by that time there were 350 in his regular congregation. The majority of these were people born in the village who had always been nominal Christians but whose faith had long been dormant until revived, thanks to Rufus' diligence in the task committed to him. He preached regularly every Sunday in a warm and friendly way which inclined people to listen. Gradually he came to abandon the habit of reading his sermons; he prepared carefully but worked from a minimum of notes when in the pulpit, preferring to look straight at his congregation as he spoke. He used always his own Javanese language, his mother tongue, although his education had been mostly in Dutch. Yet the secret of his successful ministry did not altogether lie in his preaching, for which he had average rather than outstanding gifts. Day in, day out he followed up what he said in public by close and continual contact with the lives of his people. He did little reading, and his correspondence was negligible. He had no radio. Budi's house was next to his own and the gardens of both were cared for by Budi rather than by Rufus. The household was entirely in the hands of Mrs Rufus, who also managed to share actively in her husband's work in the village, so that Rufus devoted most of his waking hours to the propagation of the gospel and the care of souls. He visited the sick and the elderly, sharing their sorrows, spending time with them, and praying for them. He was continually in motion, a familiar figure in all sections of the village; and he always had a timely exhortation on his lips so that people were not only drawn to him but reminded of the existence and claims of the Master whom he served. Thus in an inconspicuous way there took place in Karangan during those five years a reviving of spiritual life. Dead bones lived and a new spirit was breathed into an old church.

But it was not only Christians born in the village who were affected. Several Muslim families, who had settled around the fringes and begun to form a noticeable minority in the community, were also won to Christ. They saw in Karangan standards of conduct and of family life which were new to them, and attractive. They also met a pastor who did not pass them by as belonging to another faith, nor argue with them on points they regarded as controversial, but who spoke to them freely and happily of a Saviour, taking it for granted that they would have a need in their hearts and lives which only He could meet—and this was often the case. When such people began to turn towards the gospel and were willing to receive him, Rufus would go and preach in their homes at night while the neighbours gathered round. Karangan was such a widely scattered place that this often meant an hour's walk and a homecoming long after midnight. He got into the way of taking a group of young men with him to share in these evangelistic cottage meetings. Among them was a youth named Tilosa, who thus had his first introduction to aggressive Christian witness among Muslims.

Yet the aggression was always very gently done, without antagonising the people to whom they went.

These years of fruitful service, of putting into practice the lessons learnt in the cell, and of regaining his position as an accredited minister in his church, were also the years when his country asserted, fought for, and achieved her independence from the Dutch who had for so many centuries ruled the Indonesian islands. In the turmoil and ultimate triumph of those days Karangan and its pastor shared with the rest of their people, animated by the same aspirations and hopes as other Javanese. Dutch planes circled overhead on a number of occasions, but they escaped the attacks made on some Christian villages. Yet the fact that the valley was identified in religion with the faith commonly regarded as that of the national enemy put them in rather an invidious position. Troops of their own side, fearing that larger buildings might be used as barracks by the Dutch, burned down both the church and the village school. There were no casualties in these events, but it was an era of great strain and tension which at last gave way to emancipation, independence, and the joy of entirely new prospects for the whole Indonesian people.

When peace came back to Church and State, the value of Rufus' ministry at Karangan did not escape notice and he was assigned to a new and more difficult task. The Christian villages of East Java, established by emigration not conversion, are all in the neighbourhood of the Indian Ocean and in mountainous country, blocked off from the bulk of Java where tens of millions of Muslims toil upon the willing land in villages which are so close to one another that the whole countryside is one vast residential area. While the method of emigration preserved the infant Christian community and enabled it to multiply into a discernible element in the life of the new nation, its main disadvantage was that it physically divided Christian from Muslim and encouraged a false idea of the nature of Christianity. It became easy to feel that a Christian was anyone born in a Christian village and a Muslim was anyone born in a Muslim village; it grew progressively harder to conceive of a person passing from Islam to Christ unless, as had happened at Karangan, Muslims chanced to become residents in Christian communities;

indeed there was always a real possibility that when Christians became residents in Muslim towns and villages they in turn would conform to the prevailing faith. In each case the accepted religion of the locality seemed to play an important part in determining the religion of the individual. A Christian family living among Muslims tended to keep quiet about its beliefs, observing Christian customs at home but making no parade of them and doing nothing active to spread the gospel. And as the Christian villages multiplied so did the number of their sons and daughters who no longer lived in them. Office workers, administrators, medical workers, and school-teachers were especially likely to find themselves living outside among the Muslims. Their unspoken witness to the value and worthiness of the gospel was very considerable; their spoken witness was usually slight, for they felt themselves aliens in a potentially hostile environment.

Into this waiting Muslim world Rufus was now asked to step. It was rather a sad moment for the little family when they had to break up their home down by the sea and toil up the slippery path with all their worldly belongings. They took a small house in the village of Ringit, close to the market. Rufus' assignment was to keep in touch with several Christian villages near the Indian Ocean but to give the bulk of his time to evangelism among Muslims in the district of Sabrang, in which Ringit lay. The central market village called Sabrang was only a mile away; the population of the whole Sabrang district was a quarter of a million; there was no church building anywhere, except over the mountains in the Christian villages. Christian families were scattered here and there through-out the area, but the majority of them were dormant in faith. In Ringit itself Rufus knew of only one professing Christian, a widow. In Sabrang there were five families, but no meetings were held unless a pastor from a Christian village came on a visit and gathered them together; this did not often occur. Having become used to an orderly congregation of 350 people on Sundays, well trained in singing, it was a great change for Rufus. For the first time in his life he found himself called upon to live and work as a pastor in an area where there was virtually no Christian church in existence at all.

The widow in Ringit proved to be a rather unshepherded member of the Pentecostal Church. She was truly glad to think that a pastor had come to forgotten Ringit, so when he asked if she would care to get her neighbours along one night to hear him preach she consented to do so.

The sun went down across the rice fields and sank behind the volcanoes to the west. Lamps were lit in hundreds of homes in Ringit as men came back from field and factory for their evening meal. Kneeling on her kitchen floor the widow pumped up her pressure lamp and hung it on the verandah. She put out benches and chairs enough to seat thirty people; there was water on the stove and trays of cakes in the cupboard, for she would be responsible for providing light refreshments later on. She had mentioned Rufus' proposal to a good many families and expected a full house, nor was she disappointed. By 8 o'clock most of the seats were taken and she had to slip across to Mawardi, her one-armed neighbour, and borrow chairs from him. He was smoking on his verandah when she got there, watching the lights and the people gathering at her home. After a day in the fields he had just had his bath in the brook and was ready for a quiet evening. He asked again what was happening, so she reminded him, saying she hoped he would come, and hurried back with his children, who helped her carry the chairs.

Mawardi did come, but not till later. He waited till after 9 o'clock on his own verandah, watching. Nothing had happened by then, except that in addition to the forty people on the widow's verandah there were about a hundred on the road and down the lane, standing in the shadows where they might hear something without being too conspicuous. About 9.30 p.m., two hours after the first guests had arrived, Mawardi saw a stranger rise and begin to address the visitors, so he opened his gate and strolled along, still smoking. He jointed the half-invisible company in the lane just as Rufus began to pray for God's blessing on their meeting. Mawardi watched him as he had so often watched players on the stage. Although not a religious man, he was none the less a Muslim, so that belief in the existence of God and the desirability of praying to Him were second nature. But the words that Rufus said in his prayer were quite unintelligible, partly because others around him were talking as they watched.

Rufus then preached for ninety minutes. What struck Mawardi was his free-and-easy manner; he just chatted to the crowd, smiling, sometimes laughing outright, turning this way and that, compelling attention by a certain winsomeness of manner. When he sat down there was an interval as the widow served coffee and cakes to those who were actually sitting in her house. Some of those in the lane moved off, but others stayed, Mawardi among them, and after twenty minutes Rufus began again and continued till long after midnight. His text, to which he returned repeatedly, was the words of Christ, "I am the good shepherd: the good shepherd giveth His life for the sheep". His theme was that in spite of all the advances of mankind, including the independence of Indonesia, the human heart still needed a shepherd to rescue it from its enemies and to look after it in this life and the next. With many a half-humorous, homely illustration drawn from the life of the people of which he himself was part, he showed that no one is able to be such a shepherd to another human soul—save only Christ, who laid down His life to save us.

Sheltered by the night, Mawardi listened to the way of salvation for the first time in his life, which had not been a good one. Maimed in youth in his body, he had soon become maimed in soul as well. He had married many times. He had grown to look sly and un-reliable, not without reason. And now suddenly he was brought face to face with Jesus Christ through the words of a man he had never seen before. He had not been to school, though he had taught himself to read a little. There seems to have been no real conflict in his heart that memorable night. The message was simply received, as it was by those multitudes who heard the Apostle Peter preach in Jerusalem on the day of Pentecost. From that moment, little though he understood, Mawardi was Christ's man.

When the meeting finally broke up towards 2 a.m. he strolled on to the verandah where he was greeted in some surprise by the widow, who introduced him to Rufus. He hardly knew what to say to Rufus, but they sat together for an hour and through his halting questions and jerky expressions of opinion Rufus perceived that

God had spoken to this man. No defined church organisation existed in the area. He was on his own. So Rufus baptised him three days later.

But Mrs Mawardi was furious. "Dad has become a Dutchman", was her verdict, and she told the children that they were to have nothing to do with him. She would cook him no food, not even their usual early morning cup of coffee. If he wanted coffee, she told him, he could get it from the kitchen himself. And so, with his one arm, he lived as an outcast in his own home for three weeks. Each evening he strolled along to Rufus' house and sat chatting with him. These conversations began to open up his understanding so that he grasped more clearly the truths of the gospel. But for three weeks his wife remained adamant. Christianity was the religion of the Dutch, the enemies of Indonesia, the imperialists, the colonisers, and she would have nothing to do with such a husband. And then one evening he was sitting alone reading the parable of the Wise and Foolish Virgins in the gospel of Matthew when she took a chair, sat behind him, and said, "Tell me what it's all about." The children gathered round her and without turning he tried to explain what he had learnt from Rufus, falteringly, being only a babe in Christ himself. But however imperfectly he may have expressed himself, the whole family decided to join him and thus found their reunion in submission to the Lord Jesus. Once again, in these early days, there was no church organisation and Rufus was on his own. And so the wife and daughters were all baptised on the third day. How much they understood at the time would be hard to say, but Rufus believed that if Muslim people received the message and desired baptism this was evidence of a work of God in their hearts so remarkable that they should on no account be refused or asked to delay long. To him the closing verses of St Matthew's Gospel were sufficient warrant for maintaining that becoming a disciple of Christ and receiving baptism might well precede learning much about what was really involved in these decisive acts. And it was his experience that in most cases it was not possible for an unbaptised person to attend Christian meetings and receive regular instruction. Nor was his faith in the genuineness of Mawardi and his family misplaced.

Mawardi himself was overjoyed at the turn events had taken. Within one month new life had come to him and all his. Pensioned early on account of his physical disability, he suddenly found that God had given him an entirely fresh life-work—to win others for Christ. He thought first of his old teacher, Rekso. Many Javanese villages, crowded with thousands of people, have their own local wise man, some of whom attain a wide reputation as medicine men or as sages who can explain and embellish the age-old lore and traditions of their people. Rekso, who believed that he had been married twenty-seven times, was one of these local sages, a bent and battered old man. In his struggles to get into contact with the God whom as a Muslim he acknowledged, he had suspended himself upside down from the rafters of his home. This had so damaged his hearing that he was now almost stone deaf. But Mawardi went to him and shouted into his ear that he wanted him to come and hear a Christian preacher called Rufus. The old gentleman came and planted himself in a small meeting one night in Ringit. Knowing that he was deaf Rufus had not much hope that he could profit from being there, but he preached Christ as usual, and from that evening Rekso counted himself a Christian. Unable to read and unable to hear, it was extremely difficult for him to make much progress in understanding the gospel, but he and Mawardi spent part of almost every evening at Rufus' home and gradually some at least of the truth of God penetrated his fuddled mind. He was baptised and the community marvelled that two such men should declare themselves believers in the Lord Jesus Christ. Rufus often took them out with him when he was invited to other villages, where their very presence and appearance were a testimony to what the power of God could do and an inducement to others to commit themselves to the Good Shepherd, who gave His life for the sheep that were lost.

In the course of time news of these happenings came to the attention of a group of people in the village of Barek not far away, a large and beautiful place scattered across ricefields and wooded hills hard by the Southern Mountains. There were 4000 people there, a quarter of them being Madurese. For some years several families, influenced by a farmer who had had contact with Christians in another part of Java, had been in the habit of celebrating Christmas. Although they did not understand its meaning, they made it an occasion for a social evening together and put lights on a tree. Hearing that a Christian pastor had moved to the district, for their village lay in the Sabrang area, one of them called on Rufus and asked him to come over for an evening. He cycled across after dark and found seventeen people awaiting him. After an hour's chat they asked him to address them, so he spoke openly of Christ and of our need to receive from Him forgiveness of sins, which none other can give. They listened so intently that he was encouraged to go on at some length, explaining the gifts of God to all who become His children through faith in Jesus Christ. When he finished, his host rose and said he had no idea Christianity had anything to do with so cheering and encouraging a message. Rufus was invited back the next night to tell them more. After that he was at Barek regularly several times a week and within two months a number of people were asking for baptism. Seeing the hand of God in this series of events he felt compelled to grant their request. Not long afterwards it was repeated and thus it came about that within six months of his first visit to Barek there were seventy baptised Christians there, this figure including the children of believers, none of whom wished their families to continue as Muslims and to be regarded as such by everyone else. Several of those baptised were prominent men in the village, so that the sudden emergence of a Christian Church could not easily be gainsaid. One of the Christians named Chamim had a large, roofed-in threshing floor immediately in front of his house, and this became the meeting-place of the new church. Benches were bought, a lectern was made, Christian posters were hung on the walls, and they began to learn hymns.

Among these new believers in Barek was a man named Susilo whose home was in the neighbouring village of Triwung. Although a local man he had been educated elsewhere during the Dutch days and had once been given a New Testament by one of his teachers. He had tried to read the book and found it more interesting than the Koran, but in course of time he laid it aside. Later he married the daughter of a very ardent Muslim who had built a small mosque in his own garden. They moved back to Triwung, where he was related to the most important men in the district. His own wider contacts and natural abilities soon brought him into prominence; as an employee of the government his work took him all over the Sabrang district and he was known to village headmen everywhere. But with the coming of Rufus and the emergence of the new church in Barek he came face to face with the message he had never properly comprehended in his school-days. In spite of his wife's rigid Muslim upbringing they both decided that they too needed Christ and together with their four children they submitted to be baptised and commenced to associate openly with such Christians as there now were in the district. On these occasions Susilo himself said little; although accustomed to lead among his fellows, he felt himself to be a newcomer to the Christian faith. Lacking confidence, he did not assert his gifts.

Thus Rufus had, single-handed, laid the foundations for the remarkable expansion which was to follow. His home was established in Ringit. Mawardi, Rekso, Chamim, and Susilo had been won to Christ along with many others, and one entirely new church had arisen at Barek. Already the events in Sabrang district were drawing the attention of Christians throughout East Java.

CHAPTER 4

INTERLUDE IN BORNEO

MY position on returning to Java was at first conditioned by several factors not destined to be permanent. For one thing my wife and our youngest son, Rupert, were delayed in England for almost nine months, so that I had no home of my own. This meant that I lived in the Bible College in the city, but at the moment of my return the college was just closing for the long vacation, so that I was not involved in a daily round of teaching. This was just as well, since I had been appointed Acting Superintendent of the missionaries of the China Inland Mission in Indonesia, who were at that time scattered across Java and West Borneo. For several years we had been praying that God, who had taken us to Java in association with Chinese-speaking Christians, would enable us to get a house in a Javanese village not too far from the city, so that we could get to know and understand the people of the great island in which we had come to live, the Javanese themselves. Hitherto we had been segregated from them by the very closeness of our links with Chinese, who were also foreigners in Indonesia, and by the fact that we spoke Chinese but not any Indonesian language. The house, and with it experiences beyond anything of which we had dreamed, was waiting for us twenty miles away, but we knew it not, though it would be ready for us just when our family was reunited. But the road there was to lie through Borneo and Madura Island.

May 28th. My first major assignment was to preach at the funeral of one of the Bible College students. There were 200 Chinese Christians present and I can hardly see how a funeral could have been more noble and worthy, more glorifying to God, or more encouraging to the stricken relatives. Then I caught the evening express to Surabaja, travelling with the son of a Chinese pastor on Bali Island. Being an English teacher he was very pleased to chat with me in English. The electricity failed, so the carriages were lit only by an antique brand of lamp, but the train was a true express, screeching and hooting its way down to sea-level while lightning, thunderclouds, and sunset streaks girded the volcanic peaks in wild, fantastic patterns. And so I write this from my Surabaja home, Mrs Tan's house in the dense warren of streets north of the heart of the town. She has fed me regally and put her enormous car and chauffeur at my disposal while I am reporting to the various authorities scattered across this big city. At night she invited me to go with her in the car to call on some of the leaders in the Chinese Churches with which I was closely associated in former years. While we sipped coffee with the Chairman of the Board of Deacons he told me that back in China his grandfather had been a Christian and his father a pastor. Then he searched for words, chuckled, and said, "Why, I was a Christian before I was born!" Twenty years ago their church consisted of a mere dozen, but now they have over a thousand members. This great transformation has been the outcome of the visits in 1939 of the evangelist of the overseas Chinese, Dr John Sung. Next day I called on the Chinese pastor of a different church. However, I fear that he has become so deeply enamoured of philosophical, psychological, and theological study that he is neglecting the ministry of the Word and the care of souls. He has a large library and showed me book after book, massive, well-marked tomes. He had made an exhaustive study of Niebuhr, Kierkegaard, and Karl Barth. We talked for an hour and prayed together. I hope I gave him no offence.

Back at Mrs Tan's home I was delighted to have the chance to give time to her, for she has proved a "mother in Israel" to me and to many others. Her large establishment is a kind of free Christian hotel to which all who work for Christ among Chinese-speaking people are welcome. Her husband died while still a young man as a result of a terrible fire at their home. She herself was in hospital for the birth of one of their children at the time. The child of a relative was staying with them. When the alarm was raised her husband, who was running a large business, was distracted between getting everyone clear of the house and salvaging valuable documents and records. In the confusion two of their own children and the visiting child were lost. He was never able to get over the shock and died not very long afterwards. Mrs Tan has carried on the business very successfully ever since. She works hard all day and employs about a hundred workmen. She dresses less well than they do and from her appearance you would never guess her wealth. She is a determined believer in Christ and feels that the way she is called to serve Him is by the use of her home. When I go out, she and the children stand on the steps waving; when I return, she sends milk and coffee to my room. Having for years enjoyed her hospitality whenever I am in Surabaja, I brought her a present of Irish linen and Australian apples (which are expensive here). She accepted them, but then took me seriously to task and explained that I was not to use my money in such a way again on any account. She said she was no preacher, but God had given her the house and the means to run it, so that she did not want the Lord's servants to feel they had to give her presents of any kind.

June 5th. I had a long talk with Pastor Meng, the Principal of the Bible College, about the lectures he wants me to give next term. In spite of an inherent shyness which prevents him from being much of a public figure, he has run the College most successfully for several years; he is an admirable secretary-treasurer with books in perfect order and every detail thought out and provided for. It is amusing to see a great transition taking place in his elderly and con-servative brain. The first real sign of it was when he capitulated to the delightful Indonesian custom of wearing pyjamas about the house after dark. Formerly he had taken strong exception to the students doing this and even declared that no man could reverently pray in his pyjamas, but now climate and custom have won him over and he is to be seen any evening, perfectly relaxed, in good Hongkong pyjamas, strolling through these halls. But I could hardly believe my ears when he said to me today, "Christian work among Chinese is not the most important thing in this country now. The Chinese Churches have more help, more understanding of the gospel, and more active and enlightened workers than the Javanese Churches. Work in Indonesian and in Javanese is more important than work in Chinese." There cannot be very many Chinese Christian leaders who have eyes to see this, yet I believe it is true and

I greatly admire him for comprehending it and being bold enough to say so. I have preached almost daily to the students in the College and to hundreds of children in the Middle School associated with it; I always marvel that they listen so well to a white man.

In the evening I met Sutikno, a young Javanese pastor who has been living on Madura Island. He introduced me to several men from over there, quite an intelligent-looking group, all aged about twenty. Through his faithful witness in a rigidly Muslim community all these have turned to Christ. We spent two hours together and I asked them to tell me their stories. One fellow with a big shock of hair said, "I am the first of my people to become a Christian", meaning the first of his family probably, since there are just a few Madurese believers and quite a number who are half-Madurese and half-Javanese. "I met a school-friend from Java who gave me a New Testament," he went on. "I found I could understand more of it than of the Koran. Then I met Sutikno here and asked him if God could forgive me, since I had not been a good man. He told me I could indeed be forgiven if I believed in Jesus Christ. The news that God loved me and sent Christ for me, attracted me." Then another told how he had met Sutikno playing badminton. He was in training to become a Muslim religious teacher, but when Sutikno showed him John 3: 16, "God so loved the world that He gave His only begotten Son", he at first found the last three words very difficult to understand. I asked him what he had found in the gospel which he had specially lacked in Islam, and he at once replied, "The forgiveness of sins." Before meeting Sutikno he had started to investigate Roman Catholicism, but had been repelled by their use of images. The night after he first read the verse John 3: 16 he had a dream in which he saw a beam of light falling across his path. However, his uncle became very angry at his interest in Christianity and whipped up opposition in the family. He felt he could do nothing but pray and one day his uncle fell unconscious at his feet. But his people refused to feed him any longer and eventually he was ejected in the clothes he was wearing and disowned. The more he compared the Koran with the Bible the more sure he felt that the latter propounded the way of salvation. But the attitude of his family was such that he felt he must choose between death and flight to Java. He chose flight, but kept writing to his brother until the latter and a friend took the same step and identified themselves with his new faith.

A third man told how after he had met Sutikno and started to read the New Testament he was locked out of his home and told, "You can ask God to feed you. We would sooner see your grave than you." So he too crossed over to Java, for the islands are separated by only two miles of water opposite Surabaja. Before going home I led them in prayer and gave a brief message on Philippians 4: 13, "I can do all things through Christ which strengtheneth me". Later in the evening three of them called on me at the Bible College.

This remarkable and unexpected development was not to have quite the sequel for which Sutikno hoped, but for the moment I was called away from these new friends by the necessity for visiting West Borneo in my capacity as Acting Superintendent for the C.I.M. Overseas Missionary Fellowship in Indonesia.

June 8th. After tea Pastor and Mrs Meng escorted me to the door of the College and when he had prayed I left to catch the 4.5 p.m. express to Surabaja, warding off the attentions of a cheerful individual bent upon selling me a live crab. Darkness had fallen before I reached Mrs Tan's home and next morning her chauffeur drove me to the docks where I boarded the good ship *Toboali* bound for the city of Pontianak in West Borneo. There was only one class, the fourth, which meant deck passage and I at once perceived that all the other passengers, to the number of a hundred or so, had arrived before me and secured for themselves the more desirable parts of the deck. Furthermore they were almost without exception Madurese people.

June 9th. And now I am writing from my camp bed twenty-four hours after leaving Surabaja. Accommodation, by which I mean the surface of the deck, is packed tight. I am in the bows, down below the bridge, under roofing from the edges of which tarpaulins dangle to give the rough effect of an unfurnished shed. All the other passengers are lying or sitting on mats with their suitcases as pillows. Banana skins, orange peel, and refuse cover every other inch. The whole area is festooned with washing lines, from which not only clothing but also many bird-cages dangle. Smoking is heavy and illumination after dark very dim. Cocks are prominent; one is tethered a yard from my head and another a yard from my feet. My arrival caused quite a sensation, as no one was expecting a white man to put himself in such a position as this. Sea breezes mitigate the heat. Food is doled out thrice daily from a huge tub and consists of a big spoonful of rice and one piece of fish or meat three times a day, but you are expected to have your own bowl and spoon. However, the Indonesian petty-officers have very kindly insisted that I eat with them in their tiny mess, so I don't have to queue up with the other passengers; they are from Northern Celebes and thus Protestant Christians by religion. I have seen nothing at all of the three Dutch officers in charge. Every single thing I do is a matter of the greatest interest to my companions. Unfortunately I speak no Madurese and my command of Indonesian is as yet very imperfect; no Chinese has presumed to thrust himself into such a situation, and not a soul understands English here. However, I have spoken freely about Christ both to the petty-officers and to the Madurese, who are going to Borneo for a temporary tree-felling job. They have never had such a chance to examine a European in their lives! Whenever I open my case there is an audience in position to peep under the lid. I live day and night in exactly the same clothes, unwashed and unshaved. Everyone is very friendly and I have many chats with people, but few of them are at all fluent in Indonesian. Their capacity for slumber is amazing—and enviable in these conditions. The women are not at all shy and bring their babies to observe me. I have been surprised to note that although the Madurese are known to be such staunch Muslims only two young men have made any attempt to observe the hours of prayer, and then only at sunrise and sunset. They stand with folded arms, bow down with hands on their knees, and finally kneel right down with their foreheads on the boards. There is no drinking and no flirting, in remarkable contrast to behaviour on the liner from England. Their main occupations are dozing, or chatting quietly in small circles.

June 11th. No change. I watched Venus set into the sea last night and the petty-officers most graciously handed me the key of their bathroom, so that I was able to clean up and enjoy five delightful minutes of privacy. After dark seven Madurese fellows invited me over on to their mat to talk. A row of babies was bathed within two feet of my bed. I have beguiled the tedium of the days with the study of Indonesian and Chinese. Happily the sea has been calm but at no time have we sighted land. After lunch we ran into a heavy rainstorm, which drove furiously across our company in spite of the flapping tarpaulins. With much gaiety all persons and possessions were huddled into the centre of the deck, while the brighter spirits had shower baths under the leaks in the roof. When it was over the tarpaulins were hoisted up and the good sun dried out the planks, so that in two hours from the first alarm we were all stretched out again as usual, with cocks crowing.

June 12th. And we are still there, proceeding at a snail's pace in order to synchronise with the tide at Pontianak. At 3 a.m. there was a threat of more rain and I have been up since then. After three days and three nights of this business the expense of a two-hour plane trip seems negligible, yet it is good to have the experience of being part of elementary life. I have been specially struck by the affliction of illiteracy. What can fellows do all day long, if they cannot read, except eat and doze on their mats? I produced tracts yesterday evening and limited interest was shown. One was torn up and I thought I sensed a less cordial attitude towards me. Several Javanese crew-members have squatted by me to chat; they have more Indonesian than the Madurese and I have utilised all such opportunities to speak about Christ. A youth from Surabaja asked a string of questions about the gospel. It was good to see folk all across the deck poring over Christian tracts. Being landsmen they show great interest in the ships and islands we are now passing, but I shall relish freedom from their ever-scrutinising eyes. With the approach of civilisation two of my companions have attempted to shave, an operation of which no one save myself stands in any apparent need. One of them grasped a tiny mirror and chopped away with a naked blade. His companion was less well equipped. He had a mirror all right, but instead of using a blade he endeavoured to imprison his whiskers between two small coins and snap them out.

At noon we anchored a few miles off-shore; to the south lay a long, flat, jungle-girt coast, to the north an attractive array of hills. And there we lay, roasting on the equator, unrevived by the slightest breeze, for seven hours. After dark, when the tide had risen, we slid up-river towards Pontianak. The lights on deck failed, so I deemed it wise to stand sentinel over my luggage. The moon showed up an endless line of trees very close on our left, among which lights occasionally twinkled. Then came a meeting of water-ways, houses all around us, the death-squeals of a pig, boats, steamers, and by 9.30 p.m. we were alongside the jetty at the port and metropolis of Pontianak. With much pleasure I joined the mob scrambling straight over the side of the ship and jumped down into Borneo.

Don Houliston was there to meet me and I revelled that night in the luxury of a room to myself and clean sheets. The town rather attracted me, a place more Malayan than Javanese in appear-ance, only less smart and tidy than Malayan cities. There was a far greater proportion of Chinese in evidence than in Java. The streets were much quieter too, lacking the teeming throngs, heavy pressure of traffic, and desperate struggle for survival of the smaller island. These first impressions were to be confirmed by all I saw in West Borneo.

June 14th. Last night I preached to fifty people at the mid-week prayer meeting of the Chinese Christian Church in Pontianak. This morning Don and I rose at 4.30 a.m. and crossed by sampan that branch of the mighty Kapuas River on which the city stands, fascinated by the beauty of the scene as daylight dawned. From the north bank of the river we caught a bus which took us in five hours the ninety miles to Singkawang, the second city of the area. On this road the actual equator lies only three miles out of Pontianak. The road surface varied from good to very bad and we met not a single private car, only buses, jeeps, and lorries. All the way I found the scenery reminiscent of the state of Johore in Malaya in which we formerly lived, save that coconut palms took the place of rubber trees. Otherwise there were the usual Malayan characteristics—limited visibility at all times due to trees, many narrow creeks and ditches with boats in them, muddy paths leading away through the trees to scattered homesteads, practically no cultivation of the land, atap-roofed homes raised well above the ground, and villages on stilts over mud and water. Chinese and Indonesians seemed to be present in about equal proportions, as in Malaya, the countryside being chiefly Indonesian, the hamlets and villages chiefly Chinese. The landscape is also like Johore in its flatness with only occasional isolated hills until you approach Singkawang, which is backed by a noble range, while before that there are picturesque, hilly islands close inshore. There seemed to be no jungle save on the hills, nor were there uninhabited stretches, the population being thinly spread everywhere.

And now I write from Singkawang, the most completely Chinese town in all Indonesia. A Buddhist temple stands at the main crossroads, where a mosque would be in Java. The people are 80 per cent. Chinese and the Hakka dialect is the prevailing language. We have spent hours in conversation with the church leaders, especially with Pastor Lung, who shows most gratifying sparks of zeal and of call from God to preach the gospel in this hard place. It seems that he is the only full-time preacher in Chinese on all this coast. At night we met for supper in his home, an attractive house on a nice suburban road. He showed me the spot in the living-room where Miss Lo was murdered by unknown persons only eighteen months ago. We sat for a long time in a circle on the verandah after supper and they asked me to tell them how I had myself come to faith in Christ.

Next morning Pastor Lung escorted us to the bus for Pemangkat, the third city of West Borneo, another stage northwards. It is a bustling, Chinese town at the mouth of the Sambas River, lying pleasantly between hills. We at once boarded a passenger boat which conveyed us inland for four hours. The estuary of the Sambas River is wide and beautiful, and for a long time the river remained about a mile across, with tree-girt banks and background mountains. We stopped at several places on the north shore, tiny jetties behind which villages were shrouded in foliage. Once we turned into a creek to pick up passengers, but usually they came out from their hamlets in sampans to hail our boat in midstream. At the largest place we touched there were forty Chinese shops at the water's edge. At last the river forked and we turned off to the market of Kartiasa, lining both banks of the stream, which we crossed in a sampan.

There we got seats in a taxi which in twenty minutes bumped us to our destination at Sambas, a riverside town built of wood with a population of about 25,000. Bob Peterson met us and took us to his home in a shop house, the last of a row, with a little verandah overhanging a muddy creek. At night we strolled down the main road to the house on another creek where he and his wife first lived in Sambas, a tiny place, right on the road but at a lower level. The very sight of it made you catch your breath—so confined, so exposed, so brazen—but in this place during the past year more than twenty young Chinese men have turned to Christ, none of whom had ever entered a church or had any Christian connections before. They trooped in and shook our hands with great joy. Don Houliston and I preached to them for ninety minutes. Within a month the first nine are to be baptised. They are already a fellowship, if not exactly a church, and they now rent this original, defiant, little Bethel since the Petersons got the other house after their first baby was born. Would God I could transport to such an apostolic spot those at home who have prayed faithfully for the spread of the gospel in the world— dark night, clear stars, narrow street, aromatic creek, cinema crowds, packed room, open Bible, and Bob with his guitar! Both his wife and their servant are down with malaria at present, but he used to run his own restaurant in America so he has taken charge of the kitchen. Excellent meals issue from it and he roars with laughter at the idea that Don and I might assist. We called on a blind man aged fifty-four who was brought to Christ six months ago. "The Roman Catholics have been here for fifty years," he said to me, "but Christianity began with Mr Peterson." Quite a crowd assembled in his front room overlooking the river as we talked, so I preached at some length on Christ healing the woman bent double for eighteen years, one of the young Christian men interpreting my Mandarin into Hakka with warmth and understanding. It is marvellous to see and hear what God has done in Sambas. After supper we cycled again to the rented "church" on the creek for the children's meeting. Fifty-eight were present, though others and many adults watched from the road. Five of the Christian men led the meeting between them. The room is 28 feet by 15 feet. The back part of it was formerly partitioned off as the Petersons' bedroom, which boasted no window. Into the rest they have packed as many as 125 children, all Chinese. The roof is low and the hubbub terrific, but Bob knows how to control them, while his clear Christian character shines out and gives the lie to the notion that pioneer evangelism cannot now be done by missionaries. Five of the men sat with us for a long time at the end and I told them the story of their own great apostle, John Sung, of whom they had never heard. They are amazed to learn that there are large Chinese churches in the cities of Java, for they have never met any other believers nor seen any building used for Christian work save the creek "church". Their one and only model is Bob.

CHAPTER 5

MADURA AND THE WEDDINGS

NOT long after returning to Java from West Borneo I was invited by Sutikno to accompany him on a visit to Madura Island. Having already been there four times I was delighted at the chance to go again. As we travelled to Surabaja in my Triumph Mayflower car, he told me something about his own background. He was born in a Christian village near the Indian Ocean, like the majority of pastors in the East Java Church. His parents had three sons, of whom he was the second, and they were very poor. His father had four cows and Sutikno spent his youth toiling in the ricefields and caring for the cattle, in fact he attributed his short stature to the years spent bending down to cut grass for those cows! However, to me he seems to have developed into an attractive, distinct personality with a warm and genial manner. He was baptised when six months old, but it was only slowly that his parents were reconciled to dispense with his help on the farm and permit him to train for the Christian ministry. During his years of theological training at the seminary he eked out his meagre resources by acting as barber to the staff and students. It was at that time that we first met, for I had been invited to take some classes in English conversation at the seminary. After graduation he was sent to Madura Island to care for the scattered groups of Indonesian Christians (Christians, that is, from other parts of Indonesia whose work had taken them to Madura) and at the same time to do what he could to extend the gospel among the Madurese themselves.

On reaching Surabaja we spent a night with an Indonesian naval chaplain and his wife. For me the occasion was memorable, as although I had lived in Java for several years in association with Chinese, this was the first Javanese home in which I had ever eaten and slept. In their courtesy and humility they attempted to give me a Chinese rather than a Javanese meal, though I would much have preferred the latter. The chaplain himself hailed from a Muslim home and became a Christian along with his parents when he was ten years old. He told me that a remarkable work of God had recently broken out among Muslims in the area of Sabrang in East Java, where many had been baptised. In view of the usual antagonism of Muslims to the very name of Christ I asked him how he would account for such happenings. "Firstly," he said, "the Javanese soul is a seeking soul. Secondly, Muslims here are often impressed by the home life, unselfish service, and social contribution of Christians. Thirdly, in the evenings Christians spend many hours explaining the truth in people's homes. Fourthly, when Muslims come to compare the gospel with other religions they feel that it is superior."

Early next morning we drove down to the docks to catch the ferry to Madura, which is separated by only two miles of water from the great port of Surabaja. Stately ocean-going Bugis junks from Celebes, little Madurese fishing smacks with steeply swept-back masts, and freighters from the outside world lent colour and variety to the scene, all bathed in freshest sunshine. The ferry to Madura holds only four cars per journey so we had registered the day before to make sure of our place. It took twenty minutes to get across and as we mounted the ramp on to the wharf the other side a soldier thumbed a lift with us to the nearest large town, Bangkalan, a sprawling place with the crenellated walls of an old fortress standing authoritatively beside the main square, a large mosque, picturesque houses overhanging the river, and streets of Chinese shops. Sutikno expounded to the soldier the way of salvation through faith in Jesus Christ all the time he was in the car. He then took me at once to see a local official to report our arrival. The man was, of course, a Muslim and so much at leisure that our business occupied an hour and a half. He had lived at Mecca for three years and maintained that the Indonesian community settled in the Mecca-Medina area numbered two million. He was an intelligent man and our discussion ranged over many topics. Sutikno chatted in a leisurely way but was frank and unashamed in his references to "the Lord Jesus Christ" and to the cross. The

Muslim questioned him searchingly about the Christian view of marriage, divorce, and remarriage. He stated, though without bitterness, that defection from Islam would automatically dissolve the marriage of the person so defecting.

My guide and companion then decided that we would visit the chief of police, who turned out to be a Javanese Roman Catholic. He and his wife served us with coffee, which was succeeded by a meal, after which they would not hear of our leaving, so that we made their home our base and stayed the night with them. As usual Sutikno made no secret of the gospel; before each meal he prayed, not briefly, and at the end I was always asked to do likewise. In the evening they took us to visit the homes of several important people in Bangkalan. I learned that there are six million Madurese, the majority of whom live in East Java. On the island itself there are about two million, among whom I was told that there are but four qualified doctors and one dentist working. We called on one of the doctors in a well-stocked house lined with books. Although they were Muslims his wife asked me about the disagreement between Luther and Zwingli at the Marburg Conference in 1529.

Next morning our hosts went early to Mass and then accompanied us to the meeting of the Indonesian Protestant Church in Bangkalan, for which Sutikno is responsible. There were thirty people present in the front room of a private house, not one of them being Madurese. Before the service began we visited the homes of several of the Christians, praying with them and exhorting them. All these days Sutikno devoted himself to the work of the gospel wholeheartedly. He seemed oblivious of time and gifted with clear and arresting speech. He illustrated what he had to say with anything that came to hand—glasses, plates, cigarettes. I noticed that the cigarette was regarded as essential to male life. Before the meeting began all the men present were smoking, including Sutikno. There was a table in front of him; on it were placed New Testaments, hymnbooks, the offertory bowl, cigarettes, and a lighter. We sang in the Javanese language but everything else was in Indonesian, since most of those present were from Sumatra, Celebes, and the Moluccas.

From Bangkalan we travelled round the whole island, which is a hundred miles long and approximately twenty-two miles broad. The average density of population is 1300 persons to the square mile, so that Madura is as crowded as Java.

Madura has little appeal to tourists, while the fanatical Islam of its people has given it a rather forbidding reputation even in Surabaja. None of my Chinese friends in the big city had ever visited it. "The ferry turns turtle once a year," I was told. Even a Sumatran who lived on the island warned me, "They always fight with knives. They will tear up your tracts." However, we invariably found that a generous measure of unbelief in man's fears is a valuable companion to faith in Christ. We had thousands of Christian tracts with us in the car and as we travelled along we threw them out at the feet of the people we encountered on the roads. This is a method often employed in Java by those advertising public rallies, political meetings, and theatrical or cinema shows. This encouraged us to employ it rather than to pass through such a populous region without giving any sign that we had a message from God for the inhabitants. Without exception the literature was eagerly received. People would drop their work and rush into the road to collect it. We soon found that cyclists would always dismount provided the tracts were dropped ten yards ahead of them. I remember a horseman riding with a richly decorated saddle, who leapt from his mount, held on to the reins, and dragged the horse after him as he caught up with a fluttering leaflet which would speak to him about Jesus. But more commonly we left crowds scrambling for our wares.

The road to Ambunten on the north coast marches over the hills through long avenues of tamarisk trees. There were still people everywhere, although the density of population decreases somewhat in this extreme eastern end of Madura. Ambunten perches like innumerable tropical fishing villages amid luxuriant undergrowth and palms beside bays of golden, untrammelled sand, separated by rocky headlands. A mile beyond it we stopped to enjoy the breakers of the Java Sea and to drink coffee. Men and women soon collected around us, so Sutikno spoke to them about Christ in the Madurese language which he has had to learn. Moving westwards we came down to a bridge spanning a rushing, dark-brown torrent, on the opposite bank of which a large village clustered in heat and dust. To the right the river raced 200 yards to the sea, both shores lined with the characteristic, swept-back mast, Madurese fishing junks. Then as we passed through the village, the crowds raced behind us in surprise and delight to get their share of the multi-coloured leaflets fluttering to the ground.

July 28th. And now I am back in Surabaja where Mrs Tan's eldest daughter was married today. Both she and her husband are young people of character and ability, brought up in the Chinese Christian Church from infancy. Somewhat contrary to the traditions thereof the bride returned from her sojourn overseas with her great natural charm touched off with lipstick, nail paint, elaborate earrings, and a very large engagement ring, not to speak of the most dazzling attire. The church was packed with four hundred visitors for the occasion. The couple arrived one hour late and cut a magnificent figure: he in black trousers, cream coat, and bow tie; she in the most gorgeous dress and train. Children scattered rose petals down the aisle in front of them. The ceremony was wholly in Mandarin, tastefully and beautifully conducted by the pastor, and the chief place and honour were given to the Lord Jesus Christ. After solemn question and answer they exchanged rings and then, in a delightful gesture, the bridegroom lifted back her long veil and folded it carefully over her head.

August 3rd. Pastor Meng is an ordained minister of the Church of England and sometimes he has to conduct the Communion Service in English at the British Community Church in Surabaja. He finds this a severe ordeal as his English is very limited, so today he invited me to tea in his room to help him with it. When I arrived I found his tape recorder all set and at his request I read through the entire service so that he could play the tape over and over to improve his own pronunciation.

August 9th. Pastor Meng announced that there was going to be a Thanksgiving Service in the College this afternoon, but no one quite knew why. At lunch I pressed him for details and he became covered with confusion and pleasure. "A family affair," he said. Later he drew me aside and with trembling joy confided, "My old mother in Macao is eighty-one today." At least seventy people came

to the Thanksgiving and a young pastor gave an address on
Genesis 1. At first I doubted that this was a very suitable text for
such an occasion, till he gradually revealed his thesis, which was that
while each "day" was in itself pronounced "good', only the whole
lot in retrospect were described as "very good", and so it is with the
lives of those who yield themselves to the Lord, right up to eighty-
one. Pastor Meng then rose and since I was translating into English as
he went along, writing it out hurriedly for an Australian couple who
were sitting on each side of me, I got down the gist of what he said,
which was this. "Praise God for this message, and now I want to
tell you of God's great goodness to my mother. I am specially happy
today, because it is her birthday. Ten years ago today she came to
know Christ as her Saviour and now she is eighty-one. I myself was
saved when I was thirty-eight, consecrated myself to God's service
when I was forty, and became a minister of the gospel at forty-
seven. But I still had a heavy heart, for my mother was not a
Christian, although all my children were by that time clearly converted. So we prayed much for my mother. But she was from a
heathen home and it was very hard for such an old lady to believe.
But praise God, He answered our prayers, and on her seventy-first
birthday she turned to Christ and was baptised. My burden was
gone! But then she was ill for nearly three years and an operation
for cancer seemed essential. For months we hesitated but she got
weaker. We prayed much, for we did not particularly trust the
doctor who might have to operate. Then God sent a very competent surgeon to Hongkong and the Bishop himself asked him if
he would operate on my mother. All went well. The lump
weighed seven and a half pounds. In a week she was home again
and today she is eighty-one. She can walk faster than I can; she can
run upstairs; she can thread a needle; and when I am with her she
mends my clothes. Her hearing and eyesight are unimpaired. Please
pray for my mother, and when she is ninety-one and I am seventy-
one please come again to our Thanksgiving Service."

September 13th. Another week of daily lectures in the Bible
College ended at midday on Friday and I felt almost reluctant to
go straight off for a week-end of meetings in Modjokerto. I took
the drive quietly to snatch some relaxation, pausing to verify the

astonishing fact that at least 4000 of the baby volcano's 5500 feet are intensively settled and cultivated by mankind. On arrival I found that the Chinese pastor had arranged for me to stay with a Mr and Mrs Pang; their house was so large and contained so many people that I had to ask whether or not it was a hotel. Apparently it is the Lord's hotel. My bedroom measures 30 feet by 18 and the bedstead would match the King of Bashan's. At 6 p.m. I preached to eighty people in Mandarin, interpreted into Indonesian.

September 17th. My three-day Modjokerto trip ended at Djombang. The narrow, stuffy church was crammed up to and outside the doors, and half the congregation were men. The attraction was the novelty of a foreigner speaking Chinese and also the Human Heart posters which I used in preaching. Afterwards the pastor and I were entertained to supper in the back of a chemist's shop. Our host graciously insisted on filling up the car with petrol and at 9 p.m. I pulled away with eight miles to go—a hazardous venture in their eyes in these difficult times. The road was clear and wide, the night fine, and the car on top form, so in spite of climbing to 2000 feet I did it in two hours. On the way I was startled to see what appeared to be a colossal, twisted, fiery serpent in the sky. For a moment I wondered about atomic bombs, but it was a big-scale, planned burning of jungle at about 5000 feet on the baby volcano.

September 24th. After a full week of lectures I am just back from another eventful week-end in pastures new. I have long looked forward to visiting Java's remoter east and this was the chance. I drove in five hours to Djember along a magnificent, twisting, populous mountain road, and preached there in the afternoon to forty persons of Chinese race in a small house down a back alley. After dark we drove up to Bondowoso, which is the hub of these parts and the local pastor put me in a hotel. Early next morning, which was Sunday, we drove to Situbondo. Some might think that these are far-away places (with glorious names!), but they are anything but uncivilised. The towns are very large, set among mountains and gorges all over which humanity is settled on the usual fantastic Javanese scale, only that here the people are predominantly Madurese. The main roads into Situbondo are magnificent boulevards, running dead straight for miles, lined with beautiful trees and houses behind them. Of the mountain road from Bondowoso to Besuki I can only say that it is like a vision of the Garden of Eden.

At Situbondo I preached to seventy people at the morning service of the Chinese Christian Church and then talked for a long time with its leaders while we sipped coffee in a near-by home. They wanted to detain us for the afternoon, but we had to return to Bondowoso where I addressed 130 people at 3.30, and then carried straight on with forty young people till 8 p.m., by which time the long-suffering interpreter into Indonesian was too exhausted to understand my Mandarin any more.

Next morning we visited a Javanese factory owner, a wealthy man reared in Islam. He and his daughter had taken to reading the Bible, which they enjoyed but could not properly understand. A Chinese Christian helped them and they turned to Christ some while ago. Leaving them at 7.30 a.m. I started the long trek home alone, refreshed by the beauty of the sea, the breaking waves and the fishing fleets. At the town of Probolinggo I paused for an hour with a Mr Lin, an elderly man, Confucian in outlook, who had never worshipped idols and who became a believer in the Lord Jesus ten years ago. Time was short, but he swept me round to three Christian homes, back to his own for a cold drink, and then escorted me for a mile with old-time courtesy. What open doors! What welcomes! What smiles and handshakes and eager hopes of help and fellowship in the work of God! In four hours I was home and reflecting that in the last two week-ends I have been warmly received in seven cities far to the east and far to the west—a ridiculous situation when one is trying to teach in a Chinese Bible College and already has one eye on Madura Island and another on the Javanese Church.

Further visits to Probolinggo followed. On one occasion when I had been invited there Pastor Meng came purposefully into my room shortly before I was due to leave. The Suez crisis was at its height and he said that he had been uneasy about my trip and after praying over it he felt he should come and advise me to stay quietly at home for the time being. I bowed to this good counsel. Next time when I was due to go he simply informed me that he was sending one of the students with me, a boy named Li from West Borneo, and I realised that he did not think it was wise for me to be travelling alone in the car. So the two of us drove down to sea level in 100 minutes and were warmly welcomed by old Mr Lin at his high-ceilinged home which is fast becoming the Chinese Christian Church in the town. It was 4 p.m. on a Saturday. After cold showers and iced drinks we sallied out to visit Chinese homes under the wing of Mr Lin, who is an old inhabitant. Vividly I can still see the people we met:

A heavily-built, grey-haired Hakka, materialistic and un-believing, most astonished at our approaches, in which he only became involved because of his son's interest in the gospel.

An elderly man from central China who ekes out an uncertain living selling lottery tickets.

An ice-cream vendor, saved through Dr John Sung in Surabaja in 1939, who has just been back to mainland China to visit his old mother.

A garrulous dentist, full of Mencius, but reading the Bible now.

A prosperous family running a big general store, the wife a Pentecostal believer, the husband unbelieving and threatened with blindness.

A merchant explaining that it was impossible to be a Christian at present since he was obliged to lie in making up his tax returns, but he would like to become one when he had retired and handed over the business to his sons.

We exhorted, encouraged, expounded, invited, and distributed tracts for dear life, night having fallen and a cool breeze blowing off the sea to freshen up the crowded streets and alleys of Pro-bolinggo after the day's long grilling.

Every Friday night there is a meeting for testimony and prayer in the Bible College. We sit around in a large circle, students and staff, all dressed in white. This week we had an entertaining con-tribution from one of the men from Borneo. He told how the Lord had helped and delivered him when he was held up by a Madurese rickshaw driver in a dark street at night in Surabaja. For good measure he threw in a couple of murders by Madurese, dropped dark hints about knives, and advised everyone to avoid rickshaw men in black shirts. This evoked much mirth and left the company looking at me on account of my known interest in the Madurese, so I spoke at some length on 2 Timothy 1:7, "God hath not given us the spirit of fear, but of power, and of love, and of a sound mind", stressing the possibility of victory over fear and our duty to conquer evil with good and to rescue these people from their sin instead of shunning them like the plague. It is a live issue, for there are six million Madurese on our doorstep!

Next day I embarked in the Mayflower with two Javanese students to attend the wedding of Sutikno, our friend from Madura, which was to be held in his home village down by the sea. The drive took four hours by the awe-inspiring route skirting the Great Volcano. I took a thousand tracts in Indonesian and initiated my companions into the simple art of throwing them out whenever we passed people or houses on this long, rugged road. They took to it eagerly and diligently bombarded their willing victims. The practice adds interest to a journey as well as promoting faith in the power of God and a sense of responsibility towards all men. On these occasions I always pray in the car before starting and this seems to appeal to people so well that they want a prayer of thanksgiving on arrival too. The population is absolutely continuous, one village joining straight on to the next. Our destination was a Christian village so close to the sea that we could hear the breakers thundering on the rocks. Like all the Christian villages in East Java this was not a Muslim village which had turned to Christ, but an entirely new settlement established by the migration of believers from the Modjokerto-Djombang area some seventy years ago. The present population is about 2000. To picture it you must first abandon all ideas of an English village such as streets, shops and lines of houses. Imagine first a rather large wood; space the trees not too thickly and turn half of them into towering coconut palms. Then envisage your wood neatly divided by well-planned, broad, dusty paths about ten yards wide with neat hedges down both sides. Next pepper the wood with four hundred houses made of brick, stone, and bamboo, with tiled roofs, each with bamboo gateposts surmounted by a cross and its own drive-in, so that the house stands back fifty yards from the path and about the same distance

from the nearest house on either side—and there you have a noise-
less, secluded, woodland city, which has nurtured not a few pastors
and leaders of the East Java Church.

I stayed in the bridegroom's house on the eve of the wedding,
in fact I slept on his broad bed with him. Everything in the house
was clean, tidy, and simple. Lamps were few and dim, the food
plain and not over-plentiful, the precious cow very tough, the
bathroom doorless and semi-public, the bedroom minute and
devoid of all furnishings except the bed. I was introduced to
Sutikno's father, mother, aunts, uncles, brothers, and more. After
a very late supper we strolled over to the bride's house and met her
parents, aunts, uncles, and still more. Towards midnight I prayed
with him in our room and then slept so heavily after the long drive
that by the time I woke he was dressed for the wedding in a brown
sarong, a white shirt, white bow tie, black coat, and a small brown,
batik turban. With a fresh buttonhole he looked splendid. He
has taken the whole occasion most seriously, and yesterday before
we arrived there was a two-hour preparation service for the
marriage. At 9 a.m. I had the great privilege of driving the couple
and Sutikno's parents to the church in the village. The next four
hours were not altogether easy for me as everything was in Javanese.
The bride wore a buttonhole and a sarong similar to Sutikno's.
She had on a very pretty blue blouse, while the bun of her hair was
elaborately and colourfully arranged. There were 400 people
present, but apart from this coincidence I was more impressed by
the contrast between this rustic celebration and the gorgeous
ceremony I had so recently witnessed in Surabaja. Since it was
Sunday we had the regular morning service with the wedding
fitted into the middle. The couple sat on two chairs, three yards
apart, right at the front throughout; each had a cushion to kneel on.
There was question and answer; at one point he took her by the
hand; but I judged that the actual marriage was when they were
both kneeling and the presiding pastor prayed over them with one
hand extended above each head. And so we emerged into the
brilliant sunshine outside and the couple walked along very slowly
side by side under a large umbrella held over them, the congregation following. The reception was at the bride's house. The bride

and bridegroom sat in a large double-chair, almost akin to a throne, draped in white with flowers placed around it. The rest of the company took their places at long tables under a pavilion which had been specially built on to the front of the house for the occasion. Speeches followed, all still in Javanese so that I could not understand a word. Interesting as the whole morning had been, this language barrier wearied me somewhat, so that it was a relief when I realised that a short, military-looking man who had risen from a near-by table to make a speech was using Indonesian. It dawned on me as he spoke that he must be doing this for my sake, since I was the only non-Javanese present. I turned round in my seat and struggled to follow his meaning, for my own command even of Indonesian was still very limited. This much was clear to me, that he was speaking with warmth about Jesus Christ, as though he really knew Him and meant it. Somehow his manner delighted me and I wondered who he could be. When the company broke up, feeling probably that by using Indonesian he had to some extent already attracted my attention, he came over and introduced himself to me, shaking me warmly by the hand and adding other remarks which I could only vaguely grasp. He told me that his name was Rufus.

CHAPTER 6

TONGUE-TIED IN SABRANG

ONE evening while I was reading in my room at the Bible College after supper three of the Madurese boys, who had fled to Java after meeting Sutikno and turning to Christ, came to see me. With my mind full of the Chinese language it was not easy to converse with them in Indonesian, but I did my utmost to seize the opportunity and strengthen their faith in Christ. After a long talk we read the Scriptures together and I suggested that we should pray. When they left I escorted them out to the road in the manner customary among Chinese and then returned with joy and reached for my pen to record my impressions of the evening. It was a Parker 51 and I was surprised not to be able to find it. After a long and fruitless search I was driven to the depressing conclusion that one of them must have taken it while we were praying. I fear that this was the case, for the pen never turned up and the men never came to see me again. Gradually it seems that they lost touch with Christians; some of them eventually went back to Madura; one of them married a Buddhist; most of them were dazzled by the more varied and exciting city life of Java and in course of time I altogether lost contact with them.

One day Rufus called on me. I recognised him at once as the man who had spoken so warmly at Sutikno's wedding reception. But here again there was a language barrier between us. I found it exceedingly difficult to grasp more than the general drift of his Indonesian. However, I got the impression that he was having an encouraging time in the Sabrang area. He told me of a roomful of sixty Muslims who had listened to him and questioned him for four hours till he became hoarse with talking. We prayed together before he left. I greatly regretted that my lack of Indonesian prevented me from getting to know him better and learning more from him.

Shortly afterwards Pastor Meng asked me to represent the Bible College at the twenty-fifth anniversary celebrations of the East Java Church, of which Rufus is a minister. There were more than 300 people present at the service, which was conducted by five robed ministers, their names as formidable as their appearance. All spoke in the same heavy, slow, solemn manner. The secretary of the Synod of the East Java Church read a short history of the movement, which he divided into the period in the womb of its mother, the Dutch Mission (1848-1931), its birth on December 11th, 1931, with Dr Kraemer as the midwife, and its growth since that time under parental care. There are now said to be sixty-four congregations, sixty-seven ministers, and about 80,000 Christian believers, making it probably the largest break-away from Islam into the Protestant Church in the history of the world. The proceedings were recorded on tape, including the message of a missionary of the Dutch Reformed Church, who was the only speaker to bring a personal and spiritual message.

The next evening I was back in the Javanese Church once more to attend the graduation ceremony of the Javanese Theological Seminary in the town. There were ten graduates: three from Java, five from Celebes, and two from Bali. They wore white suits and sat in a semicircle in front of the flower-bedecked platform. Behind them in two larger semicircles, like guardian walls, were arrayed no less than forty pastors of the East Java Church, clad in full Genevan solemnity of shiny black robes and white cravats. I noticed Sutikno and Rufus among them, as well as the naval chaplain in whose home I had stayed in Surabaja. It struck me that the Dutch Mission had begotten a babe of remarkable proportions. In years to come the evening was to have a sequel which I should have regarded as totally impossible at the time.

After the graduations the annual Synod meetings of the East Java Church were held in the Theological Seminary close to the Bible College in which I was living. One afternoon three of the pastors, men I had never seen before, called on me. They had heard that I had bundles of Christian tracts and they wanted to get stocks for use in their churches, the idea being that I would give them to them for nothing. Their hopes were high and it happened that my supplies were low, so that I was not keen to hand them over in the way they proposed. They were greatly taken aback at my reluctance and I got the impression that they were accustomed to missionaries giving them what they wanted without charge. I suggested they should use funds derived from their weekly church collections to buy for themselves literature needed for the work of their churches, but it seemed to me they were unlikely to act on the hint.

December, 1956. On Christmas Day I drove four girl students from the Bible College to the Salvation Army Hospital at Sabrang. Deborah, Phoebe, Pearl, and Ruth looked very charming in yellow, red, blue, and green respectively. We took with us a hundred Christmas parcels and a good supply of tracts. There were seventy Muslims in the wards that day, but two died and one was born before we arrived. Gwen Crawford, an Australian nurse loaned to the hospital, stood between a pair of wards and announced the visitors through the open doors in a loud voice. Deborah and Ruth entered one, while Phoebe and Pearl stood in the other. They then preached boldly and clearly in Indonesian. In the men's wards I moved up behind them to give moral support. The patients sat cross-legged on their beds and listened in perfect silence. "What do you call the Lord Jesus?", said Deborah, expecting the answer, "A prophet". "Muhammad," called out a man in a turban. "No, no," she said, "Muhammad is Muhammad and arose from among men. Jesus is Jesus and came from heaven." After ten minutes' preaching she prayed, Muslim heads all reverently bowed. Then the four girls stood together between the wards and sang carols, after which they took the Christmas parcels and tracts from bed to bed. This process was repeated in each pair of wards.

As the year 1956 drew to a close I drove Pastor Meng down to Surabaja for the Christmas celebrations of the Chinese Christian Church, for which we have both preached frequently over a number of years. It is standard procedure in these Chinese-language churches to have a semi-dramatic performance on these occasions. A school auditorium was hired and 600 people were present, entrance being by ticket only. All the performers were children, but training had obviously been thorough and production was first class. There were ten different items, all involving singing about the gospel and the Christmas story, which was beautifully enacted in four tableaux. With musical interludes the performance lasted three hours and at the close the great company was entertained to a ten-course Chinese banquet punctuated by choruses and carols. As I looked around the sea of Chinese faces I felt the honour and responsibility of being about to address them from their pulpit for the eleventh time on the last week-end of the old year.

On Sunday morning I drove back to Surabaja alone, contending with hordes of cars fleeing the heat of the city, bound for the hill stations. After a rest and a shower at Mrs Tan's I preached at noon at the Cantonese Church, returned to Mrs Tan's for lunch and a siesta, and then spoke at the big 5 p.m. meeting to 500 Chinese believers crammed thirty-five to a row from the rostrum to the rear. This is probably the biggest Chinese-speaking Church in Indonesia, indeed in the whole southern hemisphere. The choir of a church in Djakarta was paying them a visit, thirty strong, vying with the local choir in beautiful singing. Truly God has done great things in the Chinese dispersion. I spoke on Psalm 108:13, "Through God we shall do valiantly, for it is He that shall tread down our enemies." After the long, hot day at sea-level, I drove back to the Bible College in the cool of the night to find it invaded by fifty Chinese Christians from Bandung. Yet the place was big enough to absorb them all, sleeping on mattresses covering the whole floor-space of several rooms. It was interesting to see Pastor Meng in the midst of such a mob. By nature he would crave peace and seclusion, but he is an excellent organiser and since he took over the leadership of this College in his old age the Lord has enabled him to develop the gifts which the task requires.

Then everything changed with the long-delayed arrival of Jess and Rupert, from England. They reached the Bible College just as a Chinese Christian Youth Conference commenced there. With over 200 guests living in we had to crush into the little room I had previously occupied alone. But we already knew that our destiny lay elsewhere. For years we had worked with the Chinese churches of Java amongst Chinese-speaking people, but the longer we lived there the more we realised that God wanted us to get to know the language and life of the people of the land, the Javanese, and to share in bringing the gospel to them. So for a long time we had been praying for a house in a Javanese village, where we might serve a new apprenticeship, yet not too far from the city so that I could still continue a limited amount of teaching in the Bible College. Now that our family was reunited we urgently needed a place to live and we knew that the time when our prayers would be answered must be close at hand. Six months previously the house Gwen Crawford was occupying at Sabrang had been offered to me, but without Jess it would have been impossible to run it and I had to let it go. Gwen was still there, but in the meantime I had met Rufus and we had the impression that there might yet be room for us in that district. On two afternoons we drove out to Rufus' home at Ringit and he came with us in the Mayflower to look at several houses in Barek which might be rented. None of them proved to be quite suitable and then suddenly there was a change in Gwen's affairs; she decided to move into the hospital where her work was and offered us the house which I had originally allowed to go to her. Thus with very little effort we were able to rent 122 Office Street, Sabrang. Six weeks after Jess' arrival Pastor and Mrs Meng stood a little disconsolately in the Bible College courtyard to see us drive off in the Mayflower with our effects loaded on a lorry ahead of us; although I was still to help them to a limited extent they realised that our days of close co-operation were over.

The road which was to become so familiar to us led for several miles through the suburbs of the city, then out past village after village in the country, separated by oceans of sugar-cane eight feet high, across the infant Brantas River foaming deep in its rocky bed, through teeming townships, past green fields of rice full of croaking frogs, and round the edges of the Great Volcano, whose peak towered majestically into the cloudless sky. Then it dipped to a ravine, crossed by a long narrow bridge, and rose into Sabrang with its brief bustle of cars and lorries, buses and carts, shops and cattle. From the market quiet arcades radiated in all directions each one full of homes, each home full of people. Office Street, so called because local government offices had once been evacuated there from the city during the independence struggle, ran east for a mile from the main highway. Along it lay houses, shops, and tailors' workrooms, several of Sabrang's ten schools, the lock-up, the Salvation Army hospital, the police station, the mosque, and the post office. Close to the hospital, next door to the police, and opposite the lock-up was No. 122.

The house which God had given us stood back from the road about twenty-five yards with its own circular drive-in around a clump of trees. It was typical of the more substantial village houses of East Java, though there were several better ones in Sabrang itself. It was built of stone with a tiled roof and consisted of six rooms arranged in two rows of three. There was first an open verandah behind a balustrade. From this the front door led into the sitting-room, which we also used as a dining-room. Beyond that was a third room which we turned into our kitchen. From each of these three a bedroom opened to the left. Originally extensive rear premises formed part of the house but when our landlady's husband died she remodelled them, moved in there herself, and rented out the main part of the house. Her name was Mother Daro and she lived with her old mother, known to us as Granny, and two servants. One of these was a woman and the other a hunchback who was addressed simply as Man. He had no room of his own but existed on a cheerless bamboo construction called a bed outside his employer's back door. Mother Daro was barefooted and illiterate, but she was a respected local magnate, owner of ricefields and property.

We arrived in the morning. Mother Daro welcomed us, unlocked the front door with the key which hung round her neck, and handed it to us. We could not have much conversation as her knowledge of Indonesian was almost as limited as ours. The curious stared from a distance at white people moving their belongings into a village house. They had fought similar looking people for many years and in the course of the independence war ejected most of them from the country and burnt down their houses. In colonial days Sabrang had had many Dutch residents and a Dutch chief of police, but that order of things had long passed away. So the sight of a white family moving in against the course of events could but provoke some questions. Time and again as we reported ourselves to the police, to the head of Sabrang village, and to other local authorities, we were asked, "And why have you left the city and come to Sabrang?"

We explained truthfully enough that we felt the time had come for us to withdraw from Chinese society and get to know the language and life of the Javanese people. While this attitude may have been quite gratifying to them, it probably also left many thinking that we must surely be doing it to obtain some more tangible advantage.

For the first four days we kept our doors shut most of the time while we cleaned the house, unpacked, and arranged our belongings; Yeny (who had formerly worked for Gwen) cooked for us. Gwen had often spoken to her about Christ and shortly before we arrived she had declared herself a believer in Him. A few days after reaching Sabrang we took her with us to the local Javanese Church, which was the first time she had ever been to a formal Christian meeting. The church lay midway between Sabrang and Ringit, where Rufus lived. It was really just the home of a Mrs Rakes, widow of a Dutch official; her bed stood beside the pulpit; the vestry was her kitchen.

We found ourselves up against a formidable linguistic problem. Among Sabrang's 7000 inhabitants there were 300 Chinese, but most of them could not understand Mandarin. In any case we had moved from the city to Sabrang deliberately in order to escape from Chinese society, so we were not expecting or wanting to use Mandarin. We had both already spent some months studying Indonesian, the national language of the new state. But in Sabrang, as in all Javanese villages, the language in common use was Javanese, a much more difficult tongue. Schools, newspapers, the radio, and official and political life were conducted in Indonesian, but the language of heart and home was Javanese. Jess felt that if she was to reach the women of Java with the gospel she must get Javanese, and so she started on the long and arduous task of learning a highly complicated language without any grammar or dictionary to help her. I decided that rather than stumble along in both languages, I would aim to become proficient in Indonesian. For many months we each had a teacher three nights a week and gave hours every day to language study. In effect, Jess was studying both languages at the same time, since the only way her teacher could help her with Javanese was by using Indonesian. But for the present what we could accomplish was severely limited by what we could say and understand. Day after day very heavy rain fell each afternoon, continuing till after dark, and this also had the effect of walling us off from the people at the beginning. Furthermore I was still lecturing three days a week in the Bible College in the city, leaving after breakfast in the Mayflower and returning after dark. Being accustomed to regard a white man as their enemy rather than their friend, people were slow to approach us. However, there was a school just down the road and it soon became the fashion during the brief breaks between classes for gangs of boys to come across and stare at the new arrivals from the road; before long they ventured down the drive-in to the front steps; finding that we were glad to see them they swarmed on to the verandah, fifty at a time. This would happen repeatedly every morning and constituted quite a problem in view of our limited command of Indonesian. If I made any remark to our serried ranks of visitors they burst into peals of laughter at the extraordinary noises I produced; usually they simply mimicked what I had said and made no attempt to treat it seriously. If I spoke to any individual he became covered in confusion and would at once look over his shoulder at the person behind him whom he presumed, and hoped, that I was addressing. As missionaries we were very glad to see so many young people coming to our home, but to achieve effective contact with them was far from simple. We tried handing out tracts so that, even though we were unable as yet to explain much about the gospel, they might at least carry home some written message which they could study at leisure. But to produce tracts was to invite a riot on the verandah; everybody scrambled and snatched for as many as possible, while the news spread like wildfire and fresh crowds of children came rushing into our premises to share in the fun. Those who secured tracts immediately hid them and demanded more. Only the bell ringing in the school across the road delivered us from the mob, which returned with further reinforcements at the next break. We soon decided that it was not really profitable to give out hundreds of tracts daily under such pressure. An alternative method proved more satisfactory. When the rush came upon us I took the gramophone out on to the verandah and played gospel records in Indonesian and Javanese, sitting in the centre of a densely-packed crowd of boys. This method made it infinitely easier to preserve law and order, since they were all curious to hear what was said on the records. It was not hard to hold the attention of sixty boys at a time in this way, and then in a flash the school-bell snatched the audience away in the middle of a record, a stampede across the drive ensued, and we were left to study in peace once more. If there was any spite or unpleasantness in these visitations our relative ignorance of the language hid it from us; the children seemed to us to come in good humour, bent on fun and diversion from school life.

On the days when I was away in the city Jess had to bear the full brunt of these invasions on her own—along with Rupert. Indeed Rupert was one of the main attractions. He was three years old, the only fair-haired child in the whole district. The desire to touch his head and his face proved almost irresistible to adults and children alike, but he naturally found it irritating. We had to keep an eye on him the whole time, though he was some-times capable of looking after himself. Once when an exceptionally large crowd of older boys gathered at the verandah steps he hap-pened to be the first to meet them. Jess found him armed with a little pile of stones, prepared to do battle to the death. On such occasions our main concern was lest he give a wrong impression of our attitude to visitors and arouse antagonism towards us and the message of the gospel. This general condition of morning tumult was to continue for more than a year. Jess was better able to stand it and manage it than I was. I confess that before long I awaited the invasions with some dread, feeling doubtful whether they served any useful purpose. At least they proved that we were not stand-offish; the report of what our home was like must have been carried all over the district by the children; and the same could be said of the gospel tracts which we gave them. The afternoons and the rain gave us relief; quietness descended on our part of Office Street; if visitors came, they came singly and could be met as individuals; the children who pattered up the steps were our near neighbours, who soon became real friends, their first curiosity more easily quenched than that of children who had less opportunity of viewing such strange beings. It was some time before individual faces stood out clearly from the mass we encountered in those first days, but in a few weeks we were permanently captivated by the family of our nearest neighbours ten yards away—Riti, a girl of eleven dressed in tatters, Misli her six-year-old sister in equal humility, and their baby brother Pooh, for whom no garments at all were considered necessary. The first person in Sabrang with whom I achieved full understanding was Pooh. Words were unnecessary between us. He clambered up the verandah steps in a state of nature and presented himself before me with a twinkle; we solemnly shook hands; I gave him a tract with a picture on it; and he scampered back to Riti, chortling with glee, to be hoisted on to her strong back. These three children remained through all our days in Sabrang our most faithful and affectionate friends.

It was *February 11th* when we moved in. At first Rufus left us alone to find our feet but on the 20th he came round on his bicycle, parked it under the trees, and stepped on to the verandah, holding out his hand. It was a relief to be with an adult who had some comprehension of what we were up to. Yeny brought out tea while we sat and chatted. I would have enjoyed it immensely had it not been so difficult to apprehend his meaning in Indonesian. But on this very first visit to our home he asked me if I would like to accompany him on trips to Muslim villages, preaching the gospel. I indicated that I most certainly would. At night the woman captain in charge of the Salvation Army hospital, a Norwegian, came to supper with us and stayed talking for a long time, for we were close neighbours and felt it desirable to come to a good understanding at the very outset.

February 21st. In the afternoon I drove Mrs Rufus and four of her children in the Mayflower thirty miles to the east on the twisting road around the Great Volcano, which thrashes and fights its way across the ridges and gorges running down from the upper slopes. Our destination was Trawas, where we met Rufus, who had preached there until 3 o'clock in the morning. We drew up outside the clinic, which is run by a Christian medical named Suharta. I call him a medical for want of a better term; such men are partially trained doctors; they treat all cases that are not too serious and pass the rest on to the hospital in Sabrang or to the larger ones in the city. Suharta and his wife have eight children and seem to be the only Christian family in Trawas. As we sat at the table in their little front room sipping coffee and eating fried bananas I asked him, "When did you first believe in Christ?" He nudged Rufus and said, "We were schoolboys together thirty years ago and he led me then—and now we meet again." Before long Rufus prayed and we departed, though not before he had pointed across the tangle of hills to the south of us, and said, "There are many believers in the mountains over there, about six hours' walking from here."

We did not drive straight back to Sabrang but turned aside up the ever-steepening flank of the Great Volcano until we reached the village of Gondang, where I was to experience my baptism in evangelistic work with Rufus. With eight souls on board, the Mayflower slithered on bottom gear over muddy tracks. The huge mountain is one enormous human ant-hill. When Tias, the headmaster of Gondang village school, received us into his bleak little house I innocently asked him how many pupils he had. "Six hundred and seventy," was the answer, "and sixteen teachers." He was a tall, lanky, rather dishevelled kind of man, with untamed hair and protruding teeth; it soon became obvious that he was not at all well. Although born in a Christian village he had lived so long among the Muslims of Gondang that I felt he had not only lost much sense of being a Christian but also gone to seed in other ways. The floor of his sitting-room was so uneven that no chair would balance properly on it. The concrete had worn away, exposing the bricks underneath, many of which were also broken and crumbled. His wife was infirm, and stout to the point of immobility. I wondered what sort of an influence such a man could possibly have among schoolchildren. The things that God would do were then all hidden in the womb of time.

Since it was not yet dark Rufus suggested we should visit another home. I nosed the car down the lanes he indicated, all of them lined with houses standing back in their own gardens on the hillside. We called on the head of the village, another gaunt figure with a young and energetic wife. I was struck with the bareness of their home, although they were obviously people of importance. In truth my eyes were not yet accustomed to Javanese rural life in the tropics. There was nothing on the concrete floors except bare tables, bare chairs, and bare bedframes. Sweetened tea was served to us in glasses without saucers. Our host wore a bright yellow shirt and the round, black, national hat of Indonesia. While we were there another visitor called and chatted to Rufus and our host in Javanese, which I could not understand. To my eyes he was just a country yokel, but after he had gone Rufus told me that he was a Muslim priest. The local medical man, a Christian again, whose name was Lukas, also dropped in, a stocky, muscular, wrinkled, worried-looking person. Although all the talk was in Javanese, Rufus kept drawing me in by using Indonesian, and I gathered that Lukas had married a Muslim and was now completely out of touch with the Christian Church, though there was in any case none within reach.

When we returned to the house of headmaster Tias it was 7.30 p.m. and time for the meeting which had been arranged. This was to be held in the schoolroom which adjoined his house, so we moved across there. The scene was unpromising. An ancient pressure lamp shed uncertain light over the room, which was undusted and uncleaned. The children's desks were small and narrow; a few men sat in them uncomfortably, smoking. Not taking much notice of them, our party took seats near the front. There was a pause of an hour and a half while others filtered in. By about nine o'clock forty Muslims were in the room and forty more in the darkness outside the open door and the glassless windows. The headmaster removed the lamp and pumped it up, the company waiting in almost total darkness as he did so. Then he took his seat at a table, methodically extracted his spectacles, cleaned them, and put them them on, with the air of one who is about to do something important. At last Rufus rose and faced the audience, smiling. Since everything he said was in Javanese I could understand nothing at all. He preached for two hours, breaking up his talk by using gospel posters, gramophone records, and Scripture verses. The posters hung on the wall behind him and he explained them in detail. I noticed that the men listened to him intently, their eyes not straying, their cigarette smoke curling continuously upwards. Rufus' gramophone was an elderly machine; his son operated it, sitting across the table from the headmaster; the records contained singing and preaching in both Indonesian and Javanese; since none of those present possessed hymnbooks, or would have wanted to use them if they had done so, the records served the purpose hymn-singing serves in a meeting of believers. Although Rufus held his New Testament in his hand and could easily have read from it himself, he did not do so. Whenever he wished to refer to a verse he turned to the headmaster and gave him the reference. A prolonged pause then ensued, while Tias laboriously found the place. Then he adjusted his spectacles, rose to his feet, moved closer to the lamp and read the verse in the manner of a town crier making a public proclamation. I perceived that this method, like the long delays of the evening, involved no strain or difficulty for the congregation; rather did it tend to lend authority to the text of Scripture, as well as giving a pause in the flow of Rufus' talk and a chance for him to sip a glass of water. At 11.30 p.m. Rufus asked me to give a short message in Indonesian, which I managed to do. He translated sentence by sentence into Javanese. This may sound a clumsy performance to those whose lives are set in a land where one tongue prevails, but it is otherwise in a multi-lingual region. From this first meeting onwards Rufus and I almost invariably used this method; people liked to hear their national language spoken, while the translation into Javanese ensured that everyone got the meaning properly; for the elderly and the uneducated only the translation had any meaning at all. Soon after midnight Rufus closed the meeting in prayer, we shook hands with those who had attended, sat for a while in the headmaster's house, and then squirmed our way down the mountainside back to Sabrang. Thanks to the Mayflower it was a brief evening's work for Rufus.

Sunday, *February 24th*. Last night Rufus and his wife and children came to supper with us, so we are seeing a lot of them. Since Siat, the eldest, is only twelve, they have their hands full. Rupert brought out his toys on to the verandah and they all had a gay time romping together. Just as this house seems made to measure for us, so does Rufus look like God's appointed colleague. He is in his early forties, short and spare, but wiry, with a slightly military cut about him, rather good-looking like so many Javanese, meek and quiet, but full of joy and thrilled at the work with which God has entrusted him. This morning Jess drove him to the morning service at Chamim's house at Barek. After lunch I went to Surabaja, preached once in Chinese and once in English, and came back by 11 p.m., but 150 miles' motoring and two sermons all on a packet of sandwiches were rather too much, although the meetings were well worth-while.

February 26th. Today I spent twelve hours in the city, lecturing four times and hearing Pastor Meng preach. He is starting a weekly meeting in the College in Cantonese, since there are many Cantonese among the Chinese community of 30,000 and nothing is being done to reach them with the gospel in their own tongue. I drove home to Sabrang at night in torrential rain. Tomorrow is a public holiday in honour of the prophet Muhammad. Our landlady, Mother Daro, went into the city in the car with me, but I feel she did not greatly enjoy it, because I ran over a hen. It was virtually unavoidable since the hen rushed right under my wheels at a moment when I was meeting traffic and could neither swerve nor stop, yet I feel the incident must on no account occur again. This road from Sabrang to the city is one I am bound to traverse several times every week we are here; it is heavily populated the whole way, so heavily that in twenty miles there are 150 side turnings; mine is the only Mayflower regularly using it, so I am easily identified. and I don't want to get a reputation as a hen-killer.

March 4th. Last Sunday Jess went with Rufus and his wife to a place called Lakar, where there is a sugar factory employing 2000 men. Most of the fields between us and the city are covered with sugar-cane. Twenty-one persons were baptised that morning at Lakar. Then today we had a visit from Chamim, the host of the church in Barek. He is a man of 50. He stayed for two and a half hours and had lunch with us, the first meal he had ever had with a white man. He is a farmer and gets three crops a year off his land on the edge of the Southern Mountains, one of rice and two of maize. He told us that the population of Barek is one-fifth Madurese and among the seventy-two people who have been baptised there is one man from Madura, who had four wives but has now put away three of them. Rufus dropped in and mentioned that he had been preaching the whole night long at Wates, a place ten miles from Sabrang and higher up the side of the Great Volcano; the meeting only ended at 7 a.m. It seems that many people in these parts hold to the tradition that we each of us have an "elder brother" somewhere, strong and kind, able to help us if only we can find him. Of this view Rufus takes full advantage, declaring that the Lord Jesus Christ is the One we need and grope for. Is it not wonderful that we should find a light burning so brightly in this old East Java Church?

March 8th. This evening we entertained thirteen Javanese police-men who have asked me to teach them Chinese for an hour every Saturday night. Although not optimistic about their chances of making progress at it, I felt we ought to accede to their request. I am glad to be able to do something for them which they value. The Inspector in charge opened with a little speech in which he thanked me for my "goodwill", using the English word. They all brought notebooks tucked into their shirts. We moved chairs and blackboard on to the verandah and I wrote up the Chinese charac-ters for them to copy.

March 9th. This morning we packed Rufus and all his family into the back of the Mayflower, which made eleven persons in the four-seater, and drove for an hour through teak and coffee plantations on the broad-backed Southern Mountains to the Christian village of Ponen, a small place of 700 souls, many of them of mixed Javanese-Madurese parentage. We attended the Sunday morning service, which was packed tight like an English parish church in the Middle Ages with the village elders and their wives in high pews beside the pulpit. The pastor preached for ten minutes on the sin of Uzziah the king. Like everything else this was in Javanese, but when I asked Rufus about it he smiled and said it was "an old man's sermon". After the benediction both Rufus and I were asked to speak. It was the first time I had opened my mouth at a formal meeting of the East Java Church. At the close it was remarkable to see the colourfully-dressed villagers streaming home from church in brilliant sunshine blazing down through the dense blanket of trees which shrouds the whole place. Ponen stands up on a hillside from which one can gaze south to the limitless Indian Ocean ten miles away and 2000 feet below. The church council came to the manse when the congregation had dispersed, and Rufus regaled and stimulated them by stories of conversions and baptisms, all night meetings and open hearts. The old pastor filled up the boot of the car with hundreds of bananas and clusters of coconuts, and we got home for lunch at 2 p.m.

March 15th. Study of Indonesian and Javanese is still our main occupation. Gwen Crawford comes over twice a week to run in this house a children's meeting and a girls' Bible Class which she started when she lived here; Jess helps her in these, which our language is at the moment insufficient to run without her. Yeny is still doing our cooking most satisfactorily and we have employed another local girl for laundry, which is a daily business in this climate. This second girl has proved rather difficult, and I doubt she will stay long. She is young, large, and strong, but her astonishment at us and our ways knows no bounds. Whenever she sees me she becomes frozen at such an extraordinary sight, following me with her eyes until I get away. Yesterday her mother came to call on us along with a younger sister who was not feeling well. The mother's idea was that since her older daughter was working for us we would be responsible for the medical fees of all the family and she wanted a chit on the hospital. We tried to explain, with Yeny's help, that we could not do that, but she went away disappointed and angry, saying that she had walked several miles and brought no money, counting on our help. After she had gone Yeny assured us that we had done the right thing in not agreeing to her request. The older daughter creates suspicion by her manner and we have decided that we shall have trouble if we keep her in the house, so this morning when she arrived Jess met her on the doorstep and gave her a week's wages instead of notice, Yeny having advised us on no account to allow her into the house once she knew she was being dismissed. And now an old friend of ours named Loti is our guest for two weeks. She was formerly our servant when we lived in the Bible College in the city. She has had malaria and anaemia and is suffering from the sorrows of being a second wife. When we first knew her her husband had recently died, leaving her with a son who was adopted by her brother. Later she married again, without knowing her husband already had a wife. When she discovered this she refused to live with him. He departed and some months later she gave birth to another son, who is now a year old. She and this boy live with her sister-in-law who is devoted to Loti's child. Life has thus treated Loti harshly and at 35 she looks somewhat spent. When she first worked for us in the Bible College she was a Muslim, but Jess took her once to the East Java Church in the city and thereafter she attended it regularly on her own. We are delighted to be able to have her in our guest room for a time. Nothing would please us more than if she could get well and work for us once again.

The rainy season is now easing off and each day at 5 p.m. we go out for a family stroll, taking bundles of tracts with us. The whole of Sabrang is like a wood, so that you do not see many houses at any one time. The roads are well-shaded avenues, wide and clean, but unsurfaced and therefore soft and silent. The houses stand back under innumerable trees and shrubs, each with its own little bridge over a stream, its fence, and its front garden. Everything is simple but orderly, and there is no squalor. On these occasions Rupert rides his tricycle and my job is to steer him happily through the embarrassing attentions of hordes of children. The people seem delighted to see us coming their way. The presence of Rupert, and my preoccupation with him, disarm suspicion. Both Jess and I give tracts on these occasions to adults and older children. We have found that to give to children under about twelve leads to confusion and disorder; they follow us everywhere in increasing numbers, pestering us for more tracts and spoiling our relationship with other homes. As we go along we bow and smile at everyone and Jess gives out a large number of coloured tracts, each with its message about Christ. I have to keep Rupert moving to save him from getting exasperated with the attentions of the people, so that we often get widely separated. We left the road filled with people, quiet and pleased, standing in groups at their bridges, and all around stretches a vast chequerwork of these long, shady avenues, where multitudes emerge as if by magic the moment we appear.

On Sunday, while I was away in the city, Jess and Yeny went to the Sabrang Church. The preacher was supposed to come from the Christian village of Paru, but he never arrived. The congregation

sat hopefully for ninety minutes and then dispersed unfed. Rufus
was not there, as he is normally away preaching somewhere else on
Sundays. He is not the pastor of the Sabrang Church, which is led
by a headmaster named Suwarso. Rufus is evangelist at large in
the Sabrang areas and the organisation of the East Java Church is
such that, although he is a fully trained pastor and has been in the
ministry for fifteen years, his present evangelistic assignment means
that he has no voice in the conduct of any one church.

April 1st. Last Sunday we went together to the Sabrang Church
and this time it was Suwarso himself who led the meeting and
preached. There were twenty-five present. It is a worthy kind of
meeting and gradually I hope we shall comprehend something of
the Javanese which is used. In the afternoon I walked over again to
Mrs Rakes' house to attend the Pentecostal service which is held
there every Sunday afternoon. The preacher was the Pentecostal
pastor from Paru. He strummed a banjo while leading the singing
of choruses and then preached with vigour and skill on Hebrews
12: 1-2, using Indonesian, which meant that I was able to understand.
There were twenty people present, of whom only four were men,
and the moment he stopped speaking they sprang up and closed all
the window shutters. Most of them then knelt around the preacher
on mats at the front and a woman prayed loudly and emotionally
while the others accompanied her noisily. The preacher then jumped
back on his bicycle, his trousers still wet from the knees down from
riding out in heavy rain.

When I got back Rupert ran into my study to say that the policeman on duty with his rifle outside the cells was calling him to cross
the road. I escorted him over and he solemnly gave tracts to the
guard and then to the prisoners, who cheerfully reached out through
the small square holes in the massive doors by which alone they
communicate with the world.

In the evening Rufus came round with Susilo, whom I had not
met before. I was struck at once with the forcefulness of his character
and the ardour of his faith. He quoted Scripture with delight, as one
might parade a new and enriching discovery. He also took me to
Lakar to the home of a Madurese named Hasan, another powerful
personality converted only a year ago and now expounding the

gospel each night in his own home. I notice that Rufus has won a number of influential and prominent men to Christ.

And then it was today that Loti moved in to live and work with us. With her and Yeny our home base is firmly established. They are much more than servants, they are real friends, and fellow-workers for Christ too.

CHAPTER 7

TRACTS AND INSANITY

April 10th. After I got home from lecturing in Chinese in the city—having caused much entertainment by being forced to change a wheel on the way—we took the car a mile out of Sabrang and parked it beside an inviting earth road leading off between ricefields and towering sugar-cane with the Great Volcano gazing down at us from 12,000 feet. Jess embraced a huge pile of Indonesian tracts published by the Christian Witness Press in Hongkong and the Scripture Gift Mission in London. These earthen roads, which cut the land in every direction, are wide and level and could be used by cars. On this occasion, after passing through fields for 300 yards we came to a cross-roads and a village straggling under the trees. Timid women carrying babies, neat schoolchildren, shrivelled grannies, well-dressed youths, workmen stripped to the waist, and imposing village elders were either at their doors on the streets or soon got there as the children spread the news of our arrival. Everywhere we met with courtesy, gentleness, shyness, curiosity, and friendliness, as we moved along giving several different kinds of tracts to each person.

We are now half-way through the term at the Bible College in the city and I have not fully resolved the problems raised by my dual role as lecturer in Chinese in the city and evangelist in Indonesian in the country. For weeks the preparation of lectures and sermons in Chinese has left me no time for the study of the Indonesian language, yet I am no longer really part of the Bible College staff. Last night I was at a feast in the city to welcome home a young Chinese couple who had spent six years studying in America. They were greatly in need of reorientation and planned chiefly a rapid return to the U.S.A.

On *April 12th* I was back in the city to lead the weekly fellowship meeting at the Bible College. The twenty-four students made a fine sight as we sat in our usual large circle, and I judge many of them are set for lives of useful Christian service. The evening was entirely taken up by a testimony from Pastor Tang of Billiton Island (between Sumatra and Borneo), and I hope and pray the students deeply absorbed his admirable words. With dark face and closely cropped hair he looked unprepossessing at first. He told how he was born in a non-Christian home in Indo-China and converted in Hongkong through his uncle when he was 16. God called him into full-time Christian service at 21 and he studied at Wuchow in south China where he met Mr Jaffary of the Christian and Missionary Alliance on the latter's return from his travels in Indonesia. He had previously rather dreaded the prospect of becoming pastor of a church and longed for purely pioneer work, preaching Christ where He was unknown. So when Jaffary told him about the Hakka Chinese on the tin islands of Bangka and Billiton in Indonesia these places at once became the goal of his prayers. "When my wife and I landed there in 1936," he said, "there was no Christian and no church on either island. Today there are 900 Chinese believers on Billiton and 600 on Bangka." I was impressed as much by his right spirit and his twenty-one year adherence to a God-given task, as by the remarkable results he had achieved. He pointed out the necessity for Christian workers being willing to suffer hardship and antagonism, not seeking wealth or greatness for themselves, and doing menial tasks cheerfully. He had taken as his life-motto the words "not to be ministered unto but to minister" (Mark 10: 45). In this wealthy, sophisticated Chinese society of Java it was most salutary for the students to hear him describe his vigils by the dying, and tell how he had washed and dressed the dead, digging their graves with his own hands. Thanks to such men—unknown and unsung—the gospel has taken deep root in Chinese hearts in Southeast Asia.

April 19th. It is Good Friday evening. The lamp is lit in our home in Sabrang; Jess and Rupert are singing at the harmonium. In the Bible College in the city classes have been dropped for a week over Easter, none too soon for me as I was ready to drop myself under these two diverse tasks we are attempting. Having caught up a

little on accounts, letters, and sleep we sallied forth about 4 p.m.
armed with tracts in Indonesian and Javanese. We put Rupert's
tricycle in the boot of the Mayflower, drove east for a thousand
yards, parked the car, and launched into the unknown down a
mysterious, shady lane marked "Old Hospital Street", the buildings
having been gutted as part of the price of independence. After an
initial rush on literature we cleared into open farmland richly filled
with rice, sugar, and tapioca. Then we struck a large village where
we were soon the sensation of the moment. The main street was
wide, wooded, and dusty now that the rains are over. We did
stupendous business, special favourites being red tracts, tracts in
Javanese, and tracts in Arabic script. Outside the village mosque the
men wanted samples of all we had. We never even discovered the
name of the place as we did not want to seem to be fact-finding.
A Mecca pilgrim in his white skullcap appeared on a bicycle,
avoided us, and then doubled back to ask for tracts, overcome by
his curiosity. We returned to the car after ninety minutes as darkness
fell. Our present policy is to push out like this in a slowly-widening
circle, scattering tracts, seeing where the people are and how they
live, and at the same time giving them a chance to see us and get
familiar with the idea of European Christians living nearby who
are delighted to meet them and share the gospel with them.

On this *Good Friday* morning we drove over the rocky, racing
Larsti River to the village of Barek where seventy-two people were
baptised last year. I made two trips, ferrying Rufus and his children
the first time and then returning for our family, including Loti and
Yeny. As I did so the road was dotted with groups of Javanese
Christians converging on foot, cycle and cart upon Barek, for this
was a great day for the country believers, and soon the roofed-in
threshing-floor outside Chamim's house held 150 souls. Although
we are still rather tongue-tied in Indonesian one can begin to say
that we are becoming known by face to the Christians south of the
Great Volcano.

The proceedings began at 9 a.m. and ended after noon. Rufus and
an elderly Javanese pastor shared the leadership, both dressed in
shiny black robes and white cravats. After hymn-singing, prayer,
and the reading of the Scriptures two men came to the front and

sat down on the rush mats spread before the lectern. Hasan, the Madurese from Lakar, who had come over for the occasion, stepped up and showed them that they were expected to kneel, not to sit. They were Christians who had repented after falling into sin, and asked to be taken back into the fellowship of the church. The old pastor questioned them, prayed over them, and extended his hands in blessing above their heads. Three choirs then sang in turn, the third being that of the Barek Church itself, whose young people had never before attempted such a thing in front of others. Then five women knelt on the rush mats and five men behind them. Rufus stood over them with Chamim beside him carrying a silver bowl of water. Taking up a handful of water each time, he thrice sprinkled the forehead of each of the ten while the congregation sang the Javanese translation of Cowper's hymn:

> "There is a fountain filled with blood,
> Drawn from Immanuel's veins,
> And sinners plunged beneath that flood,
> Lose all their guilty stains."

Next, three couples stood in a row at the front, hand in hand, none of them very young, while Rufus sanctified their marriages, which had been solemnised according to Muslim rites long before. Their ten children then knelt on the mats, the parents squatting among them, and Rufus baptised them all. The old pastor preached and pronounced the benediction to close a wonderful morning. Loti and Yeny had never seen the like of it, and neither had we. The inclusion of women gives the gospel a strong appeal in contrast to Islam with its very masculine emphasis.

After a rapid lunch we drove into the city and by 3 p.m. I was conducting the Easter Communion Service at the Bible College in Chinese, which brought vividly to my mind the difference between the Javanese Christian world and the Chinese Christian world. In the morning we were in a village farm surrounded by trees, among brown-skinned people speaking Indonesian and Javanese, simply dressed and often barefoot; in the afternoon we were in a massive concrete building in the city surrounded by houses and shops, among a yellow-skinned people speaking various Chinese dialects, all beautifully dressed in white with leather-soled shoes. The same Lord Jesus Christ is precious to both groups and working in the hearts of all to bring forth the fruit of the Spirit, yet in secondary matters there is a great linguistic, cultural, and economic gulf between them—and we straddle the two. This is the tension of our present situation. Which is it to be, the College or the villages? The present arrangement can only be transitional, and already we know which choice we shall be forced to make.

On *Easter Sunday* I made an unsuccessful, and perhaps unwise, attempt to bring the two worlds together. I was eager for our Javanese friends to meet Chinese Christians (since to their minds these two words are almost a contradiction in terms), while on the other hand Pastor Meng was acutely interested in what I had told him about Rufus and the work of the Spirit of God in the villages. So on Easter Sunday, Pastor and Mrs Meng and three other leaders in the Chinese Christian Church in the city drove out to our home and I went with them to Barek. Rufus did mention to me that it was Communion Sunday, but I saw no difficulty in that and felt it would be a splendid chance for the two groups to meet around the Lord's table. I did not at the time understand that it is not customary for anyone in the East Java Church to join in the Communion Service unless he has attended the special preparation meeting some days before. The Chinese Churches have no such preparation meeting and welcome "all who love our Lord Jesus Christ" to join with them in the Lord's Supper. Among Chinese Christians not to receive a person at the Lord's Supper would be tantamount to showing doubt whether he were a true Christian at all. Had my command of the Indonesian language been sufficient we could perhaps have avoided the awkwardness which followed. In fact it is only as I look back years afterwards that I see just how difficult the occasion was.

The Communion at Barek that morning was to be conducted by the pastor from Paru, not the Pentecostal pastor of course, but the pastor of the East Java Church there, whom I had never met. On reaching Barek I introduced my visitors as best I could and Rufus received them warmly. In spite of his invitation to the front they courteously insisted on occupying the back row of seats on the

threshing-floor outside Chamim's house. The Paru pastor was
very late, and a delay of ninety minutes in beginning the meeting
was trying to Pastor Meng, accustomed as he was to the punctual
ways of the city. When at last the pastor came he greeted me
without enthusiasm and shook hands rather curtly with the Chinese
delegation. Already my guests and I were somewhat isolated in the
back row—and isolated we remained. The proceedings were very
long and in Javanese, which was incomprehensible to my visitors.
I could sense that Pastor Meng was exhausted long before the end.
When the time came for receiving the bread and the wine it was not
at all clear that we were invited to the table around which Christians
of the East Java Church take the Lord's Supper. It seemed wiser to
stay where we were, and thus we remained spectators. The language
barrier and mutual shyness prevented that cordial fellowship which
I had hoped to bring about. At the close an opportunity was given
to the visitors to address the company, but to my regret none of
them felt they should do so, nor could I really blame them after the
protracted and ambiguous situation in which they had found themselves. Rufus was most apologetic afterwards and had he been in
charge things would have been different, but as a pastor seconded
to evangelism he is devoid of all authority even in churches called
into existence through his ministry. Later I found out that the pastor
of Paru strongly disapproves of Rufus and of us too because we are
associated with Rufus. The experience was part of our slow re-
education in a school that was not Chinese.

Although he never expressed any desire to repeat the experiment,
I think Pastor Meng was glad in retrospect that he had seen a rural
Javanese Church with his own eyes. It did not escape him that
during the sermon one of the rustic believers started to light a
cigarette, from which he was vigorously dissuaded by his neighbour. During the Lord's Supper another man, for whom the experience was entirely new, took three sips of the cup instead of one and
even spilt some of the wine down the front of his tunic, which
suggested to me one way in which the Roman Catholic custom
of withholding the cup from the laity might have arisen!

That same evening six Chinese students from the Bible College
came out to Sabrang and preached in the Salvation Army hospital

across the road from our home. Afterwards they came over to us and I collected Rufus to meet them, hoping to erase the unfortunate impressions of the afternoon. This time no mistake was made. Rufus told them how he had himself come to true faith in Christ and although there was much which I could not understand the students obviously enjoyed it and appreciated the fact that they were listening to a man of God. Loti joined us, and after the students had gone back to the city she stayed on, so Rufus switched from Indonesian to Javanese for her benefit. We were delighted that she had this chance of meeting Rufus and hearing him speak to her personally about Christ. Before he left he turned to us and commented on the hard lot of most Muslim village women. "They are not much respected," he said, "and are married and divorced on a mere whim. They truly need someone to lift their heavy burden, and that is just what the Lord Jesus is able to do."

A normal week of teaching in the Bible College was relieved by two long late-afternoon walks with tracts around Sabrang. I think the benefit of these walks is threefold:

(1) They spread tracts and Scripture portions in an area which we can easily revisit and which is adjacent to villages where God is manifestly working.

(2) They familiarise us with the lie of the land and with living conditions and at the same time make us known to the country people.

(3) Until we have a better command of the Indonesian language and some knowledge of Javanese they provide us with an outlet for active Christian service.

May 1st was a great occasion in this country. Not only was it Labour Day and Javanese New Year's Day, 1888, but it also marked the end of the Muslim fast month of Ramadan. Rufus wanted to take his family to his wife's home about eighty miles away and Jess offered to drive them all there. Of course this saved him quite a big expense, but it seemed to us an innocuous way of helping him and a chance to meet his relatives. They had an adventurous day. All the children were car sick on the twisty, mountainous road, and when Jess and Rupert headed back alone they were advised to take a short cut which involved her in fording several unbridged rivers, one of which consisted of four streams separated by islands.

As I had anticipated, the complexity of the Chinese language is slowly strangling my Chinese class for policemen, but it has been worthwhile as a remover of prejudice. Only three came this week and I doubt whether any of them will continue. This afternoon a policeman suffered a serious eye injury while playing football. They asked for my help in getting him into the city to hospital at night, and I was glad to assist in this way, and pleased that they had asked me to do so.

May 2nd was also a public holiday. Everybody put on new clothes and paraded about in the brilliant sunshine thinking how splendid they looked, which was perfectly true. We caught the carefree infection, abandoned work, and joined the charabancs, buses, and carts heading for the Indian Ocean. So broken is the terrain to the south of us that even from Sabrang it takes two hours to reach the sea by car. Twice we crossed the Brantas River, running deep in magnificent canyons. Climbing the Southern Mountains we looked back across the great tilted upland plain in which we live, lying below us in awesome splendour. The tangled mountains are well populated until the last few miles, when the road descends precipitously through jungle to a wild, forbidding coast where breakers raging in across 5000 miles of open sea pound inhospitable promontories and soaring cliffs, slashing rocks and islands into fantastic shapes, undercutting them as beavers do trees. We found a deserted beach and spent three hours paddling and collecting corals, bathing being too dangerous. We took with us Man, our landlady's servant, who had never seen the sea before. He felt embarrassed to eat with us, so took his picnic lunch off to a ledge of rock and had it alone, gazing childlike at the foaming waves.

On Sunday, *May 5th*, we felt we should go to the morning service at the Christian village of Paru, since the church there is officially responsible for the groups of new believers around Sabrang and we also hoped to achieve more cordial relations with the pastor. The church holds about 500 people and was packed to the back wall. This is the normal state of churches in Christian villages in East Java —no empty pews and large numbers of young men. At the end we walked round to the pastor's house; he shook hands with us politely at the door but did not invite us in, so there was nothing we could do but withdraw. Nobody else treats us in this cold manner.

In the evening Mother Daro's servant, Man, came with me to the gospel meeting at the Salvation Army hospital, to which Loti never fails to go each Sunday. He had not attended a Christian meeting before and at the end cheerfully announced, "I liked it." He is an unofficial attachment to our establishment, an amusing character, dogged and reliable, with head deeply sunk into massive shoulders, aged about forty, apparently quite alone in the world, extremely rustic and simple. Each day he draws water for us from the well beside Mother Daro's kitchen. He loves work and does everything thoroughly. The big water tank from which we bale out for our baths, and the buckets of water used by Loti in the kitchen, are always brimful with Man in charge. He has also taken over the care of the Mayflower and washes her whenever I come home. He is alert to help us at any point, such as when the roof leaks (which is frequently the case), if a puncture has to be mended, or if a ladder is needed, and for his manifold services I have agreed to give him a monthly wage, although he remains Mother Daro's servant and gives to her the bulk of his time. He gets no holidays and works no fixed hours.

We could not know that Man was to die soon after we left Sabrang, breaking his neck as a banana tree he was pulling down gave way unexpectedly. Like Loti he remained through the years our true friend and helper, but unlike Loti he never confessed himself a believer in the Lord Jesus. Apart from Mother Daro he would perhaps have done so, but she must have forbidden him to attend any more meetings, for he never came to another, with the exception of Christmas celebrations. But he often asked for our tracts and used to give them to his friends and take them across the road to share with the prisoners in the lock-up.

May 10th. A busy week in the Bible College—from which I sometimes long to be free—has kept me away from further adventures with Rufus. One night, after I got back home to Sabrang, a jovial policeman came and sat with me on the verandah. We gave him coffee. He spoke very favourably of the Dutch, which surprised me and made me guarded in my comments.

Schools reopened this week after the fast month. The one opposite us disgorged close on a thousand pupils filing past our gate in brilliant sunshine.

Saturday, *May 11th*. At noon we shut the doors leading on to the verandah, had lunch, a sleep, and showers, and then took the initiative in our turn in a side road off Office Street. To conserve energy we drove half a mile in the car, parked it in the ruins of the old Dutch police headquarters, and launched out along the well-populated lanes around us. Ninety minutes of crowded life followed. We meandered in leisurely fashion from house to house, often retracing our steps as extra people were produced to claim a share of our literature. As 6 p.m. approached the populace thickened and business became overwhelming. Somehow we managed to withdraw.

At such times most of the men are engagingly friendly, though we encounter a few sullen faces which refuse a responsive smile. This, however, is for political rather than religious reasons. Most of them are very good-looking. Almost without exception the women are cordial to us. In these walks we notice that miserable homes are rare, simple ones common, nice ones very frequent, and luxurious ones by no means lacking. Tidiness is nearly universal and many a humble residence shows taste in its garden, its curtains, and its furniture, while at this season soon after Javanese New Year clothes are new and made from the loveliest materials. Loti cooks for us in a beautiful multi-coloured fabric! She had supper ready on the table as soon as we got back. Of course Jess has invested a great deal of kindness in her, from which we reap a rich return. Each day we have morning prayers with her and Yeny, using a mixture of Indonesian and Javanese. Yesterday Loti prayed aloud herself for the first time. At night she lights a little lamp in her room and we hear her reading the Javanese New Testament.

May 12th. This morning we drove Rufus and four of his children to the large village of Semen—and by "large" I mean that the population must be about 10,000 souls. We attended a meeting of the East Java Church held in a private home on the banks of the

Brantas River. Forty people were present and the preacher was the local medical, or semi-trained doctor. There is a Government clinic in this place as well as a church clinic; both are run by Christian men born in Christian villages on the south coast. If these medicals could be ignited with aggressive zeal to spread the gospel their opportunities for doing so would be very great. As it is, although the clinics are no small testimony to the honour of Christianity in a general way, there is probably little or no witness for Christ by word or by literature carried on there. The equally large village of Lakar joins on to Semen, so we took the chance of visiting Hasan again. He brought out his Javanese Bible, Indonesian New Testament, an exposition of the Creed in Javanese, and a beautifully bound volume of daily meditations on the Scriptures also in Javanese, printed in Amsterdam. It was very moving to me to see a Madurese so eager to serve Christ, but I must admit that he seems to be a self-centred kind of witness, prone to blow his own trumpet. I long to have enough Indonesian to be of real spiritual help to such a man, whom one can but admire while recognising his need for a more sanctified life.

In the afternoon I walked two miles to Rufus' home to check over with him the text of the Christmas tract in Indonesian and Javanese, which is to be published by the Christian Witness Press. There cannot be many people around here who do not know us now that we have been in Sabrang for three months. Wherever we go we get charming smiles which imply not "Who on earth are you?" but rather, "I got tracts from you in our village last week". If only we could speak Javanese, or even decent Indonesian! It looks to me as though the hearts of multitudes are open to the sower and ripe for the reaper. We can at least do a little bit of sowing, and Rufus is a diligent reaper.

May 27th. Lately we have had a good deal of ill-health. Rupert got dysentery, recovered, and now has it again. Jess was in bed for four days with malaria and I have had a mild malarial condition, so for two weeks tract distribution has been halted. It is just a year since I landed back in Java and we are feeling that in July we must get a good holiday at a higher altitude, although Sabrang is not nearly as hot as places down on the coastal plains.

Yesterday I paid my monthly visit to Surabaja. I drove down on Saturday night, fighting a headache, and managed to win through the three Sunday sermons, ending with supper in the sumptuous home of the American Vice-Consul. At 9 p.m. I started the exhilarating drive home and did it in exactly two hours.

One morning the local police inspctor with whom we deal came to see me. He had not heard of the Old and New Testaments, so I showed him the lovely Javanese volumes, printed in Holland. He dallied long over them and, to my astonishment, found John 3 : 16 and asked about a marginal reference to Isaiah 53. This suggests to me that he has had some contact with Christians before.

The policeman who formerly visited me at night and spoke so favourably of the Dutch has come several times since. Then one evening his son arrived with a note asking me to lend him a hundred rupiahs, promising to repay it in a month. I felt that it would be a great mistake to comply with such an irresponsible request, so I went at once to his house to explain that I was not a business man and that it was in any case against my principles to lend money. He was very embarrassed and quickly changed the subject. I now perceive that the whole purpose of his visits and his adulation of the Dutch—whom most Indonesians strongly dislike—was with a view to making this request. We prayed about it and I am sure it was right to refuse. The man has a good job. He is a heavy smoker, like so many others here, and no question of the relief of genuine need arises.

A few nights later I was just locking up the front door before we went to bed when I noticed a cyclist turn into our drive. He put his bicycle against the trees, walked over towards me, came briskly to attention, saluted, and mounted the verandah steps. The light there, which must burn all night, is a very dim one, so that I could not properly discern his features. He was imposingly dressed and was obviously an important person. He handed me a letter and sat down. I took the letter to the light and struggled to understand it. I soon saw that it was another request for money, a larger sum this time, to be repaid a month hence. Had my command of language been better, and had I recognised him, I might have been able to express my refusal more tactfully. As it was I started to explain that I was not able to lend money to people who asked me for it, whereupon he at once rose, took the letter back, and excused himself politely. It was only long afterwards that I realised I had been face to face with a supreme authority whose signature would be essential if I was to continue in Java at all or if I ever wished to return to my own homeland. However, even had I known this, I should not have acted differently.

On *June 1st* I set off for twenty-four hours with Rufus in the Mayflower. Before we left his home Mawardi of the one arm arrived along with Rekso, the old village wise man. It was the first time that I had clearly distinguished these two and my friendship with them dated from that occasion. The four of us prayed together, old Rekso going on vigorously for a long time, until Rufus tapped him on the arm and persuaded him to stop.

We drove first to a place called Wates, where Rufus recently preached through a whole night, and stayed for an hour with the leader of the weak church there, which only meets once a month. He used to be a Dutch Mission evangelist, but has grown lukewarm and timorous. However, he was persuaded to join our party and we proceeded through hilly country packed with villages, at one of which we paused to sip tea and encourage a lonely Christian family, who were in charge of a clinic. After praying with them we went on to Wagir, where stand the ruins of a great Hindu temple built in the days before Islam invaded Java. Long ago the Dutch erected a chapel in one of the suburbs and there are some Christian families there still. We were generously feasted and then at 8 p.m. our party, swollen to fifteen, started out to walk by the light of a petro-max lamp to yet another place where there was to be an evangelistic meeting. It took forty minutes to get there, our cavalcade tramping cheerfully through a straggling country town, then away across the fields beside rushing torrents and huge trees looming sinister in the darkness, over a wobbly bamboo bridge across a rocky stream, arriving at last among dancing lights and mobs of people. All packed into and around a square room where the village elders sat smoking at an ancient table—dark, turbaned, wizened, weather-beaten men, looking far more "tribal" to my eyes than their more accessible brethren. I estimated that there were 250 people present. After our party had sung hymns for ten minutes and Rufus had led in prayer, he preached for an hour and a half, aided by posters and gospel records put on by his boys. Attention was excellent—rows of country lads, village belles with heavily powdered faces, battered-looking matrons, gangs of youths, and the calm table of village elders. Most of the latter, and most of our own party too, smoked while Rufus preached, for the cigarette seems to be as necessary to them as breathing. When he had finished he asked me to speak, interpreting my Indonesian into Javanese. Then old Rekso thundered until midnight, when we broke up with hearty handshakes all round and trudged back for an hour through the glorious night. When we reached the house at which we had had supper it was 1 a.m. and I was more than ready to sleep, but nobody else seemed to feel likewise. Rufus put the gramophone on and a dozen men settled down to listen to the gospel again from it. I excused myself and went into the bedroom I had been shown. It was for Rufus, his two boys, and me, but there were only two beds, one of them equipped with a mattress, pillows, clean sheets, and a mosquito net, the other merely a wooden frame covered with a mat. I decided that while Rufus and his family could all sleep on the better bed they certainly would get no proper rest on the other, which I accordingly took, though I think our host's intentions had been otherwise.

Next morning, which was Sunday, I refrained from a shower as the "bathroom" stood in the open between several houses and its walls were only three feet high. Rufus suggested the river, but this glaring publicity I also declined, although that is the way of the land. At 9 a.m. there were fifty people in the church. Rufus preached and then called upon me. I spoke on Romans 8:13, "If ye live after the flesh ye shall die: but if ye through the Spirit do mortify the deeds of the body, ye shall live." We returned to the house for another square meal and then fifteen of us wedged into the sitting-room for prayer and singing before we crashed our way back over the wide, dusty, broken road to Sabrang, earning a puncture in the process. I must emphasise that all of this was in Javanese, of which I understand only isolated words. No one spoke any Indonesian except myself, or those directly addressing me.

June 7th. As a result of my reports to him about the progress of the gospel in the villages, Pastor Meng invited Rufus to speak at morning prayers in the Bible College in the city. He used Indonesian, which was translated into Mandarin. I drove him both ways and Pastor Meng gave him a hundred rupiahs for "travelling expenses", which was quite a windfall for a hard-pressed evangelist with six children. It was an ordeal for him to address Chinese, and I also realised for the first time that not being able to speak in Javanese was a serious limitation for him.

The great flu epidemic seems to have reached here from Malaya. Four children died in the little corner of the city from which Loti comes. Our milkman also died; he was a kindly and courteous man, cycling seven miles to Sabrang with his heavy load every morning; we had given Christian tracts to him.

After almost a month out of action Rupert is well again, and as a result there are at this instant nineteen children on the verandah within a few yards of my desk. Jess is in the sitting-room reading the Scriptures with Mrs Rakes, the Javanese widow of an old Eurasian, who is hostess to both the Pentecostal and the East Java Churches in Sabrang, though she herself leans to the former.

One evening, seeking pure diversion, we went out in the car, persuading Loti and Yeny to come with us. I do not think they will be keen to do so again, for we got lost in a maze of lanes and hillocks among ricefields and tall sugar-cane. Darkness overtook us and our road home was blocked by a broken bridge. Happily we were able to keep on course, thanks to the outlines of the main volcanic peaks around Sabrang. We passed through many large, remote villages set in rich and beautiful country.

Tonight, *June 8th,* we went out distributing tracts in the by-ways of Sabrang. From the start we were smothered by hordes of children, from whom we rarely got free. Indeed it has been an exacting day, as relays of schoolboys invaded us all morning. They are marvellously well behaved, and at one stage listened quietly to gramophone records, but it was not easy under such constant pressure to prepare for messages I have to give on Sunday.

On *June 9th* I was in the city for twelve hours, preaching three times in different Chinese churches.

Our nights have been rather disturbed lately. There have been several nearby *wajang*, Javanese puppet shows, with persistent musical accompaniment until dawn. In addition a poor demented woman named Sri shouts about the house at night; she has pestered the police on guard outside the cells opposite and they throw stones to force her off.

June 11th. After a day lecturing at the Bible College I got home to Sabrang for a late tea and then we went out for a stroll, taking tracts with us, but intending to relax. However, this proved quite impossible and we had a tempestuous and delightful hour in paths we had never before struck, heavily shaded by coconut palms and clumps of bamboo. Gangs of excited children followed us for hundreds of yards before handing us over to the enthusiasm of a fresh lot. Perhaps the word "paths" may give a false impression. Most of them are grassy "rides", quite wide enough to be country roads if they were surfaced. A sense of the vast untouched multitudes awaiting the message of salvation comes over me at such times, for one is ever striking fresh "rides" branching off through richest grain to further villages shrouded in the next expanse of trees, and so it seems to go on, world without end.

Poor crazy Sri is becoming more and more of a problem. It is said that she goes out of her mind annually. She roams around and her pet aversion is the police. Since we are next to the police station and opposite the cells which they guard, she comes to our house, yelling at them, singing, cursing, and attacking them. The police are sometimes long-suffering, but at other times they retaliate with kicks and stones. Jess is the only person who can handle her adequately, and as a result she behaves more normally when inside our house. She takes luminal obediently, has a nap in an armchair, reads Rupert's books with him, enjoys a cup of coffee and a plate of rice, and then returns refreshed to the fray, shouting lustily.

June 12th. We have been out in the by-ways of Sabrang with tracts once again. On these occasions one sees many interesting sights—a house festooned with cages of rare birds; most distinguished, serene-looking couples, beautifully dressed; Madurese youths, obviously more rigid Muslims than the easy-going Javanese, and less cordial towards us; gardens exquisitely cultivated; a religious school where blank-faced young men come curiously for our wares.

Yesterday a prominent Chinese Muslim died on the very day when he and his Javanese wife were to have left to start the pilgrimage to Mecca. Since both the Javanese and the Chinese communities were involved he was accorded an imposing funeral procession, of which the rites were Muslim not Chinese. His coffin, draped in a magnificent green cloth and covered in flowers, was carried at the head of a long line of people walking slowly in the sunshine. We never met him, but it appears that we distributed tracts outside his home recently, and for that we are not sorry now.

Today Jess had a long talk on the verandah with two young men. A good many youths come to see our posters and it often seems better for Jess to see them than for me to do so. I am too large and official, so that they are struck dumb or smitten with the giggles! For most people it is not easy to meet a foreigner in a normal, personal way. Schoolboys often gape at me as though I were a passing giraffe, but tracting has made us widely known, and as our grasp of the languages slowly improves we are hoping to come to closer grips with individuals.

Crazy Sri is continually in and out of our home. She slept on a mat on our verandah last night after her brother had locked her out of her own place. This morning she shared our family prayers, singing loudly, and then departed to raid the nearby school with her parasol. Later on forty schoolboys swarmed on to the verandah and I sat stuffily among them playing Javanese gospel records and preaching in Indonesian. Half of them milled around for an hour until Sri reappeared, when a prolonged fracas ensued. Meanwhile my teacher was interviewing the head of the village to arrange for her removal to a large asylum not far from the city. But when he

came to give me an Indonesian lesson he was still more impressed
with the desirability of official action as she entertained him to a
song and a tambourine jig. We marvel at Mother Daro's patience:
neither crowds of children, nor Christian evangelism, nor lunacy
seem to worry her in the least. At night we drove into the city,
taking Loti and Yeny with us, partly to attend the weekly fellowship meeting at the Bible College, partly to escape from insanity.
We left food on the verandah for Sri and she was fast asleep there
when we returned.

June 15th. Sri, who spent part of the night on our verandah and
part lying in the middle of the road, put in no appearance till noon.
However, she then arrived with a basket on her head containing
her basic possessions—in fact she moved in on us. By vicious
language she then so sorely provoked some men that first Jess, and
later I, saved her by narrow margins from serious injury. In hopes
of forestalling worse trouble I again appealed to my teacher, who
at once called on the authorities. Later an official came to see me
and she performed a dance on the verandah for his benefit. We feel
that we need to be careful lest we appear to be complainers or
trouble-makers, or in case her exasperated family shift responsibility for her to us. So I simply represented to my caller the urgency
of getting her into a mental home for her own sake, for the sake of
the police, and for the peace of the district. I offered my services as
chauffeur for the thirty-mile trip so long as we were accompanied
by a representative of the village who would take full responsibility. Rufus came round at night and we told him our tale
and asked for his advice. He too has a squatter, a Bohemian-
looking youth from Sumatra who reckons to be an itinerant
evangelist with a strong emphasis on doing little and praying
much. He has been with them for the past five weeks, which has
been a heavy burden as they have six children and no domestic
help.

Since Sri did not reappear in the evening we turned in at 10 p.m.,
but shortly afterwards we heard her muttering on our verandah.
She then walked down the road, shouting, and roused the hospital.
Next she pestered the mosque before returning to us. About
midnight two policemen laid hands on her screaming on our doorstep,

carried her off by the arms and legs, and locked her in the cell just across the road, where she battered the door with her fists. Being unable to sleep against such competition we donned dressing-gowns at 2 a.m. and went across with food and a sedative in the bright moonlight. The policemen, standing around a charcoal fire at the foot of a tree, seemed glad to see us and got some relief after we had gone. Their action in locking her up has relieved us of the task of caring for her, so in the morning Loti carried her basket over to the lock-up.

At 7 a.m. next morning Jess drove off in the Mayflower with Mrs Rufus. Rupert and I walked the mile to church, while Loti and Yeny went on their own. Midway through the headmaster's sermon Sri burst in, half dressed. He paused while she was shepherded out. Our own policy now is to keep hands off and leave her to the police; she obeys them, thanks to a bamboo stick.

Monday, *June 17th*. Sri is now back on us, clean out of hand and badly bruised. At 7 a.m. three grievously-provoked men were at the door. We managed to persuade them not to enter our house and ill-treat her again; as we were doing so she crept up behind us and threw a glass of water at them. She was in and out of our house all day. When she was inside Jess controlled her, while I patrolled on the verandah to keep children at bay.

June 18th. The crazy business continues, though she was only here three times today. I had a good chat with a Madurese who was after her with a stick. The policemen took tracts from us and allowed us to distribute them to prisoners in the cells. I have managed to do quite a lot of Indonesian study during these stormy days, but it must be admitted that having a lunatic squatted on us rather takes the shine off our otherwise happy home. In ten days we are due to go on holiday, so some relief is in sight. Since Sri has discarded some of her clothes and torn others, Jess gave her an unwanted dress. Having thus acquired what she considers to be a Dutch garment she is under the delusion that she is Queen Wilhelmina of the Netherlands. Her appearance in the dress caused much amusement, but tragedy predominates—foul language and foul deeds.

June 19th. This was a very stormy day. After breakfast Sri appeared—in scant clothing. While we were having lunch she was in the room with us, dancing round the table at which we were eating, and crawling about on the floor. Men came in by the back door and hid in the kitchen. The moment she moved out on to the verandah they dashed past us, pounced upon her, knocked her down, and dragged her by the arms across the drive, over the road, and into the cells, where for several hours she entertained far too many people by yelling and bashing the door with a tin plate. This time, however, they kept her there. After tea we decided to escape from the neighbourhood of our house and took tracts away behind the market. Such walks are quite adventurous, for the ground is so broken and trees so abundant that you never can tell what lies just ahead. From the first moment people and children swamped us; again and again we had to tear ourselves away from enthusiastic mobs. Our teachers came at night; we have taken to working on till 11 p.m. as that part of the day is quiet compared to the senseless din and squalid folly of the rest.

On *June 21st* we all went into the city, for I had examinations to invigilate at the Bible College. Next day the authorities asked Jess to help them in getting Sri to the asylum. One of her relatives went round from door to door with a subscription list inviting assistance with the expense involved. Looking down it we noticed that most people had given five rupiahs. The man suggested that we might give fifty, but we decided it was right to be like the others and give just five. Sri was raving mad in the cell, keeping up an astonishingly vigorous and sustained hammering on the door. However, with the aid of the lieutenant from the Salvation Army hospital, injections, bathing, and much kindness, the trip went off happily, but it was unsuccessful, for when they arrived there was no spare bed, and they were compelled to return to Sabrang.

June 23rd. This was my Sunday in Surabaja. Jess had a turbulent day; Loti ran a high temperature and Sri was let out of the cell and came in repeatedly as an alternative to lying half naked in the road at our gate, throwing stones at cyclists, and getting beaten up by exasperated persons.

June 24th. At last the police were notified that there was room in the asylum for Sri. Two officials and the Javanese lieutenant from the Salvation Army hospital were to go in the Mayflower with Jess and Sri. But then she vanished. So Jess went off alone in the car to look for her, found her down near the market providing public entertainment, and persuaded her to get into the Mayflower. The whole party had coffee at our door without disembarking and then drove off—which was, I hope, the end.

June 26th. Yes, it was the end, although not without some adventures for Jess on the way to the asylum. A stop in the city was necessary, in the main square. Sri succeeded in emptying a jug of water over herself and then, under the impression that she was Queen Wilhelmina and exceedingly beautiful, danced about for a space in the public eye until she could be jostled back into the Mayflower. She had been to the asylum before and got a warm welcome back from some in as sad a state as she herself. And ever since then we have been enjoying our liberty from three weeks' siege.

We spent the *25th* attending the wedding of two of the students from the Bible College at a big town on the coastal plain. They were, of course, Chinese, and the bridegroom's family have long been members of the Pentecostal Church. The couple looked splendid, dressed magnificently. A two-hour feast followed at the mansion of the bridegroom's uncle, which was well adapted to seat several hundred people, while a Christian band played the songs of Zion with splendid vigour. There is something very fine about these Chinese Christians, so godly and so wealthy, which seemed to be epitomised in the massive uncle in his gorgeous cream coat, diligently organising everyone, a man whose home, money, and life are devoted to the service of Christ.

Most of our household were ill during the final days before our holiday, but we got away according to plan at 9 a.m. on Saturday, *June 29th*, drove into the city, and then—in full holiday mood and in perfect morning sunshine—away up into the mountains to the Hotel of Peace. The first period of our sojourn at Sabrang was over.

It had been an experimental phase, a prelude to greater days to come. The only people we really knew personally were Rufus and his wife, and the main reason for that was the difficulty of expressing ourselves and of understanding what was said to us in either the Indonesian or Javanese languages.

CHAPTER 8

RISING TIDE

THE Hotel of Peace stands several thousand feet above sea-level on the heaving, luxuriant side of one of those great mountains which surround the city at a respectful distance and lend such infinite charm to this part of Java. In former years tens of thousands of Dutchmen found here their earthly paradise, building lovely villas all the way up the road, along the colourful boulevards of its towns and villages, and then on still more steeply to the luxurious hotels, country houses, and swimming baths of the highlands. These villas were not just holiday bungalows, but solid stone mansions, surrounded by picturesque garden walls, approached by a wide drive bridging the wayside stream, gloriously illuminated and furnished, tended by old retainers. With marvellous skill, learnt in the far-off struggle with the North Sea in Europe, the tropical torrents were harnessed to their will, streams diverted, locks built, huge hillsides irrigated from top to bottom by cutting off rivers near their sources and training half their power to meander high above the parent stream, fertilising the steepest slopes where formerly the jungle held undisputed sway. Then in the war after the second world war this culture and splendour was smashed to the foundations: every villa, every hotel, everything Dutch, was blasted and burnt off the face of the earth, rejected as a thing alien and unloved. Upon this ruin the uncoordinated efforts of the local people reared at first but shacks and sheds, utilising only the foundations of the palaces of the past. Crops to feed the hungry millions soon obliterated the lawns and flower-beds, while third-class hotels arose upon the ashes of the first-class ones. The roads remain, but the secondary ones are decaying; the garden walls often remain, incongruously enclosing rice or maize with pitiful flattery; the bridges over the wayside streams remain, their stonework ridiculously unimpaired, leading nowhere; the swimming baths remain and earn good money; the irrigation systems continue to irrigate; and the rebuilding includes a percentage of attractive homes. One might think the result would be repellent, but it is not so, except perhaps to those who lived there in the past, whose opinion no longer counts. Such is the speed of tropical growth, such the innate beauty of the land, such the immensity and diligence of the population, that the mountainsides which have experienced so vast a change are lovely to this day and we always turned in their direction with refreshment and delight.

July 30th. We are back in Sabrang again to find that Mother Daro has enlarged the verandah at the front of her part of the house and the kitchen at the back. She has altered and extended her farm buildings and made a new concrete drying-floor for her harvests. Last night a young man came round to our home with a message from Rufus asking me to go to Ringit at 7.30 p.m. When I got there I found that all the furniture had been moved out of their front room, except for two long tables, round which sat twenty-five men, some very rustic, some typical of the enlightened country folk of Java. A like number of women were in the inner room, which was divided from the first by a doorway without a door. After some while I gathered that we were waiting for guests from Barek, three miles away, so I volunteered to go and fetch them, which was just as well as they had not even started the walk to Ringit. At 9 p.m. Mrs Rufus made a little speech of welcome and then handed over to her husband. Everything was in Javanese, so that I was groping for scraps of meaning here and there. Rufus launched out from Ephesians 2 and preached with vigour, interest, and charm for fifty minutes, standing in the doorless doorway so that everyone could see him. Then we sang hymns; those of the company who were believers produced hymnbooks from inside their shirts. Rufus then prayed and asked me to speak. I did so for half an hour in Indonesian, which he interpreted into Javanese, taking as my text a wallcard beside us reading, "I am the Bread of Life", for there had been no warning and no chance for preparation. Refreshments were served on a generous scale, rice and vegetables, tea, cakes, and coffee, while eight children sang solos in turn and then again in unison. Rufus' squatter, the strolling evangelist from Sumatra, then took the floor; he read the Parable of the Good Samaritan first in Indonesian, then in Javanese, and expounded it in Indonesian. By this time it was almost midnight, but after a pause Rufus pinned up the seven Human Heart posters and preached from them one by one! Jess was at home with Rupert, but Loti shared the evening with me and revelled in it; I think it was the first evangelistic meeting she had ever attended. Rufus has a friendly, informal way about him which is much appreciated, and the work of the Spirit of God is spreading to other villages.

Then we had to break off again to attend a conference of our Mission in Djakarta. We spent a night at Mrs Tan's in Surabaja and boarded the 6 a.m. air-conditioned express for the capital next morning, arriving there seventeen hours later. Close by us in the Pullman coach was a huge, pathetic, abandoned tourist from Winnipeg. He drank heavily and then slept with his feet up on another seat, whose owner politely vacated it. His conversation was vicious and highly critical of the country in which he was a guest. Half the carriage was eyeing him and listening to him; for most of them it was no doubt a confirmation of their bad impressions of Europeans. When the train broke down for two hours in open country and local beggars took the chance of crawling through the carriages, I moved beside him but could not pierce his guard at all. He remained impenetrable and hostile, until a chance remark revealed that he was an emigrant to Canada from Germany. I switched at once from English into German and his whole attitude changed as he related his miserable tale of debauchery and divorces. When it was my turn to speak I told him of the power of the Lord Jesus Christ to deliver us from the grip of Satan and sin. He listened so meekly and patiently that I was reminded of the publicans and sinners who attended to the words of the Lord better than some more respectable people. I have rarely met a man sunk so low as he. When we had finished he wanted me to join him in a drink, but I declined. "Oh, make an exception!" he suggested, to which I explained that that is precisely what a Christian does not do.

When we got back to our village home at Sabrang the children poured over us in their enthusiasm. I counted twenty-seven who were with us without intermission all morning. Sports heats at

H

the school across the road made it heavier still next day, with fifty around for hours. On Sundays Jess now has a class for six of Rupert's closest friends after which she and Gwen Crawford run a girls' class. Another recent addition to our attack is a bookcase of Christian literature which stands on the verandah outside our front door.

A youth of unsound mind living in a village five miles north of us hanged himself last night. When the news reached the police station here they had no car available, so they asked if I would drive them out. I spent an hour in the home of the head of the village and had a good chance to expound the gospel while the police were interrogating the family concerned. Later on Rufus came round with two men from Ringit, one of whom was Mawardi. They stayed till 10.45 p.m. We drank Ovaltine, talked, and had a time of prayer. Rufus said that he had long been praying for a colleague who would be really one with him in the work, implying that that was the way in which he regarded us. He said that the brief messages in Indonesian which I have given in the village churches had been of a character quite new to the Christians and they wanted further visits. I think perhaps the evangelical approach of taking a Scripture text, explaining it, illustrating it, and applying it, is something they have not met. Rufus said that the upbuilding of the churches is top priority now. It is remarkable the way circumstances have conspired to reduce the number of occasions on which I have been able to accompany him for preaching trips, but we plan to do more together now that my command of the language is increasing and my responsibilities in the Bible College in the city decreasing.

August 17th. This is Indonesian Independence Day. From early morning Radio Djakarta set the tone by filling our house with bright and victorious music. We patriotically erected the red and white flag on a bamboo pole at our gate, where Man lashed it to the fence. At 8 a.m. I walked to the sports field armed with an invitation skilfully negotiated by my teacher and stood for nearly two hours with several thousand people in the hot sun. The three volcanoes visible from Sabrang, the gentler southern mountains, and the luxuriant ricefields, made a magnificent setting. Most of those present came in processions, school after school, the police, and the army; many people carried flags and some were in fancy dress. I was alone and glad to fall in with Susilo, who graciously kept me company the whole time. After the district head had made a speech over the loudspeaker there was a pause till 9.49 a.m. precisely, when we joined the rest of the country in the reading of the famous proclamation made by President Sukarno in Djakarta in 1945. The flag was raised slowly to the masthead while drums rumbled. The Christian headmaster, Suwarso, conducted with vigour for the singing of the national anthem. Then there was a read prayer for which we bowed our heads, although some people chatted and the majority probably kept their eyes open. Finally we formed a large square for an excellent display of clubs by thirty men and women dressed in white singlets and blue shorts under the leadership of another Christian schoolmaster. I thus observed the truth of the remark that the Christian community in Java, though so small a minority, is an influential one. After that I strolled home, the processions dismissing in the field outside the school opposite our gate. Thus the whole community had a good look at us, and at our home, which was an excellent advertisement.

After lunch I attended the next public event, basketball at Sabrang's only Chinese school, my higher motive being to meet its headmaster and thus at last make contact with the local Chinese-speaking community, which I have so far avoided. Above the gate the flag that is red and has five stars on it fluttered proudly beside the red and white of Indonesia. A youth escorted me to a very prominent seat which I declined in favour of a humbler one, but I found myself in a bunch of elderly Indonesian-speaking Chinese, isolated from the type I was after. Later on some young men moved nearer, but they were so embarrassed when I addressed them in Mandarin that they could neither understand nor reply coherently. So I was awkwardly marooned for two and a half hours although among hundreds of people; yet to leave would have been a conspicuous breach of courtesy. The game was fast and furious, sportsmanship excellent, and when the Sabrang men trounced the challengers from the city there was great jubilation. The games continued after darkness fell, so I decided to escape, no one showing any interest in my presence. However, a smiling young man cut me off and shook hands. It was the headmaster himself. In front of everyone he chatted most cordially and then walked all round the ground to escort me to the gate. I arranged to call on him later and be shown over the school.

After supper there was a nation-wide broadcast by President Sukarno himself. Loti, Mother Daro, and Man joined us beside the radio for the event. For the first time I really appreciated the power of his oratory, his rich, compelling voice, fully rounded language, and dexterous piling up of synonyms to demand acceptance of his points. Then there was a torchlight procession starting from the school opposite us. We stood for a long time as the bobbing lights in their hundreds moved slowly down Office Street and out of sight. Finally, at 10.30 p.m. Jess and I went to the parade ground to watch for a while the *wayang*, the famous Javanese puppet show, which means as much to people here as soccer does to those in England. We came away at midnight after a not unworthy Independence Day, full of laughter and fun, geared largely to the children.

Next morning, *August 18th*, I went with Rufus, Mawardi, and Rekso to Lakar where Rufus and I preached in Javanese and Indonesian respectively to forty people. He took John 4:14 and I Matthew 11:27-29. As we left, after a very happy time, Hasan filled my tank with petrol. With Rupert sick and Jess thus tied to the house our operations have been fairly quiet. Few children come to the house and for a lone man like me to roam about outside is hardly desirable. So I took the chance of calling upon the Chinese headmaster. To my surprise I was able to speak to him about the Lord and he told me that many of his friends were Pentecostalists. At first he wanted to call me "Father Taylor".

One night we got our teachers to come to supper with some of their friends. We thought these modern young people would enjoy having an English meal, so we made no attempt to serve them anything Indonesian. However, the result was rather too much for them. They were all beautifully dressed. None of them being Christians we played games after supper. They stayed on, as one of the girls named Wagini wanted to hear the jazz from Australia at 10.30 p.m. We did not realise this, so when it started, I switched it off, much to her surprise.

On *August 25th* I was preaching in Surabaja all day. There were about a hundred at the Cantonese Church, a steady increase since they got their own pastor. At night there were fully 500 at the Foochow Church, and I finished up at the British Community Church where there were twenty-two, which is not a bad congregation considering that the potential attendance is under 100. I have given notice to this last church that in view of our enlarging opportunities at Sabrang I can no longer preach for them every month, so they gave a farewell supper for me at the home of the American Vice-Consul. I got away in the Mayflower at 10 p.m. and on an absolutely open road made Sabrang by midnight.

August 26th was for several reasons a day to be remembered. At dusk I drove to Rufus' home and prayed with him and Mrs Rufus and Mawardi. Joined by two of Rufus' children we then went to the village of Triwung several miles away on the far side of the Larsti River. Once we turned off the main road the lane was unsurfaced, but such tracks are sometimes kinder to a car than unrepaired metal roads, except in wet weather. Triwung has about 2000 inhabitants and is thus not a large place, but like all these villages the name applies not to a few streets of houses and shops but to an extensive area in which houses, trees, and fields are all mixed up, a sort of oriental garden city. We drew in under an exceedingly feeble lamp outside the half-built house of Susilo, the key man in this place, over-garrulous perhaps, but spiritually alert. It was the first of very many visits to his home, a place which tragedy and triumph were to stamp indelibly upon our memories. Mrs Susilo served us coffee and cakes, and we all prayed together again, before moving off by cycle and in the car over grassy tracks among ricefields, streams, and homesteads, where I suppose the makers of the Mayflower hardly contemplated her venturing. The meeting to which we went proved to be on a very small scale, the smallest in fact to which I ever went with Rufus. There were just thirteen people present in the home of a timid-looking farmer named Hastari. "Islam is thin around here," said Susilo, "and animism also, so there is a vacuum." Hastari's home stood at a rural cross-roads amidst many other similar village homes whose lights shone out through the enveloping trees. It was a strongly-built place, with a lofty roof, no ceiling, and no furniture except a bare table and benches. An ancient oil burner hung dustily from the rafters and shed a dim light upon the scene until it was replaced by the glare of a petromax lamp. At 8 p.m. Rufus rose and started to address the company, preaching for almost an hour before he called on me. I spoke for thirty minutes on 1 Timothy 2:5-6, "There is one God and one mediator between God and men, the man Christ Jesus, who gave Himself a ransom for all." Most of those present were men; they listened in perfect silence, while the youngest of Hastari's sons slept peacefully on a wooden settee. When we had finished, coffee was served and Rufus then took me into one of the bedrooms where the old grandfather sat on the edge of a wooden bed with two other grandsons asleep beside him. He was introduced to me as Daddy Tain. He was ill and looked to me as though the end of his life might not be far away. Rufus took his hand and talked to him for a long time about the Lord Jesus, exhorting him to repent and believe the gospel. Then he got Daddy Tain to follow him in a prayer, insisting that he get the words "Lord Jesus Christ" correct, which he failed to do at the first attempt. The others stood behind us and in the doorway. Rufus then called out to his wife and asked her to lead us all in prayer for the old man. When she had done so we shook his hand in turn and filed back into the other room. It was the first time that I had seen Rufus with the aged and so little did I comprehend his art that I hardly expected much outcome from the time devoted to an old man whose days were in any case numbered.

At 10 p.m. we crossed the road to a large house whose front room was littered with musical instruments, stacks of sheaves and piles of grain, underneath pictures of President Sukarno and the nineteenth-century Javanese patriot, Diponegoro. I was not at all clear what was going to happen. We sat at a table until a very old, wrinkled woman tottered in from the back premises. She was given the best chair and Rufus moved across to sit beside her and at once started talking to her slowly and clearly about Christ. Then, as she was unwell, he anointed her with oil and gave her a small glass of water to drink as a symbol of John 4:14. All eyes were then diverted to the door from the living quarters, through which

there emerged at minimum speed a man over a hundred years old—
in fact the general opinion was that he was 125. His great-grandchild
was asleep beside us. He sat by his wife, who suddenly appeared
quite juvenile. Rufus stood beside him, bending down, and
shouted the gospel into his ear, grasping his shoulders as he did so.
The old man kept nodding and grunting. Then Rufus prayed over
him, and finally the whole party shook hands with him most
respectfully, using both hands. We visited two other houses before
getting off to bed at midnight, though Susilo told me he was then
going to another meeting in the same village. It seems that the
wayang, the historic Javanese form of recreation, has accustomed
people to staying up very late at night and this affects the form of
Christian work too. Indeed so far I have been let off lightly in this
matter.

We were rather sceptical about the 125 years, but Loti said to us,
"Well, my great-grandfather only died last year, aged 140," and my
teacher assures me that the ceiling is about 150. He attributes it to
hardy, open air, farming life combined with the leisurely, calm,
monotonous round of simple customs which characterises the huge
rural areas.

August 28th. We had Jonathan, the Dutch missionary, professor of
theology and philology, to supper and he stayed a night with us.
As a master of Javanese language and culture there is much we can
learn from him and I hope his stay may have helped to iron out
some misconceptions about our presence in Sabrang, for all this part
of the world was formerly the exclusive mission field of the Dutch
Reformed Church and there are some who not unnaturally wonder
whether we intend to build up the East Java Church or attempt to
divert it to some other ecclesiastical alignment of our own! I took
him across to Rufus' home and enjoyed listening to his easy
flow of Javanese. He is full of their history and folklore, able to
discourse entertainingly on antiquarian and philological niceties.
I believe it is important for us to have his understanding and
sympathy.

I was then compelled to leave Jess and spend ten days in West
Java. I did so not without some misgivings, for we are in a phase of
being overrun with children and boys, who are not always polite or

wholesome. But she is really better at managing them than I am. Recently there has been a young girl in one of the cells opposite and each evening Jess has sent over to her, through Loti, some dainty thing to eat. In this way she also got our tracts and when the police guards saw them they asked for a set too.

On the evening of *August 29th* I went by train to Surabaja, battled all night with mosquitoes at Mrs Tan's, and caught the 6 a.m. train to Djakarta via Jogjakarta. It was a lovely day and the scenery in Central Java very splendid. I spent the last four hours locked in conversation with a young Chinese, President of the Beko Picture Corporation. His heart seemed to be untilled ground; but he was quite interested to hear about the gospel.

On *August 31st* I travelled to Bandung with our Mission Superintendent for the first Indonesian Pastors' Conference called by the National Evangelistic Commission of the Indonesian Council of Churches but financed and led by the World Vision organisation and Dr Bob Pierce. This momentous event was held in the Homann Hotel right alongside the site of the famous Asia-Africa Bandung Conference. The 570 pastors and delegates were housed there and in an adjacent hotel. Nothing more extravagant could have been conceived, but in some other respects the conference was good. One of the speakers was the Right Reverend Dr Alexander Mar Theophilus, bishop of the Mar Thoma Church in South India, clad in a pink robe and adorned with a mitre on which were twelve crosses, with a larger one on the back-flap and a gold one on a scarlet thread hanging just below his flowing beard. Everything that one had hoped these serried ranks of pastors would hear was given to them by the celibate, 44-year-old bishop in perfect English and with great charm and spiritual force. His testimony to his mother, his call to the ministry, the life of faith, the self-support and evangelistic outreach of his church were admirable. He based his three talks on 1 Peter 2:9, "But ye are a chosen generation, a royal priesthood, an holy nation, a peculiar people, that ye should show forth the praises of Him who hath called you out of darkness into His marvellous light."

The opportunity for Christian fellowship provided by the conference was most valuable to me. I renewed and strengthened almost every important official contact of the past four years with leaders of the Indonesian churches, officials of the Ministry of Religion, West Java pastors, Central Java pastors, East Java pastors, Chinese pastors, Indonesian-Chinese pastors, and Pentecostal pastors. Rufus was there and so too was Sutikno of Madura, the man through whom I first came to know Rufus; I think the Bishop gave them both a drink of the wine of heaven such as may never have come their way before.

The day after my return we had a very full Sunday in Sabrang. We attended the Javanese Church in the morning and in the afternoon Jess had her usual class of small boys followed by the girls' Bible class. Being so often away on Sundays I have no part in these. Early on Monday morning I left for Surabaja to collect Max Orr and Mrs Orr off their ship. They are to replace us at the Bible College in the city. Max slid smoothly into position, having had many years of experience in China, and Pastor Meng glowed with pleasure.

All this crashing around Java has exhausted me and today Rupert and I are alone at home with Loti and Yeny, as Jess is taking Rufus' mother-in-law back to her home village, a round trip of 170 miles. The old lady is permanently bent double and three bus changes would be almost beyond her, so this seems a way in which we can help. Jess was gone for fourteen hours and thoroughly enjoyed meeting Rufus' relatives for the second time. Rufus is most enthusiastic about the recent conference at Bandung. "I went hungry and came back filled and overflowing," he said.

On Friday, *September 13th*, we launched into what proved to be quite an adventure, our first visit to Karangan, where Rufus used to be pastor. The original plan was that I should go with him and Mrs Rufus and three of their children, Jess driving us for twenty miles until the point in the Southern Mountains where the road ends and we would have to walk. Then on Sunday she was to return in the car to the same point and pick us up. We left at 10 a.m., never having been that way before. The road was third-class and soon began to deteriorate as it climbed into the hills which bar off the Indian Ocean. We wound through the uplands amidst rubber, coffee, and teak plantations, the area being well but not densely populated. Gradually jagged stones and deep ruts became normal on the road; several of the party got out and I became seriously alarmed for the survival of the car, for we were often in danger of becoming straddled on some rocky ridge. We decided that it was impossible for Jess and Rupert to go back alone over such a surface and then return to get us on Sunday. Although neither of them had brought anything but what they were wearing, the only course open to us seemed to be that we should all go on to Karangan for two days.

I have already described the approach to Karangan and the unique beauty of its situation. In two hours we were down at sea-level among the palm trees and the houses, fording the three rivers which bisect the village, the bridges which used to span them having all been washed away. Rufus and his wife had not been back to Karangan since they moved away to live in the Sabrang district, so we became eye-witnesses of the delightful welcome they received. Old and young gathered around them, shaking hands, sometimes kissing and hugging them. At last we reached the house of the present pastor, in which our family slept.

Next morning we were rash enough to walk to the sea for the sake of the children. Although it seemed so near the trip took us over an hour and we were out in the blazing sunshine all the time, with ricefields on either hand and no cover at all until we reached the final jungle belt, where we had to ford a sinister, tree-girt stream. Budi, Rufus' old friend, came with us, and at the stream he cut down with his knife a number of stout sticks, walked ahead over a water-logged tree-trunk, and stuck them through the water into the slimy bottom to make a rough support for the uninitiated behind him. We were richly rewarded when we actually reached the long, curving beach by the magnificent breakers of the Indian Ocean crashing in fullest power upon the steep shore. Budi and I kept on the seaward side of the children as they paddled, for every wave bowled them over and dragged them back—to their enormous delight. A nick from Budi's knife in the top of a coconut meant a nice drink of cool, coconut water; a slash or two and a spoon meant a feast from inside it. The trek back was exhausting once we left the shelter of the trees; Budi carried Rupert and he went fast asleep on his bare, capacious back, an experience which made them friends ever afterwards!

After lunch we were invited to an evangelistic meeting in a corner of the Karangan plain not far from the sea and that involved another long walk across the fields. Rufus and I both preached to about eighty people, but my address on Romans 1:16, "I am not ashamed of the gospel of Christ, for it is the power of God unto salvation to everyone that believeth", was translated from Indonesian into Javanese by the young pastor who led the meeting, and I sensed that he did not do it at all well. When I asked Rufus about the translation he was suspiciously silent. Once it was over we had to walk fast to get clear of the tiny paths through the ricefields before the sun went down. As soon as supper was finished we were off again to another distant corner of the plain where a farmhouse was packed full of men and women awaiting our arrival. We were there till midnight.

Next morning came the main church service which took the form of a wedding, attended by 300 people. Once more Rufus preached and then made an opening for me to do so in spite of the young pastor, who was keen to close the proceedings. We then began our trek home, moving slowly across the plain towards the house where the wedding feast was in progress. Many guests had been there earlier and were on their way back, so we met them all dressed in their best clothes. Perhaps we got too rosy an impression of a Christian village as the stream passed us, everyone shaking hands with each person in our party, while Rufus and his wife lingered over them individually, exhorting them to continue in the faith. Many others were still at the wedding feast and we were urged to join them there. Yet again I preached, using Romans 6:22 this time, and then we tore ourselves away, though not before visiting a big house where a very old lady lay dying. She solemnly shook hands with us all and then we prayed. Her husband, a tall, grey, thin, timeless figure, led us in prayer and I understood enough to know that he was no merely nominal believer. Then we plodded up and up for an hour, men carrying the children. The car survived the road and after dark we were home in Sabrang, to find that a search party from the Bible College had been out to rescue

Jess, fearing that she and Rupert had got stranded somewhere. But really there is little to fear among these country people; we meet with great kindness everywhere. Next day I was fit for nothing and Rupert went down with amoebic dysentery, his sixth attack this year. In the days that followed numbers of young men began to come often to our home. A group of them asked me to run a Bible class for them. They were all Muslims and seemed to enjoy it; however, they never came a second time. Mountains of manuscripts in Indonesian pile up on my desk awaiting checking and correction, as though I had nothing else in the world to do except prepare tracts for publication, but the Christian literature we have all along kept on our verandah for visitors to read has been stolen. Not long before a youth asked me point-blank what would happen to anyone who just took it and never brought it back. My answer could not be very precise, so I presume he realised he could take it with impunity. We feel it may be best not to replace it just yet. So with Rupert in bed, the books on the verandah gone, and schoolmasters clamping down on their pupils for mobbing us, we live more quietly.

September 21st. Yesterday was a terrific day here. Time and again boys of 15 and young men came to the house asking for English classes or a Bible class. A boy named Samari came three times and said, "How can I enter the Christian religion? How much do I have to pay?" He said he wanted to "learn the Lord". Loti's comment was, "Many of our people are in this enquiring state of mind." As we were going to bed Rufus came round on his cycle. He is always the same, quiet and humble, but ever happy, cheerful, victorious, and thrustful. He had just had a long talk with a policeman, first about the devil and then about Christ. He too is overrun with visitors. He moves quietly, following up contacts rather than plunging into raw communities where he might arouse antagonism. Since June we have had no time for the tracting walks of our first days in Sabrang, but a large village in which we distributed tracts four months ago is now asking Rufus for an evangelistic meeting. Yet Rufus has his own church problem, for some pastors are sceptical of what he is doing and are jealous I fear; but the flow of people turning to Christ continues and the task is to gear this new life into the old congregations. At 10.30 p.m. we prayed and he departed with joy.

September 25th. While Jess and Gwen Crawford were teaching forty children in the children's meeting, twenty-five youths chose to swarm on to the verandah as observers, so I had to improvise another meeting on the steps in order to divert them. They scrutinised the large pictures of Bible stories which we keep hanging on the walls. One of them showed the armies of Israel storming over the fallen walls of Jericho. "Are those soldiers Christians?" asked the boys, which shows how confusing some things can be!

Samari, the bright fifteen-year-old boy who asked how much you had to pay to be a Christian, drops in to our home frequently. I gave him Rufus' address at Ringit and he has been there too and came back with great joy. He is an only child and seems to be seeking light. The same day three Muslim schoolmasters came to Rufus to ask, "How can we enter the Christian religion?" A man living not far from Rufus had a dream in which he saw himself washing rice in the crystal-clear water of a spring. Groping for the meaning of this he went with his wife to see Rufus, who read to him the passage about the "well of living water" in John 4, which strongly confirmed his desire to know the gospel. Tonight I was with Rufus again. He was sitting alone in his little room at dusk, accompanied by many mosquitoes, nursing one of his children with an injured foot. His wife came in too, so we reviewed the latest encouraging developments and prayed together. He had been at Barek the night before, where another twenty-five people are asking for baptism. Then he was at Triwung with Susilo till midnight. I don't know how he stands the pace, let alone visitors and squatters, but he has the easterner's enviable knack of appearing fresh and at leisure.

September 25th. All odd moments are now packed tight with correcting new and old manuscripts in Indonesian for the Christian Witness Press in Hongkong. Inevitably my Chinese is beginning to wilt a bit under such rivalry. This morning I held my first English class for boys of seventeen; there were twelve of them. A boy of nine bought a gospel of Luke for his adult brother, but came back later with instructions to swap it for "the book which tells about the cross". Jess insisted that the gospel of Luke did just that in Chapter 23 and the child ran off repeating to himself "23, 23, 23. . . ." It is difficult even to remember and record all that the Lord is doing in these parts now. The seventeen-year-olds want a Bible class in addition to the English class. Lots of small children drop in here to get Jess to put medicine on their minor cuts: if the patient is older or the injury at all serious she insists that they go to the hospital across the road. Last night we called on Rufus again, as one of his children has been quite ill. As we left at 10 p.m. four other guests, all recent converts, arrived. He gets little peace and seeks it little. Next day he came to us and invited me to join him on another trip to the south coast. He asked if I could spare any more of the booklet *The Way of Salvation* and from now on he will stock in his home a selection of every book in our bookcase, as he finds people often want to buy off him. This is good news and virtually means a second literature depot. Since it was Saturday we knocked off work after lunch, dozed through the hot afternoon, and I then drove down to Surabaja with Max Orr, partly to introduce him to the Chinese Christian Churches there so that he might take my place and set us more free to co-operate with Rufus. "He understands our customs," said one of the deacons to me with a twinkle, "foreigners usually go into a church alongside their wives, but Mr Orr was five yards in front of his." I preached all day on the text, "Ye are the temple of God". It will be a welcome relief to hand over these Surabaja tasks to Max and yet I confess that I surrender with some regret such glorious opportunities for preaching Christ among Chinese. I drove home alone at night at high speed in two hours, long lines of overhead lights leading the way into each town, the full moon standing straight over the perfect peak of the baby volcano and the lights of a holiday resort shining high in the sky on its flank. The streets of the city were strangely deserted at 11 p.m.; then came the silent road to Sabrang through sleeping multitudes, save where the night shift was pouring into the sugar factories or villagers sat gossiping on the clean tarmac, tucking their feet in as I swept past.

September 30th was devoted to literature matters. I mailed off to Hongkong a priceless packet of sixteen corrected tract manuscripts in Indonesian, only to collect at the Post Office precisely the same sixteen uncorrected manuscripts in Javanese. The proof of the Javanese Christmas tract was finally passed and the script of "The Story of Daniel" fully checked. A stack of literature was prepared for Rufus to take south. I visited and prayed with him at sunset. Meanwhile Jess labours at the Javanese language and has a steady stream of meetings and visitors, while Loti and Yeny keep our household in clockwork order.

On *October 4th* we went tracting again for the first time for over three months. We chose a corner of Sabrang formerly occupied exclusively by workers in a tapioca factory now closed, since many children who visit us come from that part. Never have we covered so small an area. In a full hour we walked for 200 yards in a tiny circle back to the locked car, which acted as our supply depot, while the people poured in upon us from every side. The children who visit our home tried to act as a bodyguard, but Jess existed in the midst of a gay and tumultuous mob, through which an old gentleman marched with solemnity to shake hands with her. There is great demand for *The Way of Salvation* and Susilo tells us of many people, not yet clearly Christian believers, who take it to work with them as a kind of vade-mecum. We had some splendid contacts and were confirmed in our former judgement that this strenuous kind of service has manifold values. But how the very ground sprouts people here! Sabrang is a far-away corner of Java and we were in an insignificant nook in Sabrang, yet in one hour we could describe a circle of but 200 yards! A vivid film of personalities flashes past the eye on such occasions—bright girls, old hags, busy mothers, students, sly coves, magnificently dressed people, urchins, responsible elders, and many eager youngsters brimming over with anticipation.

Then on *October 5th* I started off in the Mayflower to visit the famous Christian village of Kabat for the first time. I took with me two of Rufus' children and the boy Samari, who is so acutely interested in the gospel. Rufus himself had gone three days earlier, visited two other Christian villages near the coast, and took a boat round to Kabat to meet us. Meanwhile from Sabrang we climbed fiercely up into the Southern Mountains on a rough, twisty road and then wound through the high plateau country, covered with beautifully kept rubber plantations, till the hills grew wilder still and began to drop far down towards the coast. From a height we sighted the sea and wormed our way on bottom gear amidst a jagged jumble of peaks and crags to the rich valley of Kabat, where live 6000 people, the majority of them Christians. The place lies about two hours' walk from the Indian Ocean, divided from it by a last, lofty, jungle-covered ridge. We stayed with Muljono, the head of the village, a very striking young man. His home was exceedingly large and after supper there we drove through the long avenues of the village, parked the car, and climbed a precipitous hill to find that 142 people had been sitting in a farmhouse for the past two hours awaiting our arrival. This did not deter them from sitting for another three hours while we preached, the meeting closing at midnight. There are no rows of gloomy tenements in the Christian villages of Java, no semi-detached houses, no blocks of flats. Every man dwells at a discreet distance from his neighbours under plenty of his own vines and fig trees. This means that the village is very widely spread. A river flows through it and at one point there is a high, rather dangerous-looking bridge, but we crossed by a ford which Muljono cheerfully assured me was not very deep. It was night and the headlights beamed hopefully across the water as we splashed through and up the steep bank on the opposite shore. Rufus preached with great vigour for one and a half hours so I restricted my remarks to twenty minutes, conscious that I was on trial before a critical audience.

Next morning they took me early to visit an old farmer, only survivor of the eight righteous men who founded the village of Kabat sixty years ago, trekking through the jungle from the crowded country to the north, clearing the trees to win land for themselves, sending for their families, hacking out the ricefields with infinite toil, attracting other Christian settlers, and building from the first a village which was genuinely Christian. After twenty-five years the government helped them to introduce an irrigation system and today the plain is a sea of glorious rice. The old fellow sat pensively in his large, barnlike home, surrounded with farm implements and piles of grain, while long rows of sheaves lay on the threshing-floor at the door, and the others treated him with the respect due to a Pilgrim Father.

The church building in Kabat stands on a spur above the river and seats 700 people. It was packed full when we got there at 9 a.m., the big windows opened wide to catch the breeze and allow views of sun-kissed hills and fields. Since the pastor was sick it fell to Rufus to lead the morning service. Clad in his black robe and cravats he stood below the massive pulpit which occupied the centre of the end wall of the church. Facing him in a hollow square were thirty young mothers adorned in all the colours of the rainbow, carrying thirty similarly attired babies. Behind them stood thirty fathers, all dressed in white, barefoot like the mothers. For three hours these family groups stayed at the front of the great congregation, joining in the singing and hearing Rufus preach. The thirty mothers controlled the thirty babies with consummate skill until the great moment arrived. Then the thirty fathers moved out in front and each secured his baby. In careful order the couples advanced upon Rufus, and knelt in front of him, the father carrying the child in each case. An elder held a silver bowl of water while Rufus, pulling back the sleeve of his gown, dipped his right hand into it and slowly sprinkled each child thrice, baptising him in the name of the Father and of the Son and of the Holy Spirit, and then stretching out his hands in blessing over it. The comings and goings were well organised, but it took some time and with so many people involved there were a few near misses between bald heads which the papas skilfully steered through the throng. As each mother regained her seat, each father replaced the relevant baby on her lap and took his own place behind her again. Mighty singing accompanied all this, the 700 turning on full pressure for hymns they had known since infancy. Then, to my astonishment, thirty grandmothers meandered to the front and secured temporary possession of the thirty babies. Thus freed, the thirty fathers and thirty mothers knelt a second time before Rufus, forming now a solid mass on the mats at his feet. He addressed them and prayed over them, and when they then returned to their seats, one of them acted as spokesman, rising to thank the church for the welcome given to their children. The thirty grannies then advanced with the thirty babies, who were restored to their original positions and slept happily throughout Rufus' sermon. This kind of thing happens every two months in the Kabat Church. It was on New Year's Day 1949, just after the close of such a morning service that the village was machine-gunned by three Dutch planes which came over without any warning; the large congregation was still streaming homewards and although a great many houses were hit there was not a single fatality, but this sad incident is still remembered and if I had been a Dutchman I should not have been welcomed in Kabat.

After a merciful hour for sleep we started out on the three-mile drive to Tanggung, a small satelite village of only 300 souls, entirely Christian. Although so many of its roads are good enough, there does come a point in Java, as anywhere else, where three miles assumes formidable proportions. It was a beautiful trip across the centre of the plain through golden waves of rice, where the pace was 5 m.p.h. on the better stretches. Eventually we reached the bank of a river and the road became a ledge at the foot of a ridge of jungle. I dismounted to inspect the pitch and after prolonged study it was decided that if all passengers got out it might be possible to edge the car through. The bank being insecure there remained the possibility that the Mayflower and I would tumble into the river, but eventually we contrived to slip through the gap. It was a good thing we did, for after our arrival we learnt that no private car had ever been in Tanggung before and they had built up the road specially for our benefit. We got a great welcome, most of the population being out in the lane to stare at us. The local evangelist received us with great delight into his rambling home, bare of all furniture except a table, chairs, and heaps of lime. There was a meeting at 4 p.m., a communion service, and the entire adult population of Tanggung was present. I suppose it would hardly be possible to parallel such a situation in England today, but there it was in a remote corner of Java near the Indian Ocean, an outpost of civilisation so generously baptised in flood water each July that the people take to the roofs of their homes on the worst nights. It was the first time I had received the Lord's Supper in the East Java Church. Rufus led and preached and at the end I was asked to address them. In view of their labours to build the road for us I took the text,

"Prepare ye the way of the Lord". Darkness fell and no lights being available, Rufus and I were asked to stand over by a window as gathering gloom descended upon the rest of the congregation. While we were having supper in the evangelist's house men were working again on the road, and since it was pitch dark when we reached the danger spot I was glad they had done so. Back in Kabat I had to wait alone in the car at a cross-roads while Rufus went for the pastor's wife. Men gathered round me in the bright moonlight with the huge church towering above us; in a Muslim land it seemed strange to be able to assume some Bible knowledge in talking to them. "Many people are interested in the gospel these days," said one figure, "for the coming of the Lord is surely not far off." We then drove back to the home of Muljono, the head of the village, to find no less than 439 people assembled on his huge verandah. They had been there since 7 p.m. and we continued in splendid singing, prayer, and preaching until 12.30 a.m. Muljono himself expounded the Christian Witness Press poster called "The Sinner's Dream", Rufus preached next, and at the end I was asked to tell about the work of the Lord in China and Malaya. Refreshments were handed round and a collection taken up to defray the expenses of them. I got to bed at 1 a.m. and by 8 a.m. we were away in the Mayflower back over the big hill to the plantation plateau, from the crest of which we gazed out over the glory of the plain on which lies Sabrang.

This visit, confirming the impressions of our trip to Karangan, showed us beyond a doubt that the Christian villages of East Java, of which I have now visited six, are a far more formidable and remarkable factor than I had realised. The deity and death of Christ and all the great foundation facts of the gospel are believed in them, and I could not detect any special doctrinal lack. Personal response and surrender to Christ in view of the great facts could probably be stressed more and there may be too easy an assumption that baptism makes a Christian, but there is amazing achievement to offset any such deficiencies. When one looks at the forbidding jungle and then contrasts it with the mountains of sheaves piled in the Pilgrim Fathers' hall, and adds to that the great church, the multitude of fine houses, the wide, shady avenues, and the tradition of faith maintained through more than half a century, typified in the sight of the head of the village expounding an evangelical poster to his people and in the fair approximation to a theocratic society, there is very much indeed to be admired. Furthermore, in the minds of such men as Muljono, and partly through the remarkable movement of the Spirit around Sabrang initiated by Rufus, there is a growing sense of responsibility to bring the gospel to the vast Muslim north, the other side of the Southern Mountains.

CHAPTER 9

OPEN HEARTS IN STORMY TIMES

October 13th. Jess drove the Salvation Army captain into the city on an emergency call. The Army run a Children's Home there and one of the older girls in it was correctly accused of stealing a sum of money. At the first opportunity she ran away and made for the main railway line which runs into the city from Surabaja. The police keep a watch at the spot as there have been many suicides recently, and it was they who apprehended her, not the pursuers. She was in a hysterical condition, and in despair the younger workers in charge phoned to Sabrang to ask the captain's help. She handled the distracted girl with much kindness but also firmness, throwing a glass of water in her face and threatening to pour a bucket of water right over her if she did not calm down. She and Jess brought her back to Sabrang in the car and she is now in the hospital.

One evening we went out with tracts to Samari's village. He saw us and came to help me push Rupert along, sharing in the distribution of tracts and finally taking us to meet his parents in a tiny back room into which a horde of children followed us. Darkness fell, but the news had spread and people seemed to find their way to where we were easily enough. It looked at the time as though Samari was deeply interested in the gospel, but an incident which took place soon afterwards terminated our connection with him. He wanted to buy a small, red New Testament from the bookcase on our verandah. I told him that it cost thirteen rupiahs. He offered me ten, but I explained that we did not bargain over these books and that they were sold at minimum price with a view to wide distribution, not to profit. After thinking for a time he suggested eleven rupiahs. Since I was keen for him to possess a New Testament and read it I would gladly have made it easier for him to buy this one, but it occurred to me that it would be unwise to make interest in the gospel a means of getting literature at lower prices, and in any case if I let him have the book cheap I would have to do the same to others. So I stuck to the price of thirteen rupiahs. He opened his wallet and after counting the notes in it announced that he only had twelve and that he would bring the thirteenth another time. Unfortunately for him we had already found it inadvisable to part with any book before receiving the proper amount. To do so almost always meant that the purchaser conveniently failed to pay his debt which then became a barrier between him and us, preventing him from having anything more to do with us or the gospel. So I told him I would be delighted to give him the book if he brought me the thirteen rupiahs next day. He did so and went off with the New Testament, but with rather bad grace, and I hardly ever saw him again. He had, I fear, hoped for financial advantages through being friends with us.

October 16th. This is a quiet week as the local schools have ten days holiday which cuts our visitors by 90 per cent and our noise by 99 per cent, making No. 122 a peaceful and secluded spot. In the city the Bible College took one day off and we joined them in an outing to the Indian Ocean, taking Loti and Yeny with us. We had six hours on the magnificent beaches and while there scaled a steep hill which becomes an island at high tide. From the top the land drops sheer for 400 feet to the raging ocean. There is a rough shelter up there and I noticed a man sitting in it gazing out over the water, with a fire smouldering at his feet. He came from the city and I spent twenty minutes chatting with him. He told me he had walked there in eighteen hours and planned to stay for twenty-one days on a very scanty diet; water was beside him in a hollowed bamboo pole. His business was not doing well, he said, so he had withdrawn for this period to seek God, his aim being financial gain. "It is very peaceful here," he added. "My father often came here. One is removed from the temptations of city life." He listened well while I expounded to him a more excellent way. Twenty other holiday-makers reached the top, so I walked down to the car, got tracts from it, climbed up again, gave some to the holiday-makers on their way down, and found the hermit-merchant alone once more. Seeing that he had plenty of time to read I gave him plenty of material.

On *October 18th* Rufus and I spent twelve hours in Gondang on the side of the Great Volcano, the first place we ever visited together. Although it is only forty-five minutes by car from Sabrang, Rufus' letter, posted a week before, had not yet arrived, so the evening meeting had not been announced and attendance was therefore only fifteen, but it included Tias the headmaster and Lukas the doctor and lasted for three hours. We also paid prolonged visits to four homes, in each of which I had good opportunities to speak of Christ after Rufus had done so. He is very tactful and allows conversation to run along naturally until an opening comes; then he takes command almost invisibly and gets his message in. The four families all had slender Christian connections but were obviously delighted that we gave time to them. There is no regular Christian meeting in Gondang, the slightly less sleepy so-called Christians preferring to go very occasionally to distant churches in Christian villages. Mawardi and Rekso were with us so our kindly host, the headmaster, provided two square meals for six people, but he appears to have capitulated completely to the careless standards of a remote spot. He is also a diabetic.

One result of these away trips with Rufus is that country people whom I have met in their own homes come and call on us when they visit Sabrang, so that our adult visitors are on the increase. Most weeks I drop in to see Rufus some evening, when we sit for an hour rejoicing over what God is doing, comparing notes, and praying. On *October 25th* we held our fourth Bible class with the seventeen-year-old boys; there were nine of them and as their shyness thaws away we are slowly getting to know and enjoy them. Sales of literature from our verandah are also increasing, but we are striking some difficulties as our prices are low and this exposes purchasers to the temptation of profitable resale. Rufus has heard of some items originating from us being offered at five times our price!

October 28th. While all is still fresh I want to relate the tale of our second visit to Karangan, where Rufus was formerly pastor for five years. The party consisted of Rufus, Mawardi, Rekso, and three of Rufus' children. Knowing this time how bad the road became, we left the car outside a Christian home on the southern edge of the plantation plateau and walked for forty-five minutes through the late afternoon sunshine into the village of Wonoredjo, Rufus resplendent in a jockey cap and full of conversation about the wonderful works of God. As we passed through Wonoredjo we gave out a lot of tracts. We had hoped to have an evangelistic meeting in this place of 2500 souls with only one Christian family, but the plan had fallen through. Nevertheless we felt that if we sprayed the neighbourhood with tracts there might yet be an opening for us.

Rufus and I walked ahead. Mawardi, tall, thin, and talkative, came behind with old Rekso, massive, heavy-footed and silent. These are our usual companions on all expeditions, but I cannot get to know them very closely as neither has much command of Indonesian. We were down on the Karangan plain by dusk, a lovely sight with sea and mountains ringing the plain and innumerable palms waving in the breeze. I supped alone with an elderly gentleman, headmaster of the local school, a rich man. I much enjoyed talking with him about the Lord and hearing his story of the terrible Japanese days. He said that twenty-four men were taken from Karangan to the city, only twelve coming back alive. He himself was tortured with electricity, immersed upside down in a tub of water, hung up by the thumbs, and beaten. Naked and bound, they ordered him to show them how he prayed, and he told me of the joy which filled his heart as he thus had the chance to pray for himself and for them in Javanese, being fully persuaded at the time that he was about to die.

His eldest son is the only medical worker in Karangan. In former times a Dutch doctor used to come over the mountains from the city once a month, but as part of the price of independence the son now has to function entirely single-handed. He is also the only midwife, delivering about eighty children each year. In emergencies there is nothing to do but take a chair up the precipitous hillside for two hours to the road and then a jeep for two more into the city. At 3 a.m. one night he attempted this journey with an expectant mother, but somewhere out on the plantation plateau the baby decided to arrive. He stopped the car and with the assistance of the driver delivered the child; since there was then no point in going on to the city they returned triumphantly to Karangan!

At 9 p.m. there was an evangelistic meeting in a non-Christian home perched on the hillside under the palms. A hundred people were present and they seemed to receive the message of the gospel warmly. Rufus preached with liberty for an hour and a half and then called upon me. In spite of the infelicitous and pompous remarks of the young pastor, it was a happy evening. At the risk of offending him I insisted that Rufus should translate my Indonesian into Javanese, as otherwise I feared the message would be spoilt. Next morning the headmaster escorted me to the school and I gave my testimony to the senior class in Indonesian without interpretation. After lunch there was a double wedding in the church; Rufus presided and I sat at the back as an observer. The ceremony was civil and legal only; the spiritual ceremony was to be held next day but the church leaders had refused it to one of the couples, who were shortly expecting their firstborn, unless there was real evidence of repentance. It was, however, to their home that we went for a feast at the close. The humble farm was enlarged for the occasion with bamboo walls and tables spread for a hundred guests, loaded with plates of food. During the meal one table was invaded by a frightened hen which flew up on the end of it and then proceeded down the full length with wings flapping and feet flashing, crashing over every dish without breaking or spilling a single one. At the end I was asked to speak, which I did from Galatians 2:20.

Next morning was Sunday and the church was packed with 350 people for the wedding, which was conducted by Rufus, since the young pastor was unwell. He preached on John 11 and after the benediction called upon me. It was a great chance and I spoke for thirty minutes about Peter walking on the water. After lunch Rufus suggested we should go to the house of a middle-aged man crippled by the Japanese and permanently bedridden. Mawardi, Rekso, Rufus and I sat around him and after some initial conversation Rufus asked me to give a message to him, since he could never get out to meetings. The man sat upright with legs crossed for the occasion, his eyes staring straight at me. I preached at some length on "Ye have not chosen Me, but I have chosen you and ordained you that ye should go and bring forth fruit and that your fruit should remain". After this Rufus led in prayer and told the man himself to pray, which he proceeded to do.

Rufus frequently left me and went off visiting on his own, for everyone wants to have him in their homes. I think they are finding the young pastor a great trial after having enjoyed so competent a shepherd. As we walked back from the cripple's home I had some interesting glimpses of Rufus' briefer visits. He abandoned the rest of us on a stony path and cut through gardens up to the front door of a house where men and women were standing to meet him. He shook hands with them all and then hopped through a hedge and across another garden to the next farm, without returning to the road. This progress through the gardens continued, men coming from their work, wiping hands on pants, to meet him. At other times we spent fairly long periods sitting and talking with people, or just sitting. The pace was that of the unchanging countryside, where no car has ever been seen. Men sat placidly, sipping coffee, letting the smoke of their cheap cigarettes curl slowly upwards. Hospitality was unstinted and one night after a meeting we were given supper by our host at 1.30 a.m.

Towards evening on the Sunday we started to leave Karangan, shaking hands with everyone we met and finally setting out up the mountainside, where darkness overtook us. It was invigorating, in spite of the stiff climb, to be in the wilds at that time, with the stars overhead and the crescent moon to light us on. At last we were back in Wonoredjo, where we had distributed tracts, and found that there was to be a meeting after all. We climbed another steep hill inside the village, for even in such a remote part of Java the population is dense and villages seem to spread out and continue interminably. On the hilltop we found a large and beautiful home neatly arranged with benches. The non-Christian owner, a motherly, grey-haired woman, treated us with great kindness and spread for our band an enormous feast. Then all nine local school-masters trooped into the main room and sat at the back. The village elders followed, then many others, and a motley crowd gathered about the door and windows, to the total of a hundred souls. Bowls of flowers stood amidst the company and tea was served to all. Then Rufus began, standing under a strong light. In spite of the fatigue of the climb up from Karangan, he seemed to have much liberty in speaking. I followed him and then he called on Mawardi, who on this trip made his debut as a speaker and gave his testimony demurely and effectively. At the end there were more refreshments (at our host's expense) and I gave tracts to everyone, which were received with acclamation. It is hard to find words to express the greatness of the opportunity for proclaiming the gospel which faces us here in Java. The people are so often seekers after light. The suitable approach is not so much "You are a sinner who needs to be saved" but "Here is the way to God, for whom you have been searching"—although in practice we mix the two. Any doubts we may have had about how clear Rufus himself is about the gospel have quite melted away. He goes right out for the evangelical truths, but with a Javanese quietness and grace, and with much personal charm and thrust. I have the impression that his words are delivered in the power of the Spirit and that very many of his hearers do in varying degrees receive and embrace them.

By midnight the work was done. We bade farewell to friends new and old and launched out with the three children for the hour's walk back to the car, all of us full of joy at the things we had been privileged to share in and delighting in the beauty and stillness of the night. At 1 a.m. we reached the Mayflower and with no danger of meeting any other car I let her fly up and down the mountains across the plantation plateau and then down, down, down on to the wide plain, and so to Sabrang at 2.30 a.m.

I often get little notes from Rufus delivered by sundry boys and one came this morning. "I hope you have slept off your weariness all right. I lay in for a bit this morning. Praise the Lord for the wonderful time we had together. May His blessing rest on all those souls."

November 1st. The other day Rufus got caught in the rain on his bicycle and sheltered in a roadside stall at a country town several miles from here. He gave the proprietor *The Way of Salvation*, and the man answered that he had already had one from "Pa David", a name which is increasingly becoming mine, since my surname is very difficult for Indonesian tongues.

Yesterday, while I was in the city, Jess took out her flannelgraph board and pictures and asked the first bunch of women she met whether they would like to see them. The response was immediate and so she had a little doorstep open-air meeting, using Javanese as well as Indonesian. She recently began a women's meeting on Wednesday afternoons and has got Mrs Rufus to help her. It is a tremendous step for a Muslim woman to attend it, and almost involves a degree of committal to the Christian gospel. This week one woman got right to the door but suddenly remembered that she must go at once to the market and decamped! Jess and Mrs Rufus also go out visiting together now. In one nominally Christian home they found deep sorrow over the death of a little girl of twelve months, while in another they met a very pretty woman with a small child whose husband went to the city two years ago and has never returned.

November 2nd. Pressure of schoolboys has been unrelenting, and they can be very difficult to manage. After tea we decided to escape and drove in half an hour to the top of the Southern Mountains where we noticed a path meandering up a steep ridge through a plantation of thousands of young teak trees widely spaced and only a foot high. In this delightful place we achieved a complete getaway and roamed as one might on a lonely hilltop at home, with glorious views over our parish from 3000 feet. It was the last time we ever felt it wise to do it!

November 3rd. This morning I went with Rufus to Barek, where there have now been ninety-six baptisms. It was delightful to see Rufus in his black silk gown preaching to these people whom he has himself reaped in to Christ. One couple from far away Djakarta was baptised, the man being the son of Suprapto, the headmaster at Barek, who was converted in 1956. It appears that he has been writing to his schoolmaster son in Djakarta ever since and this week the son came, bringing his wife and asking for baptism. It is not the custom of this place to refuse such approaches, nor is it for me to affirm that the two will not prove genuine. I had a good chance to exhort them both. They had formerly been married in Muslim fashion but, having baptised them, Rufus resolemnised their marriage vows before the Lord. So they were nicely knotted into the church —and thus does village evangelism reach out to great cities!

Back at home, wave after wave passed over us. Two young men from Kabat came to buy books and stayed to lunch, which is one way in which we can return the unstinted hospitality I received when away with Rufus. At the close came Jess' class for small boys and then the young people's Bible class, the two spanning four hours. At the close of the latter some children pointed out that two new mouth-organs had vanished. We have learned that the only hope of recovery lies in immediate detection, so we jumped into the car, pursued the probable offenders, spotted them crossing a field playing the instruments as they went, met them to their immense confusion as they rejoined the road, and secured prompt and painless return. But wear and tear is heavy and we retired to bed at 8 p.m.

November 4th. This morning I had a ninety-minute chat on our verandah with Susilo of Triwung. He is a most unusual character, tall and commanding in presence, prone to gaze vaguely into space as he talks, and still only tentatively groping his way in spiritual matters, although I suspect he is one of the most important men in the church. He is disposed to give the prophet Muhammad rather more credit than I care for, feeling that at the beginning at any rate he was genuinely inspired by the Holy Spirit, although afterwards he deteriorated. We had a long review of such matters. Meanwhile I press on with the revision of all Indonesian manuscripts printed by the Christian Witness Press. My teacher and I are deep in "The Story of Joseph" at the moment. He gets absolutely absorbed in the job on hand, Muslim though he is, and is so linguistically sensitive that he will not pass anything unless he is fully satisfied.

This week has been one of the stiffest we have had in Sabrang. Petty thieving has increased and some bigger boys have been unpleasantly rude. There is a big drive on for the recovery by Indonesia of West Irian (New Guinea), at present held by the Dutch. Unhappily the word "Dutch" is used here not only in the sense of "a man from Holland", but also in the sense of "a man from Europe". Thus it can be said of me, "He is a Dutchman from England", and to this extent we become involved in the animosity felt towards the former colonial power. In addition of course people are not normally able to distinguish one European race from another so that all those who do not know us personally imagine that we are from

Holland. In spite of all this, however, we were greatly encouraged
when eleven women came to the third women's meeting. Apart
from Mrs Rufus, attendance on previous occasions had been one and
two respectively. After tea we distributed tracts about a mile from
our home. Darkness fell before we finished; but it was then that we
did some of our briskest business, young men coming around us in
the friendliest way. We give five tracts to each person, feeling that
thus they have a real opportunity to grasp the significance of the
gospel, one of the five being a Scripture Gift Mission booklet. We
are finding that the best language for such work is Javanese, rather
than Indonesian, for in their homes people use always their own
dialect, not the national language.

November 9th. Jess and Mrs Rufus were out visiting for four hours
today. One old grannie said, "How I wish we had heard these things
years ago when we lived in the city." We have now been nine
months in Sabrang and hope to make it two and a half years before
we go home on furlough.

Sunday, *November 10th.* Rufus preached this morning in the Sabrang Church on "I will, be thou clean". There were seventy people
present and since the ten benches provided only hold sixty with a
fearful crush, the beginning of the meeting was delayed while more
seats were found. Three small boys who attend Jess' class, dressed in
their brightest and best, asked us to take them with us to church for
the first time. Last night I spent an hour chatting with Rufus in his
home. It seems there are to be further baptisms in the district before
Christmas and he has won his point that these shall be in the villages
and not at Paru Christian village, with whose leaders Rufus has no
easy passage. I sense that he is under some pressure these days, but
perhaps it is just the fatigue of many labours and late nights.

This was Heroes Day, corresponding to Remembrance Sunday in
England, but with a Guy Fawkes touch added since an effigy of
imperialism is to be burnt as part of the present campaign over
West Irian (New Guinea). Many hundreds of schoolchildren with
flags and banners gathered outside the school opposite us. We sat on
our stone balustrade at the roadside with many friends, waving to
the children, a large number of whom are now well known to us.
With us stood Mother Daro, who had spent much of the day at the

cemetery tending the graves of the fallen and joining in Muslim ceremonies there.

November 13th. Muljono, the head of Kabat village, called on us yesterday and I drove him over to see Rufus at Ringit. He is a strong supporter of Rufus' evangelistic work and very indignant over those in the church who deprecate it. There has been some trouble about the literature which Rufus and I took to Kabat in October. The strolling "evangelist" from Sumatra, who squatted on Rufus for a time, was there when we were, and since not all the literature was sold during our visit he asked Rufus if he could take charge of the rest and sell it for us. Neither he nor the books have been seen since. Rufus has written to various places where the man might turn up but the probability is that he will move right out of the district.

I drove into the city under huge banners announcing that the patriots were ready to shed their blood over West Irian. It is best to stay where you are well known at a time like this.

November 16th. Today we became vendors in Sabrang market for the first time. It is quite a busy one, serving tens of thousands of people. We rented six feet of concrete under an awning, set up a table of literature, and stood beside it for two hours. Business was brisk thanks to low prices, attractive covers, and the appeal of Genesis and the gospel of Matthew in Javanese. One man bought a New Testament, saying that he had never read it. Two Madurese took Luke's Gospel in Madurese. At least a hundred people bought from us; the market authorities were most cordial; and although we had a thermos of tea with us there was no leisure to drink it.

November 19th. After our teachers had left us at 9 p.m. last night we drove over to spend a delightful hour and a half with Rufus and his wife, leaving Loti in charge of Rupert, who was fast asleep. Rufus' little sitting room just nicely contains four chairs; they show no signs either of wealth or of pressing poverty. He had been visiting some homes in the large country town of Gerbo east of us. Apart from a Chinese Pentecostal church there are only four Christian families in Gerbo and they are too frightened to meet together. Such "Christians fast asleep", as Rufus called them, are often found, since the East Java Church is 125 years old now. Rufus has a very winsome way. His approach is gentle and quiet, but perfectly clear and strong, and combined with a maturity of character which makes him a most effective advocate. He is continually finding new contacts and confirming old ones.

November 22nd. Today I accompanied Rufus to an evangelistic meeting in the outskirts of Lakar. We took with us several men from Ringit who have recently turned to the Lord, Mawardi among them of course. We turned off the main road on to a lane churned by rains and lorries into a creamy morass. I was obliged to shed my passengers and then slithered for a mile in bottom gear to a well-lit home where fifty people sat on benches with many more outside in the darkness and twenty women and children crowded into the kitchen doorway. An old, retired pastor was in charge so Rufus played second fiddle and I third. After over two hours' preaching and singing the old man elected to close the meeting in the middle of Mawardi's testimony. We moved back to the centre of Lakar and stopped for an hour in the home of Hasan, who was the first man to believe in this area apart from those brought up in Christian villages. He is a Madurese and marked by the extra vitality and self-assertion which distinguish them from the Javanese. Formerly he had four wives and was so poor that he wore shorts and rented out his trousers. It is his testimony that the Lord has caused him to prosper only in this last year since his conversion. His wife was formerly a teacher of Arabic in a Muslim religious school. Many Arabs come to their shop and he gives them tracts.

November 24th. At 7.30 a.m. we prayed with Loti and Yeny and then rented our market stall for the second time and sold literature till 10 a.m. Business was steady but never brisk. The head of the market, who proved to be from a Christian village, joined us and exhorted the people to buy. Most of the time Jess played gospel records on the gramophone and in this way many people who would never dream of entering a church heard something of the message of salvation. I am sure a number who stood close and long beside the books only did so in order to hear the preaching without appearing to be doing so! Genesis is very popular, but the books we would think attractive sell slowly. The sacred text fares better than anything based on it. Books in Arabic script sell well, the language used still being Javanese, which can be written in Arabic script, in Javanese letters, or in romanised, the latter being the common method nowadays. Who can tell what any one purchase will lead to, or the real motive of the purchaser—shy, timid, gruff, curt, polite, hesitant, meditative, casual? Time expended: *two and a half hours*. Total sales: 19s. Profit: *nil*. Loss: *considerable*. Perspiration exuded: *plentiful*. Satisfaction: *immense*.

After these things I departed for the last time this year to Suraja —seventy miles down at night and a tyre to change en route amidst a group of curious, friendly, young men; three meetings on Sunday, 100 at the Cantonese church, 500 for my eighteenth visit to the Foochow church, twenty at the British Community church, where the American Consul led the service with sincerity and reverence. His Vice-Consul was also present, as were the British Consul and his Vice-Consul, plus all four consular wives. A business man took me to his home for supper and a good English hot bath, and then at 9.15 p.m. I started home on a glorious night and there was no real check in all the seventy miles to Sabrang.

November 28th. This day, like every Thursday, was spent in the city lecturing at the Bible College. On these occasions I usually do some of the family shopping. In one shop, where I am well known, they courteously asked me to give my name and nationality in case they were accused of serving Dutch people, which is not now permitted. I called on Jonathan, the Dutch missionary, to see if they were all right and found it so, except that the school bus would not take their child and she had to cycle through the town.

November 29th. Early this morning I had a note from Rufus asking me to help Susilo of Triwung whose little boy was ill and needed to get to the hospital in Sabrang in a closed-in car. One of Susilo's daughters came with me in the Mayflower to Triwung. We were taken into the bedroom where both mother and father were very concerned at the child's condition. He seemed to have tropical malaria and convulsions. They wrapped him up warmly and we drove straight back to the hospital in Sabrang just across Office Street from our home, which I reached as eight young men were trooping in for the weekly seventeen-year-olds' Bible class. Before long Susilo joined us, having left his wife at the hospital with the child. He was accompanied by the young farmer Hastari, whom I now distinctly recognised for the first time. I completed my message and tea was served. Susilo then spontaneously backed up what I had said, giving the men an admirable statement of the gospel, the first they had ever heard from the lips of one of their own people. They listened spellbound while we ourselves were greatly encouraged to hear his clear exposition, for we have sometimes wondered just what he really believed in. He is a diligent evangelist, ignited by Rufus. It was then that he turned to me and said, "If I am not wrong, the Church has sent out no man like Rufus", meaning of course the East Java Church. His rustic companion, Hastari, after apologising to the boys for being only an ignorant farmer, gave a lovely little testimony, to which I listened with amazement. It appears that he turned to the Lord about three months ago when we went to Triwung at night with Rufus, prayed at the bedside of Daddy Tain, his father, and later met the old man of 125. About that time mice were damaging his crops and he went through the fields next morning crying to the Lord Jesus for help. He was one of those baptised at Barek three weeks ago, when the headmaster's son came from Djakarta. It was grand to see this gnarled and weather-beaten man testifying to more sophisticated lads, and whether it be by mice or by illness the Lord has certainly captured him. Just as we were rejoicing over our departed guests five girls came in, followed by a rowdy gang of fifteen boys, led by two familiar and unpleasant figures. After a while Jess decided to run the girls home in the car, but the boys mobbed into it as well and the leaders had some strong things to say when she would not capitulate to them. The same afternoon we went with Rufus and his wife to visit three country places to the north. In the first, Wates, which is much larger than Sabrang, there are only three Christian families and they were in the doldrums. At the second, on a high plateau soaked in rain and mud, we gave out many tracts and stopped at the only Christian home, hard by the mosque. In appalling conditions I then drove the overloaded car on to Wagir, where there are a hundred believers. However, as is apt to happen in the rural depths, Rufus' letter had never been received, or if received had not been read to others, and only fifteen people were in the church. Twenty Muslims sauntered in as well and I had a good chance to address them, but they decamped before Rufus preached. Jess missed the meeting as the church secretary asked her to drive to a neighbouring village to tell them we had come and invite them to join us. He assured us that the road was perfectly all right, so Mrs Rufus and the children went with her for the trip of a few miles. However, the road proved to be unsurfaced and after the heavy rains it was highly dangerous; moreover, there was a broken bridge at the foot of a hill. Before they got as far as that, however, they had skidded off the road and been lifted back on to it by a cheerful group of men they met. From this time on we decided not to trust the judgement of non-drivers, as we continually found that they presumed our Mayflower could traverse any road which a jeep or an ox-cart had at some time used. Loti shared the evening with us, but for once we were not given any food, so we enjoyed our own supper back in Sabrang at 1 a.m.

And the night was short, for there burst suddenly upon us the tragic and transforming event which was to herald a far more extensive acceptance of the gospel and lead to the salvation of many souls.

CHAPTER 10

TURNING POINT

WE were still asleep at 6 a.m. on *November 30th* when Susilo strode on to the verandah to tell us that his only son, the little boy I had driven to hospital twenty-four hours before, was with Christ.

For the next twelve hours the Mayflower plied back and forth to Ringit, to Triwung, and to Paru, the Christian village which is supposed to shepherd the sheep and does nothing of the sort. We kept with the stricken family as much as possible and several times we prayed with them beside the cot in the ward. I greatly admired Susilo for his bearing under the ordeal, radically though he was tortured by it. He became determined to avoid the mortuary, so for the first time the Mayflower carried the dead, Susilo sitting in the back with the child's body wrapped in a blanket across his knees. On the way we collected Mrs Susilo from the market where she had been buying supplies for the many guests and sympathisers who were already filling the house at Triwung when we reached it. I met the head of Triwung village, a kindly Muslim, and had a good opportunity to speak to him about Christ. Willing hands soon rallied from all sides and by 10 a.m. there were a hundred people in the stricken home, which was rapidly transformed for the funeral. The child's body lay on a bed under a canopy, his head exposed and flowers around him, text-cards among them such as "The Lord is my Shepherd, I shall not want," and "Jesus said, I am the Way, the Truth, and the Life, no man cometh unto the Father but by Me". It was the first Christian death in Triwung and Susilo was determined to make the funeral in every way a testimony to Christ —in which he wonderfully succeeded. I drove Rufus to Paru to collect the pastor, a man who finds it very hard to meet anyone from the western world. On the way back I stopped to fill up with petrol at Sabrang market, but the man's mate refused to let him serve me, thinking that I was Dutch. Ten men gathered around, all of them on my side, and soon I got the petrol, though the objector remained displeased.

The funeral began in the Susilo home in Triwung at 1.30 p.m. There were at least 125 present, men standing packed in the main room, women jamming each other, and the coffin in the centre— Triwung's first coffin, for the Muslims do not use them. After some singing, in which only Christian believers were able to join, of course, the old pastor from Paru spoke, and then a terrific storm burst upon us, against the noise of which Rufus and I struggled to preach. As Rufus was doing so there was an exceptionally violent crack of lightning low overhead, part of the force of which travelled down the radio aerial and tumbled into confusion a dozen women who were grouped near the radio. Thank God, no one was hurt, so after a few minutes' confusion we continued. After I had preached the Paru pastor did so for the second time and had the misfortune to tell the Muslim audience that what I had just said about heaven and seeing God in heaven was incorrect, since God and heaven are here. Rufus told me later that he himself had been publicly rebuked by the same man on the same point on a previous occasion. Suwarso the headmaster, leader of the church in Sabrang, sat in an easy chair in a corner, smoking and reading a magazine when everyone else was standing.

Heavy rain continued outside, so Rufus suggested we should wait for a while and pray that it might stop. We did so and before long the weather improved, though there was still a drizzle. Hastari and other Christian or semi-Christian young men of Triwung then shouldered the coffin and we walked to the village cemetery through the rain and mud. Hundreds of Muslim graves, all dug on a north-to-south line, the bodies lying on their sides facing Mecca in Arabia, lay under the trees, which met above our heads and gave some shelter. This grave was dug from east to west, and the child lay in a coffin on his back, facing heaven. There was further singing and prayer at the graveside, while flowers and wreaths were showered upon the coffin. Then the grave was filled in, many hands including my own sharing in the work. Finally Susilo himself planted on top of the grave a simple wooden cross, right in the middle of a Muslim cemetery! Heavier and heavier grew the rain, so banana leaves were hacked down to augment umbrellas; I moved up to the old pastor to give him some shelter under my umbrella, with the ulterior motive of thawing out his attitude towards us and Rufus. I marvelled at the fine spirit of Susilo and his wife and daughters, while the love and helpfulness shown by other Christians were truly outstanding. Loti and Yeny were with us throughout and I think it was a great experience for them, as indeed it was for us. "May my child's passing be the means of drawing others in Triwung to Christ," said Susilo.

On the Sunday morning the Barek congregation moved their service to Susilo's home at Triwung, The meeting lasted for three hours and was memorable for the splendid singing of the believers and the excellent bearing of Susilo and his wife. I was asked to speak, among others, and did so from 1 Peter 1:3-5. These people are spiritually so hungry that any morsel one can give them is not only gladly accepted but passed on to others. In my talk I suggested that all Christians are rich, having an inheritance in heaven. Unknown to me there was a wealthy non-Christian man from Gerbo present, a friend of the family. At the end Mrs Susilo sat down beside him, slapped him playfully on the knee and said, amidst general laughter, "There you are, you're poverty-stricken!"

December 6th. One evening we had to supper Mrs Rakes, the lady in whose house in Sabrang both the small Chinese Pentecostal Church and also the swelling Javanese Church meet. We gathered that she had played Abishag in her youth to an elderly Dutchman fifty years her senior. She bears his name and lives off the rent of his property. There are many such in Java whom the tide of the world has stranded on the beach. She played our harmonium nicely and rather enjoyed slipping back for an evening into a European home. The family did invite her to Holland, but the winter cold and the colour of her skin deterred her. At forty life is over.

Another visitor was our host at Karangan, who came to urge me to accompany Rufus on his proposed visit there this month. The letter of invitation from the young pastor only mentioned Rufus and so, although Rufus said, "You must come too", I demurred, feeling that they should be free to invite their old pastor without necessarily being burdened with me as well. Rufus wrote back explaining this and our host's visit was the answer. "I am the letter in reply," he said. "We want you too." We gave him a square meal in return for the dozen we have had in his home.

December 8th. Last night we were in the city with Rufus for a very important gathering at which many leaders of the East Java Church were present. I was conscious that both Rufus and ourselves were on trial, for news of the happenings in the Sabrang area has spread among the churches. Rufus spoke first, then armless Mawardi gave his testimony, and lastly I spoke on Romans 6: 22. Rugged Mawardi quite captivated them, for what answer is there to a brand plucked from the burning? At the close we were rather horrified to find that Susilo's eldest daughter, aged about fifteen, was in hospital in the city with a raging fever, suspected to be typhoid. We called with Rufus and prayed with her and the parents, who had come in from Triwung. At night we phoned for news and she is said to be a little better. Thus it was 9 p.m. before we got home. Loti had supper all ready on the table as usual, but she came out on to the verandah the moment she heard the car, anxious lest some evil had befallen us for these were still the days of the "Suez Crisis" and feeling was running strong against the white man. However, there seems no reason why we should not go straight ahead with the work of the Lord.

A Chinese Christian from the city drove over to see us with his nephew, home from Singapore. The young man was ardent in faith. "Are there sound assemblies here?" he asked. "Are the churches influenced by liberalism? Do they believe in the infallibility of the Bible?" Such echoes of half-forgotten Anglo-Saxon theological controversy sounded most odd in my ears. The worthy uncle was completely mystified. But the work of God around us marches forward.

On each of the past four days I have had to drive into the city and twice I have taken with me the head of Triwung village, to whom I first spoke in Susilo's house after the child died. We have together visited Susilo's daughter, who has pulled back from a temperature of 105·8. He is a fatherly kind of man and it was delightful to see him standing over her, feeling her wrists, forehead and cheeks, while his wife rubbed one shin and the girl's mother the other! He is not far from the kingdom of heaven and these trips have thrown him together with Christians, so that on five occasions he has bowed his head in prayer. It is part of the special situation in East Java that non-Christians can join in prayer without embarrassment.

Sunday, *December 8th.* This was Loti's baptismal day and a great occasion in Sabrang. The little church was bursting with 200 people as Christians from other villages gathered on foot, on cycles, and in lorries. Rufus made no secret of the affair, for a loudspeaker hung in the trees and carried gospel records in Javanese far down the main road. Ten young men, ten women, and seven children were baptised by threefold sprinkling, while four couples had their marriages sanctified. The heat and crush in the building, Mrs Rakes' only room, were terrific. Refreshments were served, and during this interlude Rufus asked me to give the people a message. There should have been about twenty more baptisms but these were deferred not by enemies of the gospel but by the unhappy desire of Paru Christian village to have all baptisms in their church. I have no full understanding of this situation, for Rufus has gone into no details with me and I do not think it is necessary for me to know everything that is going on.

Yeny was not baptised. For some time she has apparently wanted to confess herself a Christian in this way, but she was held back by the misgivings of her family, although Mrs Rufus feels that she need not have bowed to their opinion. Her parents live apart and have both married again. It was a hard day for her, but both Rufus and his wife spoke encouragingly to her. For Loti it was a day without clouds, the culmination of years of true faith and association with Christians. I have already stated that baptism by sprinkling in the East Java Church requires much courage. It is done publicly, solemnly, with the participants marshalled at the front of a large gathering for several hours, with repeated kneelings when others stand and standings when others kneel, so that no one who was not prepared for the world to know of his new allegiance would dare to go through with it.

December 13th. I went with Rufus to Paru Christian village to address the senior class in the church school. The old pastor was civil for a few minutes, but he does not believe in giving religious teaching in the church school. The next day we paid our third visit to Karangan with Mawardi, now a vocal and active colleague. He was late in joining us as three men had called on him at 6.30 a.m. and he had been talking to them about the gospel. A young man from the village of Tulen completed the party. Tulen is not far from Barek and there are now twenty-four believers there. This young man said cheerfully, "I was baptised seven months ago and converted three months ago." I asked him why he had been baptised when he was not yet converted and he answered, "I followed my father"—and it often works like that.

Driving through the Southern Mountains, we left the car at the beautiful home we have used for this purpose before, and set off to walk for the last two hours on a path which wound in and out of the hills from farm to farm in a lovely, far-away region where I gave tracts to everyone we met. After a while cloud and rain settled down upon us. Mawardi removed his trousers, hung them round his neck, put his mackintosh over his head, and marched on in black pants. Rufus took off his shoes and stockings, rolled his trousers above the knees, put up an umbrella, and strode on barefoot. I did likewise, but stuck to gym-shoes. The weather became most disagreeable and dank, the path muddy, slippery, and steep. In this state we paid five pastoral visits. Rufus gave himself wholeheartedly to one family on the hillside where an old lady lay crippled in bed. He leant over her holding her hand, exhorting, comforting, questioning, and getting all present to pray at the end, a first-class demonstration of what a faithful Christian pastor can accomplish in spite of rain and mud.

Our escort down the mountain was the herculean young man Budi, "an Israelite in whom there is no guile". He met Rufus in another part of Java, came as his servant to Karangan for five years, moved slowly from Islam to Christ, and is like a son to Rufus now, ready for any humble service. As we reached flat ground he told us that one of the unbridged rivers which bisects Karangan was now 5 feet deep. We waited on the bank for an hour while the level of the stream dropped a little and then formed a trouserless line led by Budi, who bore aloft our garments, holding hands to steady one another against the current, and thus we got over.

There followed twenty-four hours of intensive ministry in home after home. At night I preached to forty persons in the headmaster's house, using Indonesian without interpretation. The audience included all the schoolmasters from Karangan and Wonoredjo, who were gathered for the wedding of one of the former, a young fellow named Lantip. This man came two years ago from a Muslim home in the city and, lodging with the Christian headmaster, turned to Christ, was baptised, and chose a Christian girl as his wife. His parents gave their consent and asked the headmaster to act for them in the whole affair. Lantip himself, probably not being much used to meeting foreigners, was reserved in his attitude to me. I was not to see him again for eighteen months but then he was to step unexpectedly into our lives so that in retrospect we thank God for this first occasion when he crossed our path. I am much impressed by the headmaster. He is elderly, friendly, rich, influential, and altogether helpful in Christian work. But the young pastor is a sore trial. It appears that the Karangan folk, fed spiritually by Rufus during the five years of his ministry among them, are still nourished only by his occasional visits. On Sunday morning the church was crammed with 350 people for the wedding, which took three hours. Rufus preached and the young pastor led. Then the latter turned to me and said, as he has done before, "I give you 300 seconds." However, since the country people are not much tied to time I took a good deal longer than that in speaking about the Lord's return. Then Mawardi was also given "300 seconds". He shut his eyes, laughed, and then faced the biggest audience of his Christian life, his empty sleeve tucked into his pocket and his black Indonesian hat still on his head, as it was on the heads of most men in his audience. This testifying by a convert seems to be something absolutely new to people and each time Mawardi tells his "father-has-become-a-Dutchman" story he gains in effectiveness. He was so droll and artless that the congregation was convulsed with mirth at one instant and then immediately hushed to catch the next remark. "My wife used always to put a white cloth over her head when she prayed, but now we pray without any special garb and use the white cloth as a pillowcase." Only the young pastor kept an absolutely straight face. In visiting homes Mawardi now speaks out boldly too, which also has the effect of reducing the number of cigarettes he can consume. At the wedding reception which followed, the man from Tulen gave his testimony for the first time. Then at 3 p.m. we should have started up the steep track for home, but some rural imp got into Rufus and for two and a half hours we just sat, sipped coffee, chatted, and relaxed. Then of course we got benighted on the mountain. Darkness, rain, mist, mud, water, and slush were our lot till at last we gained the comfort of the car and home before midnight.

Next day, *December 16th*, we held a children's party, which was our main Christmas celebration. Fifty, who have often attended meetings, came to it, and there were fifteen adults present, so we served sixty-five suppers.

On the 18th we had a Christmas party for the Women's Meeting from 4 p.m. till 7 p.m. and served forty-five suppers to the women, their children, and several elderly men who invited themselves. The success of the evening was beyond doubt when Mother Daro won her heat at musical chairs! Rufus preached from flannelgraph pictures, wearing white trousers, a yellow shirt, and a flowered tie. One could wish for nothing better than the grace, charm, clarity, and joy with which he puts the message across. Mawardi was present too and took his turn at pinning the tail on the donkey. By way of contrast we called next day on Jonathan who was "feeling very isolated" and wondering whether they ought to evacuate women and children. Being mistaken for a Dutchman by strangers we too get cold looks and frowns, which casts a shadow over Christmas.

Then on *December 20th* Rufus, Mawardi, Rekso, and I started off on a four-day trip to Sidoredjo, another remote Indian Ocean settlement of 10,000 people, 2000 of them Christians. We travelled east for two hours on the main highway in driving rain, curling around the Great Volcano. At one busy market called Srengat we stopped to get coffee and refreshments in a restaurant, where we attracted a good deal of attention by giving out tracts up and down the road.

In years to come we were often to remember the little gospel seeds dropped there on this occasion when there was no Christian witness of any kind in Srengat. Not long afterwards we turned south into the wild tangle of hills between the Great Volcano and the sea. Almost at once the road became impassable for the May-flower, so Jess and Rupert, who had accompanied us up to that point, took the car back to Sabrang while our party transferred to a big truck which bumped and slithered through deep mud in magnificent country covered with farms and plantations. Eventually the truck also could go no further and at once a little problem arose. When our party was in my car I bore the expense of the journey, feeling that this was the one and only material contribution I could suitably make to the expedition in hand. However, I felt it undesirable that I should finance any other travel, so as we dismounted from the lorry I asked Rufus what the fare was, gave him enough for myself alone, and left it at that. I suspect that Rufus paid for the other two himself.

For the next four hours we walked south, shouldering our belongings until we could find a man to carry them. It was a tedious, winding, downhill trudge in drizzle, with the ocean in sight far below. I gave the Javanese Christmas tract to many people we met and stayed close behind Rufus, so that as other travellers came in sight it was not my white face which they first observed. At one village a severe-looking man in a singlet called out as we passed and asked to see my papers, saying that he was the police. We all went into his home and he served us coffee. Mawardi and Rekso proceeded to preach to him, the latter rather crudely and violently. The man was not very pleased at this; he seemed to be a kind of Buddhist, believing in self-culture. For a long time Rufus said nothing and then very quietly and gently began to explain our business and expound the gospel. In a short time the man's attitude changed and after much conversation we parted the best of friends. Before dark we dropped to the floor of the Sidoredjo valley, a glorious expanse of richly cultivated and populated land stretching inland from the sea for a distance of seven miles.

We stayed with the evangelist who has worked in Sidoredjo for over twenty years. It is not really a Christian village, since it was established earlier in this century by Muslims, but so many Christians have emigrated here that they now own most of the land. I had an hour's good talk with the young pastor, who welcomed us very warmly indeed. There was a meeting in a non-Christian home from 9 p.m. until midnight that first evening. After the strain of the long walk I dozed off many times but revived when it was my turn to preach, using 1 Timothy 1:12-15. There were sixty men present. It is probably misleading to English readers to describe these Javanese places as villages, which suggests something small and compact. In fact they sprawl prodigiously and Sidoredjo must cover twenty-five square miles!

Next day we visited several homes and in the evening we were again with sixty men till midnight. The pastor and Rufus spoke first and then I followed, using Hebrews 12:1-2. On Sunday morning there were at least 300 people in the church for a wedding, at which the pastor asked me to give the address. Afterwards heavy rain fell and at night I had an exhausting cycle ride. A Christmas celebration had been arranged near the sea, and so extensive is the valley that this meant an hour and a half cycling. It was held in a windowless farmhouse crammed with eighty people and another fifty outside. There was a 10-foot Christmas tree; twenty-five Christians read a text in turn and each lit one candle on the tree after doing so. Then the pastor, Rufus, and I preached and at 10 p.m. we started back. I had a lady's bicycle without a light, so that I had to grasp a thick torch in my left hand as well as the handlebar. The pedals were so slippery that I could never keep my feet on them for long at a time. It was a desperate struggle to keep the beam of light on the narrow, grassy, bumpy, muddy path. Then the saddle broke and pointed skywards, leaving me to sit on an umbrella tied to a brief-case on the carrier!

We left at 8 a.m. on *December 23rd* and walked for six and a half hours to our rendezvous with Jess and the Mayflower, at the Suharta home in Trawas. For an hour we were still on the Sidoredjo plain, and then we climbed into a long valley between towering hills. How blest Java is! The humble country people in windowless shacks, the children naked, the men clad only in short pants, live amidst oceans of rice, maize, bananas, oranges, coffee, rubber, melons, mangoes, and all good things. An earthen floor, a large table, a bamboo bedframe, some benches, a peg for the cap, a shirt for special occasions, cups for coffee, an old curtain over the bedroom door, a photo of President Sukarno, unlimited tobacco, unlimited time—what else could heart desire?

We stopped several times for coffee and cakes at cafés by the roadside. On these occasions there was always just one bill presented and again I was anxious that neither Mawardi nor Rekso should count on my paying for them. The plan I hit upon was to pay for everyone once myself, and after that leave it entirely to others to deal with the bill. Every time we stopped in this way Rufus, barefoot and becapped, looking rather like an army officer on holiday, would chat about the gospel in such an easy and joyful way that everyone had to listen to him. "I suppose these people have never heard the gospel before?" I said in one hamlet. "Indeed they have," he said, "for I stop here every time I come, and I really think this family already believes, only they are so far from anywhere that they have never attended a Christian meeting or been baptised." It is wonderful to see a man at work for Christ in this way, a mature and skilful fisherman. He hails from the poorest of the poor, but he is an enlightened and educated man, though not an academic type of person, just one of the millions of Javanese, and the grace of the Lord rests upon him in a remarkably vivid and winsome manner. In the Javanese puppet-show, which is a national form of entertainment, there are two well-known characters, Petrus and Gareng, the long and the short, and to these Rufus and I, because of our disparity in height, are repeatedly compared. At other times I am "one of those wicked men" and without the companionship of Javanese friends it would not be possible for me to be out in the country like this at all.

On Christmas Eve 200 people gathered in the tiny Sabrang church. After our long trip both Rufus and I were jaded. Suwarso conducted the proceedings in a lifeless manner and in explanation of the large Christmas tree in the room read a paper on its European origins, of which the refrain was "before Europe became Christian . . . after Europe became Christian", a lamentable point of view in oriental lands where the main obstacle to the spread of the gospel is the impression that it is the European man's religion. Rufus spoke next but I felt he was too tired to get his message across effectively, so in the end it became my responsibility to try and seize the opportunity.

At 9 a.m. on *Christmas Day* we lit up our own little tree and had a homely meeting for our household and immediate neighbours. Rufus and his wife called on us at 11 a.m. At noon we had a Christmas party for ten small boys who are Rupert's special friends. Cutting another local celebration I drove Rufus at night to Semen where the proceedings lasted five hours and included a series of ten Christmas tableaux, elaborately conceived and beautifully executed. Almost 300 people were present, most of them Muslims. Rufus was allotted only twenty minutes on the programme, of which he gave me five and another five to Hasan's wife, who testified bravely and clearly to what it had meant to her to turn to Christ. Since she had previously been a teacher in a religious school of another faith she was summoned to appear before certain authorities next morning to clear herself from the charge of fomenting strife.

On *December 26th* Rufus, myself, and Mawardi were in the Mayflower on our way to Gondang when we received the lamentable news that Hastari's eldest son, a boy of five, had died of tropical malaria in Triwung, not far from the home of Susilo which had been so recently smitten in the same way. We at once turned aside down the now familiar track to Triwung, but as we reached Hastari's house we met the funeral procession on its way to the grave, and it was quite obviously a Muslim funeral. The parents, who had so recently helped Susilo to bury his son, were very brave and a goodly company gathered in their big kitchen to comfort and encourage them. Hastari himself, the perfect type of simple, rugged, Javanese farmer, was only baptised three months ago at Barek. His wife and children, including the dead child, were to have been baptised at Paru the previous Sunday, but being very rustic in their ways they turned up after the service there had begun, and the old pastor—the same who rebuked me in Susilo's house for saying that the child was in heaven—refused to receive them. They returned rather dejected and made arrangements to be baptised next Sunday at Barek. But now, in the intervening week, the older child was snatched away, and since he was unbaptised he was officially not a Christian so that the Muslim relatives demanded a Muslim funeral and carried it through at top speed in spite of the wishes of the parents.

Our party followed the procession to the graveside. The body, not in a coffin like Susilo's child, was wrapped in a white shroud and it was at once lowered into the grave, two men placing it with the face turned to Mecca, lying close against one earth wall. Split bamboos were then piled to form a kind of lean-to shed over the body, beside which fruit and some small round bricks were laid. While the two men still stood down in the grave, the earth was shovelled to them. Although there was no coffin the bamboo shed kept the earth from actually touching the body, on which Hastari stooped down to place one of the Christian Witness Press children's painting books. When the grave was covered the Muslim official who deals with such matters stepped forward and emptied a bowl of petals over it. Then he squatted down along with about fifty Muslims who were present and prayed in Arabic, the fifteen Christians, including Hastari, remaining standing.

It all seemed rather sad after the triumphant tone of the Susilo funeral. But then there was a dramatic change. The moment the Arabic prayer ceased one of the young men believers called out "Please rise". As all did so, Susilo stepped to the head of the grave and read the Scriptures loudly and clearly—and the position was captured! So far as we were concerned this marked a turning-point in Susilo's life, his first act of Christian aggression. The moment he stopped reading Rufus cut in and gave a brief gospel message to which all listened in silence, his bright and cheerful face contrasting sharply with the grim appearance of the man who had led Arabic prayers. Then he prayed in the name of Christ and as soon as he stopped Hastari butted in and led in prayer in Jesus' name. Then Christian and Muslim alike crowded to the grave to scatter each his handful of earth upon it. I shook hands with the Muslim official, wishing him God's blessing and a happy Christmas, and our party separated with much affection and warmth from the Triwung Christians in the sight of all.

After that we continued our journey to Gondang, which had

been interrupted by news of the child's death, working our way up
the towering flank of the Great Volcano. There are only three
Christian families there, weak and timid, but the schoolroom was
crammed with a hundred men wedged into the little, uncomfortable desks and we continued with them from 7 till 11. First Rufus
spoke, then Jess and I collaborated in the showing of flannelgraph
pictures to the accompaniment of slow Scripture reading. Next
Mawardi spoke and then came refreshments generously served by
headmaster Tias and his wife. When that was over Rufus preached
once more, and then Mawardi again. It was a great evening in
Islam, the people smoking, whispering, cheerful, interested,
appreciative. At the close there were many warm handshakes and
we got to bed rejoicing at 1 a.m. In retrospect this also was to be
seen as a turning point in the progress of the gospel in Gondang.

Next evening, *December 27th*, I joined Rufus for the last of the
country Christmas celebrations. We drove first to Barek, where the
first break-through occurred two years before, and sat with six men
in the house of Suprapto, the local headmaster. All the men in the
room owed their Christian faith to Rufus. Suprapto and Chamim
decided to join us and we drove on for an hour to the home of the
Suharta family at the crowded market of Trawas. Endless delays
ensued and for two hours we played gospel records on the gramophone to the village lads, who contrived at the same time to let the
air out of one of the Mayflower's tyres under cover of a line of
men standing between it and the light in the house. The meeting
began at 10 p.m., but by that time most of the Muslims had moved
off. Suharta's room is very small indeed and with fifteen people it
was painfully full. We were there till midnight and it seemed to be
a useful time. Rufus and I spoke. At the end Chamim found the
deflated tyre and pumped it up. So at 1 a.m. I was still swinging
the car round the innumerable hairpins on the road south of the
Great Volcano while the others slept around me.

December 29th was the last Sunday of the old year. Jess has been
down with malaria for ten days, so I took Rupert with me to Barek
where we saw five men, three women, and five babies baptised.
Two married couples had their marriages sanctified before the
Lord. This was a delightful time of fellowship. The old pastor from

L

Paru presided and to my great joy showed a cordial spirit towards me. We were detained for lunch in Chamim's house and I sat by the old gentleman. Rufus was having his too brief holiday with relatives.

As the year died away we slipped up to the tranquil House of Peace for a week of our own annual holiday, which we always took in two parts. There we were refreshed after the storm of Christmas events, save for one unfortunate incident. We had strolled higher up the mountainside, as on our previous visit, when we were turned back by labourers on the hills, of whom there were a large number in sight. The appearance of a family of white people strolling leisurely along drew the attention of everyone in a rather unpleasant way. They obviously thought that we were Dutch and in the prevailing tension they were not prepared to see us go by. Their young foreman strode across to head us off. "There is a path here," he said, "but it is not for you."

CHAPTER II

EMERGENCE OF A RAIDER

IN our first week back from the House of Peace we were both ill with a combination of malaria, food-poisoning, and fatigue, so we kept our doors shut and lived privately for a change. But by *January 17th* we were fully in action again with the regular six meetings in our home every week and our teachers coming to help us with language study three nights a week. We have visited quite a lot in the homes of Rupert's pals, where hordes of children romp with him under the palm trees while their parents stand at their doors, calling us in with smiles, and away down the long avenues other family groups sit watching to see if we will reach them. Yet it is true that those who have had no personal touch with us find it very awkward and embarrassing to meet a foreigner and know not what to do with their eyes.

On the night of *January 23rd* Rufus, Mawardi, and I went with a youth named Garit from Ringit to the home on the Karangan road where we have several times left the Mayflower. Garit was brought to Christ in the early days, not long after Mawardi, and through him his parents have also believed. He is very ardent and rather immature, but an attractive character. The meeting lasted from 7 p.m. till after midnight and our host rounded up fifty men to hear us. As usual Rufus spoke first and continued for an hour and a half. I followed him, using Psalm 19:7, "The law of the Lord is perfect, converting the soul". Mawardi followed me, then Rufus again, then Garit, and then Rufus yet again, making three and a half solid hours of preaching and teaching. In the course of my talk I used a harmless illustration involving the name of Nehru of India, which I afterwards regretted as it possibly gave the impression that I intended to make some political allusion. We got home at 2 a.m. and by 9 a.m. next day twelve young men were sitting in our home for the Bible class for seventeen-year-olds, the best attendance we have had yet. With growing facility in the use of Indonesian an era of more intensive teaching seems to be upon us and a major theme in our prayers and discussions with Rufus is a projected Bible School to be held once a week at our home.

January 25th was my birthday. During the morning we celebrated by escaping to a beautiful swimming pool not far from the city, which we had entirely to ourselves, picnicking under the trees and relaxing in a seclusion rarely to be achieved in this land. At night we held our delayed Young Men's Christmas Party for those who have been attending our Bible Class. Two new fellows, who had attended for the first time the previous day, asked if they might be allowed to come. Wishing to encourage them to associate with us and get to know the Lord, we unwisely agreed. Seventeen men were present for games, supper, and evening prayers. We got Rupert early to bed, but knowing that many visitors were coming he could not sleep. The doors of rooms are not normally closed in Java, owing to the heat, and our bedroom in which he lay was divided only by a light curtain from the fun of the party. While I was heavily occupied conducting the games two of the men stood in front of this curtain while another slipped in behind them and took Jess' fountain pen from the darkened bedroom. Rupert saw enough to call out to Jess, who became aware that there was trouble brewing. She went into the bedroom, missed her pen, but could not be sure which boy had taken it. I knew nothing and she had no chance to communicate with me. Then, during a violent game of "Dog and Bone" a pen fell from one fellow's shirt pocket. He looked startled but recovered it, and I suspected nothing. Jess, however, kept her eyes on him and he began to feel uncomfortable. Edging round the room he quietly placed the pen on the edge of her desk, behind a picture, probably in order to get it off his person for the moment and to find out if it had been missed. In due course Jess moved casually round to that corner of the room and slipped it into her pocket. The evening proceeded and at the close I gave a message about the Lord. Then they all filed out, shaking us warmly by the hand. As soon as the last guest had gone Jess closed the doors and told me what had happened and we rejoiced together over this deliverance—but not for very long. Inside her desk had been another pen and this was missing. So were her spectacles. So was the cloth on the table on the verandah. We slept fitfully, wondering what we ought to do. Not to do anything would merely encourage further robbery, and I had previously lost my own pen while some of these very men were in the house. My English umbrella had also vanished. As foreigners in a strange land we knew we must be very careful not to make enemies. As Christians we did not wish to call in the police nor to repel those who were in great need of Christ to save them from evil ways. Yet we felt that inaction on our part would also be no help to the culprits, whoever they were. Rufus was away, so we consulted our excellent teachers instead and they drew in other local schoolmasters and also two more responsible fellows who had been at the party. The latter were able to identify the culprits and thus the facts of the case were put beyond dispute. As an outcome of a meeting of ten persons the following evening two schoolmasters called at the house of the man primarily responsible. He denied all knowledge of the matter, so they simply stated that if the goods were not returned to me by 10 a.m. next morning there would be serious trouble. One of the masters, a Muslim, linked his fingers together and said, "Mr Taylor and I are like that and I will not stand for this."

At 8 a.m. next morning four men were on our doorstep. I was deliberately not too cordial towards them. They apologised profoundly on behalf of an imaginary "friend" who had taken the things, and handed them back to me. They sat on for some time and I attempted to bring home some sort of conviction of the wrongness of what had been done and to commend the gospel. We feel that the whole incident has been salutary and will prove a protection for us in days to come.

Susilo, father of the first of the Triwung children to die, came round with another schoolmaster saying, "We talked all night. He has repented and turned to Christ." They stayed a long time and the other man bought a New Testament and hymnbook. Other guests continued without intermission all day long and there were sixty children in the house for the children's meeting, when it is my task to cope with and distract rude observers. After these things my strength departed and I had to lie low for some days.

We had wondered very much whether any of the young men would come to the next Bible class in view of the attempted robbery at my birthday party, so we were highly gratified when twelve of them walked in, including three of those who had returned the stolen things. Somebody has reported the incident to the police. A plain-clothes officer came to see me and asked me to go back with him to the station and report on the matter. I asked to be excused, saying that everything had been returned and that I was in Java to help people to know the true and living God and had no desire to accuse anyone. He graciously did not press the matter. Later I was having my hair cut in a little shack close to our home when I observed in the mirror a group of the boys emerging from the police station and sauntering down the road together, so they had evidently been called in. So far as we know, no further action was taken against anybody. From that time we were not troubled with the danger of robbery, but it must be admitted that in a few weeks the Bible class died out and we lost touch with that particular group of young men, although they continued for years to greet us cordially whenever we met them in the streets of Sabrang. Gradually we came to realise that most of them belonged to a bad set and that in many cases their motives in coming to us had never been high. One day we trust and pray that the seed sown in their hearts will spring up and bear fruit.

The night of Saturday, *February 1st*, was a momentous occasion, for we inaugurated the Weekly Bible School on our verandah. There were twenty-seven persons present, mostly men, drawn from various villages. I divided the time into two sessions, beginning the study of 1 Corinthians in the first and devoting the second to doctrine. Next morning I was for the first time the appointed preacher in the Sabrang church. Headmaster Suwarso interpreted my Indonesian into Javanese with confidence. This too was a milestone, for I am now on the monthly rota of preachers. Inch by inch our unofficial penetration into the East Java Church is merging into full co-operation and integration into its programme.

Later the same day, as the children were gathering for Jess' long Sunday afternoon labour, Rufus, Mawardi, Rekso, and I left in the

Mayflower for a five-day expedition right out of the Sabrang area. We went first to the north coast town of Probolinggo, travelling in heavy rain all the way. As we entered the town it turned into a cloudburst, water swirling and raging across the roads as we crawled around searching for the pastor's house, to which we eventually had to wade. Then we continued to a remote, widely scattered place, inhabited mostly by Madurese. Fifteen people had waited a long time for our coming and the four of us preached to them in turn till 1 a.m. and then had supper at 1.30 a.m., by which time I was utterly exhausted after the early meeting in Sabrang and the five hours' struggle with the elements.

We slept in a tall old house set in a spacious, walled enclosure and when Mawardi woke me at 8.30 a.m. Rufus was already sitting at the breakfast table, New Testament in hand, preaching to a large and important-looking gentleman. I shut my eyes again, partly for the pleasure of sleep, partly to listen and rejoice that at first waking one should behold so beautiful a sight.

After breakfast we continued eastwards, stopping in a big country town for two hours at the home of a Christian medical who bought a lot of our literature and showed real concern for the work of the Lord. This town, like all the northern coast of Java's eastern promontory, is predominantly Madurese in race and language. Further on we drew off the road at the house of another medical hailing from a Christian village. To start with he was rather cold towards us, for a few days before he had given hospitality to a "Christian" lady who had taken several thousand rupiahs with her when she left. He asked Rufus to prove his identity, which he did by producing his papers and accredited photographs. Eventually this man too bought a good deal of our literature. Then we ran on eastwards through the teeming land with the glorious sea on our left, until we branched off into the equally crowded mountains in which lies the city of Bondowoso, the great metropolis of Java's further east. At 4 p.m. we preached there to thirty people, using Indonesian only, the audience consisting of Javanese, Madurese, and Chinese. Mawardi's testimony caused great interest. Rufus is always restricted when he has to use Indonesian, so I took more time, preaching for an hour.

At night we moved on to another place in these wonderful highlands where there has long been a single wholly Madurese Christian Church, perhaps the only one in the world. There are said to be about 200 Madurese believers in these Madura-lands of Java where 4 million Madurese live. It was first necessary for me to report in person to the main police station in the area and this involved quite a long journey in the car. Back in the pastor's house there was a plain-clothes officer present as a precaution and he also attended the evening meeting to hear anything I might be saying. Forty people were present and I felt that the Lord was with us. Rufus and I spoke in Indonesian and even the Madurese women could understand us. Mawardi, whose Indonesian is too limited for preaching, used Javanese and had to be interpreted. Meanwhile one of the Mayflower's tail-lights was stolen outside the church and a back tyre deflated. No westerners have visited the Christian church in this part of Java since the Japanese invaded in 1942, so that our operation was from some points of view hazardous. There is no manifest working of the Holy Spirit, as there is around Sabrang; Christian work is static and there is crying need for help.

Our party moved on to another big town. Pressure was heavy on us, meals irregular, nights very late, sleep limited. A young man slipped into the room I was sharing with Rufus and asked me how to live the Christian life successfully. He was intensely delighted with what I told him and said that for years he had longed to have a spiritual talk with someone. When I prayed for him he burst into tears. In the afternoon we preached to eighty people in the church, and again I spoke for an hour on Psalm 1. Then we drove on to a Christian village where 400 people sat before us from 9 p.m. till midnight. After that Rekso talked loudly to some of the leaders until dawn so that I got hardly any sleep. But these are great days. Rufus has not been this way before; we are breaking new ground and the type of message we bring seems to be new too.

Next morning, when I contrived to awake, Rufus was already in the big front room of the pastor's house addressing twenty church leaders with Indonesian and Javanese Bibles open on the table in front of him. They were seeking advice on how to evangelise. The great idea up to now has been that "we cannot do anything because we have no money", so I related the story of the origin of the China Inland Mission. Rufus spoke for a long time about the way in which the Holy Spirit had worked around Sabrang.

After lunch we moved three miles to another Christian village along a road cut through the ricefields by the Japanese, muddy and unsurfaced. Heavy rain was threatening, the car was overloaded, and I was thankful to arrive in safety, my passengers walking as the Mayflower slithered forwards. The storm then fixed the car where we were! For half an hour we walked through mud and rain, fording two streams, to a near-by village, half-Muslim, half-Christian. An elementary type of house was filled with sixty people who listened in rapt attention for the brief hour which was all we could spare them. I persuaded Rufus to use all the time and only spoke myself for five minutes. Old Rekso was asked to close in prayer, but being deaf he launched into a vigorous testimony. After a while he had to be called to order by Rufus, so he then prayed through the Lord's Prayer and continued straight on with the Apostles' Creed!

Returning to the stranded car and the pastor's house we had a belated supper while 200 people waited in the church. The team then occupied them for three and a half hours. Others were present who felt it necessary to explain that my presence in the group was permissible, legal, and even beneficial. There are almost 4000 "Christians" in these twin Christian villages. There is a third not far away and I contrived to pilot the longsuffering Mayflower through the mud to get there. It is a small place of only 700 souls. We spent three hours with the pastor and twelve church leaders, speaking in turn about the gospel and the work of the Spirit around Sabrang. It seemed a really valuable time, and as usual I was the first missionary they had seen for sixteen years. The pastor had suffered imprisonment and torture at the hands of the Japanese because of his association with the Dutch; then when the Dutch returned after the war and the Indonesians were fighting for their independence, his wife and son were shot dead by a Dutch sentry as they worked in the ricefields, the soldier being under the impression that they were creeping up on him. Such experiences are not uncommon.

We then went on to another big town and addressed eighty people for three hours, and, as I write this, the four of us—Rufus, Mawardi, Rekso, and myself—are about to turn in on only two beds in a tiny sealed room. Our clothes are now filthy; they want us to stay for three more days, but it cannot be. However, the trip has shown us the need of this part of Java and the warm welcome we can expect from the churches. The people are so hungry for help that our very ordinary testimonies and Bible messages come to them as the revelation of a new world. Now that Mawardi has gained in confidence and I in language we each require about an hour on the platform!

Next morning I awoke to see Mawardi enveloped in his sarong sitting motionless in prayer beside Rekso's prostrate bulk. We left early with the local pastor and drove twenty miles to a country place of 2000 souls where there are ninety Christians. They most earnestly besought us to stay several days. We had planned to push straight on for home, but as they have invited their Muslim neighbours to an evangelistic meeting tonight we feel we must stay. The head of the village is a Christian and in his house we have been most pleasantly entertained. They gave me a room where I prepared in peace for the Weekly Bible School, while for another two hours Rufus and I lay on our beds trying to shake off fatigue. Once again, no missionary has been here for sixteen years. In former days many Christians from the Moluccas and North Celebes lived here, as well as Dutch people, but not one of these outsiders remains. Heavy thunder rolled around us, so we had a time of prayer for fine weather, not wishing to be cut off by impassable lanes from regaining the main road.

Rain started but could not get going and it soon cleared for a moonlight night which drew 300 people around the house for the meeting. Three rooms were tightly packed with people. We stood under a strong lamp. The verandah and the garden were full and all along two roads Muslims stood under the trees in the dark, listening. Mawardi and I were disposed of in an hour and a half and on to this Rufus piled seventy minutes of forceful exposition and exhortation. He is ten times the man in his own Javanese; in Indonesian he is enfeebled and restricted, for it is his third language, as he was educated in Dutch. Resisting requests to preach on till 2 a.m. we tore ourselves away at 10.30 p.m. for the three-hour journey home to Sabrang over big mountains, where the scenery under a full moon was most magnificent and we were all elated at the joy of the Lord's work. The self-starter was dead, the engine roaring like an aeroplane, two of the tyres in dubious condition, one door and one traffic indicator broken, but the gallant May-flower kept going and in fifty miles we met only one car and, to our delight, one tiger asleep on the grass verge! I was home to supper at 2 a.m.

On *February 8th* I endeavoured to recover from this kind of a life and dozed away much of the day, speaking at night for two hours at the second Weekly Bible School attended by twenty-four people on our verandah. Rufus came, but he had spent the day in the city where the child of another pastor had been drowned in a pond, and was too weary to translate my Indonesian into Javanese. However, this gave the job to Susilo and the plan now is that he and I carry on this meeting together, thus freeing Rufus not to attend if he is otherwise occupied. Since Susilo is spiritually receptive and enthusiastic to share more fully in the Lord's work this is an excellent arrangement. It was thrilling to see the folk turning up verses in their little-handled Bibles and to introduce them for the first time to such great chapters as Isaiah 53 and 1 John 1. So these eight eventful days, during which I have driven 300 miles (often under very bad conditions) and preached in Indonesian fifteen times, are over.

Malaria, influenza, and general fatigue followed the trip, but I managed to conduct the third Weekly Bible School with Susilo, who interprets excellently and takes initiative. At the end the people just sat on singing hymn after hymn till they had been with us three hours. Many manuscripts and proofs lie on my desk, some from the Scripture Gift Mission in London, others from the Christian Witness Press in Hongkong. This literary work forms the basis of my days.

Rufus has a grey-haired visitor called Akas, who has been ten days in his home. Akas is selling up his business to devote himself entirely to evangelism, but I am somewhat doubtful about him.

He reckons that the East Java Church, in which he formerly worked as an evangelist, is now a hindrance to his call. He has had connections with the Pentecostal Church and two years ago the East Java Church suspended him for some misconduct. He has come to study Rufus' methods of evangelism and may want to work with him. Perhaps he has given Rufus money.

We are not overrun with children as we used to be and since the robberies schoolboys no longer invade us at every break-time. This is really a good thing; it is not easy to handle those who are only out for a spree, who repeat anything you say to them without answering it, and whose main objective is to stroke my hairy forearm!

Recently Jess has often been in the hospital visiting a girl we know, normally bright and vivacious, who was involved in an accident with a cyclist. She was not actually injured at all, but the shock of the incident has induced a hysterical condition and she is behaving almost like a mental case. The Women's Meeting continues to be held here each week and this year Mrs Suwarso, wife of our local church leader, has allowed herself to be sucked into it, to be induced to pray, and to become an active fellow-worker of Jess and Mrs Rufus. She is a gracious, motherly soul, but a little aloof and superior. The three of them take it in turns to speak and they also meet at another time for prayer and planning.

There were fourteen at the Weekly Bible School this time. Attendance is already causing us some concern, for although the meeting is only a month old the trend is adverse, 27, 24, 21, 14. Rain and a fun-fair close by may have affected us, while many believers live too far away from Sabrang to attend regularly. Yet we had a good time and Susilo translated and conducted the proceedings with delightful enthusiasm. Most of those present were from Triwung. The leader of the band of young men who have attended the Bible class for months, some of whom were involved in the abortive robbery, came for the first time. Seeing no one he knew inside the room he did not feel able to join us, so he stood in the shadows outside under the trees. Later I had a good chat with him and he said, "Knowing that I come here often people ask me a lot of questions." He warned me against "the chap in the yellow shirt"—so we have some good friends who are not far from the kingdom.

On *February 23rd* one of the headmasters gave an earnest sermon on the Parable of the Sower. I sat with two men from Triwung, both concerned over their unconverted wives. One of them, a tall, dignified, bearded man of Madurese stock called Sugiono, took up stones to pelt Rufus only a year ago, but is now on the Lord's side. At present he is under Susilo's wing, like Hastari, which is quite a good place to be as Susilo is a transformed man since his child's death, pressing on to know the Lord better. The death of the Triwung children has somehow invested the believers there with a spiritual glow.

Not long ago Mother Daro's beautiful dog was poisoned. Man, her servant, sat with him till he died and the household mourned as for a true friend. A ridiculous pup has succeeded him, glorying in the name of Breeno. Yesterday evening a thief raided Mother Daro's garden and collected piles of fruit and flowers, intending to remove them when he had got enough. The wee pup gave tongue and Man saw the thief run off. So did the policeman on duty outside the cells. Together they went to the stream by the mosque, found the culprit, hit him a few times, and clapped him into the lock-up. So today there is no work for Man; with beaming face he donned his best clothes and has gone off to Sabrang market to tell his friends all about this great feat.

The Bible class for seventeen-year-olds still keeps on in spite of the robbery and some really bad fellows attend it, including Sabrang's centre-forward; they questioned me closely about the Manchester United players killed in the air disaster at Munich.

On *March 2nd* it was my turn to preach in the Sabrang church. Headmaster Suwarso translated happily after I had found for him my text, which was 1 Peter 2:25. Later that same day Rufus, Mawardi, Rekso, and I, joined by Pastor Wen of the big Christian village of Kabat, drove up to Gondang on the Great Volcano. It seems that earlier visits to this place have aroused much interest and a considerable group of people is moving towards the gospel. They have asked Rufus to go there every Sunday evening. On this occasion the meeting was held in the home of the head of the village. Mrs Tias, the headmaster's wife, was very keen to go. As she is unable to walk we put her in the back of the car, but there has been heavy rain recently and the side-road deteriorated alarmingly. Eventually we became stranded in slippery mud rather close to a deep ditch. Everyone else got out, except Mrs Tias, who firmly stuck to her seat. After laying branches on the trail I managed to back the Mayflower out of the danger spot and find another way round to the house. There were thirty people inside it and rather more in the darkness outside. Since Rufus was already overdue at Synod meetings which were being held in Sabrang the gathering had to be cut rather short. On returning there a pastor from another part of Java came out of the house and chatted with me in the car. He is an influential figure and was planning a very late return to the city. I persuaded him to come to us for the night and thus was cemented a friendship which was an important landmark in our gradual acceptance not only by the rank and file but also by the leaders of the East Java Church.

Alone or with my teacher I still continue to revise and correct many manuscripts and we have great discussions over the exact force of Indonesian words. He revels in such work, but we are still poorly served by translators whose English is inadequate, spiritual insight deficient, and determination to succeed wanting. I have just had to recommend that all stocks of the Indonesian version of the well-known English tract "Safety, Certainty, and Enjoyment" must be burnt, though this is largely due to sheer unsuitability for translation.

On *March 8th* there were twenty at the Weekly Bible School. Preparation for this takes me the whole day from 6 a.m., except for a two-hour siesta after lunch. They stayed for four hours. Rufus, Susilo, and Mawardi all took part. The presence of Rufus is always an asset.

One night two weeks ago Jess got stranded in the Mayflower at 11 p.m. in a village called Kedok, where there are no believers, although it is close to both Barek and Triwung in which so much has happened. She had just dropped Mrs Susilo at the end of the turning to Triwung, which was dangerously muddy, and was turning the car on beyond in Kedok when the engine stopped and she could not get it going again. High on the bank above her she made out the figure of a man who, after some hesitation, came down and helped her. He was an actor and a former colleague of Susilo in the resistance movement. He had already gone to bed when he heard the car in difficulties. Today Susilo and I paid him a visit together, really just to thank him for his kindness that night. It was the first time I had ever been out visiting with Susilo. We played gramophone records to him and his household and are praying that this touch with him may lead to a work of the Spirit of God in Kedok. The car being out of action I walked home with a young man who works in Susilo's office. I asked him if he had really believed on the Lord himself. "Oh yes," he said, "one hundred per cent." In spite of this encouraging answer he is very rarely to be seen in any Christian meetings. Not long after he had left me, as I was on the outskirts of Sabrang, a man on a bicycle caught up with me and pedalled slowly along beside me, asking what was my business in this sun-bathed and rain-drenched paradise, so that gave me another good opportunity to speak of Christ. But of course I am a great curiosity and have to go along smiling and bowing the whole time. As a result many glum looks become smiles—just for the moment.

March 16th. Yesterday evening we held our seventh Weekly Bible School. We had extra prayer about it as we felt that the previous week Susilo had made rather a serious mistake. He has become a very ardent evangelist since the Lord took his little boy, witnessing for Christ at home, at work, at the roadside, on trains, anywhere, his New Testament ever in his hands. But his zeal is not always tempered with the tact and wisdom which seem never to fail in Rufus, and last week after I had spoken he demanded testimonies from everyone present in turn, including two fellows who had never before been in a Christian meeting in their lives. When they demurred he urged them on, thinking probably that they were constantly in touch with us. As a matter of fact these two men never entered our home again, probably as a result of the incident. I felt it would be wrong for me to speak to him directly about it. Would God that all the Lord's people were prophets! But I confided in Rufus and found him in complete agreement with my feelings. I suspect he may have spoken to Susilo. Anyway, he did not repeat the mistake last night when we had three glorious hours with twenty-four people, of whom fourteen were young men. Sugiono, the bearded Madurese, sat in front taking notes. They sang splendidly, especially Cowper's hymn, "There is a fountain filled with blood". At the end I asked Mawardi to close in prayer. Although the roughest and least educated man present he has a right spirit and has caught from Rufus that personal devotion to Christ which makes his prayers a benediction.

On *March 17th* I went with Rufus to Gondang for the fifth time. The zealous boy Garit and a friend came with us. The situation at Gondang is confused at present. Many are now interested, and so is the Pentecostal Church in the town of Gerbo not far away. The headmaster, Tias, who is leader and host to the people who come to hear the gospel, is a diabetic and a very sick man. As a result arrangements for meetings nearly always go astray. This one should have been held at 4 p.m., but we had to wait till 8, and even at 11 p.m. the headmaster had not appeared. The expedition took nine hours, during which we got only one small cup of coffee. Rufus went off on his own and had a grand time in one home where he found prepared hearts. I had a long talk with Garit's friend who has been to four of the Weekly Bible School evenings; that is the sum total of his contact with the gospel. Garit is very ardent in faith, tending to weep and shout when he prays, but settling down gradually. It seems to me that he is a man God may have chosen for some special purpose in this district. There were thirty people at the meeting when at length it started. One senior man, his face dulled, scarred, curious, and mystified, asked me many questions. "How can God be known?" "What do you mean by faith?" "Are you a plantation manager?" After Rufus and I had preached and testimonies had been given by Mawardi and Garit, Rufus came across to this man, who was finding my Indonesian hard to understand. Though tired and hungry, Rufus spoke to him with such delightful eagerness and joy that he could not take his eyes off him and sat as though nailed to the desk. When Rufus read him the opening verses of St John's Gospel he asked, "What does it mean when it says 'the Word'?"

The fast of Ramadan starts on March 21st and schools are closing for thirty-nine days. Rufus came round in the evening and together we worked on both the Indonesian and the Javanese translations of the Christmas tract, the job having been very poorly executed by the original translator, as is often the case. Many other visitors quite ate up my strength and since we have had no half-day for many weeks we escaped to the city for one whole day, borrowed a room in the Bible College from Pastor Meng, and just dozed and slacked the hours away till nightfall.

On Sunday, *March 23rd*, after the morning service in the Sabrang church, Hastari came round to see us with his wife, his surviving children, and his wrinkled old father, Daddy Tain. They were all baptised on December 29th, save Hastari himself who confessed the Lord several months earlier. He alone could speak to us directly in Indonesian of a broken sort, his wife and the old gentleman knowing only Javanese. Yet their warmth and kindness were very marked, a pleasing contrast to the chilliness with which we are regarded by all those who do not know us personally. This family is pleased to regard us as associated with their turning to Christ, since I was with Rufus the night in Hastari's home when he prayed over the old gentleman as he lay beside two of his grandchildren. Living close to Susilo, Hastari shares his zeal and spiritual alertness; he is as ugly as anyone can hope to be and quite uneducated, the embodiment of the vast country life of the unchanged east, and a devoted Christian as well.

It was later the same day that Susilo himself came to buy New Testaments and hymnbooks off me, to pray with us, to discuss new contacts he had made, and to plan outings together. "One needs a strong body, a patient spirit, and a joyful heart for this work," he said, and he began to tell me a tale which, God willing, shall know no ending. It appears that on March 17th, while Rufus and I were at Gondang, Susilo was required by the government department in which he serves to visit a remote Christian village on the Indian Ocean coast. Since it would take six hours' walking through the mountains to reach it, he started a day early by bus and stayed overnight with his contact man, Wirojo, the town clerk of a place called Segaran. He arrived before supper at the house, set on a

M

pleasant hillside amidst many avenues of homes and shrouded in coffee bushes. Mrs Wirojo served the two men in the big, bare, front room but as she did so she could not help overhearing the visitor's conversation. In his cheerful, bold, and sometimes tactless manner Susilo was telling Wirojo about the wonderful works of God around Sabrang and the mighty power of Christ to save and satisfy all who truly believe in Him. Now Wirojo was a youngish man with a hard heart. He had no wish for another Master. But from childhood Mrs Wirojo had longed for some surer light upon life's pathway. She had had a vague feeling that there might be help for her in Christianity, but there were no Christians in Segaran and her husband was strenuously opposed to her making any other enquiries. But a Christian visitor right in her own home was another matter. Boldly she joined the men, rested her elbows on the table, and listened to Susilo's talk. Sensing her interest he did not spare his words, and before they lay down for the night Mrs Wirojo was the owner of Susilo's New Testament.

Next day the two men walked together for six hours to the sea and the town clerk was compelled to listen to a great deal more preaching than he had bargained for. On reaching the Christian village Susilo accomplished his business and at the same time let it be known that he would be preaching in the home of the head of the village that night. A great company assembled to hear him and he continued his sermon until 4 a.m. Wirojo was present, and without any sleep the two men then walked back to Segaran. There for the moment the matter rested.

Glad enough to have Loti's Javanese face beside me in the Mayflower, I drove into the city past many a cold look. The Dutch manager of my bank, who will soon be gone himself, said quietly, "My last customers are missionaries", meaning that most other western nationals have elected to remove themselves from these parts.

March 26th, a day long to be remembered, dawned bright and sunny, like almost every day in Java. Heavy rain had fallen the night before, freshening the glorious hills into supernatural splendour. At 8 a.m. adjectives failed me to describe country so superb, rugged, deeply serrated, used to the limit by a vast population, yet preserving the divine magnificence of its Creator. Mr and Mrs Susilo and their daughters were with me in the Mayflower and we were heading east for Segaran and the Wirojo home, which I had not yet seen. Above us soared the peak of the Great Volcano, tempting my eye away from the hairpins of the road as it thrashed and fought its way across the tangle of ravines hacked out by the rivers coursing off that mighty flank. At last we turned precipitously off the main road down a stony patch into Segaran, where thousands of colourfully dressed people were packing the main street on market day. Crawling through, thanks to our horn, we crashed our way over a steep, rough road on to the rolling hills of residential Segaran above and stopped at one of a multitude of farms tucked away among coffee bushes and palm trees.

We parked the car on the grass beside the track and strode across a garden up to the front door of the Wirojo home, where the town clerk himself, looking worried and alarmed, greeted me cautiously. Until noon we sat in the big, bare front room with four young men and three women, sipping coffee. The proceedings were delightfully casual, with Susilo vaguely in the lead. I gathered that they had invited us to tell them more about the message Susilo had delivered on March 17th. We played many gospel gramophone records, interspersed with Scripture readings and preaching, while the four men smoked incessantly. At one point Mrs Susilo read an excellent passage from a Christian book which her husband then expounded sentence by sentence. Later she took a chair at the head of the table and gave an admirable little personal testimony to Christ in Javanese, repeating it in Indonesian for the benefit of one of the men who came from a remote Indonesian island and spoke little of the Javanese dialect. His name was Sumantri and I gathered that he was from a Christian home but had long abandoned the faith of his parents. Mrs Susilo was formerly a teacher in a Muslim religious school and was for fourteen years a zealous Muslim. "Two years ago I was born again," she said, referring to the time when Rufus came to Sabrang. Both Susilo and I addressed the little company five times. The main subjects he talked about were how to find God, the death of Christ, and the new birth; he smoked most of the time like the other men.

About noon Mrs Wirojo served us a handsome meal and after it, to my surprise, out came the Bibles again and Susilo read I Thessalonians 5:12-28 in Javanese, asking me to read the Indonesian verse by verse after him. Then he solemnly repeated verse 27, "I charge you by the Lord that this epistle be read unto all the holy brethren", and handed the book across the table as a present to Wirojo.

As we drove back to Sabrang I had the feeling that I had witnessed a scene of great significance. Since the death of his son Susilo has been a transformed man. He loves the Scriptures and more than anyone else around here—in a sense more even than his spiritual father, Rufus—he is able to quote and turn familiarly to any part of the New Testament and even of the Old. As a local man whose job is the promotion of rural education he has wide contacts all over the countryside, especially with community leaders, and he combines witness for Christ with his secular job.

On *March 27th* I was lecturing on New Testament Greek at the Bible College and when it was time to drive home Rufus turned up and joined me. We went first to a hospital in the town where the young pastor from Karangan, the "I-give-you-300-seconds" man, was a patient. We both went into his room. It was nice to meet him off his own ground and I prayed over him as warmly as possible. Before we left for Sabrang we came across the prominent church leader who had spent a night in our home and who used to be so cold and unapproachable. He seems a transformed person and greeted me with exultation. Then he drew me into a room and said he wanted to have a word with me privately. He sat me down, looking very serious, and I wondered what was coming. Slowly and solemnly he began, "This is a difficult time." He paused and looked at me. "There is inter-racial feeling." He was speaking in English and I wondered if I was to be forbidden the field. "You may hear criticisms and warnings," he said, "not only from outside the church but from within it as well. I just want to say one thing to you, merely a piece of private advice. Go right ahead, don't be put off by anything, go on with the work of the Lord, unafraid!"

On *March 29th* we were very uncertain what to expect for the ninth Weekly Bible School, the maximum attendance at which has so far been twenty-four. Rain was threatening, but it held off. In the end we had thirty-six, absolutely cramming our house, so that Susilo and I had to remain standing for four hours as there were no seats for us, and Jess sat outside the door on a table. At the end the verandah was swarming with young men, many of whom bought Bibles and New Testaments.

Next morning I drove into the city, left the Mayflower at the Bible College, and proceeded to Surabaja by train for my quarterly visit to the Chinese Christian Church. I travelled with a Chinese Christian formerly well known to me. "I have no home," he said, referring to his wife and children, whom he has not seen for nine years. In the big port and in my contacts with the foreign community I felt quite an oddity, so wholly have we been immersed in another world, but I was strongly confirmed in the rightness of maintaining at least this quarterly contact with Chinese believers, especially when I rose to preach to the 500-strong Foochow congregation. It was *Palm Sunday* and this provided me with my theme throughout the day. I was quite surprised to see so many white faces still in evidence in Surabaja. I slept in an air-conditioned room at the British Consulate and lay full length in a hot bath for the first time for many months. The Consul most graciously put his car and chauffeur at my disposal and when I had finished with them I borrowed Mrs Tan's and her chauffeur. Mrs Tan entertained me with her unfailing hospitality, but she finds our switch out of Chinese society into the Javanese world utterly incomprehensible.

And then the Segaran drama moved forwards with lightning speed. On *March 31st* Sumantri, the man from the outer islands with some Christian background, came to Sabrang in search of Susilo again; finding he was in the city he pursued him there. It appears that the seven people who were present in Wirojo's house on March 26th have spread the news far and wide and the whole village is now alerted to the gospel, the three women having been particularly diligent in telling others about it. Instead of being ostracised as an outsider, Sumantri is now in great demand, as word has spread that there is a "foreigner" in Segaran who understands spiritual matters. He is now overrun with visitors, asking him questions. As usual the Scripture Gift Mission booklet, *The*

Way of Salvation, is in great demand. Susilo, Rufus, and I called on Wirojo. It was Rufus' first visit and I had the great pleasure of seeing him meet and shake hands with Wirojo and Sumantri for the first time. We all prayed together that the will of the Lord might be done and many souls in the district brought to Christ.

Next morning was *Good Friday* and there were fifty people in the Sabrang church. Organisation, however, does not always match spiritual growth and the care of this whole area has recently been officially handed over by the Paru Church to the City Church, pending the appointment of a resident pastor for Sabrang at the end of the year. The result of this new arrangement was that no preacher came at all, so Rufus had to improvise a sermon on the spot, which was a pity, especially as he had been up till 2 a.m. preaching in Susilo's home in Triwung.

The East Java Church, being Presbyterian in character, has the Lord's Supper much more rarely than we are accustomed to, so on Good Friday evening Jess and I greatly enjoyed remembering the Lord's death together privately.

CHAPTER 12

THE HEAT OF THE DAY

ON *Easter Saturday* evening there were twenty-four at the Weekly Bible School. It is extraordinary how the attendance varies, partly due to the weather and partly to the fast of Ramadan. Usually it is a young men's evening, but this time there was a majority of girls present. We got to bed at midnight but Susilo, who had translated for me into Javanese as usual, never lay down at all, for at 5 a.m. there was an Easter morning meeting at Barek to which forty-two people went. I stayed at home as *Easter Sunday* promised to be heavy enough anyway and in the upshot it gave me eighteen solid hours of work. Since Rufus, Mawardi and Susilo all shared the day with me the latter had thirty-six hours of Christian ministry without rest.

I left home at 7.30 a.m., collected Rufus and Mawardi from Ringit and the Susilos from Barek and we drove east to Trawas, Segaran, and Gondang, holding meetings in all three teeming villages, though it would be more appropriate to call them residential areas. Never before have I been out with Rufus and Susilo at the same time. A more complete contrast than these two men provide would be hard to find. Rufus is quiet, composed, steady, deeply rich and joyful in spirit, the Lord's apostle in this countryside, no fighter or arguer, gentle, patient, and meek. Susilo is filled with a most unusual life-force, bursting with drive and energy. He is a man of pens, pencils, notebooks, exercise-books, diagrams, choruses, helps and aids, texts, New Testaments, and Bibles, Bibles, Bibles, which he uses, quotes and gives away in prodigal style. He is a tireless advocate of the gospel, irrepressible, and sometimes erratic. Rufus gives him his head, almost too much perhaps, though it is hard to see what alternative he has.

At Trawas we visited a man who had been baptised in the

beginning of this movement in 1956 at Barek, but has since grown cold towards the Lord. "I used to read the Bible eagerly," he said, "but now I just feel dulled." He laid himself open to help and advice and marvellously did Susilo seize the opportunity, mixing testimony with Scripture, and finally writing out a reaffirmation of faith and devotion which the other man signed like a lamb. It was done with warmth and affection and I felt that he had truly been undergirded. When at last Susilo paused, Rufus chipped in and we ended with prayer together.

Next day we attended the Easter service at Trawas, which was nothing very grandiose. It was held in Suharta's home, which is about 12 feet square, and there were twelve persons present. But Rufus and Susilo gave them as much time and care as if they had been a mass rally. They made frequent use of rhetorical questions in speaking, and these were gladly taken up and answered, while observers gathered outside the window. It is part of Rufus' genius to fan little flames until they burst into big ones.

At Trawas we got coffee from Mrs Suharta but no food and we drove back to Segaran at 2 p.m., arriving in torrential rain in which I got marooned alone in the car for an hour. We found that that very morning forty men had gathered in the home of Sumantri from the outer islands and he had been compelled to have an Easter meeting with them on his own several hours before we arrived. Then the rain further complicated arrangements; people dribbled in to Wirojo's home all afternoon and the meeting had to dribble to keep pace with them. In the rain Susilo met an old lady in a shelter at the roadside. In his own typical way he was hugging a bundle of posters put out by the Christian Witness Press and she noticed the crocodile on the "Sinner's Dream" poster. "Oh, I'm scared," she said. "Tell me what happens." She came with him to Wirojo's house and sat in the meeting for hours, proving to be quite a character, full of questions and interruptions. The encounter gave to her and her family an enduring interest in the gospel and I was frequently to be a visitor in her home in days to come. Meanwhile Susilo was plastering the blackboard in Wirojo's home with texts and choruses. He is very good at getting men to come to the front and read out verses for him. This fixes the verse in their minds and helps to commit them both to the Lord and to us. Wirojo is thus being sucked into Christian service almost before he knows whether he really believes. Although this drawn-out meeting was not quite the kind of thing we had envisaged, yet interest in Segaran runs high, hopes are great, and it well reflects the lively and unorganised state of opportunity which exists where so recently no man's eyes were turned towards Christ.

Through the mud the Mayflower slithered up to Gondang, well laden with a joyful, singing company. At 8 p.m. the wife of headmaster Tias showed her intelligence by giving us a square meal, our first since 7 a.m. We ate it by the light of a tiny lamp, with much satisfaction and thanksgiving to God. By that time fifty men were packed into the schoolroom and as many more outside it. Only three months ago this Gondang crowd was raw, silent, curious at best. But now they are used to us and the type of message we bring, so that the meetings have more of a church than of an evangelistic character. From being outsiders listening to a far-away tale many are becoming insiders listening to truths which they are embracing for themselves. It was my sixth visit. We preached for three and a half hours, first Rufus for seventy-five minutes, then myself for twenty-five on that great text 1 Peter 5:10, which I wrote on the blackboard, "The God of all grace, who hath called us unto His eternal glory by Christ Jesus, after that ye have suffered a while, make you perfect, stablish, strengthen, settle you." Then came Susilo preaching on everything under the sun. Mrs Susilo also gave a testimony, for all the family is infected with his remarkable zeal. At midnight we called a halt and I was home by 1.15 a.m. for a second supper.

While all this was going on Jess had a houseful for four hours in Sabrang and at night Loti took Rupert with her to the meeting at the Salvation Army hospital. At the close the preacher gave an "altar-call" and Rupert, aged four and a half, asked Loti if he could go out and kneel at the front. Since we were not there she endeavoured to dissuade him, but he persisted, so she agreed and he strode forwards and knelt down in front of everyone. There were many Muslims present and Loti said to herself, "I have never witnessed to Christ before a Muslim crowd like this. If Rupert has the courage to go out, surely I can too." So just as a witness to her faith she went forward and knelt beside him, and she said afterwards that it was more difficult for her than being baptised last December, because in that case the audience was Christian. Having known Rupert since infancy she has a great affinity with him.

I was compelled to expend *April 9th* on a visit to Surabaja. Jess had been summoned by the Immigration Office there. It was merely a case of their having recorded a wrong date, which was adjusted in five minutes, but it cost me the day to see to it. Yet I had some very profitable contacts on the trains. First I came across a Chinese business man who said, "My family have been Christians for three generations, but I was saved through Dr John Sung in Surabaja on September 26th, 1939." While we were talking together two other Chinese were eavesdropping, attracted by the fact that I could speak Mandarin. "To be honest with you I never had anything to do with Christianity," said one of them. "Too many sins you know! But it is strange, every time I take this train to Surabaja I come across Christians who speak to me."

Having two hours to wait for my train back to the city I took refuge from the heat in the British Consulate, where the Consul's wife most graciously gave me a quiet corner in which to work, a cool drink, and a refreshing fan. On returning to the station I met my garage proprietor, a Pentecostalist, along with his much-painted wife. "She was a Roman Catholic," he said, "but she has now joined my religion." On boarding the train I found myself opposite a forbidding-looking Javanese reading a Leftist paper. He took no notice of me, so I read my book and prayed. When he lowered the paper I lowered the book and we beheld each other, and at once I liked him. He proved to be but another sheep without a Shepherd, vaguely looking for help. He told me he came from a strongly Muslim town, but that his own views were rather different. He was most astonished when I produced the Javanese *Way of Salvation* booklet and started to read it at once. He was greatly struck by the words, "Father forgive them, for they know not what they do". I was able to speak freely to him and his heart seemed wide open—so little do first impressions count for! When we reached his destination he said, "Won't you stop off at my home and catch a later train on?" I was unable to accept and in any case I think this was just oriental politeness.

On reaching the city I managed to catch the 2 p.m. bus to Sabrang and found myself next to a schoolmaster from Jogjakarta who was visiting relatives near Sabrang. He was beyond measure astonished when I produced *The Way of Salvation* in his own language. I think the very last thing people can conceive of is that a foreigner should have Javanese literature on him! He said little but stared at me with eyes full of intelligence as I spoke about Christ. It was a queer day all for five minutes, but perhaps it was spent thus for the sake of these sheep without a shepherd. It is at times like these that the vastness of our task as Christian workers comes home to me.

After that Jess was down with malaria for some days. Four solid hours of visitors swamped my usual preparation for the Weekly Bible School, at which we had a record attendance of thirty-eight people in the house from 7 p.m. till 10 p.m. Then the end of the fast month drew near and it seemed wise for our regular meetings to be cancelled for a week, which gave us some respite.

On *April 18th* I called on Rufus and found him full of joy after attending a pastors' conference elsewhere. He seems quite undeterred by any of the alarms which are in the air these days and plans further trips in my company, though I cannot help feeling that in the last two months he has dispensed a lot with my presence, a gap which so far as I am concerned has been amply filled by Susilo and the Weekly Bible School. But in warm fellowship Rufus is quite unchanged and I do not blame him in the least if there are times when he judges it better not to be seen with a white man.

A visit from Susilo postponed our lunch for two hours. He had preached all night in Wirojo's house at Segaran and then worked in his office all day without a wink of sleep. He reported that there are now many believers and enquirers at Segaran and they have given him money to buy Bibles, New Testaments and hymn books.

On *April 19th* I went to the homes of two young men who have often been in ours during the past month. They live in a village of 6000 souls, quite close to Sabrang, and it appears that a year ago Rupert and I passed that way on one of our tract walks and gave them literature. In the first home a dignified father braced himself visibly for the ordeal of meeting a foreigner and sat with us courteously for a long time. The second one was a very humble spot, dingy for lack of windows, but with a telephone on the desk. The men asked me about Nero, Luther, Tyndale, and baptism by immersion. At the time these seemed to be profitable and happy visits, but neither man came near us again and I am inclined to think that in each case parental wrath probably descended as soon as the visitor had departed.

On Sunday, *April 20th*, while Jess was occupied with classes in the sitting room, I went to Ringit, where Rufus lives, and visited again in three homes. The first was that of the ardent youth Garit, an only child, both of whose parents are now believers as well. From him we passed to old Rekso, but did not stay very long as he cannot hear much and his wife cannot understand Indonesian. The third home was Mawardi's. Western ideas of Sunday observance have not much penetrated among these Javanese believers in Christ; he came in from the ricefields whereby he augments the pension granted to him from the factory in which he lost his arm a quarter of a century ago. Half the tiny sitting-room was taken up by a great stack of grain. He said what an immense difference it had made to his wife and his home since he was converted. "Every evening we gather round this table," he said, "and others join us to read the Scriptures, and to pray." In all these homes we were given coffee and various nameless and delectable things to eat, mostly rice products, and in every home we prayed. Mawardi took me to see the widow in whose house he first heard the gospel from Rufus. She attends the small Pentecostal church and since she is related to Garit she influences him in that direction too. Including children there are now about fifty Christians in Ringit.

Another good friend of these days is Riti, the girl who lives at our gate. She went to church with us for the very first time this week. She is now about twelve and the perfect type of oriental elder sister who brings up all the younger brothers. There has been disapproval of Riti's friendship with us, but she has responded to the gospel from the start. She rarely misses any of the meetings in our home, including the Weekly Bible School. Often she brings

Pooh and Misli with her; Jess puts a mat on the floor of our sitting-room, so that the two of them can play there till they fall asleep, and Riti is thus free to attend to the meeting. When refreshments are served in the middle of it she invariably helps to carry them round. On these occasions she changes out of the near rags she normally wears into a smart dress and jumper. She can find verses in the New Testament quicker than anyone else, with the exception of Susilo, and this is sometimes an embarrassment to senior Christians, as she is not above leaning forward to help them if they seem to be in difficulties.

At this point our Superintendent, George Steed, arrived from Djakarta to pay us a visit. Hard on his heels a note came from Susilo asking us to join him at Segaran. However, we felt we should stay at home as we had much to discuss. Shortly afterwards a similar note arrived from Rufus, and so we decided we ought to go, and in this way Mr Steed had his baptism of village life in East Java. Rufus, Mawardi, Rekso, and Suprapto (the headmaster from Barek) came with us in the car, and when we reached Wirojo's house on the hill-side above Segaran market, Susilo was already preaching to seventy people. Rufus followed him, then I myself, and then Susilo again. We broke up at 1 a.m. but were given a feast by Mrs Wirojo which kept us there till 2.30 a.m., when we managed to escape.

While I was in the city one day Jess had many callers. One young woman said to her, "I have had your tracts and I believe all I have read, but it would cause such a row at home that I dare do nothing more at present." She also entertained Muljono, the head of Kabat Christian village, who wants me to teach him English and who revealed to her that the East Java Church is considering inviting us to come into some closer and more official co-operation with them.

April 27th. In fulfilment of a promise made to some of Rupert's special friends we drove to the Indian Ocean with seven Javanese children in the car. Even paddling had to be closely supervised, as the waves rage in through rocky islands and suddenly surge dangerously up the beach. Only one of the children had ever seen the sea before; not quite knowing what to do with it they found themselves more at home in the trees which line the shore, high up which they played as though at ground level. A long black snake and a troupe of monkeys crowned the day. We were home in time for the Weekly Bible School, attended by twenty-one. On these occasions we are often uncertain whether Susilo is coming or not. I am rather dependent upon him for translation from Indonesian into Javanese, as there are always some present who have but a hazy command of the national language. But he is so busy, and so often in the city, that he nearly always comes late, while we sing on and on, postponing the moment when I must start the serious work of the evening without him. At that moment he has an uncanny knack of turning into the drive on his scooter. When I asked him to pray this evening he first had us all recite the Apostles' Creed twice in Javanese, then twice in Indonesian, then he read the Scriptures, and finally got to praying.

May 4th. The rather tense atmosphere of the past few months has eased a good deal and even strangers now smile at us again. But there is a sense of pressure at the Bible College in the city due to the temporary closing down of all Chinese newspapers. They are wondering what will happen next. I am now at grips with the Indonesian version of Dr Billy Graham's *Peace with God.* It is thrilling to handle such a manuscript. The job has been well done by an Indonesian in Djakarta, working from the Dutch version, which was easier for him than translating from the English. My task is to check his work against the original; there is about one error per page.

There is something else in the wind which I do not fully comprehend. Rufus is just as of old, but he goes a great deal to the city nowadays and has less time for the villages. What takes him there? I believe it may be connected with criticisms of his co-operation with us, though we know that many leaders in the East Java Church —and not least Muljono—favour it.

Among the hundreds of farmers who live with their families in a beautiful village area three miles south of us is a man named Sudjono, who believed with all his house when Rufus first came to these parts. His old mother was also converted. A week ago she fell sick and they sent for Rufus one evening. When he got there he found that there were many other visitors, to whom he preached Christ till 2 a.m. At 7 a.m. the old lady died. Although Sudjono explained to the relatives that she had believed in Christ and been baptised, her other sons insisted that she should have a Muslim funeral and burial. When he pressed his remonstrances there was an unseemly row and he had to give in. It seemed best for Rufus to keep away till the funeral was over; none of the Christians went.

I have already explained that this district of Sabrang, Barek, and other country churches is now under the ecclesiastical supervision of the city church, twenty miles away. Misunderstandings easily arise, partly due to the distance, partly to the difference between town and country mentality, partly to the age-old problem of fitting a new spiritual movement into an old church framework.

On Sunday, *May 4th*, there was reason to suppose that no preachers had been appointed to lead the meetings in the Sabrang area, so Rufus and I were asked to help in the emergency. En route to our appointments, however, we met students from the seminary in the city who were obviously on their way to take charge, so we hurriedly backed out—for Rufus is the meekest man in the world on such matters. The student who preached at Sabrang was Tilosa, the boy from Karangan whom Rufus had himself nurtured in the faith. He gave a stirring talk on the experiences of Noah. It is just possible that this man is going to be appointed resident pastor at Sabrang later on. This would not be in succession to Rufus, for Rufus is not the pastor at Sabrang at all. He is evangelist at large, although he happens also to be a fully ordained man, but the success of his labours has created all around Sabrang a new pastoral charge. "Many of the students in the seminary would like to be sent here," Rufus told me with a twinkle. Perhaps this partly accounts for his many visits to the city, from which he has also now secured on hire-purchase terms a motor-scooter to facilitate his many journeys.

The same evening Rufus and I went yet again to Gondang on the Great Volcano, which has troubled people lately with its rumblings. Mawardi and old Rekso came too, and at Barek we picked up Chamim, the host of the church, a gentle man delighting to serve others. We also stopped in the perfect night at Segaran to pray with Wirojo whose house stands on the concrete foundation of the tennis courts which were once used by the Dutchmen, who once worked in the factory, which once processed the rubber from the trees, which once stood on these hills, now blanketed by small-holders' coffee bushes. There were only twenty people in the meeting at Gondang, but all accustomed to us and receptive. At my suggestion Rufus asked Chamim to speak; he has been out with us several times now and is gaining in confidence. Mawardi, myself, and Rufus followed him and we were home before midnight. Rufus does not often call upon Rekso, as he is so hard to stop once he starts!

On *May 10th* I was due to drive south to Kabat once again in company with Mawardi and headmaster Suwarso to join Rufus, who had gone there the day before. However, the battery of the Mayflower was quite dead and it was three hours before we had her going. As soon as we got to the bottom of the monstrous descent from 2500 feet Muljono met me and said, "Quick, Rufus is just spinning out the last hymn", and he straightened the tie I had hastily donned and ushered me into the big church to face 600 people at the close of their morning service. In spite of the rush, the heat, and the strain of driving the mountain road I was able to preach with some freedom on Hebrews 2: 18, "In that He Himself hath suffered being tempted, He is able to succour them that are tempted". Immediately afterwards the church committee of twenty-five men met in the house of Pastor Wen. They had just been newly elected for a term of three years and Muljono called upon me to give them a message, which I did on the qualifications of a bishop in 1 Timothy 3. Thus within an hour of arrival I was given two valuable twenty-minutes opportunities of speaking in Christ's name in this important place. As soon as I sat down they called on Mawardi. Last time we were in Kabat he was still not able to open his mouth for Christ and his "sly-cove" look hardly suggests the preacher. He stood in the doorway between the two rooms where the men were sitting—white trousers, yellow coat, empty sleeve tucked into one pocket, and on his head the same black Indonesian hat that President Sukarno wears. I have never heard him so obviously effective and the men hung on every word.

Then we all packed into the Mayflower and on a steep, rocky slope scored a direct hit on a big stone which neatly punctured the oil tank, the contents of which emptied slowly all over the village

of Kabat as we proceeded in blissful ignorance. When we reached
Muljono's home having forded the river, he produced a bar of soap,
a wad of cotton wool, a strip of silk, a piece of cloth, and a bundle
of fibre. With this concoction Rufus and I spent some time lying
together under the car and contrived to plug the hole; we then
drove safely home in ninety minutes over the rugged mountains
through torrents of rain. This brief visit—for which the arrangements were, as often, muddled—was an important opportunity of
recontacting the Christian village which shows most understanding
of the work of the Spirit of God in the Sabrang area. With joy and
amazement they receive the news of Susilo's zeal and the opening to
the gospel of Gondang and Segaran. Several stiff days of labour on
the Indonesian version of *Peace with God* followed, in addition to
one in the city, which now involves me in more Greek than
Chinese.

Then on the afternoon of *May 15th*, Jess, Rupert, Rufus, Mawardi,
and I returned to Kabat. We reached sea-level at dusk, the mighty
ocean spread before us as the day faded away. After supper in Pastor
Wen's house we walked for three-quarters of an hour with forty
others by the light of a petromax lamp to a non-Christian village
on the Kabat plain. On arrival we found a big house crammed with
people; many others stood outside by the oxen; lamps and a loudspeaker had been fitted up in the trees. By count there were 551
present. The meeting lasted three hours and was led by the Kabat
evangelistic band, whose chairman kept a cigarette in his hand
throughout. Five different choirs sang to us and there were five
speakers. I preached on the birth of Moses, Mawardi on Romans
1:16, and Rufus on Hebrews 9:27. Mawardi again did very well;
he is quite a trump card with raw outsiders. Gospel records were
played and Rufus hung up Christian Witness Press posters. No
missionaries having touched these parts since 1942 our family was
esteemed a sight worth beholding. At the close we tramped wearily
back to Kabat, reaching the pastor's house at 12.30 a.m., and I
managed to keep awake through the interminable curves and
bangings of the rough road till we came out at last on the crest of
the Southern Mountains above Sabrang, from which a truckload of
people crashed to death recently when their brakes failed. We

N

treated the long hill with the greatest respect and were home by 2 a.m.

May 19th. The checking of the manuscript of Dr Billy Graham's book is still my main preoccupation. It is a thrilling task on which to be engaged but hard on the eyes, which are ever shifting from book to manuscript. Requests to teach people English are always rather a problem to me, but I have just had one which I can hardly refuse from Muljono, the head of Kabat. This gifted man is such a prominent figure both in the community and in the church that I feel I must do what I can for him. On Monday mornings he travels ninety minutes each way in order to get seventy-five minutes' English. I frankly do not think it will last long, for he is a busy man and was recently flown to one of the outer islands in connection with schemes to shift some of Java's overflowing population; it is also a shock to him to find how hard English is and to discover that he pronounces imperfectly some of the words he thought he did know! Perhaps the title "head of the village" suggests something too rustic to English ears. He is as much a pastor as leader of 6000 people, an impressive figure with a broad forehead, an immaculate cream suit, and a loud tie.

May 20th was an important anniversary of the Indonesian revolutionary movement and at night there was a torchlight procession of schoolchildren through Sabrang and Ringit. I estimated there were about 1500 bamboo "torches", a beautiful sight bobbing down the full length of the road. As usual on these occasions, we sat on the stone balustrade at the entrance to our home.

May 24th was Rupert's fifth birthday so we took our Whit Monday holiday then and drove to a beach on the Indian Ocean which we had never before visited. A massive, uninhabited island stands only half a mile offshore; since it is eight miles long and the breakers part on it, the narrow channel between the island and the mainland is a tranquil lagoon. There was just a tiny strip of beach where one could paddle, perhaps twenty yards long, a rather comical conclusion to two hours' driving through a maze of mountains and ridges. There is a small Christian village nearby and we noticed that some men working on boats close to us were singing hymns.

Next day I drove to Gondang with Mawardi and three others to join Rufus, who had been there all day escorting his rather peculiar guest, Akas the healer. On reaching the home of headmaster Tias we found him sick and with a badly swollen foot. He lay in total lack of comfort on a dirty and rickety bed without bedding—I constantly marvel at these situations, which are not by necessity. Recently I have been forced to conclude that Rufus' now strictly rationed invitations to me are due to his being forced in that direction by the difficult atmosphere of these times. However, even as these thoughts were in my mind a man asked me most cordially to come to his home, walked down Gondang's main street at my side, and took me to a house where Rufus was sitting under a lamp expounding the gospel to several schoolmasters. He at once asked me to give them my testimony. The main meeting began at 9 p.m. in the schoolroom. Since we had a strong team I suggested to Rufus that he should drop me, but he retaliated by putting me on first, a thing he has never done before. He then spoke himself and after that handed the meeting over to Akas, who was really the special guest of the evening.

Akas read the Scriptures and preached with considerable skill and grace. Then he prayed and called out in turn the six people who had come to the meeting specially in order to seek physical healing. His method was the same in each case. Tall, bespectacled, dressed in white, with a tiny beard and the black Indonesian hat, he fixed his man with his eye, talking to him quietly, and giving him total, unhurried attention. Then he placed the palm of his right hand on the man's forehead, resting his wrist on the nose, paused long, and drew his hand slowly down till his fingers touched the tip of the nose. Then the temples, cheeks, neck, chest, and shoulders were touched or massaged in the same dignified, slow, solemn manner, with whispered exhortations. Then he raised his hands high and prayed. In one case he called for a cup of water, took three sips himself, and made the man take three. There was an element of massage in it, and perhaps of hypnotism, but no abuses such as I had feared, no noise, and no extravagant claims. I felt at the time that in some cases it might be beneficial for a rustic farmer to have such close, paternal attention paid to him in the name of Christ and in connection with the preaching of the gospel. Rufus took no part at all in this; it is not in the least his way of doing things. We were home by 1 a.m.

A few days later Susilo took me to call on the head of Sabrang, a young Muslim, always courteous and kind to us. His mother was ill and after the three of us had sat sipping coffee for a time Susilo asked if we might see her. We stood at the door of her room for some minutes and then Susilo made what I am convinced was a mistake. He asked me if I would like to pray for her. I indicated that if the head of the village wished it I was certainly ready to do so. Turning to the Muslim Susilo said, "Pa David wants to pray for her," which quite misrepresented my approach to the situation. With oriental courtesy the head of the village agreed, but I found it very hard to pray sincerely, for I felt that something had been tactlessly imposed upon him which he was not yet ready to welcome.

May 27th. One night an old man who lives near us and is strongly opposed to the gospel brought round to our home a guest of his, a building contractor from the town of Gerbo, in which as yet there is no stirring towards Christ. The contractor had heard the singing from the women's meeting in our home and asked his host, "Are there Christians here?" His command of Indonesian was so limited that I could get no clear picture of his position, so I suggested we should go and see Rufus together. We drove to Ringit and found Rufus reading the Scriptures with two naval men who now spend much time with him or with us and are seeking baptism. The Gerbo man stayed for two hours and we trust that this may prove a stepping-stone to the establishment of an effective witness for Christ there; it is the largest place in the whole Sabrang district.

The child of Natmina, a woman who attends the women's meeting, played truant from school this week. She was angry with him and struck him, so he stole money from an aunt and disappeared. The mother came to Jess, fearing that the boy might have reached Surabaja. However, a phone call came from the city to say he was there; Jess drove her in and they returned with the boy in triumph.

Not far from our home there lives a retired colporteur of the Bible Society, a man who preached here in the years before Rufus

came. Unfortunately he has grown cold in heart; he strongly disapproves of Rufus and has attended no meetings for many years.
But I think he enjoyed chatting with foreigners again and telling
us of his adventures in Celebes and the Moluccas. "I just lie low
now," he said, adding that all Christians in Sabrang come from
other districts and that "none of the people from here believe".
To correct this I endeavoured to explain the great change
which has come over the work of the Lord since he withdrew
from it.

Both Rufus and Susilo are so busy in Christian service that we
do not see much of them and this week Susilo failed to turn up for
the Weekly Bible School, so Hastari translated into Javanese for
me, though it is really beyond him. About sixty people attend when
moved to do so; in practice our numbers keep steady at twenty to
twenty-five, of whom two-thirds are men.

Sunday, *June 1st.* There were fifty people in the Sabrang church
this morning and at the close of the meeting Rufus rose and cheerfully announced that Faral, who is the highest authority in the
churches here, was coming that very day to interview "Pa
David" and invite the latter into still closer co-operation with the
East Java Church. When we got home he was waiting for us, a
short man, serious and quiet. We sat in the cool of the sitting-room
for the crucial interview. He solemnly but gladly announced that
the East Java Church had unanimously decided to invite us to work
officially with them, and thus what we have prayed for and aimed
at for so long, and unofficially enjoyed for the past sixteen months,
is now formally extended to us. Having marched in by the back
door we are now invited to step round to the front. This will be a
much greater gain than might be apparent to the Western observer,
for formal agreement counts for a great deal in this country. I was so
surprised at his words that there were many things I omitted to
discuss with him, but it is wonderful to be sure of the intentions of
the East Java Church in this matter.

June 2nd. For the third Monday morning running I spent some
hours trying to teach English to Muljono. In a way this is favourit-
ism, for I would not do it for others, but exceptions are at times
necessary, and in any case I do not think it will last much longer.

Thereafter came the common round—Greek in the city, Billy Graham in Sabrang. A voluminous manuscript, and a time limit in which to handle it, tie one to a desk and tend towards a closed door, especially when a horde of children, a tricycle, two old motor tyres, a viewfinder, and sundry applicants for iodine, Elastoplast, tracts, and lumps of ice are just the other side of it.

In the ebb and flow of things there is now a marked ebb in young men. Some of the best have moved elsewhere. Some have been warned off us so that they do not dare to be seen greeting us cordially in the streets. The January 25th robbery has not helped, nor has the general atmosphere of the times. Others again realise at last that there is nothing much beyond the gospel to be gained from us, and exams press heavily in the schools. As a result, since the holiday for the end of the fast of Ramadan in April our young men's Bible class has never properly got going again.

Hastari of Triwung came round to see me one afternoon. He wanted to get clear the distinction between Zebedee and Zachariah, between John the Baptist and the Apostle John, and to make sure whether or not Paul was one of the Twelve. Although almost entirely un-educated, he is reading the Bible and pressing on to know the Lord in a way the people brought up as Christians do not. We called on the wife of a local official who is a Madurese; she has a Christian back-ground, but has left the gospel far behind her; however, she seemed glad to talk and welcomed us warmly to her home. In the early evening we both visited Rufus and his family at Ringit. He apologised that due to sheer pressure of work he has recently come to us so rarely. They have no servant now which makes life heavy for Mrs Rufus as their children are still small and they have many guests. Perhaps in these days they need to offer rather more money and give some regular time off, which seems to be a new idea in these parts. We prayed and discussed the Lord's work together and later he interpreted for me at the Weekly Bible School, to which twenty-nine people came. It always makes a difference to have Rufus there; he speaks with such freshness and glow and has an apparently perfect sense of what is fitting. Mawardi's girls now regularly form a choir on these occasions. Seen from the road the meeting looks quite enticing, two strong lamps showing up the company packed on the verandah, so that no one can attend in secret.

It now looks as though June 22nd is to witness a climax in the progress of the gospel in the Gondang-Segaran area. About forty persons are to be baptised and the two naval men will humble themselves to swell the number. Faral will come from the city for the occasion. Several hundreds are expected to attend and so the sickle will be put in and Rufus' labours there over the past eighteen months produce their astonishing harvest.

On Sunday *June 8th* I was out with Rufus and Mawardi for sixteen solid hours, from 8 a.m. till midnight (an early close for once!). We took with us the two naval fellows and a middle-aged man from the city called Rubani. Our assignment was first Gondang and then Segaran. The meeting at Gondang was to be at 9 a.m. and it was the very first time that the group of people now believing in Christ had ever convened on Sunday morning rather than at night. It was thus their first experience of what might be called a church service and in every way it was a great occasion. About forty came, all in their best clothes and with an air of great expectation and joy. In the depths of the country there is no unseemly hurry, so the service actually began at 11 a.m. and lasted two and a half hours. Rufus put me up to speak first, as he is inclined to do these days, then followed Rubani, who is an ordained man, then Rufus himself, and we all enjoyed much liberty in addressing the company so recently come out of darkness into the marvellous light of Christ.

The importance of the new man, Rubani, is that he may become the resident pastor of the large and scattered flock to the east of Sabrang who owe their Christian faith to Rufus. It seems to be between Rubani and the young theological student, Tilosa of Karangan. Rubani has quite often been in Sabrang district these past weeks, preaching and helping in the new churches, and we like what we have seen of him. He is a quiet man, rising with a smiling face and an open Testament, and his one idea is just to expound God's Word, which he does with considerable skill. He can quote many Scriptures, which is a rare feat, and he is good with chalk on a blackboard. His gift is obviously that of teaching and he appeals to me as just the right kind of man to follow up the great break-through. I spoke on the Holy Spirit in John 14, Rufus on Matthew 24:14, "This gospel of the kingdom shall be preached in all the world for a witness unto all nations, and then shall the end come", and Rubani on the last three verses of Matthew's gospel. We sold a number of New Testaments and Bibles. Some might hold that one should not do that on Sunday, but we are never there on other days of the week. After profitable visits in three homes we drove down the mountain to Segaran and pulled up outside Wirojo's house. The meeting had been fixed for 3 p.m. but it did not begin till 8. Wirojo welcomed us with great warmth; he is a very gracious man and thrilled at what God is doing all around him. "Before I was in the least interested in the gospel," he said to me, "that young fellow over there got hold of a Bible in the city. He bought it just as a history book and could not understand it at all, but as soon as we started having meetings here he came along and was well prepared to receive the gospel." Sumantri, the man from the outer islands, is in some respects the real leader of the group in Segaran; having seen in his youth how a Christian church should be run he has already organised a choir and a Sunday school. Both he and Wirojo are diligent teachers of the backward. A sewing class for girls was in progress as we entered and at the same table Sumantri was busy with two boys over exercise books and inkpots.

With so long to wait we took the opportunity of strolling about Segaran and visiting people in their homes. In so doing we caused quite a sensation, partly through the lovely uniforms of the naval men, partly because of my immense height. We called on the head of the village, an elderly man who seemed to me to receive us rather coldly, though Rufus did not quite agree with me. "Yes," he laughed, "I was told that a Dutchman had come, and come to get the land back from us too!" This good joke was enjoyed by all, but it is the universal impression of the uninformed. In this part of Java, which is plantation country, the land was formerly owned by Dutch firms; then in the independence struggle the local people simply took it over, without having formal deeds; thus the sight of a white face suggests that an agent of the ousted foreigners is nosing around to see who has occupation of what he regards as his own property.

Rufus would not translate into Indonesian for me the rest of what the head of the village said. The meeting lasted from 8 till 11.30 p.m. and the three of us preached again, but I was too tired to get my message over effectively, largely because most of the conversations are in Javanese, which I do not understand, so that such a day constitutes a severe physical ordeal no matter how great the privilege of being present.

It took me several days to recover from this affair and Dr Billy Graham's manuscript lags behind schedule as a result. A cable from Mr Steed was rapidly followed by the arrival on a day's visit of another member of the C.I.M. whose usual field of service is Borneo. I took him out to Barek after dark, when we were less conspicuous, and at 11 p.m. we were still sitting in Chamim's home as Rufus rode up on his scooter, clad in a windbreaker and a peaked cap—quite a delightful picture. We always enjoy greatly the rare occasions when we can help some Christian from the outside world to get his eyes on this remarkable movement of the Spirit of God and to meet the men who have been saved out of Islam, but it is extraordinarily difficult to do it without risking some harm to the work of God. Two white men together are a suspicious and unwelcome sight these days. They must surely be up to something, hatching something, collecting information of some sort! Our visitor took photos in the city and we were glad he survived this rashness, which we succeeded in avoiding in Sabrang. Photographs are of course invaluable when shown years afterwards to Christians and churches at home, but it was always my fixed principle to give priority to the healthy progress of the gospel in the east, and in my judgement this usually meant no photography.

Hastari, a man as active as any in the Lord's work, has often been here lately. He has contacts at Gerbo, the largest place in this whole area, where we are all praying and plotting for an entry for the Word of God. Most weeks he brings a Gerbo lad to the Bible School here and this boy's family are now interested in the gospel as well. This week, however, we have reluctantly decided to cancel the Bible School, as the whole region is much disturbed in mind by our very first air-raid practice, for which all lights must be extinguished. It would be most inadvisable for twenty-five people to be marooned in pitch darkness in our home for an undetermined length of time.

On the night of *June 14th* I called on Rufus and found Susilo there, a rare treat, for these gifted fishers of men fish best independently. We exchanged news and prayed till 10 p.m. Susilo abates not his zeal and many nibble at the message. There is excellent concentraton on the Gondang area in preparation for the baptisms on June 22nd. Rubani is living there for ten days final, intensive, personal ministry. Rufus is ever on his scooter to water the seed. As I sat in the dim light of Rufus' little room, watching the faces of these two men, God's chosen apostles, I would not have changed places with anyone in all the world.

On Sunday morning, *June 15th*, I was the preacher at Barek, my first formal invitation there without Rufus, probably a result of the news that I am to be officially invited to work with the East Java Church. Susilo translated my Indonesian into Javanese; I spoke on the foundation of the church at Philippi. Barek village, which has a population of 4000 souls, is set in the most magnificent scenery. We had a good time and at the end the people continued singing without weariness. The two naval men accompanied me and returned to spend the rest of the day with us, looking most impressive.

And now for three solid days I have immersed myself in the closing chapters of Dr Graham's *Peace with God*, determined to finish this happy but onerous task. I kept my door shut and came within sight of the end, but this sort of thing does not advance local work and I must get clear of it quickly.

June 17th. Natmina, the mother of the boy who ran away, wants to be baptised at Gondang on June 22nd. She came round to talk to Jess and then asked me to drive her over to Ringit to see Rufus. We picked up her sister on the way, a rather distinguished-looking woman. Rufus was at home with his family and rose splendidly to the occasion. We sat round his humble table and the sisters never took their eyes off him. He plunged straight into the gospel and I marvelled again at his freshness, joy in Christ, victorious spirit, and great attractiveness. He stood up and went right through the "Sinner's Dream" posters and the set of "Human Heart" posters for the two ladies, who nodded and said, "Yes, yes", at almost every sentence. Mrs Rufus brought out tea and cakes. All I had to do was to sit in silence praying and later drive them home.

June 21st. My labours on Billy Graham are over at last. I made about 150 minor corrections in the Indonesian manuscript and in addition explained in a document of twenty typed pages no less than 369 important failures to give the sense of the original English.

So the hour of baptisms at Gondang draws near and our holiday is but ten days beyond it. We are in good health, though late nights have wrecked my ability to sleep well.

CHAPTER 13

THE BRIDGEHEAD IS WIDENED

FOR the second week running we were compelled to cancel the Weekly Bible School because of air-raid practices which follow one another thick and fast and keep us lying in bed in inky darkness in the evenings. It would certainly never do to have the house filled with guests at such times, for they are very protracted. It seems rather sad, but we have to adapt ourselves to what it is practicable and wise to do. During the morning I drove round the countryside in the Mayflower to let people know that there would be no meeting at night. I found Mrs Susilo in bed with an infected tooth and prayed with her. I also called on a Chinese family who have recently come regularly. They hail from Middle Java and are Pentecostalists, as are most Chinese believers in this country district where the Chinese Christian Church does not exist.

One whom we call the Samaritan woman has started coming to Jess to learn to read. For some time she has regularly attended the Women's Meeting and is an alert and aggressive person. We feel that the Lord is working in her heart. Each week there are reading classes before the women's meeting and Jess is finding it useful to follow this up by reading with women in their own homes. We called on a rough and simple woman in a densely crowded suburb of Sabrang. She is wholly immobilised by arthritis, but after Rufus prayed for her she became interested in the gospel and seemed to be healed. She worked for Mrs Rufus for a time but probably a small house with six children was too much for her and she did not stand it for long. Although bitter and sceptical at times, she received us well.

And so we came to *June 22nd.* In the morning I preached for the second Sunday running at Barek, with Susilo translating. There is a warm spirit there, but they need more teaching and spiritual fellowship than they have had. A charming little boy of ten from a broken home is Susilo's constant companion now he has no son of his own. The child often visits him and likes to hear about the gospel, so Susilo puts him on the back of his scooter and carries him off to meetings. Indeed Susilo expands on many fronts and is always bubbling over with new information, new contacts, and new verses which he is enjoying himself and teaching to others. A school-teacher, a rather striking girl, lodges in his home and is well on the way to personal faith in Christ.

In the afternoon we drove up to Gondang for the great occasion, the first baptisms. There were actually thirteen souls in the little Mayflower: Jess, Loti, Mrs Rufus, Mrs Suwarso (now, to her astonishment, our excellent friend and fellow-worker) and seven children. A hundred and forty people packed into the schoolroom hard by the house of headmaster Tias, adorned with sixteen flags and eight Christian Witness Press posters. Rufus opened the proceedings and then the robed assistant pastor from the city did the actual baptisms by threefold sprinkling with great solemnity. Twenty-five people were baptised. Twelve of these were from near-by Segaran, where everything began with Susilo's visit on March 17th, eight were from Gondang, two from Jess' women's meeting, and three were naval men from Middle Java temporarily stationed in the district. It was a most memorable day, not least when such a community leader as Wirojo removed his black hat and knelt with his wife to acknowledge himself a disciple and servant of Jesus Christ. They and other couples involved then had their marriages sanctified before the Lord, taking Christian vows of mutual faithfulness. To have twenty local people baptised in Gondang is revolutionary indeed; it forms at once a precedent and also a nucleus to which others can later be added, for many more are truly believing in their hearts. No children were accepted for baptism on this first occasion. The brethren were filled with joy and the whole village flooded with Christians who had come from the city and the south coast in lorries for the function. Rufus and Susilo—who have been the instruments God has used from start to finish—were most inconspicuous, as the proceedings were in the hands of the city church, of which work in the Sabrang area is now officially a branch. Indeed one heard a criticism on this score, for the city visitors, including the pastor who baptised them, are unknown strangers to the Gondang and Segaran believers, who would much rather have been baptised by Rufus himself. Rufus would also have seized the opportunity to give a spiritual message calculated to edify those about to be baptised, whereas in fact the ceremony itself swamped all other considerations. These, however, are inevitable problems involved in the fusing of an old church with a new movement of the Spirit.

Next day, *June 23rd*, I drove with Rufus thirty miles west right out of our normal area to a big Christian village where 3000 people have been 99 per cent. Christian since 1875. We went on the invitation of Faral, partly (I suspect) to allow the pastor there to get a look at me in view of the proposal that the East Java Church should invite us into official co-operation. This Christian village lies in the Garden of Eden on the slopes of a huge volcano at 1500 feet. Its eight parts straggle over four square miles of matchless country tilted sharply off the wall of the volcano and deeply serrated by torrents rushing down it. In the rainy season I could never have got the Mayflower there, but it has been bone dry for weeks. We crashed and banged our way over a broken road and then wound along a grassy track with glorious dark-green coffee bushes brushing the car on either side. Then we crawled down a bumpy, unsurfaced pathway through terraced ricefields which gradually became precipitous. Never did I dream of taking a car down such inclines and I repeatedly had to ask my passengers to dismount. On reaching the pastor's house there was plenty of time to chat in his tall, airy, clean, quiet rooms, until we moved rapidly out into the garden as a strong earth-tremor rattled the tiles and shook the pillars, carved seventy years ago from jungle trees. He fed us often and well, and I slept in a spotless little room. Faral and other leaders of the city church, including a massive man who as a Muslim had made the pilgrimage to Mecca, were present and it was a splendid opportunity for me to meet and talk with these influential figures. At night there was a business meeting in the church, which can hold 700. It was all in Javanese, but the ordeal of just sitting there was well worth it, for at 10 p.m. Faral gave me the floor and I preached and testified for twenty-five minutes. Talk went on till 2 a.m., when there was a midnight feast and much rejoicing.

Next morning the local pastor took me all over the village, or rather one should say up and down it. "Do you mind if we go in the car," he said, "as everyone will think you are a Dutchman? Perhaps you remember the affair we had here. It got to the United Nations. The Dutch burnt the hospital and shot nine village leaders. I'll show you their graves."

When at last we left, Faral was in leisurely mood, enjoying the country and brief liberty from city life and business affairs. We stopped at a coffee factory employing 500 workers and the manager entertained us, a tall, grey widower, not a Christian. He took us to a Christian home where I sought to encourage in the faith the woman who brought us coffee, aiming my words also at the manager, from whom we parted with much warmth. We drove slowly through a village in which a local prophet resides who is visited annually by thousands of people. He has been in prison twice, but his fame has proved so profitable that he has been able to instal an electric light plant for the village. We saw him at the door of his large, bizarre house—a tall, authoritative, rather forbidding figure. Faral then decided that since we were not far from a famous pilgrimage mountain which none of us had ever visited this was a perfect opportunity to do so. The road proved longer and more rugged than we had expected and some of the ascents were frighteningly steep. We passed up and up over tier upon tier of mountain, with hordes of people everywhere, until we came to the pilgrim centre at 3500 feet. Even at noon on a Tuesday morning there were fifty big cars parked under the doubtful supervision of a money-hungry rabble. Stone steps led on up for another half hour, making it a modernised version of the pilgrims' way to some hilltop temple in China. Chinese were on every hand. At the top, humanity was packed together in an astonishing manner. There were several large bungalow hotels consisting of one huge room each, with Chinese lying all over the whole area alongside their piles of baggage. We passed many restaurants, stalls, and shrines, up to the tomb of a Javanese worthy and his Chinese wife, where it was necessary to remove your shoes. One rarely sees idolatry in Muslim

Java. I found the place repellent and the type of Chinese frequenting it unattractive and utterly unlike the clean Chinese Christians of the city and of Surabaja—from which places these no doubt largely came. Faral was determined to hear me speak Chinese, so he accosted a complete stranger, ascertained that he could speak Mandarin, called me over, and sat down to listen. The man proved to be the owner of a radio shop in Djakarta, off on a grand tour with his family. His whole party gathered round and I had a good chance to expound to them the way of salvation through faith in Jesus Christ, contrasting it with the folly of the idolatry around us. One of the women had had some Christian contacts but the rest of them seemed utterly raw: they listened gladly but were speechless, and so departed. Faral sat watching my face and theirs throughout and of course the immediate significance of the whole trip was the chance it gave for closer friendship with him in view of the invitation we are to receive from his church.

June 27th. We heard today the amazing news that the long negotiations for the loan by the C.I.M. of a doctor to the Salvation Army hospital in Sabrang have been crowned with success. Finding that nothing was known at the hospital about his visa having been granted, Jess got the captain in charge over to our house and told her privately. She flatly denied that it could possibly be true, but it is. The series of Weekly Bible Schools is now to be discontinued for a period of six weeks, during part of which we shall be on holiday. There were thirty-one at the nineteenth and last meeting and we have now finished the First Epistle of Paul to the Corinthians up to chapter ten. Average attendance on these nineteen occasions has been twenty-three, which we feel to be most encouraging as the weather has often been bad, homes are widely scattered, and the studies have been quite hard.

On *June 29th* I preached in Surabaja all day, my sleep badly affected by close work on *Peace with God* and late nights with Rufus. I returned in time to preach for Pastor Meng in the Bible College at a Chinese Christian Youth Conference in progress there. Two hundred were present and I greatly admired Pastor Meng for carrying through so large a venture without any specially attractive outside speakers. Driving home to Sabrang in very heavy rain a piece of iron six inches long somehow passed right through a tyre and ripped the inner tube to pieces; I was drenched to the skin changing a wheel on such a night.

Next day, *July 1st*, we drove back to the city and on up to the Hotel of Peace, whose seclusion I badly needed. However, seclusion was not easily attained, for the East Java Church had elected to hold a conference in the same hotel and as soon as we arrived we were greeted by Rufus, Susilo, and many other friends. Already Susilo is recognised by many pastors as a new figure with which they must reckon. He is so capable in Scripture quotation that they have nicknamed him "Daddy Verse". Maybe Rufus will prove in the long run not to be the apostle at all but merely his forerunner. At conferences such as this Rufus does not stand out in any way, for he is no debater and is outclassed by other sharper wits and better stored brains, but Susilo revelled in it all and sat up till 3 a.m. with Sutikno, our old friend from Madura Island, trying to commend to him his ideas about evangelism and the role of the Christian Church in modern Indonesia. His eccentricity causes general entertainment, revealed in the announcement, "Those who wish to go to bed and sleep are now free to do so; those who don't should go to Daddy Verse's room."

At length peace did descend. We walked on the mountains, basked in the sunshine (mitigated at that altitude), read, wrote, and idled. On the Wednesday night there was a meeting in the hotel, which serves also as the local Christian church, at which I preached from Ephesians 1: 13. The man at the organ had turned to Christ from Islam two years previously. The manager is a stalwart believer, but the main spokesman is his wife. When she married him she was a strong opponent of the gospel, but she was eventually converted through attending a representation of the Christmas story in the Chinese Christian Church in the city in 1951. This is most unusual, for the linguistic and cultural barrier between the Chinese and the Javanese is such that the former are not normally able to be of spiritual help to the latter. As she watched the tableaux she told us that an angel appeared to her and stroked her brow. The incident was quite decisive in her experience and she has for years been an ardent Christian. At the close of the conference in the hotel she and

o

the manager were as a courtesy asked to come in and meet the
assembled pastors and church leaders. They sat at a table with
flowers on it for the introductions, after which it was not the
husband but the wife who rose and delivered a stirring address
to the gentlemen, a sight unique in my experience in Java.
After being married for eight years they have just had their first
child.

As we strolled around on the well-worked and well-populated
hillsides we found the animosities of last January largely melted
away; on all sides we were greeted with smiles and a cheerful curiosity about our affairs. The scenery around the hotel is an unending
delight, but I think we have benefited most after the storm of life
in Sabrang just from moving easy chairs on to the terrace and brow-
sing there with the sun beating down through the crisp, chilly air,
a stream below us deadening all other sounds, a deserted village
farmyard to our left, towering cultivated hillsides to the right, a
jungle-covered volcanic peak ahead, and no sense of pressure or
responsibility.

On our return journey to Sabrang we carried out a little experiment. It is under twenty miles from the city and in itself has a
population of only 7000. However, I estimate that the road between
the two serves about 100,000 people and as we drove along it we
decided to count the side-turnings, ignoring paths and tracks which
cars and carts could not negotiate. The total was 150. We were
delighted to be back home again and found the hospital in great stir
preparing for the coming of the Doctor, for there has been none
resident there for sixteen years, although before that there were
three. Shortly after we arrived an old man called on us from a
Christian village far to the east. I had never seen him before. He was
full of fervour, longing for widespread revival in the East Java
Church. It was thrilling to find that such figures do exist. He had
served the Lord on Bali Island and is now praying that he may soon
depart in peace from this world, having told his people to bury him
in the garden with no expensive ceremonies.

On *July 26th* Rufus arrived back in Sabrang from an extensive
trip right outside our area to the village where he was formerly
pastor, the one which put him in prison. He had been most cordially

received, even by those who were then his enemies, and they had urged him to return to them, bringing me with him. By nightfall we were under way, Rufus and myself in the front of the Mayflower, Mrs Rufus and three of their children in the back. We drove for three hours on a main highway, quietened by darkness, and sailed late through a big town, under the grim walls of the prison, when Rufus nudged me and said with a smile, "That was my school". Then for several miles we followed an unsurfaced village road, raising billows of dust which caught us up if we paused at any of the numerous intersections. We then ran into the long avenues of the place which was our destination, a village of 2000 people, one-quarter Christian, fruit of some evangelistic outburst back in the last century. The young pastor started up in delighted surprise as we nosed our way between the flowerpots on his drive. Towards midnight we paid a courtesy call on the head of the village. About a thousand people were besieging his house as there was an annual theatrical display in progress on the broad verandah. Then we were divided up between various homes, I myself in a beautiful, big, stone establishment in which I have a nice room, austerely furnished. By covering my head with the quilt I succeeded in gaining a partial conquest over the mosquitoes and next morning we all attended the village church, where hundreds of people, quiet, smart, and reverent, were mightily surprised to see "a Dutchman" again after a lapse of seventeen years. After the pastor's sermon and the benediction, Rufus and I were given the floor. It was a happy time and easy, in the sense that every ear was pricked to catch what "the Dutchman" would say! Outside in the blazing sunshine they pounced on the Bibles and hymnbooks we had brought for sale and in a few minutes the stock was exhausted.

After a long sleep in the afternoon we both spoke again at night at an evangelistic meeting to which we drove through interminable avenues of houses, blanketed in their mantle of tropical trees. We drew up at a big, rambling farmhouse I knew not where, inside and around which there were packed about 300 Muslims. It was the home of the man primarily responsible for Rufus' imprisonment and this was a reconciliation de luxe. He and his wife received me most warmly and gave me a big bedroom as a refuge. I noticed that Rufus sat long with the couple in earnest conversation, straightening out the sorrows of the past. Then we had a substantial meal while the people waited, and great was the stir and anticipation when at last we moved out to the front room where they were packed in every corner. Rufus spoke to them vigorously for eighty minutes, warm, clear, and inviting, magnetic in his appeal to Christ. I followed him on "the seven sons of Sceva" though it was not too easy for me as the hour was already very late, refreshments were being handed round the tight-packed company while I spoke, and a strong light hung too close to my face. Yet their response was delightful: they hung on every word—the men in serried ranks on the benches, the women on mats laid all along the walls, children and babies fast asleep everywhere. There were two other pastors present, who had come specially to see one of Rufus' now famed evangelistic evenings, for there tends to be apprehension in the churches that aggressive witness will arouse antagonism towards Christian communities. But there is no need for such fears, for Rufus is the embodiment of the apostle's advice in 2 Timothy 2, "The servant of the Lord must not strive, but be gentle unto all men, apt to teach, patient, in meekness instructing those that oppose themselves, if God peradventure will give them repentance to the acknowledging of the truth, and that they may recover themselves out of the snare of the devil, who are taken captive by him at his will."

We got to bed in our respective houses at 1 a.m. The village looked superb at dead of night, so quiet, so luxuriant, the full moon pouring down through the heads of the coconut palms on to the homes and gardens embowered in richly productive land. Next morning Rufus and his wife continued their orgy of visiting and the sorrows of the past were wiped clean away and buried with Christ. We extracted ourselves at 10 a.m. and drove for two hours through burning heat and continuously occupied country to Mrs Rufus' old home in a Christian village of 3000 souls. Here lives still her bent and aged mother in great simplicity, the old farm shrouded in trees and bushes. It is an abode of the very humblest kind one sees in this marvellous land—earth floor, bamboo walls, just the tiles for ceiling, and scarce a window to be found. I am writing these words there now, sitting on the edge of a rickety four-poster bed innocent of any bedding, though they have put a lace cloth on the little table for my benefit and added a bottle of eau-de-Cologne. For the long trip back to Sabrang I was faced, as often, by the problem of how many people to permit in the Mayflower. When one has received hospitality it is virtually impossible to refuse a free ride to members of the family, even if the car does suffer. As a result there were ten persons in her for the next four hours and on getting back to Sabrang I found Mr Rockness, one of the C.I.M. directors, had arrived from Singapore.

Next day I took the visitor to Segaran with Rufus and Mawardi, where we spent a long and memorable evening with Mr and Mrs Wirojo and Sumantri, all of them rejoicing in the Lord and in the amazing opportunities for Christian service which they are finding. They asked Mr Rockness to give them a message by interpretation. We sang in Indonesian, "What a Friend we have in Jesus", which was already written up on the blackboard in Wirojo's home when we arrived. He and his wife have remodelled the back quarters, moved in there, and given the front part of the house to be the Christian Church in Segaran. He and Sumantri are busy with classes for young adults and have learnt Susilo's way of weaving Christian witness in with their public service. Sumantri had just come back from a class for thirty-six young adults in a neighbouring village; they have asked him always to open the class with prayer and to include every time some teaching about the Lord. Wirojo has a gramophone which they use for playing gospel records. It went wrong so he gave it to a mechanic to repair. After putting it in order the man tried out some records and he and his family were at once struck by the message they heard, so that they are now attending meetings. These Segaran believers are enjoying the bloom of first love and zeal for Christ, and they glow with heart-warming joy.

For Mr Rockness' second day with us Rufus planned two meetings. The first was at Barek, a brief but delightful time, at which he spoke in English and I interpreted into Indonesian. Then we went on, seven heavy men in the car, back to Segaran. This time Wirojo's house was packed with people inside and out. Rufus started off in his usual bright manner, intending later to call upon me and then upon Mr Rockness. He had preached vigorously for about an hour and had delivered the main part of his message when I observed through the open door that a rather forbidding-looking person was staring in at him. He was a young man, but dressed in an authoritative manner. Suddenly he strode straight into the room and was alongside Rufus before the latter had even seen him. He demanded to see Rufus' papers and I was interested to note that he had them all in his pocket and at once laid them out on the table. There was complete and rather tragic silence as the man examined them with a critical eye. "And where is your permit for this meeting tonight?" he demanded sternly. Many of the men in the audience rose and began to get out of the room at the back. Already it was obvious that we were in trouble. Rufus stood his ground and explained to the man that we had had many meetings in the house and nobody had ever suggested that we needed a permit for each one. The man was not at all impressed by this explanation and he began to cast his eye around the room. Had he been a Westerner I suppose he would have pointed straight at Mr Rockness and said, "Who are you and what are you doing here?" But being a polite oriental he began to indicate man after man saying, "This man I know, this man I know, this man I know, this man I don't know [Mr Rockness], this man I know, this man I know [me]." Then he announced, "The meeting is closed" and walked out. It was very sad and yet transmuted at once with a certain joy. Rufus wound up in dignity with singing and prayer, and refreshments were served to the twenty-five people who still remained. I moved here and there about the room, chatting with different people, and found no alarm at all about the outcome of the interruption. In fact the brethren were elated, four new men announced that they wished to believe, and books sold fast. Chamim came over to me with his New Testament open and pointed to the verse, "I came not to send peace but a sword". The general feeling, which proved in the outcome to be quite correct, was that the man's superior was temporarily absent and that he became alarmed at the presence of an unidentified

European in the district and acted unilaterally, fearing that otherwise he might be blamed for inaction; they prophesied that he would get into trouble next day for what he had done. There was satisfaction that Rufus had practically completed his message, but real regret that they had been deprived of the chance of hearing Mr Rockness. We stayed with them for a long time, parted with much affection, and got to Sabrang again at 1.30 a.m.

On *August 11th* we entered upon the last year of our service here. I had a long, leisurely talk with Rufus, still unchanged, full of a mature joy, just back from another long trip during which five churches had asked for visits from "the Sabrang team". Far out in the country, halting at the roadside on his scooter, he met a man prepared by the Lord and insisted that he must turn to Christ there and then. We also called on Susilo, who was bubbling over with news and encouragement. The whole work is on the move. And Dr. Rupert Clarke has arrived with his wife, Jeannette, both old friends of ours and seasoned warriors. They seem just made to measure, moving easily and happily into position. Surely it takes time to make a real missionary! And Dr Billy Graham's *Peace with God* is through to the printer with my 369 corrections all evaluated and in many cases endorsed and incorporated into the text with zeal by a Batak Christian, who did the work mostly at sea between Djakarta and Hongkong.

The Doctor and Jeannette reached Sabrang eighteen months to the day after our own arrival. Their home is about half a mile away, but of course they spend much of their time at the hospital, which is within a hundred yards of No. 122. Independence Day, *August 17th*, is very close so this is not the time to get meetings restarted. For the moment there is a pause. Mrs Rufus is in hospital and Rufus tied down with his children at home. I have devoted two days to concocting language examinations for the Mission in Indonesian. One evening I called on Mawardi. He was not long back from his ricefields at the foot of the Southern Mountains, sitting barefoot and in shorts at a table with the New Testament open at 2 Peter 2 and several notebooks around it; it was interesting to me to catch him at such a task.

Mrs Rufus has been quite ill in hospital and each day at 4 p.m.

I collect Rufus and their six children in the car and bring them from Ringit to see her; the drive only takes about six minutes. Before returning they all congregate in our home. She has witnessed to the other women in the ward, with the result that the patients asked if Rufus would come and preach to them. So last night he went, taking me with him. There were fourteen women present. He spoke quietly and winsomely to them, and I followed on. I then had the great joy of introducing Rufus to the Doctor and acting as interpreter between them.

On *August 16th* I was out for four hours with Mr and Mrs Susilo in a country town west of here where there has as yet been no movement of the Spirit of God. In the first home to which we went the father was the local medical man, born in a Christian village. We spent two hours with him, his wife, his mother-in-law, his eight daughters, and his one lone son, chatting about the gospel and playing the gramophone records, all twelve of them following closely. We went next to the home of an elderly Muslim named Rifai, a wealthy man whose wife died some years ago. Recently he married a girl from a Christian village. Their place was beautifully furnished and he received us warmly. I felt that his wife had some real spiritual understanding and she obviously longs for her husband's conversion. We testified about Christ, preached to them, and played gospel records. A monthly meeting for the "Christians" in the district is held there, so although the householder is a Muslim it approximates to being the local church. In his presence the wife suggested that her husband had a heart of stone, so Susilo first quoted and then found for her Ezekiel 36: 26, "A new heart also will I give you, and a new spirit will I put within you; and I will take away the stony heart out of your flesh, and I will give you a heart of flesh."

On Independence Day, *August 17th*, Rufus preached in the Sabrang church at 7 a.m. and at 9 I was one of several thousand people who attended the public ceremony on the local sports ground. In the afternoon we drove with Rufus and Mawardi to Barek for an unusual meeting, the setting apart of sixteen men and one woman as leaders of the country churches called into existence by Rufus' ministry.

August 20th. I write now at the close of a Tent Campaign at Segaran, struggling to recover from this amazing experience, the more remarkable because the whole work there only began with Susilo's visit to Wirojo's home on March 17th and in view of the trouble we ran into the night Rufus was stopped as he preached. I discovered that a Tent Campaign here is not quite what we would understand by the term. Forty Christians from all over East Java descended on the responsive village and held a conference on evangelism in a bamboo tent erected on a wind-swept hilltop. We had the hours of daylight to ourselves, but at night the local people swarmed around us. The purpose of the campaign, or conference, was (1) to encourage the new village believers by fellowship with other Christians, (2) to stimulate these other Christians by fellowship with the newly converted, (3) to swing into the gospel as large a section of Segaran as possible. The leader was a gaunt old pensioned evangelist, the co-leader was Rufus, but the life and soul of the party was Susilo.

The first night it was necessary for me to drive on to Trawas to report to police headquarters. As I came back the lights on the hilltop were visible far away across the rolling, teeming, unbelievably beautiful mountainsides, and the loudspeaker carried Susilo's voice for many miles. They asked me to give a testimony, but my own role was a very minor one, for Rufus was not in charge and officially I have not yet any connection with the East Java Church, being merely a private intruder. One day there was a three-hour Bible study on the Book of Jonah, when each of four study groups thrashed out the answers to questions allotted to it on one chapter. At the end the whole book, all the questions, and all the answers were read out! With minor exceptions the entire three days were conducted in Javanese, which was no small ordeal for me, sitting in the circle on straw in the chairless tent. There was another missionary present, Mr Larp, a very learned man, whose bearing and behaviour were excellent. I admired him for his friendliness (Rufus not only shook his hand but put his arm round him in welcome), his humility, the easy way he fitted in, and his courage in bathing in the open stream with everybody else. But what he said in the very long talk he delivered seemed to me both regrettable and unsuitable—not only excessively professorial but most sociological, psychological, and most unwisely political as well. I marvelled that anyone so intelligent and experienced should so gravely misjudge the need and the times.

The roll of events cut the agenda to ribbons. One night yet another missionary from far hence sailed in in an enormous car with film-strips and four assistants. Hundreds of the local inhabitants crammed in and around the tent in heavy rain to see the fun. Rufus became marooned in the middle of the squatting throng and preached vigorously, turning slowly round and round as he did so, a grand and apostolic sight! The pictures proved to be only of mediocre quality, but the missionary's commentary was first class, translated into Javanese by Rufus. "Wisdom is justified of all her children."

A car is useful at a conference and by day and night I drove the mountain roads on various errands, sleeping at home in Sabrang each night. Two great ladies from the city were present. "I am a Javanese," said one to me in English, "but as a babe I learnt to cry in Dutch." Seeking a way of escape from bathing in the local stream in full view of the general public, the noble ladies got me to drive them to the lovely home of a widow in Gerbo, where I too was glad enough to profit from her bathroom. The incident, which seemed so trivial at the time, was to have far-reaching effects in the establishment of permanent Christian witness in Gerbo, which is the biggest place in the whole Sabrang area. But for the most part I was in Segaran, where the conference members split up into small groups for intensive visiting. There is something wonderful about being known and accepted in such a far-away corner of the oriental world. I spent an hour alone with two men and two women in a farm where Rufus and I have often been, and found them not at all averse to hearing more about the kingdom of God.

On the last night of the Tent Campaign, Susilo arrived on his scooter after a day's absence from his office in Sabrang. He and I fell in with a hundred schoolchildren and had an entertaining time giving them Christian tracts. Then we joined up with two men from a Christian village on the south coast and strolled down a long avenue looking for some opportunity of further service. "If a man squats at his door and smiles," said Susilo, "it implies that he is open to the gospel, for otherwise he would avoid us." As we passed one door a turbaned man, prematurely grey, stripped to the waist, called us into his home and donned a shirt in our honour. This simple act was to prove another turning-point in the spread of the gospel. The farm was a large, airy place. There were several people in it and we sat down at a long table. Susilo at once asked his wife to take the lady of the house off to the bed in the corner and talk to her there, while the men stayed with us. For the next hour the two conversations ran simultaneously. Rufus joined us, but it was Susilo as usual who dominated the scene. Later he asked if I would like to add something, so I spoke from Matthew 11:27-29. Finally Susilo drew the old man aside into a dark corner of the room and squatted there whispering with him. I felt that both the man and his wife were ready and waiting for some messenger from heaven, and so it seems to be again and again in this land. At the time I did not know that this was Daddy Ren, the local wise man, to whom many people on the hills all around us looked as a leader.

It was delightful to notice the impression made on the visiting Christians by the example of Susilo and Rufus and the fruit of their work. The possibility that a Muslim could be converted, new churches brought into being, and laymen used by God, opened up a new world to them and one could see man after man catch the vision and begin to exercise his own spiritual gift. The bridgehead is being widened almost beyond belief and I am astonished how many men are becoming able to preach Christ. "We witness a development of amateurism," said Mr Larp.

Night fell, threatening rain, and the conference gathered at the historic home of Wirojo. A lorry arrived carrying twenty-five men from Gondang, almost to a man converts of 1958, and joyful was the meeting under the stars in the courtyard, warmest handshakes all round. The house began to fill up with women, the yard with men, the road with watchers. And then thirty bright-eyed village boys, eleven to fourteen years old, gay and eager, spoiling for some fun, washed and clad in coloured sarongs, invaded the conference. In a trice Susilo cast off his shoes and had them squatting

round him in a circle, roaring choruses. For half an hour hundreds
of people watched as he held them with singing, the gospel message,
and his scintillating personality and ability. A bearded man from a
Christian village, magnificent as Abraham, squatted with him in
the ring, and two young men made up the informal team, which
showed to me clearly enough that there is man-power, talent, and
spiritual gift in the old East Java Church to cope with these days
of mounting opportunity.

By this time I know not how many hundreds of people had
assembled. The old evangelist stood outside the house under a lamp
and with the blunt authority of age preached Christ to them.
Then he called on the bearded man, who cut a very striking figure
in a white suit, with his large head, glorious hair, and full beard,
as with arms extended he offered salvation through the cross of
Christ for half an hour, his voice ringing through the quiet of the
night. Then came Rufus, who still remains the major spiritual power
amongst us and the cause of the Lord's power being manifested in
Susilo and others. Rufus is usually gentle and soft, but on this
occasion he let fly a fiery attack of which I had hardly thought him
capable, while the multitude listened in perfect silence. If Rufus had
been in command he would have called upon me, Mawardi, and
others and we should have continued into the small hours of the
morning, but the old evangelist was tired and he closed the meeting
at the height of opportunity. The Javanese nature being polite and
gracious, Rufus yielded and the crowd outside melted away. The
believers, however, packed into the house, about eighty strong.
Susilo took over, whether by arrangement or accident I could not
say, and told the full story of his visit to Wirojo's home on March
17th, introducing to the visiting Christians from the south coast
villages Wirojo and his wife, the man converted through repairing
the gramophone, and other local characters. All this, interspersed
with prayer and singing carried us past midnight, when we broke
up with joy. Early next morning Rufus and Mawardi were off two
hours by lorry and two hours on foot over the Southern Mountains
down to Karangan on the Indian Ocean, and so the work is
relentlessly driven forwards with a devotion which is truly
marvellous.

August 28th. A schoolboy from a non-Christian home has been to our place a good deal recently. He has shown great interest in gospel records and asked if he could buy all the Indonesian ones we had as there was a gramophone in his home. These records are free but there is a carriage charge of one rupiah per record. A few days later he was back again, saying that his family were using the records a lot and he would like to have all the Javanese and Madurese ones we had. In the end he bought the whole lot, but there is a problem involved in this. A gramophone record costs from fifty to eighty rupiahs here and I do not deny that they probably intend to resell these records they have obtained so cheaply at a handsome profit. The records will go on bearing their testimony to Christ, but it is not always possible to prevent people using them for material gain.

On the night of *August 30th* we attended a kind of garden party at the hospital, which was the Doctor's introduction to local community leaders. Of the latter I found I knew few, for we are of no significance to them. I sat with Rufus, Susilo, and the man who once came by night to ask for money—an event neither of us has ever referred to since. The Doctor's arrival is already a major local event. We learnt that 260,000 people live in the district referred to as Sabrang.

Next day I travelled by train to Surabaja, with an Italian ice-cream merchant! At noon I preached to the reviving Cantonese Church, now 125 strong, on the closing verses of the book of Jude, but I felt dissatisfied, revised the sermon after I had had a good sleep, and had a better time with the great Foochow congregation, full 500 people bursting the church at its seams. After so long in Sabrang I am losing my instinct for the Chinese language, but the Lord seemed to overrule that and the mere sight of so great a congregation of Chinese believers is a thing to live in the memory. The day ended at the British Community Church where the American Consul led the service and I preached from the book of Revelation. I spent the night with the British Consul, who had other guests as well. On these occasions it is now standard for me to be asked to say grace before the meal. Afterwards we sat out in the garden by the Brantas River under lights hung in the trees against the background of the Armenian-style Consulate. During the night the Consul unfortunately suffered what may have been some sort of a stroke, involving temporary loss of memory. Then I returned to lecture on Greek in the Bible College in the city and to represent the College at a conference of theological students from all over Java which was held in the East Java Church. Jess came for me in the car late at night, having entertained Faral and other leaders in my absence and introduced them to the Doctor, whose aid they are most anxious to secure for certain church clinics in the villages. "You are from the Overseas Missionary Fellowship of the China Inland Mission, aren't you?" they said to him. "We want to co-operate with the Overseas Missionary Fellowship."

September 2nd. Yesterday I drove to the Christian village of Kabat on the south coast to look in on the meetings of the city presbytery, by invitation. Susilo, Mawardi, and Mrs Hasan from Lakar came with me, all of them converted through Rufus. As usual at Kabat we got the warmest possible welcome from Pastor Wen and Muljono, the head of the village. There were fifty people for supper and I was able to renew many friendships. Faral, their leader, is exceedingly cordial and delighted at the prospect of closer co-operation with us and with the Doctor. We attended the evening session at which the thirty-two elected delegates of the churches sat at tables in a hollow square behind printed notices of their place of origin, as at the United Nations! The business in hand was the election of delegates from the presbytery to the synod. This took ninety minutes and then, without a scrap of warning, I was asked to address the company. However, I am tolerably used to sitting for hours with drawn sword in case action is required. I spoke to the noble gentlemen on "God is able of these stones to raise up children unto Abraham". Rufus came back to Sabrang with us around midnight, the moon shining gloriously on the mountains as we crashed and bumped up, through, down, and along! Rufus, Susilo, and Mawardi sat together in the back and great was the rejoicing for it appears that another new development is under way. During the Tent Campaign at Segaran it seems that a leading man from a place where there is as yet no church decided that he was the prodigal son and that he must return to the Father. He sold two cows and bought testaments, a gramophone, and gospel records, and on September 5th there is to be an evangelistic meeting at his place. Meanwhile Wirojo and Chamim have gone all out to help and hold this man and his associates, for the day when only Rufus was really on the job has long passed.

When *September 5th* came nothing happened in the new village after all, arrangements not having been clearly agreed upon. As a result Rufus, Rekso, and I went to Segaran and spent two and half hours in conversation with Wirojo and Sumantri. These brethren are sorely tried by the city leaders who insist on probation before baptism and absolutely demand that the Creed and the Lord's Prayer be memorised, which is alarming and repellent to the more rustic and elderly. Among these is Daddy Ren, to whose home I went with Susilo and others during the Tent Campaign. He has shared in Christian witness with Wirojo ever since, but to learn two pages of print by heart and be examined on it by a man from the city is more than he can face. The leaders of the church in the city rarely come to the villages and their sceptical attitude towards men brought to Christ through Rufus is sorely resented. I endeavoured to mollify feelings!

Sunday, *September 7th*, was annual thanksgiving day in the city church, so they cancelled all meetings in the villages and everyone was supposed to go to the city, twenty miles away. This was not at all a good idea, for few are likely to make the effort and it undermines the growing habit of regular church attendance in the countryside.

September 11th. The last two days have been dominated by a youth squash held in our home and attended by sixty-five, lasting from 6 p.m. till 9.30. With the decay of our original Bible class for seventeen-year-olds we are hoping that this will be the start of a new Young People's Meeting, to be held each Sunday afternoon. At noon I left with Rufus, Mawardi, and Rekso for another visit to Kabat, where we dawdled for three hours and then towards dark set off to walk for one and a half hours through the ricefields to that remote corner of the village where formerly the entire adult population came to the Lord's Supper. I found it difficult to keep my footing on the very narrow track, immediately below which a stream was rushing. On arrival below the steep jungle ridge where this place lies we heard a woman singing hymns in the very first farm we reached. Soon the school-house filled up with 150 people and the meeting which followed lasted from 8.30 p.m. till 2 a.m. Pastor Wen opened and then Rufus put Mawardi on. I have never known him do better and he held them for an hour. I spoke next for forty minutes on Jude 20-21. Rufus was brief and in the end both Mawardi and I were asked to speak again. At midnight, the team having had no meal for twelve hours, we were called to the back room for supper while the audience waited. Then old Rekso addressed them till 2 a.m., but I did not wait and slept soundly close by in spite of his bellowing. Nevertheless he goes down quite well in the role of old-style healer-teacher turned Christian. It appears that Allied planes were over Ringit during some unidentified episode in the second world war and the old gentleman stuck to his post ringing the alarm although, it is said, he and his hat were well peppered with machine-gun bullets, which were powerless to hurt him.

Rufus and I shared a room and in the night he awoke with the sensation that his hand was being gripped and pulled up. He sat up, his right arm fully extended; then he drew it slowly down, but felt it was still held. He has had no such sensation before. Our entire stock of New Testaments, hymnbooks, and other literature was sold out in this remote corner of Kabat's far-flung plain. Next morning, which was Sunday, *September 14th*, the village church was crammed with almost the whole able-bodied adult population. Seven babies and two adults were solemnly baptised and then I was asked to preach, followed by Mawardi. Once more it seemed to be a time when people avidly devoured the message.

We left them at last at 2 p.m. for the blazing hot, ninety-minute walk through the shadeless ricefields back to Muljono's home, skirting at first the jungle which rises like a sheer wall from the pathway. Seen from the middle of the plain this Kabat valley is a most glorious place, the people strung out over many miles of richest land. On all hands are lovely mountains, jungle crags, heavily cultivated hillsides, mysterious long vistas into many a side-valley, oceans of coconut palms, oceans of rice.

After a brief respite we climbed into the Mayflower with Pastor Wen and drove up a bumpy road on to a high ridge where we left the car at a forester's home and walked into the jungle. In one hour we came out at a small Christian village of 800 souls within sound of the ocean breakers. On the way the pastor showed us the spot where a tiger, chasing a monkey in an overhanging jungle tree, crashed with it to death on the rocky track below. As the news of our arrival spread the house of the head of the village began to fill with people till there were 250 present. I felt rather knocked out by walking in the sun and rested some time in an inner room. Rufus put Mawardi on to speak first and then, instead of following him himself, gave Rekso the chance. Rekso certainly interests village people very much and he points them to Christ, but his vivid descriptions of his pre-Christian life are so gripping and so amusing that the audience becomes convulsed with mirth and a somewhat theatrical atmosphere is produced. Rufus did not seem quite able to recover the situation, so that the meeting left me with very mixed feelings, fully shared by Rufus, who fears that he must not again give the rustic brethren quite so much scope.

Next morning we walked back for an hour through the jungle and I learnt how a wise tiger catches a monkey. Apparently the tiger stands below a tree up which the monkey tribe climbs, chattering excitedly about him. They vie with one another, racing higher and higher, till one exceeds all and goes beyond the top of the tree altogether, crashing to the earth—and the tiger! We spent over an hour at the forester's house; he sat in tattered shorts and gave us a good hearing as we testified to him in turn. I was not to travel that way again, but apparently his interest continued and at Christmas the Kabat Church held a big celebration in his home.

Back in Kabat we had to ford the river. Seeking a shallower spot I happened upon a deeper one and the Mayflower stuck fast in soft mud and strong current. The others leapt out into thirty inches of water and as they pushed I managed to drive clear. Pastor Wen

P

was with us in all this; he is a delightful character and has now become our firm friend. Bidding him farewell, and sustained with coffee by his wife, we crashed up over the Southern Mountains, the others fast asleep in the car, and were home by 2 a.m. on *September 16th*, our literature sold out and ourselves exhausted.

CHAPTER 14

POLICE

HASTARI is Susilo's shadow, a faithful and devoted man, standing to him as Mawardi stands to Rufus. His old father, Daddy Tain, who dates his spiritual experience from the night we prayed over him in bed with his grandchildren at Triwung, speaks no Indonesian at all and reads Javanese only in the ancient Javanese script, not in the romanised which is commoner nowadays. Acting on the principle that his own time in this world is bound to be short, Daddy Tain is a diligent witness to other old men. He visits them, armed with the Javanese New Testament, of which his own knowledge is exceedingly small. His method is to bow his head in prayer, asking the Lord to guide him to a suitable verse, hand the book to any available schoolboy, ask him to read from it, and then expound from that text! "He seems to have a special gift for this kind of thing," says Susilo.

Hastari and Daddy Tain preached the gospel to Hastari's married sister. She welcomed the good news, but her husband was adamantly opposed to her having anything to do with Christians. The resulting tension affected her mind. I showed Susilo Mark 9:20, "When he saw Him [Jesus] straightway the spirit tare him"; but the issue is painful and crucial for them.

Each week the Bible School on our verandah goes on its way. There were twenty-eight present last time. It was the twenty-third evening of this kind which we have held. The morning of *September 19th* was spent mostly in assembling books to take on another three-day trip with Rufus, Mawardi, and Rekso. We met for prayer at Rufus' home at 2 p,m. On the way we stopped at the home of Mr and Mrs Rifai, the Muslim-Christian home used as a church. He is old and she is young. He is quiet, investigating the gospel and comparing it with the Koran; she is merry and apt to speak openly of the hardness of her husband's heart. "It is easier to speak to him about Christ when she is not there," said Rufus. However, it was she who made the opening for me to tell the whole story of Jim Vaus the wiretapper, to which he listened bolt upright, saying, "Yes . . . Yes . . . Yes". Rufus also spoke to him at some length. It was his last chance. A week later he died suddenly while his wife was away touring on Bali island.

We drove westwards for the next three hours, meeting the evening rush in city after city, then away on unsurfaced roads to the village which once put Rufus into prison. "This road has a history," said Rufus. "My wife used to walk these ten miles each week to visit me." As so often, letters had gone astray and arrangements miscarried. In the end we were preaching at 10 p.m. to about fifty people, though the audience increased as the night wore on. At 1 a.m. I went to bed, but they continued till 4.30.

Next morning we visited several homes close to the mighty waters of the Brantas and then drove out of the maze of village lanes on to the smooth, straight, main road again, crossing the river by a temporary bridge and entering a region previously altogether unknown to me. We spent three hours in a large town, visiting the pastor and some of Rufus' relatives. It was a tedious business for me. On such trips there is plenty of room for patient endurance through long hours of uncomprehended Javanese conversation, which is the price that has to be paid for the glorious opportunities for Christ which follow.

We were on a great mountain-girt plain at 1200 feet, and steadily nearing the south coast. On this plain lies a huge swamp, which is a well-used lake, dotted with islands, fishing huts and traps, and many homes on stilts, a scene of immense activity. Roads, villages, and ricefields skirt this swamp at the foot of the loveliest peaks. Only a few miles short of the coast the swamp is blocked by a wild range of peaks with their heads in the clouds at 5000 feet, the backside of which veers down to the Indian Ocean. The village of Tugu lies at the foot of one of these peaks on a narrow ledge beside the swamp. Rufus chuckled as we got nearer and said, "I was born here." Tugu lacks the polish of more accessible places. They told me that no foreigner had been there for seventeen years. Under such circumstances one is gazed at in a special way; small children cry and run; few can look you in the eye, and it is kinder not to look them in the eye. We drew up at a simple, rambling, bamboo house and were warmly welcomed by an elderly woman, her mouth red from chewing betel nut. "Yes," laughed Rufus, "this was my home." Both he and I badly needed a bath, so he took me down the street behind the luxury of three and a half feet of bamboo screen (three sides only). The elderly woman, who cared for Rufus in his babyhood, feasted us royally beside the two beds in which the four of us would sleep. By nightfall the house was packed full inside and out. Fifteen boys were sitting on the Mayflower, working the wipers and other fixtures. Under these circumstances it was not easy to concentrate on preaching, so I just had to commit my anxiety for the car to the Lord and forget it. Indeed this had had to be done all day long, for she has a dozen ailments and dirty petrol, but she keeps running. I was advised to shift her from under the trees lest a falling coconut liquidate her! When we began at 8 p.m. I was asleep after the heat and tension of the drive over a road patterned on the sea's surface. They listened grandly to Rufus, then to me on John 14:6, then to Mawardi, then to Rekso. "Go to bed," whispered Mawardi, "you've got to drive again tomorrow" —so I did. They served 256 cups of tea.

Next day we attended the Sunday morning service in Tugu. There were 100 present. Rufus preached on the woman of Samaria and after the benediction I was given full scope behind the table below the pulpit using Jude 20-21, a most useful text for professing Christians here. At 3 p.m. we tore ourselves away, Rufus walking ahead of the car to run in to houses here and there, for he excels still at farewells. We continued to circle the swamp in glorious scenery on a perfectly atrocious road. At one busy market we dropped in on a relative of Rufus, a young man who professed to have turned to the Lord through the Pentecostal Church before moving to this wholly Muslim place. Far from any Christian church he had no Bible, and he was not interested in buying one of our New Testaments.

Moving north we came by contrast to a magnificent stretch of main road running at one point for fifteen miles without a curve.

In this depressing spot we halted at the home of a tall, grey head-master, a gifted, authoritative, and godly man. The village hall filled up with 100 persons, but not the pure countrymen we usually face. They were all leaders of society, schoolmasters, officials, and edu-cated people, personally invited by the headmaster, so that it was necessary to use Indonesian not Javanese. This is crippling for Rufus, as Indonesian is only his third language, and I felt he was having a hard time to get his message across until a note was passed up from the back of the hall asking him to switch to Javanese, which he did with great pleasure. Mawardi and Rekso looked very rustic in such company and Rufus did not ask them to speak. On such occasions he specially needs my help and I preached for nearly an hour on John 14:6. We were most beautifully entertained by the gracious headmaster and I am writing this on my bed at midnight, while Rufus sits beside me and old Rekso holds the family enthralled close by.

There is an acute shortage of petrol with long queues waiting for it in all towns, but we have been wonderfully successful in getting what we needed in smaller places. Next morning we made for home, three and a half hours away on a good road almost devoid of traffic, scarcely anyone matching my full tank of petrol. So up the hills and across the plains we soared with little to stop us and home to find that Jess had had thirty-nine at the Young People's Meeting which she has launched virtually single-handed.

It is now *October 2nd* and I have lacked energy to write much. We have been in the city several times and have managed to keep a small amount of petrol in the Mayflower. The Women's Meeting, Children's Meeting, Young People's Fellowship, and Weekly Bible School have kept us hard at work. We have had good times, though everything has to be battled over in preparation, prayer, visiting and planning, if results are to be satisfactory. One night the Doctor and Jeannette came to supper and we relaxed for an evening, greatly enriched by having them living so near us.

October 6th. Heavy rain fell last night and we had to rise often to put basins under the leaks which affect several of our rooms. Thus ended the dry season; it has rained frequently since then and will no doubt continue to do so till next April. Inch by inch the transfer of our sponsorship to the East Java Church proceeds. Already they much regret that the Doctor and his wife were not sponsored by them, and Faral travelled out to Sabrang to ask about their relationship to the Salvation Army hospital. It is over three months since I went to Gondang and some weeks since I was at Segaran. This is due to the advent of Rubani, the man who is to assume pastoral responsibility for all the groups brought into existence by the ministry of Rufus. However, I fear that he is not commending himself to them. He is too solemn and stiff, too bound by rules and regulations, and too prone to run down Rufus. Since the June 22nd baptisms at Gondang there is a further batch of twenty-nine persons there asking for baptism, but their plea is that Pa Rufus and Pa David will return to them at once.

There were twenty present at the twenty-fifth Weekly Bible School. Mawardi prayed beautifully at the end. Rufus was there and always brings a blessing with him. Susilo arrived on foot with Hastari and two new men, having walked for an hour from Triwung carrying a stick with a fork in the top and singing along the road. Good, there is room for that kind of thing in an old and staid church fellowship. He still presses eagerly on and his daughters in the city have caused several of their schoolmates to turn to Christ, so that Susilo is often there preaching to them in the house where his girls board. Hastari's afflicted sister is said to have been healed through Daddy Tain's prayers.

October 9th. Our house was filled again for the Women's Meeting, but it has become much harder to get Muslim women to attend it now. The baptism of the two sisters at Gondang on June 22nd has perhaps been a warning to some families that that is what tends to happen if people fraternise too much with Christians. Then Mrs Rufus has probably been unwise in rather stressing the need for baptism at this meeting. If a man is baptised his whole family is split open to the gospel, so there is reason in Rufus's contention that he should not be much deferred, but the baptism of a woman whose husband is unsympathetic to the gospel is almost impossible, so that to urge her to take the step may compel her withdrawal altogether. And nicely though people smile at us in the roads here in Sabrang, the overwhelming mass of husbands are very decidedly unsympathetic to the gospel.

That same night Rufus and I were at Gondang for the thirteenth time together. The meeting was small, for we were not expected and the night dark and gusty, sharp storms blowing one after another across the face of the Great Volcano. We were just fifteen persons in the home of Sumali, who was formerly head of the village. The day was the twenty-fifth anniversary of my own conversion and I could not help noticing that Rufus called on me to speak exactly at 9.15 p.m., the time when my own decision for Christ had been made. I used Jude 20 again. At the close Rufus characteristically went into the kitchen of the house and stayed there for half an hour talking to an old hag, thin, dirty, and forbidding. Apparently she wants to know more about the truth following the sudden death of an elderly man who often came to the Gondang meetings but remained unbelieving.

On *October 11th*, in company with our Superintendent, Mr George Steed, I had a momentous interview with Faral in the city, in which we successfully talked out all the problems connected with the invitation of the Synod of the East Java Church that we enter into official co-operation with them as one of their recognised workers. No basic change in the pattern of our activities will be involved and it is likely that our official welcome and setting apart for this service will take place on December 11th.

Recently we have suffered considerable losses in Sabrang through the removal of Christians to other parts of Java, so it has been specially encouraging to see two new couples attending meetings, recently, both fresh arrivals. The first, Sardjonan, is a humble, sickly-looking man, who actually goes to the length of taking turns with his wife in staying at home with the children. He has been a Christian for some years. The second is Subir, a policeman, the rest of whose family is Roman Catholic. He himself was brought to Christ through contact with a Pentecostal pastor elsewhere and it appears that when the pastor heard he was moving to Sabrang he told him to go and see Pa David, though I know not how he knew my name. At first sight Subir is very charming, in fact he seems to be a man set apart for Himself by the Lord. He was thrilled to learn about the various meetings in our home and at the Sabrang church. He bought Bibles and New Testaments and hymnbooks in both Javanese and Indonesian. Furthermore there is marked progress in Suwarso, the Sabrang leader; his solemn frame has recently become filled with new insight and fire; he is actually friendly to us, and he now has more time for Christian work.

On Sunday, *October 12th*, the Sabrang morning service was placed entirely in my hands for the first time, to lead and preach as I liked. I spoke in Indonesian without interpretation on Matthew 16:24, "If any man will come after Me let him deny himself, and take up his cross, and follow Me." There were forty present. This was only the fifth time in twenty months that I have been invited to speak in Sabrang itself, but Faral's known intentions towards us have unbarred every door.

The new Young People's Fellowship—entirely Jess' creation—is now in regular swing each Sunday afternoon with twenty-five attending. Suwarso himself came and even gave a testimony. He was brought up as a Christian and his story was of limited value to non-Christians, but it was interesting to us to hear of the alarm he had felt on being posted by the education authorities to a non-Christian village such as Sabrang, and his satisfaction at discovering that it was possible to maintain a Christian stand even against the grain of the community.

Another speaker the same afternoon was the girl who is shortly to graduate from the seminary and become the first woman minister in the history of the East Java Church. She is rather a striking personality and gave a testimony more down to the level of the young people. It seems that she chose her present vocation in preference to an offer of marriage. In the event, however, she became engaged to a minister as soon as she was ordained and so no church would call her and the experiment of ordaining a woman was to that extent a failure.

At night Jess and I took the Lord's Supper with the Doctor and Jeannette in English. At the Salvation Army hospital they never have it and in the East Java Church it is rarely celebrated, only once in Sabrang in the past twenty months, for instance.

October 13th was, in retrospect, a memorable day. There were fifty-three children at the meeting on our verandah, including those of Subir who was on duty outside the cells opposite marching up and down with his gun, but watching our house, and with us in spirit. As soon as he was free after sunset he came for two hours' chat. We were sipping tea on the verandah, visible from the road, and it was raining heavily. Another policeman passed the house and evidently observed Subir there, for he stumped across the driveway, shrouded in his cape, came up on to the verandah, greeted Subir cheerfully and me in a slightly embarrassed manner, and slumped into a chair. I gathered that his name was Kardjo and that while he and Subir had been on duty together at night outside the cells the latter had spoken to him about Christ. Sitting there on the verandah while the rain cascaded down outside in blackest night, we had time for quite a long talk. Subir spoke freely about the Lord in front of the other man and I added my testimony. Kardjo listened to it all in a good-natured way, but indicated clearly that such as he were not really interested in matters of that kind, and he laughed and waved the palm of his hand across his face.

Much time has had to be expended during this month on securing an extension to our residence permits. Clearance has to be obtained from various offices in four different towns, where interviews have been as prolonged as they were cordial. I have also paid several visits to Jonathan, the Dutch missionary, to keep him abreast of the work of the Holy Spirit in the Sabrang area, which he is not able to see for himself. Later he and his wife came to have supper with us and we invited the Doctor and Jeannette to meet them. Jonathan ordered a taxi at 9.30 p.m. so that they would not have to spend a night out of the city with the reporting to authorities which this entails. On *October 18th* I spent from breakfast till 2 p.m. in a police office and I think the conversations held then will ultimately result in our getting the extensions without which we cannot continue in this work. On getting back to Sabrang I found awaiting me an invitation to an official reception to farewell some local officials and to welcome new ones. I went at once and had a useful evening with a number of important men, upon whose goodwill our position here is largely dependent.

On Sunday, *October 19th*, we were encouraged by an attendance of thirty-five at the Young People's Meeting on our verandah. Rufus was the speaker. As I stood on the steps welcoming the arrivals I noticed one sturdily built man whom I had never seen before. He wore flannel trousers and a white shirt. He seemed a little nervous and I noticed his eyes roving around, taking in every detail. When he saw Subir and Mrs Subir near the front he at once went there and sat by them. It was only then that I realised it was Kardjo, the policeman who had come a few nights earlier in darkness and rain. He had never before been in a Christian meeting of any kind. There is another stranger among us these days too, a fellow named Nasur. He first began to attend the Weekly Bible School back in August, his left eye shrouded in a large bandage, whether because of a genuine injury or to hide his embarrassment I am not sure. He has been coming to the Bible School and the Young People's Meeting ever since, saying nothing, a mystery to us all. Then one day he admitted that he had started attending the meetings because he heard that there were a number of girls who did so and he was looking for a wife; after discovering the kind or message we proclaimed, however, he continued coming to learn more about it. He is a very impenetrable kind of man and nobody seems to know much about him. He is said to be a salesman in the Sabrang market, the sort of vendor who spreads a cloth on the ground covered with oddments whose virtues he then extols in the manner of a preacher.

Monday, *October 20th*, proved to be an unusually hard day. I had to go to Surabaja about a technical point affecting the extension to Jess' residence permit. The train from the city was late and very crowded, so I had to stand all the way. Being on the train I failed to observe a severe earth-tremor which sent the whole countryside dashing out of doors, including Jess and Rupert in Sabrang, where hundreds of children tumbled out of the school just down the road. Up on the side of the Great Volcano at Gondang every stone house was split and as headmaster Tias shouted to his boys to run clear the old school-house, scene of so many spiritual battles and victories, cracked and slouched to its end. Having completed my unromantic task in Surabaja I endeavoured to mail to England a tape recording which we had recently made for our children there.

Not once nor twice did one office pass me on to the next, and in the end I was totally frustrated by the ruling that as a resident of the city area a parcel could not be accepted from me in the Surabaja area. The rainy season being overdue the weather was very hot and sultry, and my return trip was again delayed and the train overcrowded. Refreshed by tea at the Bible College I drove back to Sabrang in the Mayflower, arriving just as the Children's Meeting was disbanding from our home. But hardly had we sat down to supper before we were asked to help in an emergency by driving Jess' teacher to a town more than three hours' journey away, where her little brother was said to be dying. She had received an urgent telegram, but the regular buses had already stopped. The local military were willing to supply petrol, which is still exceedingly short. I was too exhausted after my day in Surabaja, but Jess was willing to go. However, oil leaked from the car. Suwarso, Rufus, Mawardi and others came to help, but it was midnight before the Mayflower was roadworthy, and at that hour Jess and four others left on this long trip. It seemed almost crazy, but human friendship and the ministry of the gospel do involve crazy acts at times. Jess got back at 10 a.m. next morning, having driven for seven hours and had two hours' sleep. She was very glad she went. The child was already dead when they arrived and in the midst of their sorrow the family were profoundly grateful for the effort she had made. The moment she got home I took over the car and left for the city, so that the Mayflower did round-the-clock service. Petrol being almost unobtainable two local officials thumbed a lift with me and in the city I met Subir, the policeman, who came back with me. We picked up man after man stranded at the roadside by lack of public transport.

On *October 22nd* Subir dropped in again and Susilo happened to arrive at the same moment. The latter is still pressing ardently forwards as a Christian and a witness for Christ. I marvel at his progress in knowledge of the Scriptures. He asked me about the English Authorised Version of Revelation 22:14, "Blessed are they that do His commandments, that they may have right to the tree of life and may enter in through the gates into the city", for the Indonesian reads, "Blessed are they that wash their robes", and he wanted to know which was the better reading. He also asked what was the right sense of the word "power" in 1 Corinthians 4:20, "The kingdom of God is not in word but in power." His next enquiry was whether I thought Timothy's grandmother, Lois, was a true Christian believer. He added a remark significant enough for any missionary among the Javanese people, that some of the most gripping and significant verses in the Bible for Javanese are 1 Timothy 6:14-16, "Keep this commandment without spot, unrebukeable, until the appearing of our Lord Jesus Christ; which in his times He shall show, who is the blessed and only Potentate, the King of kings and Lord of lords, who only hath immortality, dwelling in the light which no man can approach unto, whom no man hath seen nor can see, to whom be honour and power everlasting, Amen." Subir sat listening, weighing and absorbing the other man's faith. That night we had fifteen at the Weekly Bible School, one of the smallest attendances yet. One must admit that numbers at this meeting are slowly dropping and removals have hit us badly. Mawardi never misses and his support has meant a great deal to us.

I decided that it was high time I visited the home of the mystery man, Nasur, so one day I set out for the spot, about a mile from No. 122. On the way I met him on his bicycle and told him my intention. His face fell at once, and I soon realised that he very much hoped I would attempt nothing of the sort. The incident made me think back over my visits to some other young men and I was regretfully forced to admit that in several cases they had attended meetings up to the moment I met their home folk and then no more. It was difficult to resist the conclusion that although I had always been most cordially received by parents they had afterwards prohibited their young people from having anything more to do with Christians.

Later I called on a couple from a Christian village who attended the Sabrang church and the Weekly Bible School in our home most regularly until the birth of their first child five months ago. Since then they have never been to any meetings. Their house is a little removed from main roads and they make the darkness of the track an excuse for not coming; he also says his wife does not like to be left alone with the child at night. These things are perhaps true, yet I presume there are other reasons unrevealed. Anyway, my visit led to no improvement and they were never seen in Christian meetings again. Very different was the situation when I dropped in to Subir's home. He is a most delightful person, thrilled to have found Christians in Sabrang, to which he had rather dreaded being transferred. He is very eager to witness for Christ and always carries a New Testament in the pocket of his uniform. From him I went on to the Sardjonan family, the other new arrivals, and here again there is a firm desire to associate with Christians and share in active testimony. Meanwhile Jess was out with Rufus and Mrs Rufus visiting in Sabrang and Ringit. Knowing that Susilo and others are far from idle in the Lord's service I think we can say that there is a considerable daily spiritual attack mounted throughout the district.

On Sunday, *October 26th*, there were forty people in the Sabrang church, sixteen men, twenty-four women, and some children as well. Suwarso who is increasingly aggressive spoke well on Psalms 32 and 51. And Kardjo, the policeman, attended church for the very first time in his life. This is a far more drastic step than it would be in England. Merely to enter a Christian church involves a degree of committal to the Christian faith and is sufficient to arouse comment and criticism. Further time has been burnt up in fresh visits to distant offices, since a certain official in giving me clearance to get an extension to our residence permits omitted the word "not" from the sentence "he has not been involved with the police". However, I think all will be well and it has gone on record that I am "not bound by strong drink or opium". But we are in grave danger of being bound by lack of petrol. Miraculously we have managed to keep the Mayflower on the road, but for weeks all longer trips with Rufus have been ruled out. Public transport is much reduced and strained to the limit, so that to board a bus from Sabrang to the city means hours of waiting. If we have to lay the Mayflower up I do not know how I shall keep my lecture hours at the Bible College. Paraffin, which we use for cooking and lighting, is also gravely affected, but we have never quite been without it. It is tragic to see the huge queues waiting to buy it.

Sunday, *November 2nd*. Accompanied by Mawardi I went to

Gondang for the thirteenth time, though it was actually my first visit as formal Sunday preacher. We were shocked to see the effects of the October 20th earthquake all the way up the Great Volcano. Only the humbler homes with bamboo walls stood it all right. The attendance at the morning service was no true reflection of the progress of the Lord's work at Gondang. There were only fifteen present, for the homes of the believers are very widely scattered, none have watches, and the habit of regular attendance each week has not yet been generally acquired. But I feel prospects are good as there is obvious growth in Tias the headmaster, Sumali the ex-head of the village, and Lukas the doctor. There are already further candidates for baptism both there and at Segaran.

Just now our eyes are specially upon Kardjo the policeman. It really seems that through his friendship with Subir he has turned to the Lord. Before the Weekly Bible School formally starts, Jess sometimes leads a Bible quiz when those present have to find and read out verses she announces. He enters enthusiastically into this and is to be seen in every meeting now. Today, as he came on duty with his gun, he led his two little boys into the Children's Meeting for the first time, shy, wee mites, identically dressed in light grey. On November 9th Subir and his wife are to be baptised in a Pentecostal church in another town. This is right, for his background is Pentecostal, though he shows no characteristics which make fellowship with him difficult and he is at pains to explain that he intends to go on coming to meetings of the East Java Church. He is a fine Christian character and we much enjoy his numerous visits to our home. "My wife and I always pray together before I go on duty," he said, "and again when I get home."

At a recent Women's Meeting we were interested to hear Loti give her testimony. She reckons that she was not born again until she came to Sabrang, ill, and we got her into the hospital. One night after a ward service she could not sleep. At 2 a.m. she began to read a booklet which Jess had given to her and was gripped by John 15:16, "Ye have not chosen Me but I have chosen you", and a paralysing sense of her own badness gave way to the assurance that the Lord had indeed chosen her to belong to Him, and that has never left her.

November 4th. I drove into the city with Subir and preached in Chinese at morning prayers in the Bible College on the question of healing, which is much discussed these days. One of the Pentecostal churches has a healing campaign this week, and the handbills invite the "blind, deaf, dumb, heart-diseased, tubercular and cancer sufferers, diabetics, and the lame" saying, "If you believe on the Lord Jesus Christ you will receive perfect healing", an assertion which I felt to be badly in need of rectification.

The petrol and paraffin shortage continues to be most acute and we have had to put our refrigerator out of action. Thanks to a Chinese photographer in the city I have always managed to keep something in the Mayflower's tank, but today I got right down to zero, only to be rescued by a kindly policeman. "There are loads of Christians down our road," said a schoolboy to Jess with typical exaggeration. On investigation the "loads" proved to be just the Subir family, but the remark is some indication of the impression they have made in a few weeks.

On Sunday we had the Lord's Supper in Sabrang, conducted by Rufus. There were fifty-two people in the church, and with children added I estimate the Christian community in this firmly Muslim place to be about 120, no small miracle. The average weekly attendance at the five meetings which take place in Sabrang, four of them on our verandah, is 150. Though we are much aware of enemy counter-attack there are yet great things happening around us. Nasur, the mystery man, continues to attend most regularly. Kardjo is never absent and his younger son, aged about 4, delights to come and play with Rupert. Then through the Young People's Fellowship, still barely two months old, a great transformation has come over the school-teacher Wagini, who formerly wanted so much to hear the jazz from Australia on our radio. She has moved quietly into a clear understanding of the gospel and is becoming active in spreading it.

Sunday, *November 9th*, proved to be rather an unusual day. After the Communion Service attended by fifty-two we had lunch and our usual tropical siesta after it. I was still fast asleep and in pyjamas when three lorries stopped at the gate and 100 young people from the city debauched upon us. While I managed to wake up with a hurried shower, the guests carried all our available seating out under the trees on the drive-in, and Jess, Loti, and Yeny produced 100 cups of tea. Susilo was with the party, which came from the East Java Church in the city, and after a time I was asked to speak to them. There was no chance at all for formal preparation, so I stood on the steps of the verandah and preached from 2 Timothy 1:9, "God, who hath saved us and called us with an holy calling, not according to our works but according to His own purpose and grace, which was given us in Christ Jesus before the world began". Our neighbours gazed in astonishment at so much young Christian life. The moment they had gone our own Young People's Fellowship arrived and I preached as I had prepared to do on Matthew 22:1-14. All this took four hours and then the day ended with an evening of prayer with the Doctor and Jeannette after which we heard the midnight news from Melbourne. During it the announcer said, "A river of lava a mile wide is pouring from the crater of the Great Volcano in Java. Since the crater is blocked up an eruption is possible and local people have been warned." So we went out on to the porch and had a look at the mountain on which we live, shrouded in the silence of the night. We are about twenty miles from the crater, but separated from it by deeply serrated and heavily populated country. However, having seen the destruction of the earthquake at Gondang, I have a wholesome respect for the Great Volcano.

Next morning, *November 10th*, Subir came to tell me all about his baptism. Then Susilo arrived with Sumantri, the man from Segaran who hails from the outer islands. Yesterday there was held at Segaran the first communion service in its history. Twenty-nine were present, but Sumantri himself felt he could not join in and stood at the back. Susilo and I tried to reassure him about this matter and also about the way Segaran believers feel they are being mis-handled by the city church. In spite of all that has taken place there for the glory of God, I am afraid it may be true to say that with wiser leadership at a level higher than Rufus much more could have been accomplished at the time when a large number of people were well disposed towards the message of the gospel. There was, for instance, in a near-by village a certain important official who

Q

requested Christian baptism and Christian marriage without delay. The couple concerned, together with Sumantri, met with Rubani, the man who is now living temporarily in this district and may become the resident pastor if that seems a suitable arrangement. Rubani explained to them that these things cannot be hurried and that a probation of several months must elapse before their request could be seriously considered. Probably it was not so much his words as the intransigent and unsympathetic attitude adopted which did most damage. The man soon made arrangements to have a Muslim wedding and the opportunity of swinging him into a Christian orbit where he would have had the chance of understanding the gospel was missed. Had it been taken, everyone knew that there were many others who would have been glad to find out more about the Christian faith under the shelter of his name and company. This is typical of the sort of problem and opportunity which are constantly arising here nowadays. There are admittedly great dangers in accepting people too easily, but in the opinion of Rufus the dangers of repelling those who are groping for light are greater still. It was a mark of Susilo's amazing grasp of the Scriptures that he commented on the affair by quoting not only Colossians 4:6, "Let your speech be alway with grace, seasoned with salt", but also the first half of Mark 4:34, "Without a parable spake He not unto them", meaning that we must not be too blunt with outsiders. The three of us prayed before parting and soon afterwards the Children's Meeting was upon us. Rufus spoke on John 5:7, "Sir, I have no man", and did well, though he is not specially gifted for children. There were fifty-five present, a tight pack on the verandah. Mrs Rufus stayed at home while her husband was speaking. Otherwise she is always there and the previous week, when it was her turn to speak, she had to do so while keeping hold of a tearful little daughter perched on a stool beside her. They live under heavy family pressure.

November 11th. While I was in the city, Susilo came again to our home, bringing Wirojo of Segaran and his wife, the hosts of the church there. Jess gave them all lunch and I was very sorry to miss them as they have so often entertained and fed me in their place on the Great Volcano. They confirm that there are now three streams of lava running down its side. Jess was telling them that it is illegal to preach the gospel to Malays in Malaya and Susilo answered, "Do you know what is forbidden here?—preaching that there is no God."

In the evening Jess, Rupert, and I went for the first time to the home of Kardjo the policeman, which lies not far from our own, shrouded in palm trees and adjacent to a centre of Islamic studies. It was dusk as we arrived, and his two little boys were having supper at a table in the corner. Kardjo and his wife were actually sitting together reading John's Gospel when we entered. We sat with them for some time and Mrs Kardjo served us coffee and cakes. Jess urged her to drop in and see us, but from the way she answered it was evident that that was a risk she was not yet ready to take. "I am a man who has lived without God or religion," said Kardjo. "But I have long had a vague desire to be a Christian." He is afraid that he may be transferred elsewhere, as he has already been some time in Sabrang, and he wants to get properly established in the Christian faith before moving. He is often in our home now, and the children too. His four-year-old son has taken a great fancy to Rupert and apparently talks about him a lot at home. The other day he was playing with Rupert on our verandah when there was a sudden silence. Jess went out to see why and found the little chap fast asleep on the floor. She picked him up gently and carried him in to Rupert's bed, but he woke and was rather alarmed to find where he was. When Subir dropped in to see us the same evening before he went on duty he told us that some nights ago, as he was on guard with his gun outside the cells, he heard one of the prisoners praying aloud in the name of Jesus. The man's record was very bad and he was taken to the city next day before Subir could meet him.

Our thirty-first Weekly Bible School drew only nine people, the smallest attendance we have had at this meeting in twenty-one months. True they were most valuable people, but true too that attendance has steadily slipped since we could count on thirty in July. Yet we had a splendid time and Susilo was in great form. He is not finding it easy to draw others in Triwung to Christ— indeed his great successes have been away from home. "People are interested in us only if they are ill," he said. Nasur actually asked if he might say a few words. He apologised for his aloofness and said, "I am from a Muslim family, but I am here because I want to find the way to heaven."

I called on Garit at his home in Ringit, but at present he is in that state of excitement and tension which I am afraid the Pentecostal church in this district induces. He asked if the new translation of the Indonesian Bible was being done by "the Lord's servants" or not, since he maintained that the existing one was the work of those proficient in Greek only. When I led in prayer before leaving he prayed parallel to me throughout. I got back to find Subir and Kardjo the policeman waiting on the verandah to see me. Kardjo is concerned that his wife shows little interest in the gospel, but I quoted to him Luther's dictum, "Give men time". Then in the late afternoon I enjoyed the rare pleasure of an hour's walk. It was drizzling with rain and therefore cool, and rain also reduces curiosity. I grinned and bowed at everyone I met and encountered in return 50 per cent pleasure, 30 per cent astonishment, and 20 per cent horror. One is indeed a most extraordinary, unexpected, and alarming sight to a stranger!

November 15th. Last night Rufus, Susilo, Mawardi and I—a team rarely assembled—drove to Segaran for their mid-week meeting in Wirojo's home. It was an awkward moment owing to the visit of a theatrical company which drew 2000 of the country people. With this major attraction close at hand attendance was badly down, but fifteen of us spent a happy evening together. Rufus asked me to preach, which I did on the marriage supper in Matthew 22:1-14. By 11 p.m. we were through and it was decided that we should visit a Christian whose humble abode lay five miles further east beside the main road. He had so far kept away from the new believers at Segaran. To reach the house we had to carve a tunnel through the 2000 people watching the theatricals, who were spread right across the highway. Police walked in front of us to clear a path. When we got there the man and his wife were, not unnaturally, asleep, but they welcomed us well, having lived in this remote spot without any Christian fellowship for the past thirteen years. With Susilo in charge of the conversation I guessed that our hosts remained ignorant of Rufus' identity and probably thought the pastor was Susilo. Before we left, Wirojo chipped in, having learnt that our host was a nominal Christian from childhood and quoted most effectively Matthew 5:15, "Neither do men light a candle and put it under a bushel but on a candlestick, and it giveth light unto all that are in the house", and capped it with Matthew 25:25, "I was afraid and went and hid thy talent in the earth: lo, there thou hast that is thine." I observed that he was a true spiritual son of Susilo. We got home at 1 a.m. and at 7 a.m. Pastor Wen from Kabat was on our doorstep. This good friend bought twenty-four hymnbooks off us before preaching in the Sabrang church. Whether he used church funds or his own money, and for what price he would resell them in Kabat, I cannot tell.

I myself did not hear Pastor Wen preach, as I drove to Gerbo with Hastari beside me, a faithful, much-tried man. Gerbo is the largest place in Sabrang district, but spiritually it is in a dismal condition. Many people have prayed for it and Susilo especially has a burden for its evangelisation. In fact there are three small Pentecostal churches in the town, but they all use the Indonesian language, not Javanese, and their membership is almost entirely Chinese, so that the real people of Gerbo, the Javanese Muslims, remain untouched by the gospel. There are said to be many Javanese Christians from Christians villages there but they slumber deep, so that the East Java Church barely exists. I was the Sunday preacher for the first time and the congregation numbered six, but wedged into a tiny space it was cosy and I greatly enjoyed it and would not have exchanged my lot for any more imposing congregation. We have had ample evidence in this district that dead bones can be revived, so maybe the day of rejoicing for Gerbo will not be long delayed. They told me that in the time of Dutch rule to embrace Christianity offered some additional security in life, and that this no longer pertained as an inducement.

I have already stated that the Sabrang church is really the home, or rather the bedroom, of Mrs Rakes, derelict widow of a Eurasian. She, being ill, lay on the bed beside the pulpit while Pastor Wen was preaching, for she has nowhere else to lie. So at the end Jess brought her home and she is now established in our spare room, where the Doctor is treating her. Jess has recently been involved in quite a lot of co-operation with the Doctor. He likes to know when Christians or friends of ours come to him amidst the mass of other patients, so they often drop in to us and ask Jess for an identifying note first. This makes no difference to what they pay. Today Jess took to him a little friend of Rupert's who was suffering from a horribly infected finger, then collected the father in order to get his approval for an operation, and finally carried the unconscious little chap back to his home in her arms. I suspect that the influence of this kind of thing is tremendous.

In view of the steady decline in attendance at the Weekly Bible School (it has dropped from thirty to nine) we wondered what to expect on *November 22nd*, which was the thirty-second of these gatherings. We specially prayed about it with Loti, who shares to the full in all the joys and sorrows of the work. There was great rejoicing when our verandah filled up with twenty-four people and we had one of the very best evenings I can remember, expounding from 2 Timothy 2 our calling to be witnesses, soldiers, athletes, and farmers, while for the second session I began a series of studies on the burning issue of faith healing. Susilo, who had been up at Segaran on the Great Volcano all afternoon, sent a note to say that he was worn out and could not come, but close on its heels he arrived on his hard-worked scooter, saying that he had had no peace of mind sitting at home! He translated from my Indonesian into Javanese with tremendous enthusiasm. It is really only necessary for the sake of one or two, yet it undoubtedly hammers the message deeper into every Javanese heart—and of course it is good for Susilo himself, who has had no formal Bible training. There were nine men present on this happy occasion—Rufus and Susilo, the apostles; Subir and Kardjo, the policemen, rejoicing in faith; Mawardi, who opened beautifully in a long prayer in Javanese; Hastari, the faithful farmer; Sardjonan, the new man from West Java; Nasur, the mystery man, and a friend of his. The rest were women and girls, not forgetting Riti, who never misses. Rufus has decided that he too must not attempt to visit Nasur's home, so Susilo has seconded the task of keeping in touch with him to his rustic and unsuspected henchman, Hastari.

At the close of this thrilling evening, when all the others had gone, Rufus, Susilo, and Hastari sat on while we exchanged news, made plans, relaxed, and rejoiced till 11.30 p.m. Susilo is the most marvellous gift of God to this work. You would certainly not blame anyone who thought he was the pastor rather than Rufus, for Rufus sits quietly when Susilo is there wagging his mighty tongue. Strange to say Susilo is really the more characteristically evangelical man of the two and his overflowing spiritual life is being reproduced in others. Rufus is a child of the older, Dutch tradition, but with a later infusion of spiritual light. Yet without Rufus there would have been no Susilo!

The purifying power of the gospel was shown up by contrast the very same day by trouble in poor Yeny's family. She was the youngest of her parents' children, but while she was small her father left them, lived close by for years, and recently married again. Yeny stayed with her mother, who soon remarried and had three more children, who are still small. Yeny's stepfather is a dreadful trial to them and today he declared that Yeny's mother was about to have another child of which he was not the father. He therefore took the other three children, the youngest of which was not yet weaned, and after an unsuccessful attempt to get money out of Yeny, departed with them. At night he was back again, threatening with a knife the youngest child, who was already sick. . . .

On *November 20th* I drove into the city with Susilo and his eldest daughter, whom the Doctor has successfully treated for acute malaria. All the way we were discussing the gift of tongues. His progress is amazing. He absorbs and gives out at top speed. There is none of the slow mystical East in him—he gallops. He loves to discuss a matter with me, to check his own exposition of Scripture, and to ask about trends in other lands. Then he is clear, which means that everyone else will be clear tomorrow! He asked me the difference between the words Pentecost and Paraclete.

After teaching Greek all day in the city I drove back to Sabrang and found Jess teaching at the Women's Meeting. This is causing us some anxiety, as, for the present at least, Muslim women simply will not come to it. Yet, although attendance is under ten, there has been not a little spiritual blessing through it. Immediately afterwards I departed with Rufus and Mawardi on my fourteenth visit to Gondang. Up and up we went, collecting Wirojo and his wife from Segaran on the way. On reaching Gondang market we parked the car outside the school-house ruined in the October earthquake and walked by moonlight under the palms along a path between houses and gardens to the home of a merchant "where many were gathered together", thirty-five of them visible, others invisible, this being the regular mid-week meeting of the Gondang church, fruit of Rufus' persistent attacks. I noticed the head of the village, Sumali, Tias, Lukas, and their wives. Tias the headmaster is quite transformed in body and soul. His diabetes seems to have vanished. Last year he appeared to have gone to seed completely, untidy and drowsy, the floor of his house so broken and holed that no chair would stand evenly on it. But now, as a symbol of new life it seems to me, his floor is concreted right over and he preaches every week at this Thursday meeting. He expounded Genesis 39:5, "The Lord blessed the Egyptian's house for Joseph's sake". Rufus followed on John 10:9-10, "I am the door: by me if any man enter in he shall be saved, and shall go in and out and find pasture. The thief cometh not but for to steal, and to kill, and to destroy: I am come that they might have life and that they might have it more abundantly." Then I spoke, using 2 Timothy 2 again. It was a great evening, but for sanity's sake I managed to get the party home by midnight and in the car Rufus asked me to explain my views about baptism by immersion and baptism by sprinkling. The children of a new era have to rethink everything.

Although I have a permit for four gallons of petrol per week it is another thing to get it, for I am only allowed to buy at one designated pump, which is in the city, twenty miles away. This week I arrived with the needle pointing ominously to zero and found at my pump a colossal queue stretching through three streets. I returned an hour later, found only twenty-five cars, tacked on at the back, pushed the Mayflower up yard by yard like everybody else was doing, and stood seventh when the pump ran dry, the crew hanging the "Empty" notice on it and standing back to mop their brows. The six cars ahead of me left but I drove slowly up to the pump.

"Finished, finished," cried everyone jovially. I got out and chatted to the two armed policemen who were posted there to see fair play, showing them my permit for four gallons, explaining that I came from Sabrang and was rarely in the city, and asking their advice on what to do next. They conferred together in Javanese and then said to me, "We'll come with you," jumping in, guns and all. "What factory are you from?" they asked as we went along. I explained carefully that I worked for the Lord and that I was not Dutch. "Oh, we must certainly help you," they said. "Could you take eight gallons?" They guided me to another pump, talked to the man in the office, saw eight gallons safely into my tank, and thumbed a ride back to their beat.

It was just as well that we had plenty of petrol, for next morning, *November 21st*, a message was received from the city to say that Susilo's eldest daughter had been taken ill there. Jess drove to their home at Triwung, collecting the parents and the head of the village, continued straight on to the city and back again to Sabrang Hospital with the girl as well, a round trip of fifty miles. Then I took over the wheel and ferried them hither and thither, Susilo replenishing our petrol from a friend of his, a nominal Christian who never attends meetings. Susilo stayed the night there in order to read the Scriptures with him. Mrs Susilo came to us for the night, though she flatly refused to sleep within sheets, lay on the top of the nicely made bed all night, and escaped at 4 a.m. During these trips Susilo told me that a Dutch teacher gave him a New Testament when he was at school and that at times he read it over a period of ten years. Then he married Mrs Susilo, who came from an ardent Muslim home, indeed her father had a private mosque in his own garden. He thinks he turned to the Lord in the war years when his first child was born, and that was through the kindness shown to them by a Dutch lady. But real liberty and light came only after he met Rufus in 1956, and it was then that Mrs Susilo was converted. But it was the death of their little son that galvanised both of them into the tremendous and fruitful service of this past year. He told me that his father-in-law still knows nothing of their new faith.

On Sunday, *November 23rd*, I preached in the Sabrang church to thirty-five people, but the highlight of the day was the Young

People's Fellowship on our verandah at 4 p.m., attended by thirty-six. This meeting has the character of a Christian Endeavour gathering, the young people sharing actively in it. Susilo was the speaker, making up in glowing enthusiasm and enjoyment of verses God has given him for what he lacks in other ways as a preacher. He took the marriage feast at Cana. Both he and his wife stayed for supper with us. In her husband's presence Mrs Susilo seemed more at ease. Her background is so strongly Muslim and rural that she still hardly knows what to make of foreigners, and alone among our hundreds of visitors persists in feeling that she ought to enter a white man's house by the back door. After supper the Susilos, Mawardi, and I drove up to Segaran. Rufus was too exhausted to accompany us, this being the first time that I have ever known him unable to keep an appointment. At Barek we added Chamim to our raiding party.

On reaching Wirojo's house at Segaran we found twenty men assembled, a very special company, for he had invited just the leaders of Javanese religious-philosophy. Wirojo himself opened the meeting and was followed by Susilo, cheerful and rambling, who expounded the Scriptures in his own fashion for forty-five minutes. I then took thirty-five more on 2 Timothy 1:9, and Mawardi spoke for a quarter of an hour on John 15. Then Mrs Susilo most effectively alluded to the custom of putting a light alongside the body of someone who has died, showing that it is in life they need light and Christ is that light. The audience was just the right one for her. When she had finished Wirojo stood close under the lamp and read clearly and strongly, without any comment, Ecclesiastes 2:1-11 and Matthew 25:1-13. Refreshments were then served by Mrs Wirojo and her friends and the guests departed after Susilo had led in prayer. Our party stayed on for a happy time of fellowship together. Then came the fast drive over the twisting, plunging road at midnight, a familiar, blinking light pulling us up at the police check-point at Gerbo, coffee in the Susilo home in Triwung, then the last few miles alone with Mawardi, the final parting from him outside the deserted market at Ringit, his handshake through the window and home by 1 a.m.

On *November 24th* I went to a weekly cottage meeting which

Mawardi now arranges in different homes in rotation. This time it was in that of Natmina, the woman whose baptism in June terminated Jess' closer contacts with Muslim women in the avenues behind our home. There were twenty-five present, but not one unbeliever.

A baby was born in this house last week, Mother Daro's first grandson, and on *November 25th* Jess took the parents back to their home near the Hotel of Peace, using petrol which they were able to supply. She picked me up in the city on her return journey and when we got home at night Subir was on duty outside the cells. He came straight across to us, gun in hand, with the very sad news that Sumantri of Segaran, the man from the outer islands, the colleague of Wirojo, had been arrested and was there in the cells opposite our door. It appears that on Monday morning, not many hours after the special meeting for village leaders in Wirojo's home, which he had attended, Sumantri was tempted to take a gold watch from a neighbour's home. Subir said that we could give him refreshments if we wished to do so. We handed him coffee, sandwiches, and some pineapple through the small square hole by which alone prisoners communicate with the outside world. Sumantri was very pleased indeed, but on both sides it was hard to know what to say. He admitted his fault, suggesting that he could regard this time of withdrawal as a gift from the Lord and asked us to pray for him. It was pitch dark inside the cell, but I could see the glow of several cigarettes and later on, when I collected the plates, a number of men spoke up eagerly in thanks, so evidently they had a communal feast. Sumantri said that it comforted him to look across to our house, and indeed he can see right into our sitting room at thirty-five yards' range, and as I write these words Jess is playing hymns on the harmonium for his encouragement. But what will Wirojo be feeling and what will the Muslims of Segaran be saying? And we are not too sure that Sumantri's attitude denotes any very deep repentance.

Next evening Subir and Kardjo, the policemen, sat at dusk on our verandah. Subir is a very choice man and rugged Kardjo a real trophy of God's grace. He is not a bit ashamed to confess himself a Christian and sailed into a meeting in full uniform a few nights ago. The freshness of a new convert is a tonic to everyone, and it is of course most delightful to have the police force represented among us.

It is a constant problem to me to know how to apply such verses as, "Give to every man that asketh of you . . . and lend, hoping for nothing again". I find it hard to believe that God or man are served when base motives are gratified and deliberate deceit is allowed to succeed. The other day a youth of twenty came hobbling on to the verandah with a piece of plaster on his leg just below the knee. There were six visitors already in the house and I was overdue at a meeting. He asserted that he had travelled with Rufus and me a year ago. He said he had no money to get back to his home three miles away, and as soon as his leg (for which he had been treated in the hospital opposite us) was better he would go out preaching with Rufus. I was unimpressed either by his promises, his hobble, or his motives. In the end I drove him to the place where he lived, although it made me later still for my meeting, and put him out at the cross-roads. However, he then wanted money to get down a long lane to his home and was not at all pleased when I refused this. It was quite clear to me that he was out for money, not a lift. In contrast to this sort of thing I feel that we are obeying the text I have just quoted by having Mrs Rakes here. She has now been with us ten days, a woman needy, alone, unloved, and tolerably apprecia-tive of anything done for her. Yet even there a problem remains. She asked us to buy a thermos for her on one of our trips to the city. We did so, but having now got the thermos in her hands it seems a shame to pay us for it when (she feels) we can probably well afford it. Should we insist on payment? Where does generosity degenerate into gullibility? And does gullibility ever really help souls or advance the work of the Lord? When Sardjonan first came here from West Java he dropped hints to us about free medi-cines and free milk, which he apparently got from some missionary over there. We failed on principle to take the hints; Christians who have to be nourished on free milk are sitting targets for the devil.

Early this morning I read the Scriptures on the verandah as Sumantri's cell was being cleaned. Through its open door I could see him wave, and others with him too. Each time I leave our house a hand emerges from the hole in the cell door and is then raised in mute greeting to me. But God is not glorified when His children fail to observe the injunction of 1 Peter 4:15, "Let none of you suffer . . . as a thief".

CHAPTER 15

TRIUMPH AND TRAGEDY

November 30th. This is Sumantri's tenth day in the cell opposite our home. We are able to feed him on Tuesdays only, but the mother of Riti and Pooh, from whose little stall the prisoners are allowed to buy through their guards, has our instructions to charge us for his coffee, but not for cigarettes. There has been much lobbying behind the scenes in his affairs, and I think we have helped to form the opinion among Christians that it would be wrong to try to buy him out. Susilo is constantly working on the matter, both above and below ground. Rufus, Mawardi, Chamim, and I went up to Segaran one night to see Wirojo and get from him further details about the affair. It appears that Sumantri has had no settled job or income for some time, and he has also had marital troubles. At one time I was certainly under the impression that I had met his wife, but latterly he has lived on his own, in fact I suspect that Mr and Mrs Wirojo have largely kept him. When I asked Wirojo whether the matter was having repercussions detrimental to the gospel in Segaran, he said it was not. Apparently, the local people have never really accepted Sumantri as one of themselves, for he is not a Javanese at all, and thus his fall has not greatly implicated Javanese Christians. Wirojo came on with us to Gondang, the full moon blazing gloriously down on the cloudless peak of the Great Volcano. A meeting was held in the home of the head of the village; there were fifty people inside it and fifty more outside, and the former head of Segaran was present for the first time, a strong and influential man, who seemed to enjoy himself and bought a New Testament at the end.

Mrs Rakes left us after a stay of two weeks, which was quite a success. I imagine that her rather immature faith has not been unimportant in the spread of the gospel in Sabrang, where her one-roomed house is still the church building. She has visions and hears words in the night. One day she saw a man bury three eggs at the church door and three more outside the back door; later she observed that the congregation was sleepy, so those eggs were certainly powerful!

December 1st. I got back home at noon from my quarterly visit to the Chinese Christian Church in Surabaja and by 4 p.m. there were fifty-five children sitting on mats in our house, heavy rain was crashing upon us, twenty more were sheltering on the verandah, the roof was leaking badly, and Susilo was holding the mob entranced with his antics and choruses, notwithstanding the noise of the storm. There is something of the comedian in him. He charms the heart, sits on the floor too, goes down on all fours, leaps among the children, drags individuals out to the front to recite or sing, shoots questions in all directions, and holds everyone's attention in a vice. But as a speaker he is inexperienced, and today he had such a good time that he scrapped his Bible story altogether, which was a pity.

At night the storm continued unabated and somewhat marred the weekly cottage meeting under Mawardi's auspices, which was held midway between Kardjo's home and ours. Rufus was the speaker this time. I went rather out of a sense of duty, for I was too tired to speak after Surabaja and the children. Only nine people were present, including Loti, and beside her I was astonished and delighted to see Mrs Kardjo, who had ventured out on such a night to attend the first Christian meeting of her life. Loti had known her in former years, so they sat together and I think this helped Mrs Kardjo to feel less ill at ease.

On *December 5th* Susilo came round on his scooter to say that guests from the World Council of Churches were being brought to the Sabrang area, their names unknown. My help was requested with interpretation. So we drove with Rufus to Barek, but no guests appeared. We waited there for several hours and Susilo taught them Jess' version in Indonesian of the chorus "Open Thou mine eyes that I may behold wondrous things out of Thy law", which is becoming rather a favourite. He added another chorus concocted by him and Jess together which brings in the names of all the books in the Bible; this we use at every Weekly Bible School and it has helped many people to feel more at home with the Scriptures. Then, without a scrap of warning, he sat down and said that I would speak. My mind had flitted to 2 Corinthians 6:10, "As sorrowful, yet alway rejoicing; as poor, yet making many rich; as having nothing and yet possessing all things", so I expounded that. Rufus also preached. I could wish that Susilo deferred more to Rufus, but his own gift is of the kind that "runs over the wall", and who is called to prune such a necessary branch?

There being no sign of visitors we at last scattered. I got home to lunch at 2.30 p.m., a shower, a short nap, and the messenger from Rufus was there to say they had come. So off I drove once more in the Mayflower on a burning hot afternoon. I collected Rufus and Mawardi from Ringit, crashed over the bumps to Triwung to recover Susilo, and then raced east down the main road to Barek. There we found the massive frame of no less than a bishop from Indiana together with his wife. It seemed intensely comical to see a bishop in Barek! But at the first encounter I felt with joy that here was a true servant of Christ, and such he proved to be through the next six hectic hours. He was not a little comforted to see my white face and said, "Now look, I am entirely in your hands, so you just tell me what I have to do." I assured him that he was not in my hands at all, that I was in no sense the boss, but an uninvited adjunct to the church of Christ, and that he was in the hands of its Javanese leaders, ten of whom had accompanied him from the city. After a meeting at Barek we drove on up to Gondang and then far back to the Christian village of Paru. The Bishop was profoundly thrilled to meet so many believers who had recently turned to Christ from Islam. Of course I had to interpret everything that was said to him or by him. The humility of his character, his joy in Christ, his clear, simple, elementary Bible teaching, his quick sense of a chance to exhort and encourage, were altogether admirable. There was a matchless scene at Gondang when Sumali gave in Javanese a most excellent message of welcome and personal witness to Christ, which was interpreted into Indonesian by Susilo, and then into English by me, before being beautifully answered by the Bishop, the four of us standing in a little knot in the middle of a small, crowded room. At Paru the situation was less happy, for the pastor is not an easy man to understand. We were given a Javanese meal with tropical fruit, but both meal and fruit inflicted a total defeat upon the Bishop and his wife. They had some other nasty shocks for millions of flying ants were whirling around on that particular evening, littering everything and everybody with their corpses. And when we dropped into our home at Sabrang to give the couple ten minutes' respite from publicity, several hundred cockroaches chose that moment to emerge from Mother Daro's well and stage military exercises for their benefit. But if the Bishop may remember these things, we too shall remember him with joy. At such a distance in time and space from the Western world it seemed a delightful joke to have a bishop from Indiana in Sabrang, littered with flying ants!

On *December 6th* we spring-cleaned our house and with help from Man terminated the existence of fifteen baby mice. Next day I preached at the morning service at Barek. Although about 100 people have been baptised there in the past three years, the younger folk are apt to escape to the city, for beautiful Barek offers them nothing but a lifetime of back-breaking toil in the ricefields. Thus only seventy-three baptised persons live there now, and about half these are children. So there are often not more than twenty-five adults at the Sunday meetings, and it must be admitted that the four leaders, Chamim the host of the church, Suprapto the headmaster, Susilo, and another younger man, are not quite mutually adjusted as a team. In fact, team-work is not Susilo's strong point, for no one else goes at his phenomenal pace. On this occasion they were deeply troubled because one of their company was that very day to marry a Muslim girl with Muslim rites, repudiating his Christian faith. Chamim sadly compared this to Peter's denial of Christ, but Susilo would have none of it. "No, no, it's quite different," he announced, and he stuck to his point strongly, so that the less articulate Chamim had nothing more to say. These men have travelled far in spirit, but one must not forget how far they still have to go.

Meanwhile in Sabrang Rufus preached and Mrs Kardjo went to church for the first time in her life, accompanying her husband. In

R

spite of rain there were twenty-eight young people at the twelfth Young People's Fellowship on our verandah, four of whom took part by giving brief messages. At night Jess and Loti went to a cottage meeting. In fact on this Sunday, Loti contrived to cook, serve, and wash up all our meals and to attend four meetings as well. Next afternoon the house was packed with sixty-two for the Children's Meeting, though we are well aware that it is partly the approach of Christmas which is inflating attendance.

Thereafter our attention became riveted to December 11th, the day when we were to be formally received as workers by the East Java Church. This is really the achievement of an objective towards which we have been working for several years. We drove to the city on the 10th and at night I attended a preparation meeting. This was a delightful occasion. There was prayer, detailed explanation of the programme for the next day, and a message from Faral which strongly impressed me, partly because it was in Indonesian and I thus had the rare pleasure of being able to understand it. He based his exhortation upon three Scriptures: (1) John 21:15-16: Love to Christ is to be expressed in "shepherding" the sheep, which is the translation in the Indonesian. (2) Colossians 1:24: We are called not only to preach Christ's sufferings, but also to share in them. (3) Luke 22:36: "He that hath no sword let him sell his garment and buy one."

On *December 11th* I was not feeling well and slept for three hours before the ceremony at 5 p.m. for which I wore my Oxford M.A. gown and hood. The pastors assembled in the big vestry at the East Java Church in the city. There were fifty of them in addition to four Dutch pastors and twelve graduates from the seminary who were about to be ordained, making a most imposing host, all robed in austere black. The church was packed with about 350 people. The front of it was richly adorned with white flowers and on a table stood the empty cup and silver plate, reminders of the Lord's Supper. The pastors and graduates sat in four curved rows close to the pulpit, which occupied the centre of the back wall. The first part of the evening was a service of thanksgiving led by the man whose child was drowned in a pond. Then Faral took over and preached excellently on 2 Corinthians 5:18, "God . . . hath given to us the ministry of reconciliation". He explained carefully that whereas the twelve graduates were being ordained as pastors of the church, I was merely being received as an evangelist working with the East Java Church. This was at my own request, for they had originally planned to ordain me too, and in the ceremony not the slightest distinction was made between us. Before all I had to stand and answer three questions from Faral: (1) Do you believe that God has truly called you to this ministry? (2) Do you promise to be faithful in it? (3) Do you promise not to meddle in politics? The others were asked the first two questions, but not the third which was given to me as an alien and partly because there were non-Christian local officials present who might otherwise have assumed a political significance in my inclusion. Faral then came down from the pulpit, the twelve men and I knelt, everyone else stood, and Faral and the fifty pastors (including Rufus and Sutikno) stretched out their right hands over us (no head being actually touched by any hand) in prayer and blessing, in ordination and (in my case only) welcome!

It was a great occasion, uplifting to the soul, glorifying, as I felt, to the Lord, and a most impressive demonstration of the life and impact of this church. In the presence of all we each signed a contract form. Then the pastors filed before the thirteen of us, shaking hands warmly, followed by the entire congregation. Naturally I dwelt with special pleasure on my handshakes with Sutikno, Rufus, and Jonathan. I could but admire the Dutchmen and their ladies for being there at all and for the degree of acceptance they still have among believers. By this time my head was throbbing furiously and at 10.30 p.m. we left the city, Pastor Meng seeing us off from the Bible College, anxious (as always) at our launching out at night into what he thinks of as the "dangerous" countryside. To the north the sky was lit up by the lights of the city; we headed south into the silent village world, Jess driving.

Sumantri has now been removed to the city gaol. His attitude is not quite satisfactory. He smuggled a note to us in an empty coffee cup asking for "as much money as possible", as his salary had not been paid, and before leaving he got permission to come to the verandah steps under guard to repeat the request in person.

We felt it right to decline, but passed the news on to Susilo's office, which is responsible for him. Susilo at once said to me, "I hope you did not give him anything."

Meanwhile I preached for the seventeenth time at Gondang. The fact that New Testaments and Bibles are bought off me every time I go is one sign that the Spirit of God continues to work there. The midweek meeting on Thursday night is better attended than the Sunday morning service, for farmers do not find 9 a.m. an easy time.

And now at last the decision about a resident pastor for this area has been taken. Rubani, a man of limited vision and ability, who has been tried out here for several months, has been shunted off to Wagir, partly on our recommendation, I think. Instead we are to get Tilosa, a brand-new man, powerfully built, already married, forthright in character, a former pupil of Rufus in his Karangan days, and leader of the group of twelve who were ordained on December 11th. Our first impression is that the Synod has given to Sabrang the best man they had available, and that we can rejoice because the village churches have been delivered from Rubani. Tilosa will start work in February and live at Barek.

Arrangements for Christmas are now absorbing much time. There was originally hope of a united public Christmas celebration with the Salvation Army hospital. However, Salvation Army work is controlled from their headquarters in West Java, which is sending three foreigners to take charge, and the East Java Church (which is, I repeat, an entirely Javanese organisation) has wisely shied off. Instead we are to take the local theatre on Sunday, December 21st, and it looks like being the biggest evangelistic effort Sabrang has ever known.

On *December 15th* we held the last Children's Meeting of the year with eighty-four present, buoyed up by rumours of an outing. This is to be on December 30th, but the high cost of transport will confine it to those who have attended steadily. Six children told the full Christmas story from Jess' flannelgraph pictures, the result of many hours of preparation with them.

On *December 17th* the cottage meeting under Mawardi's wing was due to be held in the home of Mr and Mrs

Kardjo, a very important occasion for them, involving a large degree of committal to the Christian gospel on the part of the whole family. They rearranged their sitting-room and prepared refreshments for twenty-five guests, but from 4 p.m. very heavy rain set in and continued for the next six hours. I stayed indoors for some time, hoping that it would relent, and then, since there was not far for me to go, sloshed through water and mud to their home, minus shoes and socks and with my trousers rolled up above the knees. The only other person to get there was Subir. It was rather sad to see them disappointed.

Mrs Rufus has been away from her home in Ringit for the past six weeks. Eighteen months ago one of their children broke his arm in a fall from a tricycle and it was not properly set. The Doctor has agreed with others they have consulted that for the present the arm should be left as it is, although it is obviously awry. Seeking a different answer Mrs Rufus took the child to an old-style Javanese medicine man in the district where they formerly used to live. It has been hard on Rufus having his family away for so long, and he has made many trips to them, three hours on his scooter each way. We have done his laundry for him, but we have not seen much of him during this period.

The whole of *December 18th* was devoted to decorating our house for Christmas and preparing for the Women's Meeting Christmas celebration at 4 p.m., to which husbands were also invited. There were nearly forty people present. At the start I read the Scriptures, prayed, and gave a short message, and then led games for forty-five minutes—these are always greatly enjoyed. Then we had refreshments, a choir piece, messages from Rufus and Suwarso, and a small present for everyone off the Christmas tree. Mrs Kardjo not only came but actually sang in the choir while her husband, dropping in in uniform as soon as he was free, stared shyly at the floor. This was a great victory for her. Just as the party drew to a close the rain started and rapidly grew to a deluge, which made it impossible for anyone to get home. A mob of youngsters splashed through the elements to practise hymns for Christmas and with the guests stormbound we were under very heavy occupation for a total of six hours.

December 21st was our Christmas Sunday. There were twenty men and twenty women present, but many other women were absent preparing for the evening meeting, for which the local theatre had been hired. It was good to see Nasur there, silent as usual and with roving eyes; after attending Christian meetings two or three times a week for four months he must have absorbed a great deal of teaching.

At night our Christian company was on parade in a big way. Both men and women were in the mat shed theatre for most of the day. We ourselves lent balloons, bedspreads, sheets, gowns, dolls, and cakes! By 8 p.m. there were 400 people packed inside. I stood with the welcome committee in the central aisle and shook hands with them all. It was a splendid occasion, for nine-tenths of these people would not think of attending an ordinary Christian meeting. Even Mother Daro, our landlady, came. The local gentry and their wives, all magnificently dressed, were there in force, to our great delight. It would probably be true to say that their presence was due more to courtesy than to interest in the gospel, though it provided a convenient opportunity for learning more about the nature of the Christian message without making oneself conspicuous. Mawardi and Rekso also shook hands with everyone who came, as did Subir and Kardjo. Subir looked very smart in a new grey suit and he showed to their seats the most distinguished of the visitors. Kardjo, short and dark, wearing the black Indonesian hat, entered with zest into everything. It is remarkable the way these two men have become the central figures in our lives in recent months.

The stage was beautifully decorated, equipped with footlights, balloons, flowers, a large Christmas tree, and amplifiers. The proceedings, which were in charge of headmaster Suwarso, lasted from 8 till 11 p.m. As a local dignitary it was a very great ordeal for Suwarso to address such an audience and he made the concession of sometimes calling the Lord Jesus Christ "the prophet Jesus". Rufus would certainly not have approved of that, for it amounts to adopting Muslim phraseology and tacitly endorsing their view of Christ. There were several choir-pieces by children, women, and young men. The wings and the back-stage areas were a hive of activity, most of our Christian community being gathered there. Rufus, who had no part at all in the arrangements, was given the thankless task of explaining about the tree, a regular feature on these occasions and one that might well be dispensed with. But of course he did it a great deal better than Suwarso had the previous year. Then I was put up to preach. I used the text Psalm 147:3, "He healeth the broken in heart and bindeth up their wounds", illustrated by the story of the Good Samaritan. I had been specially asked to include my own personal testimony to how I found Christ. This was far the largest audience I have ever faced in Sabrang itself. After me came Faral, representing the city church, but unhappily he went astray. In some quarters great emphasis has been placed upon the gospel as the fulfilment of age-old national aspirations and cultural forms. Thus at excessive length Faral expounded ancient national traditions and sang several songs from the Javanese classical theatre, catching at allusions and words as adumbrations of Christ, the moral being that Christianity is in harmony with and is in fact the ultimate fulfilment of the Javanese spirit and inheritance. In the end his coat-tails had to be pulled. He did not hold the audience well and those we have talked to since—Rufus, Subir, and Loti— are unanimous that direct, spiritual, positive presentation of the word of God is far more effective than enmeshing your own feet by the selection of a devious and doubtful route.

At the end came six tableaux of the Christmas story, most beautifully and tastefully done by the Young People's Fellowship. On the whole it was a daring, significant, encouraging, and successful departure for the Sabrang church. I was out till after midnight ferrying people home in the Mayflower, the last being Mrs Kardjo, who had bravely sung on the stage beside Mrs Subir. Nasur, too, openly identified himself with us all. The staff of the Salvation Army hospital were present and also the Pentecostal church. Seeing the latter bunched together I was struck again with their marked racial characteristics; they are mostly of mixed Chinese-Indonesian stock.

The following night, *December 22nd*, the Salvation Army hospital held their Christmas celebrations in a military hall at Ringit. Again there were about 400 people present, though the leaders of the community, the officials, and the school-teachers, were notice-ably absent. The Doctor sat in the audience, but when the curtain rose the five seats on the platform were all occupied by foreigners. I felt that this lack of orientation to the times was never quite overcome.

On the evening of *December 22nd* I drove to the Christmas celebra-tions at Barek. Subir has not been to any of the outlying churches, so he and his wife came with me in the car and we picked up Suwarso, Mawardi, and some of Rufus' children. Happily the rain held off and the large covered area in front of Chamim's house was well filled with about 200 people, the Christmas tree standing in the centre. Susilo led the proceedings, erect at the reading desk through-out. The agenda was written up on a blackboard. Susilo is most unoriental in speed, and along with this characteristic goes a tendency to be irritated with slower mortals. At times he was distinctly curt and angry-looking with those who failed to do exactly what he required. There were many singing items, and Rubani, Rufus, and I preached in turn. The lighting of the tree was a great event. All lamps were first removed and for a few minutes we sat in total darkness. Then Rufus entered in full robes, carrying one large candle. This symbolised his arrival as evangelist three years ago. From his candle one representative from each of the seven churches which have resulted from his work, came forward, lit his own candle, and knelt. Rufus read the Scriptures over the seven, and then they rose and lit every candle on the tree till it was a blaze of light. This done, they walked round and round the tree with their own candles still burning, singing, It was most impressive and the idea, of course, was Susilo's.

On *Christmas Eve* I was out again, for the fourth night running. While Rufus went alone to Wagir, Susilo, Mawardi, and Hastari came with me to Gondang. As soon as we reached the house of headmaster Tias, Susilo was asked to take full charge of the evening. There was a delightful scene in the living-room as he sat, pen in hand, at a table with the Christian leaders crowding round him, being told what to do at top speed, while the crowd waited.

The meeting was held in the old schoolroom shattered by the

earthquake, the roof propped up and one wall down. Two hundred people braved these conditions, gathered in high anticipation around the Christmas tree, which was thus seen for the first time in Gondang. My mind flitted back to the previous Christmas when Rufus, Jess, and I showed flannelgraph pictures to 100 people who were at best curious. But this has indeed been the year of Gondang's visitation. Tias took charge at the first, which was fitting since he and his stout lady have provided the setting and basis for all that has taken place. Susilo made them repeat the candle parade which was so effective the previous night at Barek. Rufus being absent, Tias led off in great solemnity with a solitary candle in the pitch-black room, frozen in silence and expectation. From that candle the doctor, Lukas, lit his and knelt, followed by the ever-impressive figure of Sumali, ex-head of the village. These are the three leaders at Gondang and with such important men serving Christ the entire community must respect what is happening.

Then came Wirojo of Segaran, for seventeen Segaran men had walked up the hill to join in the rejoicing. Others followed and finally they lit thirty candles on the tree, which held every eye with its splendid blaze as we sang hymn after hymn. It was indeed a great evening, the best of all. I was the only preacher, speaking on "This child is set for the fall and rising again of many". Men and women alike seem disposed to pay eager attention to the gospel at Gondang now, thanks to Rufus' long perseverance last year. It was my own eighteenth visit, so there was no strangeness to be overcome. Refreshments followed, during which I was asked to explain that we do not worship the tree but use it as a symbol of the Light of the World. Four hundred tracts were distributed and at the end there was a great shaking of hands and confirming of faith. It was a crowning evening and we drove down the Great Volcano with no little joy and raced along the empty, undulating highway into Sabrang at 12.45 hours on Christmas morning.

December 25th. After four hours' sleep we were awakened by the Javanese and foreign staff of the Salvation Army hospital singing carols under the trees on our drive. Then at 11 a.m. we had a select gathering in our house to which we had invited only new believers like Mr and Mrs Kardjo and others converted or responsive from non-Christian families, who would otherwise get no celebration of Christmas at all, such as Nasur, the mystery man, Riti at our gate, the Samaritan woman and her children, and a wizened old woman named Sari who attends many meetings here and lives altogether alone. There were twenty of them all told.

The first to arrive was Nasur, dressed in spotless white, and thus for the first time I had a natural opportunity of chatting with him. We talked for a long time and this confirmed my impression that he is not an observer with ulterior motives but a genuine seeker for truth from the strictest Muslim circles. He has perhaps already found the Pearl of Great Price, but I felt it wisest not to press him too closely, but to let him keep on going at his own pace. Registering decisions, in the East at any rate, is often the enemy of true evangelism. With this mixed group we had a delightful morning—chatting, showing flannelgraph pictures of the whole Christmas story, singing, and having a Christmas dinner, buffet style. Loti and Yeny do magnificently on such occasions and as I looked round at our guests I felt how privileged we were to call these people friends and to be allowed to help them to pass out of darkness into God's marvellous light.

In a Muslim land the annunciation of the angel to the Virgin Mary is a very important passage in the Scriptures, so I spoke on it, as I have repeatedly done this year. Javanese Christians—knowing full well its strangeness to Muslim ears and the objections raised against it—are apt to skate round it, which only leaves the objections holding the field.

In the early evening we had another, more solemn and private party, perhaps reception would be the better word, just for Mother Daro, her old mother, and her two servants, a woman and quixotic Man, who has been unfailingly helpful and kind to us throughout our years in Sabrang. All these are strong adherents of Islam and ancient Javanese tradition. Loti and Yeny joined in as our guests and Jess herself served the company coffee, biscuits, tinned pears, and sweets. Then we lit up the Christmas tree again and there was a present for each one off it. I said grace before we ate and spoke briefly about the Lord's coming for our salvation. The seats of honour were occupied by the two noble ladies, one shrivelled and horny with age, the other an experienced and buxom matron. They sat happily with us for an hour. They very rarely enter our home and, although theirs joins right on to ours, they have never invited us inside.

Two further expeditions with Rufus for Christmas celebrations fell through due to rustic confusion of arrangements, which was perhaps just as well, for we have had many visitors. Chamim came from Barek and is rather concerned about the church there. He and others tell me that Susilo is too aggressive and puts people off. We have seen some truth in this in our own home. In many respects he has the virtues and the vices usually attributed to Europeans. This, and his lanky stature, sometimes make me wonder if he is not of Arabic origin. Kardjo the policeman came twice. He makes much progress in the faith and hopes he will escape an early transfer from Sabrang, for it is only two months since he turned to the Lord and he feels acutely his need of time to absorb the teachings of the Bible. Before Christmas he felt depressed and we had a long talk about the deceptiveness of such feelings and the necessity of trusting Christ, His sacrifice upon the Cross, His presence, and His promises. On Christmas Day we gave him *Pilgrim's Progress* and he said later, "I read it from 3 till 7, and then after supper straight on till 11 p.m." It seems to us that the Lord has laid hold of this man. "God really called me long ago," he said, "but I needed someone to open the door for me. Subir did that by making it possible for me to attend meetings here, though at first I was rather bewildered, especially by the way you called Jesus Christ 'the Lord'."

On *December 29th* Rufus asked me to attend a Christmas party at Ringit for his neighbours. Fifty people were present in his small house, nearly all of them Muslims. It was a little awkward for me as I was marooned at a table with men I did not know who were racially, religiously, and linguistically shy of me. Both Rufus and his wife spoke and then, without any warning, he called upon me. I used 2 Corinthians 5:19-21, the verses beginning, "God was in Christ reconciling the world unto Himself". I was tired and I do not know how well it was received. There was one prominent Muslim leader in the room, but he avoided seeing or greeting me.

Next day *December 30th* sixty-two of us went to the Indian Ocean in two lorries. Some friends of ours in Canada had sent us a special gift. We do not normally use any money other than for our living and travel and as a fund from which to buy literature for resale. We have never given any financial support to the East Java Church or its agents, neither to Rufus, nor Susilo, nor any of our colleagues, and we were anxious to use this gift wisely, in a way which would not create a precdent or encourage people to look to us as a source of material gain. This trip was the answer. We explained that it was not from us but from Christian friends in Canada in memory of their son. The great majority of the party, even the adults, had never before seen the sea, which put on a dashing display for our benefit. Choruses and hymns were sung all the way in the lorries; some of the crews, Christians from Kabat, joined in with us. Jess took Mrs Rufus, Mrs Susilo, Mrs Kardjo, and their children in the May-flower, getting back with the windscreen wipers and self-starter out of action and the handbrake on the floor under her legs. It was a relief to us to get everyone home again without any mishap. Susilo acted as leader, a whistle on a red cord dangling round his neck. While Rufus sat decorously on a rock with his family watching the animated scene on the beach, Susilo removed his trousers, tied them round his shoulders, pranced about in the shallows, and scaled the cliffs in scorn of skull-and-crossbone signs. Nasur strolled on his own and Mawardi entertained the company through getting caught by a wave from behind while he was collecting shells. It was delightful to see our friends relaxing for once and we arrived home full of thankfulness to God for the day. Human nature being what it is, five of the young people came right back to No. 122 with us at the end, sat about on the verandah, and demanded presents. We talked with them for some time and explained how big a present the whole trip had been; but they departed in a huff.

The outing left us quite exhausted for the last day of the year, which is annually observed in our Mission as a Day of Prayer. We were forced to lie low till after tea, when we prayed together; then the Doctor and his wife came to supper and we spent the evening in prayer, ending with the Lord's Supper. This brought us to 9.30 p.m. which, in the familiar words of the radio, is "Midnight.

Australian Eastern Time", so we tuned in to Melbourne to hear the clocks chiming in the New Year there and to receive the announcer's delightful personal wish, "May God bless you and give you your heart's desire and strength to cope with it when it comes".

On *New Year's morning, 1959*, we had an extended time of prayer and singing with Loti and Yeny. Then I had my hair cut in a little shack close by, during which operation the barber said, "In Middle Java fifty of my relatives are Christians; in connection with their work they have to be!" Roman Catholics, of course! But we are constantly confused with the Roman Catholics and I had a note the other day addressed to "Pa David, Chairman of the Catholics in Sabrang". As a matter of fact there is no Roman Catholic work in this area at all, but there is a vague notion current that we are all much the same, and one can do little about this. As though to offset the previous note, I had a New Year card addressed to "Mr David, Evangelist opposite the Prison". This may not be inappropriate, as one day a policeman handed me a letter from a man in the cells asking for Christian literature. We sent over a bundle of tracts and booklets, not going across ourselves as that attracts undesirable attention, and later I had a letter of thanks. We did not know the man and he seemed not to be a Christian yet, though he stated that "there is a church in the prison".

Then an unpleasant incident occurred. A betjak, which is the Indonesian style of rickshaw in which the driver pedals behind and the passenger sits under cover in front, drew up at our door and out of it stepped two complete strangers. They were both young men and the chief spokesman lacked one leg, walking with a crutch. Among our many visitors there are often those I am not aware of having met before, so I greeted them with warmth, sat them down on the verandah, and asked Loti to bring tea. They had a suitcase with them and from this they produced scarves, table covers, and badminton racquet frames, explaining that I was to take one of these in return for a donation to the "People's Fighters", though they made it clear that the donation was to be many times the value of the article. They suggested a sum equivalent to about £6 and said they had been given my address by a plantation owner at Gerbo, of whom I had never heard. By this time I was most dubious about the guests' connections and intentions; they came from far-away Middle Java, so there was no way of checking up on their identity. The more uncertain I became, the more pressing they waxed. When they saw their hopes of a handsome donation receding they tried to make me pay for their betjak. With profuse apologies I made it clear that I could not be browbeaten for cash in this manner and withdrew from the verandah until they had taken their departure.

In the evening I attended a New Year party at Susilo's home in Triwung, somewhat akin in nature to the Christmas party Rufus had held for his neighbours. Most of the sixty people present were Muslims and the programme was mixed, but wholesome throughout. For four hours our versatile host directed the proceedings, using four different translations of the New Testament, with hymns, prayers, songs, testimony, preaching, and a little conjuring whereby unskinned bananas acquired slits inside them and lamps went out at a word of command.

On the first Sunday of the New Year I was asked to preach in the Sabrang church, taking 2 Peter 1: 1-11, which is a most necessary passage in these parts. "Giving all diligence, add to your faith virtue." Seventeen men and twenty-eight women were present, but there should really be more. Mr and Mrs Kardjo did not come, which was a pity. Perhaps they had had some trouble; outside his home we passed him looking rather worried, fixing up a fence at the roadside, which he need not have been doing on Sunday morning.

And so we drew near with relief to the last fortnight's holiday we would get before leaving for furlough. The petrol shortage is now most acute, but by this time I know the inconspicuous houses in various villages which grow it in the garden. None the less, for the second time we were on the road approaching the city with the needle pointing straight to zero. Happily we got enough to carry us up to the Hotel of Peace, but in the city the garage I use misplaced my car book, which it is an offence in this country not to carry with you. A two-hour hunt ensued, during which the accountant at the garage challenged me to a game of chess. In holiday mood I accepted and five pairs of eyes followed every move for the next hour. I was eventually cornered, which was a most satisfactory result.

Then on the eve of departure I received a summons from the authorities in Surabaja and as it seemed unwise to delay I was compelled to take the morning train from the city. Business took exactly two minutes and concerned an extension of residence permit for Jess. They had already received a letter stating the necessity for me to remain in the country, but I was now requested to produce one explaining why my wife should do so. After four hours on crowded trains for all that it was a great joy to pull away in the game little car right up to the Hotel of Peace. This time I felt really exhausted. I think the toll is taken by the tropical climate, by the strain of constantly operating in a foreign language, and by the fact that our home, being a centre of much work, is not exactly a peaceful retreat. We would not have it otherwise, yet we thank God for this place at high altitude to which we may retire from time to time. One needs to be refreshed out of staleness.

Daytime at the Hotel of Peace: crisp air, brilliant sunshine, clouds capping the volcanoes, hillsides terraced to the top, miles of Indian corn on the mountains, oceans of potatoes, of flowers for the city markets, of vegetables, of orange groves, the infant Brantas hurtling over a 200-foot precipice, villages nestling thick in the folds of the hills, no waste ground, geese in the roads, glorious views, rain every afternoon, fir trees on higher ground, then jungle at last.

Night-time at the Hotel of Peace: blazing sunset and afterglow, lamps twinkling in homesteads shrouded in bamboos, the incessant roar of water, frogs croaking, the ten thousand lights of a city strung out for many miles far below, no traffic, stillness.

We have slept much, read much, and walked far. The country people are still very friendly and everyone knows that we are "walking about for two weeks". The foreman of a labour gang in an orange grove insisted that we rest a while and drink tea with him. Generations gone he thought that his ancestors were Hakka Chinese, but he looked fully Javanese. He said he had an uncle who was a Christian. Although he seemed very ignorant of the gospel and lived in an ardently Muslim community he told us that he had hung up a picture of Christ in his home.

On the late afternoon of our last day, Sunday, *January 18th*, we sat out on the hillside entranced by the magnificence of the scene as the sun went down and a myriad lights were turned on in the valley deep below us, wholly unaware of the awful tragedy which had taken place in Sabrang.

On that Sunday morning Kardjo's little boy of four woke up early and sang choruses to himself which he had learnt at the Children's Meeting on our verandah. At 8 a.m. his father took him to the Sunday School which is held at the Salvation Army hospital; it was the first time he had ever been to it. Then at 9 the family all went to the Sabrang church and the child sat right through the meeting between his parents instead of going out to play with other children. They then took a betjak home, but on the way he asked for an ice-cream so they stopped and the child and his mother crossed the road to get it. The man handed over the ice-cream and while Mrs Kardjo was paying him the child ran back with it across the road towards his father in the betjak. A taxi was passing at speed and he was killed in an instant between them.

Kardjo's first thought was to kill the driver, for this is what sometimes happens on such occasions, but "the Lord reminded me that I was a policeman and I even began to feel sorry for him." Perhaps had he been a believer of longer standing he would have said that he remembered he was a Christian, yet Javanese Christians have a very strong sense of their duty in society so that his remark was not inappropriate. In their perplexity the Kardjos turned to the Muslim authorities for the funeral, knowing no other method. However, their approach was refused on the grounds that they had already believed in Christ. And so the little boy was accorded a Christian funeral, which was all over by the time we got back to Sabrang next morning and heard what had taken place. Kardjo got Subir to take charge of arrangements and Mrs Kardjo asked for a hymn to be sung which speaks of the names of believers being written in heaven. There was a large gathering in their home, most of those present being Muslims; Rufus spoke and so did the Pentecostal pastor from Paru. The child's grave is the fifth in that corner of the Sabrang cemetery reserved for Christians.

Rufus and other believers had been with the Kardjos ever since the accident and we visited them the night we got back to Sabrang. There were a number of Muslim relatives present and we could hear prayers being intoned as we talked. They looked stunned and shattered, as anyone would. He told us the whole story in detail; then Jess spoke about heaven, I read from Revelation 7, and we were able to encourage them. I felt they were very brave, holding to the Lord. They were deeply impressed with the way the child had spent his last days and hours. He was frequently in our home, came to the Christmas morning party and on the Indian Ocean picnic, and often played with Rupert after that.

This terrible tragedy made it difficult to settle down again. Rufus came and we prayed together about everything. So did Subir. We visited Triwung and had a long talk with Mrs Susilo in her husband's absence. There is sad trouble at Barek, where the original turning to Christ took place three years ago. The four leaders have recently found it increasingly hard to pull together and the other day Chamim, the host of the church, quarrelled fiercely over financial matters with Suprapto, the elderly headmaster, who is the most influential man in the church there. It ended with Chamim punching him in the face and although Suprapto refused to strike back relationships are bad, which is not going to make a very happy start for Tilosa when he is inducted in a fortnight's time. He is to live at Barek.

On *January 21st* we called on Mr and Mrs Kardjo again, with Rupert, and came away marvelling at the grace of God in them. At Christmas we had given them a very attractive Christian calendar with a picture for every month. One of these pictures shows the Lord receiving children, about twenty of them, and one little boy kneeling at the back seems to her to be her child and this has greatly comforted her, for she has not had time to acquire much understanding of the Scriptures. It is only a month since she began to turn towards the Lord, and less then three months in the case of her husband. They went over with us again the things the child had said and done in the last days, all seen in a special light now. Their

Muslim relatives have rallied to them, staying in the house. So have local Muslims who are holding special prayers for the child for a week. But their faith in Christ seems to be standing the strain remarkably well. The police authorities have freed Kardjo from all duties and told him to report later when he feels ready for work again.

On the morning of *January 22nd* Kardjo came round to us to chat, dressed less smartly than usual as a sign of mourning, with no shirt on and his coat collar turned up to hide his vest. His father-in-law said to him, "If it had been my child, that chauffeur would have died", but Kardjo strongly dissented to this and I rejoiced to see that the Lord had freed him from hatred and given him a quiet, forgiving spirit. We talked for a long time and I urged him to be very patient with his wife, though she might prove less able to disengage her mind from the tragedy and often relapse into tears. Before his conversion he was a hard man and did not treat her well.

Since meetings do not recommence till February my immediate programme is rather lighter than usual. We called on several new officials who have recently been moved to the district. It is most necessary to pay one's respects to, and be known by, the leaders of the local community. Ideally we should have made a round of such calls when we first came to Sabrang, but since our Indonesian was at that time so limited it is hard to see how we could have done so very successfully.

On *January 24th* we again called on the Kardjos and once more we left marvelling at their triumph in this agony. On Sunday morning, *January 25th*, we were there yet again and he came with us in the car to the Sabrang church, outside which the accident had taken place. Happily, it is just possible to reach the church without passing the actual spot, so I chose the back road and as we got to the corner Kardjo beside me looked resolutely away from the scene. Mrs Kardjo did not quite feel up to going, for which we could not blame her, so we left her at home with our gramophone and gospel records. After church—the moment one week ago when it all happened—I sat with them and when I left the gramophone started up again. Loti, instead of taking her day off in the city as usual, is spending it with Mrs Kardjo.

On *January 26th* Susilo came for one of his long chats. He asked me the meaning of Leviticus 2: 13, "the salt of the covenant of our God", which was remarkable since the verse in my mind over Kardjo's child and the quarrel in the Barek Church has been Mark 9:49, "Every one shall be salted with fire". I am sure no one around here reads Leviticus except Susilo! He has spent many hours with the Kardjos and wrote out a prayer for them to use. The Samaritan woman called on Jess the other day; her husband, who is also in the police, is away and before leaving he said to her, "You go on attending those meetings and when you really understand you can join". The faith of Subir and Kardjo has been a challenge to many. The fact that Kardjo stood right beside the chauffeur without striking him and that Mrs Kardjo did not go out of her mind has caused much comment.

Then on *January 27th* we all drove to the city and at night I caught the train to Surabaja en route to spend one week in Djakarta attending various committees and council meetings. After sleeping at Mrs Tan's I caught the morning express for the west with Mr and Mrs Orr, but when we reached Middle Java the train was halted at a large town on account of a break in the line ahead of us. It was only 11 a.m., but there was no hope of getting through that day. Leaving the others with our luggage at the station I walked through the town for forty minutes and succeeded in hitting upon the house of a missionary I had met in former years. He and his wife rose splendidly to the occasion and we greatly enjoyed their capacious, old-style, Mission compound with its lofty rooms, deep verandahs, and quiet lawns. I found him to be a linguist of amazing versatility, intensely learned in many fields, and withal a delightful character. We had a long talk about the ways of various missions. He feels that the steady increase in both the Middle Java and the East Java Churches since about 1950 is due to the resumption of foreign financial and personal aid, "everything has been properly run again". Certainly Rufus, Faral, Susilo and our friends in East Java would not be able to agree with that!

Next day we went to Bandung, but it was the hardest travelling

I have yet encountered in Java. We were in an air conditioned second-class Pullman, but the conditioning had failed. No window would open and for most of the day we sat in the broiling sun at sea-level, the bad air giving us headaches, for the coach was very full. Never do I remember enjoying wholesome air as much as we did the freshness of the Bandung night. We slept in a row on mattresses on the floor of what used to be the Bible College before it moved across to East Java, and next morning caught the express to Djakarta after almost four days' travel from the city. During the ensuing week many long hours were spent in committees and there was time for nothing but business and one message at a Chinese church. Immersed in the vast, hot, humming capital, Sabrang seemed a far-off tale indeed, but for the fact that Jess and Rupert were still there. It did me good to meet fellow-missionaries once more and to laugh with others again. We are indeed thrice blessed in Indonesia, for the Lord has given us a wonderful team of colleagues.

At 5.30 a.m. on *February 4th* I left again in the air-conditioned express for the east, gliding clear of great Djakarta before dawn and racing headlong across the vast plain which divides the volcanoes from the Java Sea. In barely two hours we were tearing down upon the junction of Tjikampek, the diesel engines eating up the glorious country. Ahead of us a goods train was heading eastwards too when something went wrong and twenty covered freight cars slammed together, a dozen of them crashing down the embankment in a dreadful heap into the ricefields. Packed with people, the express pulled into the junction as I was busy revising Christian Witness Press tracts. Then we drew out, gathering speed again, with only ten miles to go to the scene of the crash, and it must have been then that the first news came through and I like to think of the station-master slamming down his phone and grabbing for the inter-com! They got a signal up in the path of the express and as we ground to a halt everyone looked up with the same thought in his mind, remembering what had taken place the week previously.

We backed into Tjikampek and rumours flew. For four hours the express stood parked while a thousand people tried to think what to do. Many went back to their homes in Djakarta. Others paid heavily for road transport beyond the break in the line. Some got a partial refund of their money and headed for Bandung on the branch line, anticipating a long hold-up on the direct route to Surabaja. At times I leant towards each of these alternatives and in such a crowd clear information was unobtainable. In the end I felt I should stick to the express, so I went back to my seat and, so far as was possible in the prevailing uncertainty, continued working. Suddenly a tall foreigner was beside me, stacking his luggage on the rack, and almost at the same moment the train started. We moved up to the scene of the crash, dismounted, walked for 500 yards through the ricefields, and clambered confusedly on to a small, crowded, relief train the other side of the wreck. The foreigner proved to be an American theatrical director, travelling alone with heavy suitcases, two overcoats, and no knowledge of the language. He was the kind of man who wears no vest and unbuttons his tropical shirt from top to bottom, revealing a hairy chest. He had been on another train, not the express, and when that was stalled behind us he somehow managed to get a taxi to catch us up in the nick of time. He was thus quite capable of looking after himself in one sense, yet through my knowledge of Indonesian I was immediately able to be of service to him and he became more or less my responsibility. For the detour through the ricefields he hired a coolie to carry his cases. When we mounted the relief train it was already packed and I was thankful to notice a tiny ledge-seat, on which I at once put my briefcase. However, a restaurant car attendant saw the two of us and very graciously said quickly, "Follow me." He led us straight into the dining-car where two window seats were still vacant. There the coolie presented himself to the director, who paid him three rupiahs, which he refused, demanding fifteen. His request was unreasonable, but he had been of service in a special emergency. I advised him to give five, which he did, but the man refused it again, talking to us hard but not unpleasantly. At that the director began to get angry, and answered simply by a raucous blather of gibberish right in the man's face, aping what the Indonesian sounded like to him. The whole dining-car became silent spectators of this unhappy display, which he continued. Feeling that something must be done to stop him, I said to the coolie quietly, "Would you be content if I gave you ten?" He at once said, "Yes," so that was the end of the matter, but I felt the atmosphere around us was not too good.

Next came the ticket collector punching tickets. I handed him mine, plus the extra ticket required for travelling on the express. When it came to the director he had only his ticket, without the extra one, for he had not originally been on the express at all. So the ticket collector asked for the further twenty rupiahs, explaining that this train was now the express. I translated this to the director, at which his indignation knew no bounds. "Why should I be surcharged," he demanded, "when I never wanted to go on any express?" In vain he tried to get me to translate his angry remarks. "If this had been in my country we would have had a humble apology for the delay, free transport across the break in the line. . . . And now after hours of delay and difficulty, I'm to be surcharged, am I?" Since I would not interpret he turned to others, asking for someone who understood English. Every eye was upon us, hating the white man. The ticket collector, seeing that he was not going to be paid, retained the director's original ticket, without which he would not be able to leave any station. I talked hard to him in English, explaining that one could not behave in such a manner with impunity, and stressing that he and I were guests in a foreign land, to whose ways we must adapt ourselves. I also talked in Indonesian to the men packed around us, apologising for his attitude and words, explaining that he was a stranger and did not understand the ways of Indonesia. It seemed to me essential to dissociate myself from the spirit he was showing. In the end, seeing his ticket gone, he paid up with a very bad grace, indignant at my failure to back him.

The long-suffering ticket collector, who was only doing his duty, turned to collect other tickets, but three men near us, one of whom was a soldier, refused in like manner to pay the surcharge, arguing back to him. To the director this seemed a vindication of his position, but I laboured to explain that it was one thing for an Indonesian to refuse to pay in his own country and quite another for a white man to do so, since his position was already precarious. In this case the three men altogether refused to yield, so the ticket collector went off with their tickets in his pocket. When the excitement had subsided I said to one of them, "How will you get past the barrier at Tjirebon?" "Oh, that's no difficulty," he replied, "we know everybody on the station there, its our own city!"

Now that the relationship between us was ruined the tall stranger was rather a problem to me. I felt he wanted to be rid of my assistance and be free to manage things in his own way. For my part, I was keen to shed his company, for nobody knew how far the train would get that night and I foresaw having to go to some hotel in a big Middle Java city with him. As I thought over it I came to the conclusion that I would not pass the night in his company. I decided I would get him into a room and then find a Chinese Christian's home on my own, which was unlikely to be difficult. However, he solved the problem for me. When we stopped at Tjirebon in the late afternoon he suddenly announced that he would get off there. The carriageful of people, who had been horrified at him at first and then came to accept his presence as a curiosity, were now genuinely alarmed to see his defiant figure stalk down the crowded platform, heading for the streets of a big town, where he had no friend or acquaintance. So he went alone, a sitting target for the devil.

By 11 p.m. we were in Semarang and thanks to the kindness of a Chinese Christian I was able to reach the American Southern Baptist Mission as an entirely unexpected guest, but one made richly welcome by a very different type of American! Yes, the "household of faith" is no imaginary entity. Their goodness, their cleanness, their godliness, their self-control, their devotion to Jesus Christ shone out by contrast with that unhappy man's behaviour, and I slept deeply, thankful for this port of refreshment. But by 5 a.m. I was on the train again with the same company of weary, dosing, congested companions and it was 6 p.m. before I was home after two days of seventeen and nine hours' rail travel respectively. I went to bed at once, but rose later and spoke at the Weekly Bible School. Susilo failed to turn up and I had been unable to prepare properly, so I told them the whole story of my adventures, based on Proverbs 3:5-6. Mr and Mrs Kardjo were there, nicely dressed again, as those that have come out of great tribulation, washed their robes, and made them white in the blood of the Lamb.

CHAPTER 16

THE RECOGNITION OF THE CHURCHES

RUFUS might truly have said, "Lord, now lettest Thou Thy servant depart in peace, according to Thy word, for mine eyes have seen Thy salvation", for on Sunday, *February 8th*, the seven scattered village congregations numbering in all some 500 souls, were officially constituted one church fellowship and Tilosa solemnly installed as its pastor. These are Rufus' children in the faith. True that a small number of them, such as headmaster Tias of Gondang or Suwarso at Sabrang, were Christian in name before he ever came here, yet they have suffered a spiritual transformation since his arrival. And for the great majority, for Mawardi, Rekso, Susilo, Wirojo, Sumali, Lukas, Hastari, and many, many others "whose names are in the book of life" he has been the doorkeeper in the house of the Lord who has thrown open the portals of life eternal. Many of them have long been his colleagues, and it is often through them rather than directly through him that souls pass out of darkness into God's marvellous light, yet he remains the instrument in the background, so much in the background that most people outside the Sabrang area still do not appreciate the force of his ministry. He is repeatedly slighted and overlooked, while his failure to shine in elegant company lends colour to the notion that he is not of much importance. It is perhaps better so.

On the eve of the crowning day Mr and Mrs Kardjo called upon us, and when they went Rufus and his wife came. It was 10 p.m. and we were already in our pyjamas, but they stayed till 11 and we had a heart-warming time of fellowship and prayer, relaxed and rejoicing in the wonderful works of God.

From 7 a.m. on *February 8th* Jess was constantly at the wheel of the Mayflower, ferrying people to Barek along the big road. They would have gone there anyway, but we could at least serve them in this little way, which is the only material contribution we give to Christian work in Sabrang. Subir called at 8 a.m., unchanged. For this month he is stationed at a remote spot in the mountains, so he cannot often be among us, but he is a vibrant witness and has already found out other Christians and stirred them into action.

Meanwhile believers converged on Barek to the tune of 550! The roofed space outside Chamim's house sheltered the whole company from the burning sunshine. After hours of rural delay we started at 11 a.m. and the proceedings lasted till 2.30 p.m. There were many choir-pieces from the various churches, some very rustic, some highly polished. Faral presided and at 12.20 p.m announced the birth of the new church, consisting of seven congregations. Then the seventeen appointed local leaders, one of them a woman, formed into an arc, inside which stood a smaller arc of robed pastors, and within that again Tilosa knelt in his robes while Faral led in prayer. Then headmaster Suwarso, the interim leader of these local churches, solemnly shook hands with Tilosa, presented him with a Bible, escorted him to the rostrum, and the new figure, striding confidently upon the scene, at once read out as his text 1 Corinthians 2: 1-5, "I determined not to know anything among you, save Jesus Christ, and Him crucified."

For me the occasion was an opportunity for fellowship, not only with believers in the area, but also with the many who came in six truck-loads from the Christian villages on the south coast. Jess continued her self-imposed task as chauffeur and while returning empty to Barek at sunset she met one of these homeward bound trucks, and all hands went up in a spontaneous yell as she passed. I must admit that there is something profoundly moving and satisfying about being so warmly accepted by the churches of Christ in the orient, even in the face of the spirit of the times. I myself, after an orgy of contacts, walked home at dusk, enjoying the chit-chat of the road—"No, all four will be turned into beef at Lakar"—"The coconuts are for my family"—"Yes, I'm building the house myself"—"Why on earth are you walking and where have you come from?"—"Stop in here with us, won't you?" and this last was in Kedok.

And Rufus? As usual, he was apparently forgotten, wholly in-conspicuous, not robed as a pastor or even invited to the platform, but standing with me among the seatless ones at the back. As the guest trucks made off, our own company was left in the banana-skin littered arena, remnants of the refreshments which had been served. Tilosa has made a good start and the brethren seem pleased to have him. He is a strong-looking, firm-spoken young man, now lodged with his family in a tiny house near Barek. Rufus and Susilo feel that they will be freer than ever to bring the gospel to the complete outsider and are elated that a number of people are now meeting every Saturday night in hitherto unresponsive Kedok.

Somehow we contrived to hold the Young People's Meeting on our verandah that evening. Nasur was there, and Kardjo and his wife too. Kardjo had missed the big meeting at Barek, as he was called to share in guard duties on President Sukarno's route through East Java, but standing rigid with arms presented as the cars flashed by he saw only his own gun and not the President at all.

Meanwhile Tilosa, his solid frame encased in black trousers, a long and immaculate cream-coloured coat, and a bow tie, sat till midnight with Rufus discussing and planning. We were already in bed after the day's labours when a scooter turned into our drive. Being exhausted we lay still, rather hoping that the guest, whoever he was, would come back another time. However, the scooter was parked and someone stood for ten minutes meditatively on the verandah. Eventually I rose, perceived that it was Susilo, and let him in. He was very concerned about one of his daughters, who has spent a lot of time in hospital recently. Still wearing pyjamas I rode most uncomfortably on the carrier of his scooter to the Doctor's home and the latter then accompanied him back to Tri-wung. The girl seems to have some kind of hysteria brought on by overstrain, and perhaps by having such a strenuous and restless father! "No wonder she's hysterical," commented the Doctor later. "She's Javanese and whatever her father is, he's not Javanese!" This independent opinion interested me as I had already formed the idea that our good friend's ancestors must have been Bedouin from the deserts of Arabia.

And then our normal programme resumed its stride. Heavy rain washed out the Children's Meeting; only twenty got through it, and were rewarded by being marooned here for three hours. Mrs Rufus led and I spoke. The pressure was just off when Mrs Kardjo, her sister, and her father visited us. After producing tea, Loti came and sat with us on the verandah, as she is a friend of the family. We estimate the ladies to be around twenty-five years old and their father fifty. Almost at once Mrs Kardjo asked a leading question about the Two-Ways poster which has been on our wall all these years. This was intended to make an opening for me to expound it to her father, which I proceeded to do. He responded by explaining that there were two good religions in the world, Islam and Christianity. For me, at any rate, it is best to avoid all controversy, so I simply laid beside his remarks others of a positive nature about the power of the Lord Jesus Christ to save sinners. We also had a general chat about other things. This family remains the focal point for us these days and hardly had they gone before Kardjo himself arrived, full of joy. His growth in spiritual things is amazing and such is his zeal to learn that he attends a meeting here or at the Salvation Army hospital six evenings a week.

On the night of *February 11th* at 9 p.m. Rufus arrived on his scooter, shrouded in cap and mackintosh, and we had a delightful evening of prayer and discussion. It is always cheering to have Rufus in the house.

On the night of *February 12th* I accompanied Rufus, Mawardi, and Rekso to Lakar for the inauguration of a regular mid-week meeting there. Although not more than ten miles from us, Lakar is out of the Sabrang district and comes under the ecclesiastical supervision of the city church, which is inclined to mismanage its children. Thus we have seen little of the Christians there, and this rigidity of organisation has made it difficult for Rufus to visit them without trespassing. We found twenty-five people crammed into every room of Hasan's house. Hasan is the Madurese engineer who was converted three years ago when living at Ringit with his family. It appears that he had the house next to Rufus and his daughter liked the singing she heard there and brought home a New Testament. Her father dipped into it and the more he did so the more his desire to investigate the gospel grew. He was actually born on

Madura Island, a Madurese of the Madurese, with many Mecca pil-grims in his family. He was baptised at Barek and has stood firm ever since, which is saying a lot. However, having moved from Ringit to Lakar he has lacked Christian fellowship. He is a bold witness and a vigorous, rather self-important Christian. "What I have done for the Lord is quite exceptional," he declared, but since he has not seen much of other keen Christians there may be truth in it. I am bound to say I like him and respect his zeal for the Lord, in spite of his immaturities. He has fitted a loudspeaker to his gramo-phone and broadcasts music and gospel records for hours a day on the main street of Lakar; he has thirty-nine gospel records in Madurese, Javanese, and Indonesian. "Him that is weak in the faith, receive ye", is a golden text. "For God hath received him . . . yea, he shall be holden up, for God is able to make him stand."

Both Rufus and I preached and then we all sat on for hours. I had a long talk with Hasan, while Rufus opened his Bible and ex-pounded the truth to Hasan's brother-in-law, a massive man who had never before been in a Christian meeting, heavy-jowled, sick, and broken-looking. This Lakar group of believers is now asking for more help from Sabrang. Shortly before midnight we took our departure. With the Mayflower laid up for repairs and all normal traffic off the roads, we faced a two-hour walk home through the silent countryside with the glow of the city lighting up the northern horizon. A policeman on a bicycle stopped us and asked where we were off to at that time of night. Then a military lorry, packed with standing soldiers, very graciously picked us up and we raced home in the finest breeze I have felt for years, standing among the men who were friendly and amused that they should have given a lift to an evangelistic band.

On Sunday, *February 14th*, I paid my first visit to Kedok since the time when Susilo and I called on the actor who had helped Jess. Up to now there has been no movement of the Spirit of God in Kedok, which breaks a long line of villages between Sabrang and Gerbo, in all of which there are Christian contacts. But now through the sorrows of Barek, the turn of Kedok has come. I have already alluded to the quarrel between Chamim, the host of the Barek church, and Suprapto, the elderly headmaster, recently pensioned off. Both these men were prominent in the community before their conversion through Rufus. After the trouble it became difficult for Suprapto to attend meetings of the Barek church, since these were all held in Chamim's house. He is a dapper, round-headed man, aged about sixty, and ever since his conversion he has been an ardent fisher of men. With time he has developed considerable gifts as a speaker, and now just as he was free from other responsibilities came this difficulty. So he said, "Right, I'll be an evangelist and work with Rufus and I'll start at Kedok." So one month ago, shedding reserve, alarm and shame, he stood with Rufus in a house in Kedok. The place was full of people. That was on January 17th, the eve of the death of Kardjo's child. On January 24th the two of them stood there again. On January 31st and February 7th, Suprapto alone preached for Christ in Kedok. Then on Saturday 14th, I joined him for the first time and he told me, "We are starting a Sunday School to-day." It was held in the home of a young widow, wife of the former village secretary, who believed in Christ in 1952 through Pentecostal Christians, but who has had very little spiritual help since then. It seems that she has responded with delight to Suprapto's interest in her village. To begin with there were twenty-two children in the room, excited, responsive, raw. Lots of people watched the house at a distance. Numbers rose steadily, first to thirty-four and then to fifty-two, so that the meeting was not altogether easy to run. When a group of lanky youths marched in, most of the girls ran out. Later the youths took their departure, the girls came back, and comparative order was restored. Suprapto conducted the proceedings with considerable skill and for his first Sunday School lesson expounded the opening three chapters of the Book of Genesis clearly and vivaciously, holding the children for no less than forty-five minutes. Then he got them to shut their eyes and pray, and he taught them two choruses. When he finished he asked me to speak. I remained sitting to eliminate my height and he interpreted my Indonesian into Javanese excellently. Then I gave out the Christmas tract to the children amidst great excitement and delight.

In the evening I went back to Kedok once again for an evangelistic meeting with Suprapto. This time there were about 200 people packed into a house on the main road, noisy, curious, pushing. Suprapto had his plan and worked it resolutely. To begin with we made an attempt to sing. Then he prayed briefly, read Romans 3: 10-20, preached with vigour, and called upon me to follow him. I spoke on Matthew 11: 28. It was a memorable night of raw evangelism amidst the yelping of babies and the chattering of on-lookers. Everybody was in gleeful mood, and when it came to giving out tracts at the end, the crush and enthusiasm were well-nigh overwhelming. No doubt numbers will drop as the more curious get their fill, but Suprapto lives close by, visits diligently in Kedok, and regards himself as spiritually responsible for the place. In other words, it would appear that yet another village church is on the way.

Next morning Tilosa, the new pastor, spoke for the first time in the Sabrang church. He put on his robes for the service, which added unusual decorum to it, and he has a splendid voice, powerful and rich in both singing and preaching. In build he is short, thick and strong, and he speaks clearly and with authority. He must be about twenty-eight years old and has independent means. He read the third chapter of I John and gave an excellent, interesting exposition of "Behold, what manner of love the Father hath bestowed upon us, that we should be called the sons of God". In manner he is warm and friendly, diligent in greetings, smiling and attractive in his cream coat. It all seems almost too good to be true. One can feel already the comforting, encouraging sense among the people that we have a real pastor of our own now. But what a tremendous job he has—seven scattered churches led by headmasters, doctors, and village officials, with other new departures simmering, Rufus rampant, and a couple of missionaries under his wing.

In the evening he came to address the Young People's Fellowship on our verandah and gave them an excellent talk about the Widow of Nain. Twenty-eight of them were around us for four hours and we had an exciting election of a new committee. Fellowship is warm and hearty and Tilosa just slipped into position as though he had always been here. He strikes me as a born pastor, on the young side, like Timothy. He is a child of the new Indonesia, confident, full of hope and expecting great things. Loti is delighted with him, and she

is always a good barometer for us to read. Both Subir and Kardjo
were voted on to the committee to represent seniors who insist on
attending the Young People's Fellowship. Kardjo looks very sad at
times, and then a strong light seems to flood over him. He and his
wife attend many meetings, cleaving to the Lord. Since our furlough is now only five months away we are anxious to turn the
children's meeting into a regular Sunday School. On February 16th,
we took a big step towards this, fixing classes and inaugurating a
teachers' preparation meeting. Furthermore, Sardjonan, the man
from West Java, offered himself as a teacher, which will be a great
asset to us. Indeed, there is an all-round augmentation of the striking
force.

A man whom I know but have not seen for many months visited
me early on February 19th. I am afraid I always respond rather badly
to gush. He roared with pleasure, held on to my hand, banged me
on the shoulder, and planted himself on the verandah. Seeing
Isaiah 53 on the wall in Javanese below a picture of Christ in
Gethsemane, he read it all, asked questions about it and laid himself
open to a prolonged explanation of the gospel, which he has often
heard both from Susilo and from Jess. He said he would make up
his mind about Christ one day, so I showed him the story of Felix
and Paul, where the governor's main interest was really money and
not the gospel. This was rather unfortunate for my visitor. He
hesitated a moment and then plunged into what he called "the
second reason for my coming to-day", which was to ask for a loan
of money. Long ago I perceived that the only way to deal with such
approaches is by refusal, for they are not genuine and if one were
granted they would soon become legion. The only way I can see to
approach keeping the letter of certain Scriptures is to give people
the gospel and literature about it, for which I had ample opportunity in this case. We get far fewer guests now that it has been
generally comprehended that we are not a source of material gain.
Plain curiosity, plus hopes of acquiring money and English (the
gateway to money), were largely responsible for the crowds of our
earlier days.

For the second week running I joined Suprapto at Kedok for the
Sunday School and the evangelistic meeting on Saturday afternoon

and evening. Prolonged heavy rain reduced attendance, yet we had forty children and eighty adults. Mawardi came too. He is a very helpful man. I marvel at Suprapto's skill. In spite of his age, he holds the children's attention easily. He drops into choruses which they rapidly learn. His theme this time was Genesis 3, and he used an empty gluepot and an old ink bottle to represent the two trees in the Garden of Eden. Both Mawardi and I addressed the children. At night Suprapto was rather brief, and it fell to me to give the main talk. Already seven adults in Kedok are asking for baptism. I rather doubt that they are converted yet, but the request is an indication that they want to go on receiving the gospel.

The same evening we had an unexpected visitor, Sumantri, from the outer islands, straight from prison. He stayed the night with us, full of the Lord's goodness to him and his wonderful opportunities of witnessing for Christ in the gaol, where it seems that he acted as preacher on Christmas Day. Holy words roll out of his mouth a little too easily, yet one feels truly sorry for the discharged prisoner, wifeless, homeless and discredited. He came with me to Kedok and spoke briefly on John 3: 16. He seemed to be in no hurry to get back to Segaran and stayed to hear me preach on Revelation 1 at the Sabrang church. Feeling sure that he was going to ask me for money, I decided to forestall it by giving him a gift of ten rupiahs, and after prayer he departed to start what I trust will be a new life.

Once again we had twenty-eight at the Sunday afternoon Young People's Fellowship, in which the young people themselves are increasingly taking control. At the close of each meeting the committee meets in my office. Soon after they had all gone, Kardjo appeared. He and his wife are under very great strain as the fortieth day since their child's death approaches. On that day there must be a big feast, and the relatives, of course, want things done in the old Muslim way, while the Kardjos themselves are none too clear what the new Christian way ought to be.

Quite an important decision was reached this week when Mother Daro, our landlady, gladly agreed that we should rent this house during our ten months' absence in England on furlough and return here at the conclusion of it. Rufus is keen for us to do this, and we feel that we are not likely to find a more suitable spot. Mother

T

Daro will guard our furniture and belongings, and whatever she does, she does well.

During the children's meeting this week Sumantri came back from Segaran to spend another night with us on his way to get a new job in the city. Perhaps it is best for him to get right away from Segaran after what has happened, though he says that the night he spent there in Wirojo's house he testified before nineteen men. On the four journeys involved in going there and coming back to Sabrang, he was in pick-up taxis without ever having to pay his fare. Three times, he says, the drivers refused to take his money, and on the fourth occasion, an elderly man paid for him, saying, "Pa David gave me a Christian tract once." Sumantri is full of joy at all this and gleefully showed me the ten rupiah note which I had given him, still unbroken. It seems to have been a good start for a discharged prisoner. At the end of the children's meeting, I asked him to lead in prayer. He did so at considerable length, but I must admit that we have never had such total silence during prayer before. He thought, as many people do, that Rupert was eleven years old instead of five, and that he was our only child. He seemed very pleased to see the photographs of our other boys, and asked many questions about them. This encouraged me to pop my question, "Are you married?" He firmly said, "No", which conflicts with what I have been told. All evening as we sat together he brought out problems which he had met with in his Bible-reading in prison. Thus we discussed: (1) Who was Cain's wife? (2) Is circumcision necessary, or is it a sin? (3) Are the Old Testament food laws binding upon Christians? He took down the Scriptures which we read together, especially 1 Timothy 4:1-4, Galatians 3:1-3 and 5:1-4 and 6:14-15, and Acts 15:1-11. Something seemed to strike him as we read Acts 15. "You mean these verses are connected, they hang together," he said, as if he had suddenly understood something. All his time with us he spends in his room with Bible, notebooks and pencil. He told us that his spiritual life really dates from Susilo's visit to Segaran on March 17th, 1958. That evening he watched Susilo as he was speaking and wondered, "Who is he? What is he after? Is that book in his hand a dictionary? Could it possibly be a Bible?" At the close of the gathering Sumantri rose and asked Susilo a question about fate and free will. Susilo marked him down and got hold of him at the end, and (notwithstanding robbery and prison) the blow Susilo struck for Christ that night may yet prove to have been a stout one.

At the close of the children's meeting, I took a car-load of children back to their homes just outside Sabrang, and as we drew near to the long bridge over the river, a cyclist crashed thirty yards ahead of me. He had a pillion rider, a strongly built, barefooted youth, whose foot became entangled in the spokes of the back wheel and brought the machine down. Although his foot was not cut, it was bound tight in a mesh of spokes. I stopped the car, told the children to stay in it, and ran down the road to help him. A crowd of other people soon gathered round, but we had to cut the spokes to free the man's foot. I explained that I must first deliver my car-load of children, but that I could return in a few minutes and take him to hospital. This I did, and he seemed very glad of the lift, a plain-clothes policeman coming with us in the car. As we passed No. 122, I mentioned to the fellow that I lived there and that my name was Pa David. Then I delivered him to the hospital and went home.

On the day of our Weekly Bible School I am always immersed in preparation, but this week I managed to do some visiting as well and went to Ringit. I called on Rufus and found him very tired after some exacting days at Karangan on the south coast. We had one of our usual sessions of exchanging news, of planning, and of prayer. Still in Ringit, I dropped into a home where three men were con-verted through Rufus some years ago. They are humble folk and one reaches their place by passing behind another house on Ringit's long back avenue, but there is something stalwart in character and faith about them. In all these villages, the backbone of the churches is farming families such as these, for Rufus and Susilo have not primarily won the young people, but rather their own age group, early middle-aged family men who have brought with them all their young folk.

Then I went on to see Tilosa, the new pastor, at Barek. He is not yet quite at ease with foreigners. After we had talked together, I wanted to ask him to lead us in prayer, opening my right hand a little as I made the suggestion. He misunderstood what I was doing and shook my hand, but then he hastily recovered and prayed. He is doing well, proving a man of action and strong character. Twenty yards from his house there is a house of ill-fame. He discovered that one of the girls there was known to him and came from his own Christian village of Karangan. Only two weeks after his arrival he contrived to pay off her debts, get her out, and plant her temporarily in the home of a Christian woman in Barek.

The fortieth day since the death of Kardjo's child fell on a Thursday, the day of the Women's Meeting run by Jess and Mrs Rufus; it seemed remarkable that Mrs Kardjo managed to attend and a sign of her genuine desire to follow Christ. Later in the evening Kardjo and Subir called on us, just as Rufus, Mawardi and Rekso also arrived. It was good for Kardjo, I felt, to talk and laugh and pray with these men again. He was shabbily dressed as a sign of mourning.

The same evening, Rufus, Mawardi, Rekso and I drove to Lakar to see Hasan, the Madurese engineer. Then we went on to Semen, which joins on to Lakar, forming together a rambling township of 15,000 people. Passing through Semen, we went on by night to a near-by village, down lanes and muddy tracks where all the others had to dismount until we finally parked the May-flower under the trees outside a big farmhouse owned by a very old man whom I had never seen before. We spent two hours with him and his family in a small, dimly-lit, ill-furnished room. The brethren devoted every minute we were there to making known the gospel. Rufus is at his very best with old people. Our host perched on the edge of a comfortless bamboo bed, a man heavy with the labour and ignorance of life in a remote village. Rufus gave himself wholly to him, with everybody else listening, and women and children packed in the doorway behind the grandfather. At closest possible range Rufus hung up the "Sinner's Dream" poster and expounded the way of Salvation most attractively, cheerily patting the old man on the knee and the shoulder, constantly questioning him to make sure that he held his attention, planting the gospel in his heart.

On the last night in February a meeting of the new Church

Council was held at Tilosa's home at Barek. Rufus and I attended by invitation, and were given the right to vote, though in practice we both abstained. There were fourteen present, of whom two were women. We started off at 7 p.m. with a handsome meal. Then we sang, and Tilosa read the whole of Joshua 3 in his magnificent voice, declaring that we were like the priests, the River Jordan was like the world around us, and we were called to stand in the middle of it with the Ark of God. Then there was a time of prayer followed by a four-point agenda, which took us until 3 a.m. Sustained by coffee, fried bananas and rice cakes, we sat doggedly and joyfully around a long table in the tiny manse and hammered out the new shape of the church. Tilosa was in the chair, the youngest present, clad in a dark red shirt, a striking figure with his big head, thick neck, splendid physique, strong forearms, and large expressive hands. He is a born pastor and seems to have all-round ability for his job. It is the nature of this country to organise everything meticulously and the duties of each office in the church were thoroughly discussed. Rufus and I acted as tellers when it came to voting. Much time was given to discussing "evangelism within the church area", which is regarded as the church's responsibility, and "evangelism outside the church area" which is regarded as Rufus' duty and mine. Everything was conducted in the Javanese language, of which I understand a little, although 85 per cent remains hidden from me. Susilo, however, sat next to me and made full notes of the discussion in Indonesian in his beautiful handwriting; these kept me on the line of the conversation.

Among the questions which had to be hammered out was where to hold baptisms and the Lord's Supper in this seven-in-one church district. The pastor is full of ideas on everything; some of these have a youthful dash that won't do much harm. He has already changed the times of several meetings so that he can visit each of the churches at least once in three weeks for the main service. I think he is God's gift to this work. My main impression of him is strength —physical, mental, spiritual strength. He has a strong voice, a strong will and clear ideas. He is very warm and friendly, a most charming smile ever flashing on and off his face.

Rufus and I did not stay to the bitter end, but left at 2 a.m., and then at 7.30 a.m. he accompanied me to Tulen, where I preached for the first time in Sudjono's home, festooned with Christian Witness Press posters. This is the man whose believing mother was given a Muslim funeral. There were not very many people present, but yet it seemed a wonderful thing to have a regular Christian meeting in such a place. Why does one family of timeless countrymen, lodged in a barn-like farm miles away down a muddy lane above the Larsti River, respond at once to Rufus' message and stand staunch, holding faithfully to the main lines of a gospel which they do not exhaustively comprehend? Sudjono is about fifty, thin, dark, simple, gracious, smiling, uneducated, locked away from me in his Javanese dialect; but he is Christ's.

From there we drove straight back to Sabrang and I preached on the epistle to the church at Smyrna. Sumantri is here again, apparently full of zeal. He borrows things and does not return them, yet it still seems to us that the Lord has done much for him.

Every Monday morning Jess cycles off to the women's prayer meeting, which is a great joy to her. We have come to regard Mrs Rufus as a soul as choice as Rufus himself. Like him, she is from the humblest type of family, living right down on mother earth, but they both belong to the Lord's aristocracy—humble, gracious, godly and faithful.

Nasur, the mystery man, still attends meetings several times a week, and is very interested in our forthcoming furlough. He even asked me if he could come with us and how much it would cost. He said he would be glad to escape from Sabrang "since my family is not of the same faith". This was the first time I had heard him imply directly that he was now a Christian. As a matter of fact he needs to make real friends of the believers here. Up to date, he has just come, and listened and gone away—a thoughtful, unrevealing, unknown man.

The first to arrive at the Weekly Bible School on *May 4th* was Kardjo and his family. We were thrilled to see them again, but first he went off to a previous meeting at the Salvation Army before coming back a little late to ours. The next arrival was Nasur, who deposited his Bible and hymnbook and then also vanished into the darkness, returning after the meeting had begun. At its close I drove Mawardi and the Ringit party home, as I always do, and then dropped in to see Rufus at 10 p.m., finding him full of joy and news and plans.

This week's Young People's Fellowship was conducted by Sardjonan, the man from West Java. The speakers were the two policemen, Subir and Kardjo. All three of them prayed nicely, but otherwise it cannot be said that they did very well. Sardjonan was a bundle of nerves and had to ask for a malarial pill before he could even get started. Subir read through the story of the marriage at Cana of Galilee, but, good man though he is, found next to nothing to say about it. Kardjo was the best of them, but at the moment it is terribly hard for him to grasp what the verses of Scripture are all about. He tells me that he thinks he turned to the Lord Jesus on November 18th last year. Nasur was present and is increasingly friendly; I had a good talk with him about baptism. Hastari of Triwung came for a long time, so concerned about a sick friend of his that I eventually drove the Doctor out to see the man. Hastari's old father, Daddy Tain, though a staunch Christian, lends more of an ear than Hastari likes to ancient Hindu lore. The other day Jess discovered that Sardjonan married his wife when she was at the tender age of twelve years, so that at twenty-two, she has four children. Mrs Subir, we find, was thirteen when she married.

March 10th. I went to the city for my lectures. The rainy season is now at its heaviest, and we drove home at 5 p.m. in dismal conditions, the heavens black and angry, torrential rain falling, visibility very low, all cars with lights on, wreaths of thick smoke from the railway beside the road further deepening the gloom, water swirling across the highways every few yards and rising in cascades from each car. On *March 11th* I drove the Doctor to the Christian village of Paru where he attended patients at the newly opened clinic in what was once the palatial missionary residence. Meanwhile, I was received by the old pastor who has taken such a dislike to Rufus and us, and in his house I addressed a group of thirteen people, including several church and village leaders. Thus was inaugurated a new venture, for I am to accompany the Doctor most Wednesdays and speak to this group of people in the pastor's house. In this way, I hope very much that there will come to be a change in his attitude towards us. That night I conducted our thirty-seventh Weekly Bible School, when, in spite of heavy rain, we had eighteen people present, including Rufus. He told me that there are now twenty people asking for baptism at Kedok, thanks to the labours of headmaster Suprapto.

Next day while Tilosa was addressing Jess' Women's Meeting in our home, Rufus and I went to Lakar and attended a meeting in the clinic attached to the big factory there. The Lakar-Semen church is enjoying a breath of new life. There were twenty-seven people present, all professing Christians, and all of middle-class type—administrators, schoolmasters and medical workers. An old man preached thoughtfully on the story of Martha and Mary. The remarkable thing was that neither Rufus nor I was asked to speak, a sign that the Holy Spirit has already imparted gifts and new life to others. We left while they were practising hymns and went on to another small factory town nearer to the city. Here we met with a similar group, twenty strong, running their own regular mid-week meeting. Rufus preached on Acts 4:12 for forty-five minutes very forcefully and attractively. It is grand to see and hear him, so quiet, clear, firm and winsome. I followed for a further forty-five minutes in Indonesian, untranslated, expounding the marks of a true believer from the First Epistle of John, which is a most useful theme here. Slowly but surely there is a great awakening going on, a rediscovery of the gospel by men from Christian villages.

March 15th. This morning I went up to Gondang on the Great Volcano, giving lifts to various friends seen on the road. It was my nineteenth visit and I was received and fed with the usual kindness by headmaster Tias and his wife. He has developed into a stalwart Christian leader and from the rather strong core of the Gondang church the brethren have fanned out and at seven surrounding places there are now groups of ten or twenty people who are responding to the Lord and want to hear the gospel regularly. Tias feels that this is partly due to the fact that in some respects the brand of Javanese tradition current in the area has points of contact with the gospel. Thus they have a kind of trinitarian belief which runs, "The Lord is Jesus. Jesus is the Lord. The Holy Spirit is the

Lord." There are now a regular forty people present on Sunday in Gondang and more than that each Thursday night. But today my audience was only fifteen as I was not expected and most of them had walked for one and a half hours along the volcano's flank to a village still higher up where a regular Sunday meeting is being inaugurated in the home of the head of the village. Thus Gondang is on the way to becoming a mother of churches.

In this pre-industrial era, when the vast mass of the population tills the soil, this type of evangelism is an injection into the bloodstream of the nation. In my judgement the once diabetic headmaster is one of the Lord's apostles; so is the Doctor Lukas and so is the ex-head of the village, Sumali. How the headmaster does anything I scarcely comprehend, for his study has not been dusted or tidied these past ten years. And now he faces the probability of promotion to be Inspector of Schools, a move which he feels may give him the chance to repeat elsewhere what has been done at Gondang. Truly, the Spirit of God cannot be restrained, and the work has run far and wide beyond Rufus' hand. The morning service seemed to be a very happy time, and once more I preached on the marks of a true Christian from the First Epistle of John. Everybody was exceedingly friendly to me. I met an entirely new man, a strong and pleasing character. He said that he had seen Christian tracts in the doctor's clinic and this had led to a chat with Lukas which had that week drawn him into the Christian group. But just to attend meetings like that is to begin to commit yourself.

I drove down the great mountain to Segaran and sat with Wirojo and five other men for an hour. Again it was a very thrilling time. Wirojo is doing the Christian and Missionary Alliance "Light of Life" correspondence course and is introducing others to it. We talked over the parable of the talents together. He marks and studies his New Testament, and I got the impression of a man who was making new discoveries, passing them on to others, and responding to the Lord with all his heart. He told me of contacts here, there and everywhere with men groping in the darkness for help. As I drove home I passed Tilosa on his motor-bicycle, heading back for the area which I had just left, and thus the work is driven forward so that one can no longer keep track of all that is going on.

On *March 20th* it was my turn to preach at Gerbo, the biggest town in this region, yet the weakest church. In truth no evangelism has yet been done in Gerbo and only six people can reasonably be expected to attend a Sunday service. When I reached the home of the local salt agent, where meetings are held, I found it locked up and deserted and it was soon evident that there was going to be no service at all on that Sunday. This, however, gave me a good opportunity to visit people, so I called on the Christian doctor, a man in whom the Spirit stirs not yet. We had a long talk on his verandah, and, to his alarm, I prayed with him. He has been there, silent, but diligent in good works for the past twenty years. His wife was out delivering a baby.

So I passed on, down a long muddy lane, to the home of the wealthy widow living alone in a fine house with a dual drive-in and closed red gates—the same widow to whom I took the two noble ladies from the city at the time of the Tent Campaign at Segaran so that they might bath in private. She was about to leave on a holiday trip to Bali Island. She is a Christian from birth and has little contact with local Gerbo people. I read the Scriptures to her, expounded the passage, and prayed with her, and I felt that she was quite glad of it. So little time has been put into Gerbo that it is not surprising the harvest is small. However, she told me that a Christian man from Ambon Island had recently moved nearby and so I went at once to call on him.

This man, whose name is Prak, received me with the greatest astonishment. After thirty years in the navy in Surabaja, he had recently retired and come to his wife's old home in Gerbo. She proved to be a Madurese lady, but had been baptised in 1931. I noticed at once that his Indonesian was bespattered with Dutch terms, and he was curious to know about what he called "the kirk". So I explained the local situation and the turning to Christ which had taken place throughout the whole Sabrang area. I felt I had a willing hearer who might possibly prove to be the key to Gerbo. On my way home I picked up Mrs Susilo on the road, and also waved down headmaster Suprapto as he was cycling home from his Sunday

School in Kedok, and then finally called on Tilosa to give him the names and addresses of the people I had visited in Gerbo. The ice seems to be broken with Tilosa and he is most grateful for suggestions where to visit in his far-flung field.

The next night there was a meeting in Kardjo's home, attended by forty-five believers from Sabrang and Ringit, a preparation meeting for the administration of Communion on Good Friday. Tilosa was in charge. Rufus was there, but sat beside him in a subordinate capacity. The younger man, by virtue of his office, is always in the position of leadership, and the yielding Rufus never for a moment obtrudes himself. But so far as I can see, Tilosa gives him room and does not ride over his head. It seems wonderful that this meeting should be held in Kardjo's home in spite of all the sorrows of the recent past.

On *March 25th* I drove the Doctor for our second visit to Paru village. The arrangement is rather a delightful one, for while he sees patients in the old missionary residence, I am free to preach in the pastor's house. It is true that not very many people attend, but I specially value the opportunity of being of some service to the old gentleman. In fact, he really seems to be quite a new man, and has even become enthusiastic about evangelism. His personal attitude to me is now delightful, and at the close of the meeting we talked together for seventy-five minutes while I sipped the glass of hot, free, American milk which he always gives me. He said, "The people everywhere are far more open to the gospel than they used to be. I have been reading about John Sung, the great Chinese evangelist, but in 1939 when he was here, the Javanese people did not pay much attention to him. Their hearts were quiet and tranquil. But now they greatly need spiritual help and comfort, so when Christ is preached they are irresistibly drawn to Him. In a Christian village like Paru, the people have been handed over to the gospel and to Christ, but their knowledge is most deficient. I only wish that every church could have a Bible class." That night we held our thirty-ninth Weekly Bible School. It is, of course, a big regular responsibility and I roam abroad little these days, but I am clear that for me the right thing is to keep on teaching, week in, week out. Mawardi and his family are most faithful in attending this meeting.

Jess is giving time to Mrs Mawardi, teaching her to read: she is sixteen years his junior and grows steadily in grace. I asked Sardjo-nan of West Java to pray. He is struggling to overcome a crippling nervousness. If he knows that he has to lead a meeting, he becomes sick, gets malarial shivers and takes to his bed, but he genuinely desires to be of use to the Lord.

CHAPTER 17

MOTHER PARDI'S KITCHEN

On *Good Friday* morning I had a visit from the farmer Sudjono in whose home I preached recently. He told me that his family had been strongly Muslim until he heard Rufus at Barek in 1956. Formerly he had himself been a heavy drinker; but, he said, "I felt that I needed a Saviour." We had a good talk together, but he sat on for two hours and I began to fear that he had another motive in coming. Eventually it came out. Would I lend him 200 rupiahs for fifteen days, that is to say, over the time of Javanese New Year? Now I am quite clear that there would be few surer ways to spoil the Lord's work in this district than by agreeing to irresponsible requests of this character. Yet I realise that everyone has times of extra financial strain and the thought that perhaps the foreigner would like to help comes easily to mind. He has a large farmhouse, many sons, smokes a lot, and is not destitute at all. Without directly alluding to him I did mention my surprise that men who smoke up their savings should try to borrow money from others. It will be a good day for the East Java Church when some conscience on this matter develops. When we first came to Sabrang I twice saw Rufus with a cigarette, but for years I have not done so and it is now generally known that he and I do not smoke, so that we are not even offered tobacco. We do not provide cigarettes for visitors to our home, and in this we are really breaking social custom, for when visitors come the very first act in Christian or non-Christian homes is to break open a packet of cigarettes and place them on the table beside a box of matches. It is almost unknown for a woman to smoke, and almost unknown for a man not to do so. Even Susilo still smokes, though he has told me that he knows he ought to give it up, but has not yet managed to part with so inveterate a habit.

As soon as Sudjono had gone I drove off in the Mayflower to

collect Rufus, Mawardi, and Tilosa, and together we went to a large
place on the top of the Southern Mountains where an evangelistic
meeting was held in the home of a doctor whose teacher daughter
has been attending the Young People's Fellowship in our home. It
was a splendid evening, three rooms packed tight with sixty-five
people, mostly men. We all spoke while they listened in perfect
silence. On such occasions when we are operating outside the sphere
of the newly constituted church it is Rufus and not Tilosa who takes
the lead. My own talk was a little unusual in that as I rose to speak
I became aware that the cane chair I had been using was broken and
that it had torn my trousers. With people on almost all sides of me
this constituted an awkward predicament and for the rest of the
evening, to the amusement of Rufus and Tilosa, I was compelled
to hold a hymnbook behind my back whenever I was standing.
Many New Testaments and hymnbooks were sold at the end and
since they wanted to use the latter right away Tilosa led them
strongly in hymn after hymn till after midnight.

Tilosa is out every evening except Saturdays and is thrilled at the
opportunities spread before him in this his first pastorate. On Good
Friday morning he conducted the Lord's Supper for the first time
in his life. It is a joy to see him, the born leader, made to be a pastor,
though he was once a soldier and before that a man of the theatre,
experiences which have given him something valuable for the
ministry. His sense of punctuality will need to yield a little to the
unhurried ways of the village world, but he is a willing learner.
That very afternoon Rufus had been at Lakar again, preaching to
about fifty people, but it was as we were driving cautiously on
bottom gear off the steep face of the Southern Mountains towards
1 a.m. that he began to speak excitedly about his adventures that
morning at a far-away place called Srengat. He reminded me that
years ago we had stopped there on our way to Sidoredjo and had
refreshments in a café with Jess and Rupert before they turned back
in the Mayflower to Sabrang. On that occasion we gave out
tracts around the market. Apparently a few days ago he was visited
by a man from Srengat who besought him to go there, and this
morning he was welcomed in a doctor's home by twenty-five
people who hung upon his words and requested him even with

tears to go often and teach them. I have not seen Rufus so moved as when he recounted this experience. He told them how very busy he was with developments in and around the newly constituted church, but the doctor actually knelt down in front of him and said that no matter how busy he was he simply must make time to help them.

After this storming Good Friday the flesh craved peace, but got none. At 7 a.m. next morning we had fixed a cycle outing with the Young People's Fellowship to a bathing pool some miles away. In the end I joined twelve gallant cyclists, while Jess took Mrs Subir, Mrs Kardjo, and Mrs Sardjonan, with their children in the car. The outward trip in early sunshine was delightful, but Jess got stuck with total brake failure and we spent several hours having the car repaired. I did manage to join the others at the pool, which proved to be a dammed-up village stream surrounded by giant trees, in which everyone bathed under the close and rather trying scrutiny of rows of village lads. Then on the way back Jess became stranded again, this time with dirt in the petrol, and so most of the day was spent salvaging the car, the mothers, and the infants.

At night we had a guest, a girl Jess had come across, the illegitimate child of a European by a Javanese woman. Her father left Java when she was an infant, but she has a great longing to meet him. She is now about eighteen. Having been married against her will at the age of twelve and become a mother at thirteen she is now being badly treated by her husband, who last week brought a new wife home, which is not wrong for a Muslim. She would like to go back to her mother in the Southern Mountains, but for her little girl; in such cases a daughter would stay with the father, and she fears that in her absence the child would get the violence which is now meted out to her. So what is she to do? She is very good-looking and charming with the child, who stayed to supper too and played with Rupert. She seemed to know absolutely nothing of the gospel. In spite of Jess' efforts to keep in touch with her she soon vanished from Sabrang; I was unsuccessful in trying to trace her in the city, and we do not know what became of her or the child.

Next day I was due to pay my three-monthly visit to Surabaja, so I drove to the city and travelled from there by train to save the exhaustion of taking the Mayflower down into the heat and contending with crowded roads. Opposite me in the carriage was a Javanese man with a girl, probably his wife, though she looked slightly Chinese. For a long time he leant over, whispering to her. She raised a newspaper up to her forehead and cried behind it. It was his talk which made her cry. I felt sure she was in much the same plight as the Eurasian girl. Then a chance came my way and I asked him who he was. "I am a Madurese," he said, and enquired in return from what plantation I came. So from this cue, on Easter Sunday morning, I was able to proclaim Christ as Saviour from the devil (looking at him) and from sorrow and need (looking at her). He was at least outwardly friendly to me, but she never spoke a word. There was some dreadful trouble in their lives, but the train drew into Surabaja and I know not just what it was. But it is good for the preacher, even on the steps of the pulpit, to be reminded of the whirlpools of this world in which men and women around him are drowning.

> *Oh, strengthen me, that while I stand*
> *Firm on the Rock and strong in Thee,*
> *I may stretch out a loving hand*
> *To wrestlers with the troubled sea.*

At boiling noon I preached to the Cantonese Church and then at 5 p.m. to the great Foochow congregation. After that came the British Community Church, where I addressed twenty white people and then had supper with the agent of the Blue Funnel Line, the American Consul, and a Shell Oil prospector. I was asked to say grace. It is good and profitable for me to retain this slender link with the European way of life, thought, and speech.

On *Easter Monday* I returned by train to the city, meeting on the platform a young pastor from Celebes. Several such have found life there intolerable and after months of hiding in the jungle this man felt he must escape altogether from misery and violence. He had just arrived, battered and bewildered in teeming Java. I drove home from the city very slowly and went to bed for eighteen hours.

Meanwhile one of the Young People's Fellowship boys had been home to Karangan for the Easter holidays. After church on Sunday morning he and six other boys walked through the rice-fields to the jungle belt on the shore just as we did years ago. They stood watching the breakers racing in over thousands of miles of open sea to pound upon two miles of glorious sand curving between rocky headlands. The temptation to plunge in was too strong and for half an hour they splashed about in the water, continually bowled over by the waves, shouting back and forth above the roar of the surf. And when they came out there were only six of them! Without the slightest indication of struggle or distress the power of the sea had simply absorbed a boy of nineteen, the only son of a widow. In recounting the tale at the Young People's Fellowship the fellow from Sabrang said that it was a call to him from the Lord to commit his life fully to Christ and also to keep Sunday more strictly for His service.

Kardjo came round for another long talk and prayer. He knows the husband of the Eurasian girl and is trying to draw him to Christ. While I was speaking at the Weekly Bible School, alluding to verse after verse, it was thrilling to see Kardjo find them himself in the New Testament and then turn round to help the man behind to do the same.

We are now in the middle of the fast month which the more devout Muslims observe by not eating, drinking, or smoking during the hours of daylight; to make up for it they have a feast at sunset and another at about 2 a.m. So each night men go round Sabrang clanging gongs to arouse the faithful for the nocturnal feast, yelling out the name at each house. Last night as they were clanging near us somebody shouted out "Pa David" amidst much mirth, so we seem to belong to the community all right. On Sunday it was my turn to preach in the Sabrang church. Whenever I do so, I just take the next section of the letters to the seven churches in Revelation 1-3. On this occasion there were only thirty present, as some are away during the fast, which is the holiday month, and others are distracted by it. For instance, the two sisters who were baptised at Gondang last year, being seamstresses, are so busy making new clothes for the great annual holiday season which follows the fast, that they have excused themselves for the month from all Christian meetings.

U

When the end of the fast month came Jess went with Mrs Rufus'
family for another visit to her home far west of here. In the evening
many people came to the house; gradually the children ceased their
playing and listened to the adults talking till one by one they lay
back on the beds around the walls, like swotted flies. After Jess
and Rupert had crawled under a mosquito net they could still hear
Rufus preaching on and on behind the partition, until they fell
asleep. Next day she was taken to visit an old gentleman completely
crippled with arthritis. Since he could neither turn his head, nor
move his arms, nor change the position of his legs, he lay sideways
across a double bed with his bent legs resting on a chair. Mrs Rufus
said that the old man was always happy, rejoicing in the Lord, and
that his wife was equally triumphant. Jess noticed mysterious ropes
hanging from the ceiling behind a curtain on the wall, and as they
saw her interest they explained their purpose. One simple bamboo
contraption, with clothes-pins attached, enabled a book to be
suspended above him, which he could move by a bamboo stick
which his thumb could just grip sufficiently, and thus he read for
hours at a time. Then he had what he called "my cross", also suspended from the ceiling, to the bar of which his mouth-organ was
attached by rubber bands. His wife told Jess that he loved to play
hymn tunes on it. These contraptions he had himself devised. So in
the vast, elusive, mysterious, crowded, countryside Christ has His
children and His witnesses.

One night I edged the Mayflower through the interminable
labyrinth of lanes and houses behind Triwung until we reached the
dimly lit farm of Hastari, who received me with delightful charm
and courtesy. He said that from childhood he had been seeking light
on life's pathway, and since he could not command enough cash
for the pilgrimage to Mecca he studied Arabic as the next best
thing. "This room has been full of young men studying Arabic,"
he said. Then a visitor from Sumatra, a Batak Christian, stayed in
his home and gave him a different hope, which flowered when Rufus
crossed his path three years ago.

On Sunday I preached in Gerbo in the home of Prak, the sailor.
This was an outcome of the visiting I did three weeks ago when the
salt agent's house was closed up. We had a maximum attendance,

seven adults and seven children. It is the third regular Sunday meeting to start this year in addition to the newly constituted seven-in-one church.

Meanwhile headmaster Suprapto is forging ahead in Kedok and the group there have again asked for baptism. If Rufus were in charge I suspect that their request would be granted and Christian witness in the place thus put on a firmer footing. However, Tilosa is new to this kind of situation and tends to share the scepticism of the city church about converts from Islam. Furthermore, living in Barek himself, he knows that Suprapto is partly motivated by the desire to have a Christian Church other than the one which meets in Chamim's house in Barek. Kedok adjoins Barek, and Tilosa's feeling is that rather than duplicate work by establishing yet another centre it would be better to move the meeting-place of the Barek Church a little nearer to Kedok, thus getting it out of Chamim's house and making it easier for everybody in either Barek or Kedok to attend the same meetings.

Sardjonan of West Java has become increasingly active for the Lord in Sabrang since Jess introduced him to the Christian and Missionary Alliance correspondence course. He was present for the forty-first Weekly Bible School, with twenty-one others. Tilosa came on his motor-cycle, attending this meeting for the first time. He looked splendid, all in white with the black Indonesian hat atop his large head. He is a man of outstanding personality and everybody was cheered to have him. He took over the harmonium and filled the house with music, but showed his immaturity by missing half the meeting struggling to mend a broken lamp, which he succeeded in doing just as the proceedings were terminating. His gifts, his youthful energy, and his confidence, are most delightful. Who would have dreamed we would get such a pastor? Mawardi and his girls were there as usual, and so were two soldiers from Celebes temporarily stationed at the local camp. They say there are forty-four Celebes "Christians" among their colleagues, for parts of that tormented land are Protestant by religion.

On *April 16th*, while the Women's Meeting was in progress in our house, I went to Lakar to attend the mid-week meeting of the church there. I had suggested to Mawardi that if he cared to go we might return together. I made for the home of Hasan the Madurese and found Mawardi already with him, reading John 14:1-6. Hasan, in fact, was thoroughly depressed over his daughter's affairs. She has married a young man who promised to become a Christian, but now that the wedding is over he has stated that he has no intention of doing anything of the sort. Since the son-in-law works at the same factory as Hasan, the latter has been made to look rather ridiculous. When eligible Christians in any one place are few this problem of matrimony becomes very pressing. Hasan is rather a carnal believer, ever harping on all he has done for the Church, and it is a great pity that Lakar's ecclesiastical link with the city has cut him off from the developments at Sabrang. But Mawardi's attitude and message greatly cheered him. He and his wife threw off depression, changed into their best clothes (which were very smart indeed) and we all climbed into a pony cart and went to near-by Semen, where the meeting had already begun in a schoolmaster's house hard by the mosque.

The Water Controller was preaching to about thirty people, his Bible open in his hands, which is a new touch in these parts. I wondered if I would be asked to say anything, but it appeared unlikely, for I had gone uninvited, simply to keep in touch with the group. The meeting ended, refreshments were served and I afterwards learnt that as the local doctor passed the cakes to Mawardi the latter whispered, "Aren't you going to give Pa David a chance?" The doctor took the hint, and I spoke for some time about Jeremiah's escape from the dungeon, telling them of the expansion of the gospel east of Sabrang. Jess collected us in the Mayflower at night and on the way home we had a puncture. Mawardi held the torch with his one hand while I changed the wheel; he is indeed a good man, steady and reliable.

Next day I was teaching Greek in the Bible College in the city as usual and took the opportunity of spending an hour with Jonathan, who is vitally interested in all that goes on around Sabrang. It is sad to see the many villages on the road between Sabrang and the city with its 150 side-turnings and no witness for Christ anywhere except at Lakar-Semen. Although we pass through it so often this seems to be a wholly unevangelised area; Rufus and everyone else have been so occupied with developments to the east that we have none of us had time to do anything on the northern road. However, there is a group of girls from a place two miles out of Sabrang who come most faithfully to the Children's Meeting; it was when I was driving them home that we saw the accident to the cyclist with a pillion rider.

On Sunday, *April 19th*, I preached at Barek. Things are not too healthy there, for the quarrel between Suprapto and Chamim has been most damaging. Susilo led the meeting and translated into Javanese for me. There were twenty-five present, but two years ago it would have been fifty. One Madurese believer never comes to the church for some reason, but he is glad to have his home used for meetings. Another man turns out to have two wives; he is faithful in his own way, but sorely pressed at home and his daughter has just married a Communist. The schoolmaster who used always to lead the singing at Barek has rarely come since he married and moved two miles away, though he married a Christian. While rejoicing in all the wonderful things that God has done one must not overlook the severity of the conflict and the grievous problems which have to be faced by those who turn from Islam to the Lord Jesus Christ. Not in a day is the battle won.

The same evening we had the biggest Young People's Fellowship yet, thirty-seven guests in the house. The fast month, and with it the school holidays, is over; so is the rainy season, so everyone is feeling fresh. But it was a strange meeting, for it was Nasur's turn to lead. Instead of just leading, he gave an impassioned testimony of which we had not thought him capable. It was a bit of a mixture, but he stressed with refreshing force that Christ is the one and only Saviour. Loti was not much impressed by his effort, but although we always find her opinion worth getting, she perhaps made little allowance for the darkness out of which he has come. He has actually read Luke's gospel up to Chapter 22, which is quite a feat here.

Rufus often drops in to see us late in the evening, usually travel-stained, always rejoicing, and generally with news of fresh victories. On *April 23rd* I launched out once again with him and Mawardi. Tilosa was sick and could not join us. When we reached his home he appeared in blue pyjamas, a yellow scarf, and his black hat, and we prayed with him before going on to Segaran, where we added Wirojo to our party and called at the farm where the elderly woman lives to whom Susilo spoke the day he was carrying a bundle of posters. She is rather odd and thumped me on the back and chest in most unoriental fashion. We prayed with her and her married daughter and then continued east with the peak of the Great Volcano towering 12,000 feet above us, a thin wisp of smoke trailing upwards for another 1000 feet. At Trawas we drank coffee with Dr Suharta, the local church leader, who is now much revived. His wife is shortly expecting her tenth child. A tyre was flat, so Mawardi and I changed it. This meant that for the next twenty-four hours on rugged, mountainous roads we had no spare tyre and one nail would have badly stranded us; but from this predicament we were preserved.

Crossing on a very high bridge the yawning chasm of the Tantring River, we reached Srengat at nightfall and for five minutes paused at a large farm at the roadside, where I beheld for the first time the faces of the newest believers, young and old. Promising to stay longer with them next day, we crashed on, rounding innumerable bends, till we were over the top of a high pass and began to drop down through jungle towards the plains of Java's eastern peninsula. About 8 p.m. we reached our goal and went supperless into action in the home of the local doctor. Arrangements had somewhat miscarried. He had invited thirty persons, all community leaders, but two political meetings were being held close by, so only five of them were able to come, in addition to fifteen from "Christian" families. But the five included the district head— a man whose very manners were redolent of President Sukarno— the head of the village, and the second of the latter's wives, a most distinguished-looking lady. It was the first Christian meeting they had ever attended. Months ago these last two met Rufus and such is the mysterious and marvellous way of the Lord, recognised at that first encounter that they needed to find out more about the Light of the World. Both Rufus and I preached, but conditions were not at all favourable: we were tired and hungry, and the audience was sitting in three different rooms, so that we could not see them properly. At midnight supper was served and after that I asked chauffeur's leave to sleep. The others continued talking till 2 a.m. and at 6 a.m. Mawardi was playing gospel records on the gramophone. We then called on the head of the village. "The Christians here are scared," he said, "but there is no need to be afraid. Young men come here to my home every evening and I give them the gospels to read." Rufus' view of his position is, "We must not hold them off because he has two wives. The salvation of their souls is the vital thing. If they have truly turned to Christ we must receive and baptise them. Then the Holy Spirit will in time show them what to do about their family affairs." We prayed with them and parted with much warmth. They all stood out in the road and, as usual when leaving any of our friends, I banged the roof of the Mayflower in greeting as we moved off. At the foot of the jungle pass we paused to see a minute country church in the vast Muslim countryside, just a tiny bamboo box.

By 10 a.m. we were over the pass, round all the hairpins, and back at the farm in Srengat where fifty-eight were gathered for the Sunday morning service. Thus the newest baby of the churches, altogether outside the seven-in-one church, is already the biggest, born big on the pattern of the Jerusalem Church in the Acts of the Apostles. Truly "the earth bringeth forth fruit of itself". Srengat is a very fine place where the main highway writhes its way upwards between wide, green swards and the houses stand back in big gardens, swathed in fruit trees, while above them towers a tangle of jungle-covered peaks, wild country from which the Great Volcano springs up into the clouds. I am now gradually piecing together the story of this new development. It seems that among those brought to Christ through Rufus at Barek in 1956 there was a humble farmer, who in February of this year moved temporarily to Srengat in search of work on a coffee plantation. The district oozes coffee and the grains are often laid out right across the road to dry in the blazing sun. On reaching Srengat he missed the Christian fellowship and meetings which he had enjoyed for several years at Barek, so he enquired whether there were any Christians in the district.

He was directed to the only partially trained medical in Srengat,

Dr Darmo, a short, dapper man in his middle forties. "Are there any Christians here?" asked the farmer. "No, not really," said the doctor, "I am from Paru myself, a Christian village, but all the people here are Muslims and none of them have ever believed in Christ." "Do you hold any meetings, then?" continued the farmer. "No," answered the doctor, "as I said, they are all Muslims in Srengat." "How long have you been here?" was the next question, to which the doctor laughingly replied, "Oh, twenty-odd years, a long time." "But you have never made known the gospel at all?" said the farmer. "No, no," said the doctor, "they are all Muslims around here and you can't do that sort of thing." But after the farmer had left him he felt most uncomfortable and his conscience rebuked him for utter coldness of heart, even though he had been born in a family supposed to be Christian. "I went into the bed-room," he delighted to say in after days, "opened the cupboard, and took out my long unread New Testament." From this a spiritual earthquake has ensued.

He tried to read the book and called on a few friends to see if they would be interested to do so too. In early February, on the very day when Tilosa was inducted at Barek, six men sat with him in the clinic and some sort of a Christian meeting took place. By the next week their numbers had doubled. Several families with long-sterile Christian connections were drawn in, as well as many Muslims. Not till the fourth week did they get into touch with Rufus, that most inconspicuous of evangelists. Since then their souls have basked in his care. As numbers increased they were compelled to move from the doctor's house to Mother Pardi's farm, and this is now the meeting place of what is fast becoming the Srengat Church. Everything is done decently and in order, for Dr Darmo remembers from his childhood what a Christian church should be. Flowers stand in a vase beside the preacher. Good collections are taken. The walls are adorned with Christian Witness Press posters.

After Rufus and I had preached and Mawardi had given his testimony, Mother Pardi tapped me on the shoulder and drew our party into her capacious kitchen. There we sat at an enormous table surrounded by years of junk and soot, by pots and pans hanging on pegs, by women and babies resting on beds around the walls, by old cronies and grannies encamped amongst dogs and cats, with great logs burning on the hearth and chickens snapping up the scraps. Mother Pardi stood over a big basket full of steaming rice and kept our plates full till we were satiated. I gazed in amazement at a new world of friends and fellow-believers into which I had been so suddenly projected when but three months remained to us before we left Java on furlough. Mother Pardi, her mouth crimson through chewing betel nut, is the Lydia of the church. Having but one child, a married daughter, she has room in her heart for other troubled souls and assured me that she has adopted many children and keeps a sort of open house for all who need help. Hence, I presume, the motley collection of persons in the kitchen in addition to all those in the wide-spreading front room, which is now in fact a church.

Wirojo shared all this with us and was thrilled to see the finger of God, but he truthfully said, "You know, at Segaran it is so different. We haven't a single family from a Christian village. All of us are absolutely new to the Christian faith and I, who only believed a year ago, have to be the leader." On the way home we paused at Segaran to drop him and to visit the mechanic who was drawn to Christ through mending his gramophone. This man is in deep distress, for because of his new faith his wife has left him and married someone else. So at least I understood, though of course he may not be without fault in the matter himself; for those who have lived without a Saviour have generally marred and seared their lives so badly that much time and patience are needed to set things aright. He now wanted Rufus' help to find a Christian wife. "Any race will do," he added, "only not Madurese!" Rufus asked me to lead in prayer and the man stood with tears in his eyes as he shook hands with us before we drove on to Ringit and Sabrang. The Young People's Fellowship followed as soon as we got back and Rufus was the speaker. Although so good at the personal side of pastoral care he does not really have much gift for Bible teaching. At its close two young men whom I did not recognise came on to the verandah. Then one of them said to me, "Don't you remember helping us when my foot got entangled in the spokes of my friend's

cycle that day?" They stayed some time and it is just possible that
the incident has opened their minds to receive the gospel. The pillion
rider is a distant relative of the poor old woman, Sari, who lives
alone. She is often in our home these days. She gets eggs from
neighbours and brings them to us on her way to market; to help the
old soul Jess buys them off her at a higher price than she would get
elsewhere; she then settles down in our kitchen on a stool and has a
long chat with Loti while the latter works. Almost daily I find her
there. She is friendless and we are delighted to see how she gravitates
to Loti.

On the night of *April 30th* I went to the weekly cottage meeting
in Sabrang, which was being held in the home of one of the sisters
baptised two years ago. Our hostess had arranged everything
beautifully and was rewarded with a full house. Rufus spoke on
1 John 3:8-9 (a text he has stolen from me, but I see no harm at all
in the procedure), followed by Tilosa on the excellent 2 Corinthians
3:3, "Ye are manifestly declared to be the epistle of Christ, ministered by us, written not with ink, but with the Spirit of the living
God, not in tables of stone, but in fleshy tables of the heart". Then I
closed by expounding John 15:7. There were no unbelievers present.
Our hostess has never seemed to us to be a very inspiring Christian
and during the recent fast month she excused herself from attending
any meetings at all. However, oriental politeness veils from us
many things to which Christians in Sabrang are exposed. We now
learn that she is leaving the district altogether in order to escape the
ridicule and social ostracism to which she is continually exposed on
account of her faith. She is counted as a foreigner, and the same
weapon is used against others too. Probably for this reason Mrs
Kardjo has been staying with her father in the Southern Mountains
and we have seen little of her recently. Kardjo himself is doing a
spell of duty at a remote plantation, so their home is temporarily
disbanded and the house shut up. Subir has already been away on
duty for over a month, and thus we have virtually lost both the
policemen who have been such an asset to the work of the Lord in
the past six months.

May 1st. Our lamps were lit on the verandah for the forty-third
Weekly Bible School. Old widow Sari arrived first together with

the two young men who were involved in the cycle accident. It was the first time either of them had ever attended a Christian meeting. Sari valiantly sat them down and taught them to sing hymns for a considerable time till this delightful scene was interrupted by the arrival of a lunatic, whom we were guilty of christening "Sailor Bill", an Arab from Singapore. He stayed for the whole evening, sitting facing the wrong way, harmless but thoroughly mad. I was a little concerned that he might cause trouble, so when I saw Subir coming across under the trees I went out and spoke to him, telling him that we had an unknown visitor. He was in uniform and had a good look at the man from the garden before coming on to the verandah. Then he stood in front of him in a threatening manner, staring at him, letting him see that authority was present. For two hours Sailor Bill struggled to mend his belt with a piece of twine, till Jess gave him an old belt of mine. When the company dispersed at 10 p.m. he hung about in drizzling rain. I confess that I am no good with such people, but Jess spread mats out on the verandah, gave him supper (which he hardly touched), Ovaltine (which he enjoyed), and cough mixture (which silenced his cough). He then lay prone for seventeen hours. By 3 p.m. next day we were a little alarmed lest he die there, so I called the Doctor. Sailor Bill then awoke, took up position on our front steps, grinning, and thus compelled those coming for the Women's Meeting to use our back door. I felt it wise to ask help from the head of the village and there was immediate response. Three gentle, tactful men came on their bicycles. They stood quietly under the trees while Sailor Bill shook his finger at schoolchildren who were laughing at him. I managed to shepherd the latter back from the house while the three men sat with him drinking tea. When they asked him to leave with them Sailor Bill announced that he would do "whatever that Doctor says". So I fetched the Doctor again from the hospital, who tactfully listened to his heart and then gave verdict that he should follow the three men, which he meekly and cheerfully did. They took him into the city and I presume he was lodged in an asylum. That same night at 2 a.m. we were awakened by the headlights of Tilosa's motor-cycle turning into our drive. A woman at Barek, wife of a believer, was in labour and no transport could be found to take her to hospital, so the husband had appealed to Tilosa for help. Jess went in the Mayflower, following him, and by 3 a.m. the woman was safely in hospital. Tilosa is the kind of pastor who enters energetically into the actual problems of his people's lives.

The following evening, *May 2nd*, I was at Segaran with Rufus, Mawardi, and Tilosa. We halted the Mayflower at a lonely spot on the road and had a time of prayer together. The occasion was the eve of an eldest son's wedding in the home of a man who has recently turned to Christ. He was bold enough to use the opportunity to hold an evangelistic meeting, inviting the local dignitaries. Many Christians from Gondang and Segaran were present, together with seventy unbelievers. Just as we got to the house we were caught in heavy rain and soaked in a few minutes. I was conscious that many of the guests were eyeing me askance; however, we had a good time preaching in turn till midnight, so that I found it hard to keep awake on the drive back through the sleeping countryside.

CHAPTER 18

FRUIT, MORE FRUIT, MUCH FRUIT

Sunday, *May 3rd*. I preached at the morning meeting in the Sabrang church to thirty local people and seventeen soldiers from Celebes, all nominal Christians from the island's central mountains. Our home is two miles from their camp, which is rather too far for them to drop in regularly, but three of them came afterwards and sat for some time on the verandah. So did the two young fellows who had the cycle accident, and it really looks as though they are turning to Christ. Already they are meeting with a good deal of ridicule and opposition, but they are resolved to continue. They came to examine Bibles and New Testaments and find out about prices. The encounter with Sailor Bill at the one and only Christian meeting they have attended has not put them off. Rufus also came to pray with us to stock up with New Testaments. We took the opportunity to and review the present situation. I have already realised that co-operation with Tilosa is harder for him than it is for Tilosa! The position is in some respects a little anomalous, for there are now two fully trained pastors in the area. All the believers owe their Christian faith to Rufus, yet Tilosa has the ecclesiastical position and authority. The new pin from College, so gifted, so assured, so strong, is quite a problem to the middle-aged, more experienced, less gifted man. I am often at pains to explain Tilosa to Rufus. Side by side at Segaran the other night I watched and compared them—R. thin, T. fat; R. worn, T. bursting with health; R. shabbily dressed, T. resplendent in bright shirt of the best material; R. poor, T. prosperous; R. yielding, T. pushing; R. the old-world village product, T. the new-world townsman; R. a great man in the hidden, spiritual, divine sense, T. a great man too, I truly believe, but in the making. The Church in the East has such need of men like Tilosa. What a boon he would be in so many districts where there is as yet no national church. His enthusiasm, drive, joyfulness, energy, thoughtfulness, and disinterested service, are a benediction. And he is good with Rufus, though he could be better. "Would you care to add a word?" he said to him at the close of his own talk, at the Segaran wedding feast, as though the older man's labours had not created the whole situation. But I try to tell Rufus that this is just youthfulness and he does not mean it in any unkind way.

On *May 5th* I went to the city as usual on Tuesdays, did the week's family shopping, queued for an hour for petrol, lectured on Greek at the Bible College, and stayed on in the evening to attend a most important and valuable function, a refresher evening for pastors of the East Java Church working in the presbytery to which Rufus and I belong. In the 20 million strong province of East Java there are altogether four presbyteries, forming one synod. The proceedings were held in the East Java Church in the city and since the Dutchmen who teach at the seminary were not invited I was the only non-Javanese present. Had I not been officially sponsored by the East Java Church I should not have been there either.

The meeting lasted for nine hours, starting at 5 p.m. and ending at 2 a.m. Some of the pastors had travelled far from Christian villages on the Indian Ocean and we met in a delightful atmosphere of comradeship, joviality, and pleasure in momentary withdrawal from battle. There were twenty-four men present and we sat at tables round the walls of the big vestry at the back of the church. Coffee and light refreshments were served twice during the evening. There was no agenda. Each person just went in turn to the lectern beginning with the youngest, then those from five to ten years in the ministry, and lastly the seniors. The idea was that everyone should say frankly anything that was in his heart, sharing experiences, joys, sorrows, problems, or criticisms. This was an admirable plan and I soon realised that if I sat long enough I was going to get a priceless opportunity of addressing the august company, the leading men in the biggest church ever to arise out of Islam. It was almost midnight before my opportunity came; never have I waited so long to speak and when I did so my remarks were based upon seven hours of note-taking. Many of the talks were memorable for their frankness. "I left the pulpit," said one young man, "walked down the church, shook hands with nobody, went straight home, shut the door of my bedroom behind me, and burst into tears." Another said, "I have often wept in the pulpit, I don't know why." One with more experience confessed, "With nine mouths to feed I simply did not have a cent, and I was compelled to ask the Synod for a loan." In the course of his talk Faral said, "There were four of us pastors together in prison. The Japanese beat us day after day and finally we were taken to Djakarta to be shot. On Kertosono station we picked up a filthy banana skin and shared it between us in our desperation. Yet we did not hate them and we were ready to die rather than deny the Lord." Pastor Wen of Kabat, our staunch friend, said, "I was educated in a Muslim religious school and could only read books written in the Arabic script. It was the desire to be able to read romanised which eventually took me to a mission school. One day I was given St Matthew's Gospel as a form prize. It was so different from the Koran and I was irresistibly drawn by what I read in it about the work of Christ."

The senior men, among whom I was placed, dealt mostly with points the others had raised, of which I myself took up four when my turn came at last. These were (1) The role of the pastor in evangelism. In the East Java Church pastoral work and evangelistic work are rather rigidly separated. The pastor looks after the Christians, marries them, buries them, baptises them, conducts their services, and cares for their interests. Others are beyond his duty and vision. Evangelism is the work of those seconded to it, such as Rufus and myself. I endeavoured to include evangelism among the essential duties of every pastor. (2) The value of taking the Bible to church, for traditionally here people take only a hymnbook. (3) The neutrality of circumcision. In East Java it is regarded by Christians as a Muslim rite, as sinful, which raises not wholly necessary problems for the many Muslims converted in our area. The pastors seemed amazed to hear that circumcision was widely practised among Christians in England, not on religious but on health grounds, for they have usually regarded it as non-Christian and anti-Christian. (4) The lawfulness of the baptism of individuals —even if husband, or wife, or parents, are not in sympathy. This is not at all obvious here, even to Tilosa for instance, for conversion is regarded as a family matter.

Rufus was glad for me to make such points rather than leaving it to him. He spoke after me, cheerfully and forcefully, though he is not at his best in such company. Both he and I looked up and read several Scripture passages as the basis and authority for our remarks; no others did this, for the idea of deriving one's message directly out of the written Word of God, letting that word speak to human hearts, is rather a new one. I regretted that there was no paternal, commanding, Javanese figure, no really mature father in God, to give to the younger men a compelling and adequate answer and example to help them in their struggles. We drove home in the silent night, Rufus, Sutikno of Madura, and I, and were abed by 3 a.m.

On the following evening, *May 6th*, we held the forty-fourth Weekly Bible School on the verandah with twelve men and twelve women present. I was expounding the first chapter of Colossians and the thirty-sixth of Jeremiah. Everyone was cheered by the presence of both Rufus and Susilo, and indeed by a third most welcome figure, Sutikno of Madura, our original Javanese friend, who is spending a few days with Rufus to find out why it is that Muslims are turning to Christ around Sabrang and to learn what he can for his own ministry on Madura Island. It was at his wedding that I originally met Rufus and this gives us a special relationship to him. He is a small, youthful figure, very slow in his words and ways, but twinkling, sparkling, scintillating. We notice great progress in him and he gave a most moving account of his grim struggle to proclaim Christ on Madura, which is not without fruit. I greatly admire him for sticking to so hard a task and for mastering the Madurese language. I regard him as a true missionary and it is splendid that he has come here and is going around the churches with Rufus. The two bicycle-accident boys were also present again. However, for the second week running we lost New Testaments to somebody, and we feel driven to conclude that it must be these two comparative strangers who are taking them.

May 7th. This morning the two bicycle boys came to No. 122 and bought New Testaments with such pleasure and artlessness that I find it very hard to believe that they stole any last night! It was

Ascension Day, so there were meetings in all the country churches. I drove to Segaran with Rufus and Sutikno, thrilled to have them together in the car again. We had a most wonderful gathering of twenty people in Wirojo's home. Using their brand-new rostrum I preached on "God also hath highly exalted Him", Daddy Ren, the tall, turbaned, village wise man and quack doctor, is to be baptised with five of his family on May 17th, which will be an event of major significance. My mind goes back to that first crucial visit to his home with Rufus and Susilo during the Tent Campaign last June. And yet how little such men know of the Lord, of the Scriptures, and of their Christian inheritance! They have so lately come out of such great darkness that the light in which they now live might well seem to a critical mind to be but twilight. As I sat on my stool watching their faces in that thrice-blessed home where Susilo and Wirojo had their memorable meal together on March 17th, 1958, I found myself deeply moved by this raw, new, unsophisticated company of Christ's people, so reverent, so open, so turned towards the Lord. "Can any man forbid water that these should not be baptised, which have received the Holy Ghost as well as we?" Sutikno, raising his eyebrows as he caught my eye, simply basked in such Christian fellowship with men recently saved out of Islam, and then when it was his turn to tell them about his own apostleship on Madura Island it was they who basked, their faith stimulated by his and their zeal provoked. Rufus then took him on to Srengat that he might behold the latest of God's wonderful works, over which great excitement prevails since many baptisms are fixed there for May 31st. I felt that I must call a halt and returned home to Sabrang, meeting on the way Tilosa's massive, goggled form, cornering at speed on his B.S.A., heading east. When I got back Jess told me that he had made a lamentable error at the service in Sabrang. The seventeen Celebes soldiers from the camp came again, but he preached in Javanese, of which they know not a word, instead of switching to Indonesian for their benefit. Yet I feel that in the long run he will win through. Being socially of rather aristocratic stock, he and his wife do not always find it easy to fraternise with humbler folk; people complain that they do not shake hands enough.

w

On Saturday, *May 9th*, we determined to relax, so we drove Rupert and two of his friends to a swimming pool ten miles west, a lovely, quiet spot, where we just sat in the shade of the trees and watched the children in the water. Jess drove both ways, so I had time to scrutinise the glorious land and to observe the many mosques and Muslim chapels all along this unevangelised highway. There is one magnificent place, where the mosque is unusually ornate and adjoining it are several very splendid homes. In spite of all I have written about the working of the Spirit of God, the conversion of Muslims, and the emergence of Christian churches, long and strong is this other influence. We have just learnt that our dear friend and colleague, Mawardi, was married nine times before that more memorable day when Christ found even him, and many things of this sort are slowly unfolding to us as the years of our residence in Sabrang begin to unlock more and more of its secrets to us.

Every week Jess drives over to Triwung for a Javanese lesson from one of Susilo's daughters. Today a lunatic climbed on to the back of the Mayflower as she arrived. He is the son of a wealthy home, but two years ago he married an older woman and became mentally unbalanced. Large sums of money have been spent in vain in efforts to effect a cure through local medicine men. When Jess came to leave he climbed again on to the back fender and asked her to drive him to Sumatra. Neither Mrs Susilo nor her daughters could dislodge him. Hastari then appeared and although much smaller tackled him and twisted his arm to make him get down. A struggle ensued and Jess managed to start the car and unbalance him. He pursued, but she escaped. In spite of the huge asylum not far from us there is a grave shortage of accommodation for such poor folk.

On Sunday, *May 10th*, I drove alone to Srengat in one and a half hours. In the early morning sunshine the land looked exceedingly magnificent—mighty, rolling, cultivated hillsides, exuding wealth; jungle-tipped peaks; far-away farms and villages on the mountains; and the road thrashing through ravines and gullies, coffee and rubber plantations. It was a little unwise of me to go alone and I should have taken Mawardi with me. At two points I passed doubtful looking individuals at lonely spots in plantations and, had a tyre punctured or had I been compelled to halt for any reason, I might

have constituted a temptation for them, as they would have presumed
that a white man must have money on him. At Trawas I was glad
to pick up Dr Suharta. At long last we curled over the wide bridge
that heralds Srengat, which is really the finest place around here.
The road through it is smooth, rising and cornering sharply, with
wide grass verges, well-kept hedges, richly-coloured flowers, and
mile after mile of spacious homes bowered in palms and coffee
bushes. We drew in at the church farm, Mother Pardi's home, and
there were forty-five hands to shake and much laughter as I had
to double up to get under 5-foot eaves. It was my second visit and
they are slowly learning how to handle me. A large easy chair was
put at the front for my benefit and after I had secured a perch on a
bench in the back row I had to ward off repeated attempts to get me
to vacate it and take the easy chair. I stayed back there until Dr
Darmo, who led the meeting, called me up to the front to speak.
At the end all the Javanese New Testaments, hymnbooks, and
calendars I had brought were bought up. I was pressed to another
meal amidst cats, hens, and junk in the great kitchen, my suitcase
was filled up with unground coffee, and we departed banging the
roof of the Mayflower at groups of Christians strung out all down
the road. At Trawas, I dropped Dr Suharta, spending a brief time
with him and his wife, who is expecting her tenth child in about
six weeks. On reaching Segaran I stopped at the home, right on the
main road, of the mechanic who mended Wirojo's gramophone.
He asked if Rufus had made any progress in finding him another
wife. I said I knew nothing about the matter and enquired whether
his former wife had come back to him or not. He said that she had,
in fact that she was one of three women sitting on a bench immediately behind us. Since this seemed a rather fragile situation I did not
prolong my stay.

May 11th. A middle-aged man with a bad face came to ask me
for Gospel Recordings gramophone records "for propaganda". His
purpose was obviously not propaganda but profit, since what he
wanted to get from me for a nominal charge of one rupiah he could
resell for more than fifty. The pleasant singing on these records
means that they can be a grave temptation to Christians, let alone to
such as this visitor. At the Weekly Bible School at night, during the

interval for refreshments, I asked Rufus to tell the people about his prison experiences. He recounted something of the efforts the Japanese had made to force him to renounce his Christian faith, which was the price of liberty, and stated that twenty-six of his Christian friends had died of starvation and hardship in the prison. Then when he came to talk about his second imprisonment at the instigation of a decadent church he strongly stressed the need for faithfulness to Christ under all circumstances, quoting the over-comer promises of Revelation 1-3. I feel it is very good for new believers to hear this kind of thing and to draw encouragement from the victories of others in the past.

On *Whit Sunday*, the Day of Pentecost, I preached at 8 a.m. in the Sabrang church on "The Seven Spirits of God". The little place was packed with fifty people, of whom fifteen were soldiers from Celebes. Although we do not have very much contact with these men it is good for them to see a new work like this and who can tell what repercussions for Christ there may not be in their own lives and in their island home? The marvel of a meeting of this size in strongly Muslim Sabrang should not be overlooked. We are only gradually realising how deep-seated is the animosity to the gospel here. The two cycle-accident boys were in church for the first time in their lives, diligently using their new New Testaments.

Straight from the church I drove to Gondang with Nasur, Mrs Rufus, old Sari, and Yeny. The occasion was a great one, the second Gondang-Segaran baptisms, and I do not know that I was ever present at so apostolic an occasion in my life. The meeting was held in Sumali's house, specially enlarged for the occasion. A hundred and twenty-five people were packed in—tiles and rafters overhead, bamboo partitions all round, mother earth under foot. I was the only non-Javanese present. All the rest were believers of the seven-in-one church. At Gondang too they now have a nice new reading desk, which I thus observe to be one of the hallmarks of a growing church. At this Tilosa presided, wearing full robes. On his left was Rufus, also fully robed, and given a proper part for a change. On Tilosa's right was Mawardi in a bright yellow shirt, unusually honoured, though I think his dogged faithfulness and prayers have been no small factor in all that has happened.

Having survived many hard looks directed at me in the car on the way up the Great Volcano, I received the warmest possible welcome from "the household of faith" and tucked myself in at the back, alongside Susilo and Wirojo. After singing and prayer Tilosa started the baptisms, headmaster Tias holding the silver bowl close beside him. The people were called forward one by one to kneel before Tilosa who, pulling back the right sleeve of his long black gown with his left hand, dipped his right hand three times into the silver bowl as, in his rich and powerful voice, he baptised each "in the Name of God the Father . . . God the Son . . . and God the Holy Spirit". After the first five had been baptised and the procedure was thus clear to everyone Tilosa himself started up Cowper's hymn (in Javanese, of course), "There is a fountain filled with blood, drawn from Immanuel's veins", which is a great favourite in the churches. After the first verse, however, there was a pause as Daddy Ren, local philosopher and medicine man, tall, thin, erect, aristocratic, walked to the front, removed his turban, knelt, and was baptised into Christ. It was a supreme moment, after which the singing was resumed while Mrs Ren, a massive motherly soul, and her girls, followed him to the front. It went on and on, Tilosa's voice booming out now and then through short gaps in the singing. Thirty-one adults were thus baptised, and among them Nasur, thus crowning his steady pursuit of truth through the past ten months. He was weeping when his turn came and afterwards Mawardi asked him why he wept on such a joyful occasion. He answered that he had been thinking of his unbelieving family, for in the eyes of the whole community it is baptism which makes a man a Christian, not the faith which is in his heart; thus the step of being baptised is what cuts a man off from the Muslim world. One old man, heavy and wrinkled, knelt before Tilosa with his black Indonesian hat still on his head until one of the assisting brethren caused a ripple of mirth by deftly removing it from behind. When all were finished the thirty-one stood and audibly confessed their faith. Then they were asked to kneel and the remainder of the company stood and prayed for them. Susilo was hardly able to control his emotion at the sight, but paced up and down at the back of the room praying and praising God, Bible in hand.

Then followed that splendid ceremony, the sanctifying of marriages. Nine couples stood before Rufus, among them Mr and Mrs Ren, and took in the name of Jesus those vows of mutual love and faithfulness which are not known in Islam. Next came the baptism of twenty-seven children of school age, mostly offspring of the adults just baptised. Remembering that so many girls marry at twelve or thirteen, the more Christian umbrella they get over their heads the better. That made a total of fifty-eight baptised, so Tilosa dipped his hand 174 times into the silver bowl, which was a remarkable experience for a young man in the third month of his first pastorate!

Rufus then stepped to the reading desk and preached, closing with the benediction. The moment he had finished Tilosa called out that "Pa David" would address the company while refreshments were being served. I did so from the words "called to be saints" in Romans 1: 7, for baptism is one thing and holiness in daily life quite another, and it is part of my business here to keep reminding people of this. Rufus interpreted into Javanese for me and then had the misfortune to sit down on a chair which was not there. As he and his robes struck the good earth, his foot overturned a table and a vase of flowers emptied its water on him. After the excitement of the long meeting this incident neatly relieved the tension and the whole room exploded in good-natured mirth.

For a man of Nasur's background the day was momentous. He seemed quite knocked out and drowsed in the car all the way back to Sabrang. He asked me to take him not to his home, but quite near it, which I did. I got back to No. 122 just in time for the Young People's Meeting, which was addressed by Subir the policeman. Three of the servicemen from Celebes walked two miles each way to be there.

Thinking back over the day an observer might ask, "Who has begotten all these?" I can only answer that the apparent human agents, taking new life in Christ from Rufus and Susilo, have been the new men of last year, Wirojo of Segaran, and of Gondang Tias, Sumali, and perhaps more than anyone else Lukas the doctor. Then one must not forget the "mothers in Israel", Mrs Wirojo and Mrs Tias.

Next day Kardjo dropped in once more. He is doing three months' duty at a remote plantation; by the time that is over we shall have gone to England on furlough, so the days of our close association are unfortunately over. We had a good talk and prayer; it was splendid to have him in the house again. But he sat on interminably and as 2.30 approached I got more and more hungry. I recognised the symptoms and was ready for what followed. It appears that he has embarked upon the purchase of a motor-scooter by instalments; the last instalment is due in three days and he finds himself short. Would Pa David feel able to allow him a loan for a month? I explained, as gently as I possibly could, that Pa David would not.

On Rupert's sixth birthday, since we were all exceedingly tired, we decided to escape for two nights to the Hotel of Peace. They gave us an upstairs room and we felt immensely refreshed sitting at an open window, not overlooked by anyone, gazing at the stars and the outlines of the mountains under a full moon. Of course our Sabrang house has no upper storey and all windows have the lower half curtained to discourage the curious, so that an ordinary open window was a treat.

Then followed my final Sunday in Surabaja. It was my twenty-fourth sermon to the great Foochow congregation and perhaps my last, for I wonder how my long-neglected Chinese can possibly be good enough for such use after furlough. From there I went on to the British Community Church, again preaching—perhaps for the last time. There followed an evening at the Consulate with fourteen guests, when much wine and whisky were imbibed by some. I was asked to say grace, in fact I suppose I was the guest of honour.

The same day, *May 25th*, Rufus was alone on his scooter, pressing up a hill at 20 m.p.h., when part of his mudguard broke and became entangled in the front wheel, jamming it. He shot over the handlebars and landed on his head right in front of a police station. He was wearing a topi and was quite unhurt, except that the accident awakened the old injury to his leg. I was with him on the night of the 26th in Rekso's home for the cottage meeting. There were twenty-five people at it. Nasur, who misses nothing, worked the gramophone: he has made friends with the oldest of Rufus' boys.

Mawardi led. Rufus had been resting up and two of his children were fast asleep in his arms, so it fell to me to be the main speaker. I used the text Romans 8:13, "If ye live after the flesh ye shall die, but if ye through the Spirit do mortify the deeds of the body, ye shall live", such sanctification being in too short supply among professing Christians. Some months ago, for instance, the schoolmaster who was one of the original leaders at Barek, married a Ringit girl whose family turned to the Lord at the beginning of this movement. It was the first Christian wedding ever held in Ringit. Unhappily the couple have not often attended meetings since that time; we now learn that the bridegroom struck the bride between the wedding and the reception and has continued to do so ever since. Her family are quiet people and this is a deep distress to them. The couple are now expecting their first child and the girl's father has told the husband that if he goes on like this he will kill her. To this his answer was, "She's mine and I can do what I like with her." Hence my text.

I am glad to say that the couple came to the forty-seventh Weekly Bible School just after I had written the above paragraph about them. So did a heavily-built young man of twenty-one who was fearfully embarrassed at coming face to face with me. Apparently he got a New Testament from Mawardi, whose comment was, "A son of Islam." The bicycle-accident boys were there again. I had supper with some friends and could scarcely believe that the lessons of the twentieth century could be so ignored. Foreigners were placed at the head of the table, Indonesians lower down. There was different food at each end, and thus different utensils. Happily I was on the join and could thus fraternise downstream—and get at the rice!

May 28th. This was a wild day. I had to go to the city with a local policeman in connection with our application for exit and re-entry permits to go on furlough. He is a good-natured and helpful man, but these matters involve a wearisome amount of negotiation. As I was driving down the well-known main street a cyclist hit the back of the car ahead of me and crashed headlong to the right, bringing down the cyclist behind him. Together they and their machines sprawled in the road ten yards ahead of the Mayflower

—but I was able to halt with four yards to spare. Then on the way home I twice sighted snakes crossing the road and on each occasion succeeded in running them down and killing them. When I reached No. 122 it was to learn that our cat had just killed a small snake immediately under our bedroom window. But I also learnt something much worse. Rupert had not been well for some days, but as usual children had been continually coming to borrow his tricycle. This noble machine, worn out with hard labour over several years, had at length begun to disintegrate, especially the seat, but it could still be ridden. A girl of eleven had secured it and was careering round and round on the verandah, in spite of warnings from Jess and from other children that it was broken. Then she lost her balance, fell, and ripped herself badly on the broken seat. Jess found her sitting on the verandah with blood around her. She at once got Loti to call the Doctor and Jeannette, and also the child's father, who behaved sensibly and dismissed the crowds of school-children who were gathering. Such an accident on our premises and with our property could of course lead to most serious consequences though just now the general atmosphere is not so highly charged as it has been at other times. Later in the day the girl's father came to see me and I drove him to the hospital a second time. The father proves to be one of Sabrang's twenty-three tailors, a dignified man with sixteen children, quiet and respectable, a Muslim. Far from wanting to make capital out of the incident he has been most grateful for our sympathy and help.

The same evening, as soon as the Women's Meeting was over, I left with Rufus, Mawardi, and Rekso, for a final pre-baptismal visit to Srengat. We drove through the night, passing many lorries loading coffee at farms by the light of pressure lamps. At Srengat we found fifty people in the church farm at Mother Pardi's, and Dr Darmo was preaching while children played about among stacks of coffee lining one side of the big room. Rufus followed him on 2 Corinthians 4:4, "In whom the god of this world hath blinded the minds of them which believe not, lest the light of the glorious gospel of Christ, who is the image of God, should shine unto them." Then I again expounded Romans 8:13 at some length. Old Rekso was also given a chance and he marched up and down thundering out his experiences. I hope it was profitable; there was no question that it was most entertaining. Mawardi followed and at 11.15 p.m. we were given supper in the great kitchen, Mother Pardi standing over us as usual to make sure we ate well. The house is full of tiny bedrooms and stray beds, littered with women and children. Mother Pardi, tall, thin, youngish, wrapped in a shawl, spitting betel nut, has taken many babies, children, and girls under her capacious wing in addition to her cats, chickens, and the ill-lit, undusted, impedimenta of a farm. At midnight we broke up and all stood out on the main road while they lifted high the pressure lamps so that we could admire the new signboard, red letters on a cream background, "Javanese Christian Church, Srengat". Then, after many warm and affectionate handshakes we escaped into the darkness, the moon blazing now to the right now to the left as the road hacked its way round the hills, while above us the serene peak of the Great Volcano cut into the Milky Way. We were home by 1.30 a.m. and I had driven 100 miles within our area during the day.

On *May 29th*, after teaching Greek in the city, I had to go again to Surabaja to push our exit and re-entry formalities a stage further if possible. I stayed the night at Mrs Tan's and returned on the 30th, having a good talk in the train with a twenty-four-year-old man of Arabic descent, a native of East Borneo and a relative of one of Indonesia's ambassadors in a European capital.

On *May 31st* we drove to Srengat again with a full carload for the baptisms, Jess being at the wheel each way: I had had more than enough of it. Two hundred people were present to witness the baptism of 89 souls (62 of them adults), and the sanctifying of twenty marriages. This took three and a half hours and in this grandiose manner was the Christian Church there inaugurated, all as a result of an illiterate farmer calling on Dr Darmo in February. Rufus and Tilosa shared the leadership of the meeting, baptising simultaneously. Strangely enough Rufus did so by single sprinkling and Tilosa by threefold sprinkling, the latter more impressive in its slow solemnity. A party of forty men and women from the Christian village of Puspo had walked for six hours to be there and their singing was quite a revelation to the Srengat folk. I was given a brief chance to speak at the end and did so from the Parable of the Sower, but I was too exhausted to get the message across effectively. I learnt afterwards that it was only with difficulty and at the last moment that Tilosa had been persuaded to go through with the meeting, since he feels that these people should have had a longer probation and a more systematic preparation for baptism.

Next morning a local official sent a man round to ask if he could call on me, and then came himself later. I know him and he is quite friendly to us, though a keen Muslim. In conversation he failed to reveal any reason for the visit and now we are wondering if it has something to do with the accident to the little girl. We gather she is promised in marriage within two years. In theory there might blow up a great tornado around the affair, but so far we have little evidence that this is going to happen. I have no idea what the legal position would be if they took us to court. It is perhaps in our favour that the girl had already played for several days with the broken tricycle, that on this occasion she walked right into my empty office and took it out herself, that she is reported to be very naughty, that Jess warned her it was broken, and that her sister repeated the warning just before the accident.

CHAPTER 19

FELLOW-WORKERS UNTO THE KINGDOM OF GOD

June 1st. We are now planning to leave Sabrang to begin our journey to England on July 13th, so only six weeks remain to us. I have often felt that missionaries who are nearing the end of a term of service need special prayer. Personally, in this equatorial climate, I find that fatigue builds up quite alarmingly in the last year and it becomes easier to make mistakes. Hard on the heels of the injury to the girl, Jess had a dreadful experience today when she was taking a crowd of children home in the Mayflower at the close of the Children's Meeting. We do not use the car to collect people for meeting, but we quite often take them home, especially children who walk in from places outside Sabrang and then have to get back after dark. On this occasion night had already fallen, I was not at home, and Rupert was out with me. Jess had no less than fifteen small children in the car. As she came down on to the long, high, single-track bridge leading out of Sabrang, the brakes failed completely. There was an oncoming car crossing the bridge. Jess was absolutely helpless, coasting down towards it, but she cried to the Lord, the other car cleared the bridge, and she passed in behind it with a length to spare, coasted over the empty bridge, and came quietly to rest on rising ground beyond, alongside a lunatic. Leaving the car locked she escorted the children to their homes and then walked back into Sabrang to tell a mechanic who has often helped us. Somehow this man contrived to drive the Mayflower to No. 122. The incident has helped to make us feel we ought to sell the car and we know that Tilosa would like to have her.

Meanwhile I gave my last lectures at the Bible College in the city, invigilated exams, and retired to bed for some days quite worn out. But the work goes on. Mawardi has struck a group of eight schoolmasters who all want to buy New Testaments. Tilosa has called a special meeting to discuss the continuation after our departure of work hitherto done in our home. Sales of Scriptures and hymnbooks continue unabated. Rufus disposes of a lot, making something on them no doubt, though we do not need to grudge that to successful agents. Susilo, of whom we see less than of old, still finds his own original ways of serving Christ. As a guerrilla leader he was once a nuisance to other foes, and that is still his character. The mildly Christian doctor at Gerbo calls him to dying patients and I am sure the witness of the tall, bold Bedouin will not be in vain on such occasions. We never forget that it was he who launched Wirojo and the Segaran Church. The head of Kedok village visited me the other day and pulled a New Testament out of his pocket. The Samaritan woman is strong in faith, giving glory to God. I am confident that many will find their own way into the unsearchable riches of Christ irrespective of our presence, which has never been more than auxiliary.

While I lay up for several days full meetings continued. There were actually seventy-five on Sunday at the Sabrang church and the Young People's Fellowship here later was packed. I have had valuable chats with Tilosa and we are steadily disengaging from our responsibilities. No meetings are to be held in this house after July 1st. No doubt matters will not always be arranged just as we think best, but we have had our chance and must leave things now in the hands of the Lord and those He has raised up for the job, which means primarily Tilosa. I was to have gone east with him last night but the Children's Meeting was prolonged and he, being a punctual townsman, departed on his motor-cycle without waiting for me. However, I stayed to talk and pray with Mrs Tilosa, whose faith is probably none too clearly defined.

On *June 11th* Tilosa himself attended the Women's Meeting here and this produced a full house. At the close Jess withdrew and under his chairmanship they discussed plans for the future. He is dealing with each of the regular gatherings in this way. As soon as his motor-cycle roared off, with his wife riding pillion, I snatched an early meal and then picked him up in the Mayflower at his home at Barek. I found that he had changed into Javanese national dress, a sarong, sandals, a dark-brown coat-shirt, and the Javanese brand of turban. He looked another man altogether, the epitome of the unchanged East. We drove on with two local believers, heading for Gondang. Darkness fell and a storm was raging ahead of us on the Great Volcano. With many miles of uphill, muddy, unsurfaced road ahead I was a little apprehensive, but the Lord answered prayer, the lightning passed round behind us, and the road remained fairly dry. At Gondang we joined a party of twelve Christian men and walked on up the volcano by the light of torches and a pressure lamp, via waterlogged paths through coconut trees and coffee plantations, to a village I had never been to before where there are three believers, all men. The meeting which followed was not a large one, which was indicative of no great welcome for the gospel there yet. In addition to our party there were about thirty present. Lukas the doctor started off, read Matthew 24:1-14, conducted singing, and handed over to Tilosa, who spoke for some time, using a text very popular here, Mark 16:15-16, "Go ye into all the world and preach the gospel to every creature. He that believeth and is baptised shall be saved, but he that believeth not shall be damned." Then he called on me and, as so often recently, I expounded Romans 8: 13. All this was in a non-Christian home with women and children packing the back parts. Then Sumali had his turn and also sang two solos, Christian hymns which he intoned in the age-old Javanese style. Having finished he ordered all to stand and with great solemnity we recited under his leadership that bulwark of the churches here, the Apostles' Creed. Informality followed. Tilosa, his feet tucked under him in Indian fashion, his national costume perfectly suiting the occasion, tried his hand at intoning, pleasing everyone with the power of his voice and his hearty good cheer. He then expounded the "Sinner's Dream" poster, which was taking a leaf out of Rufus' book, and the household served us coffee and cakes. Hymnbooks and New Testaments were sold, talks developed all over the room, and at 11 p.m. we rose and sang "God be with you till we meet again", everyone moving round and shaking hands as we did so. It was a wonderful glimpse of what can happen without Rufus and of how the gospel and the warm fellowship it engenders are being planted in remote places by men like Sumali and Lukas. The latter actually gave me "petrol money", this being the first time any Javanese church has helped me with travelling expenses.

Then we trudged back to Gondang by the light of the pressure lamp, steeply upwards on a narrow, slippery short-cut, while Tilosa poured out a stream of entertaining remarks as I followed his large bare feet with great care. He is extremely nice to me and seems thoroughly accepted and popular with Christian and non-Christian alike. We feel increasingly that he is the right man for this big job. He has actually solved the financial muddle which underlay the quarrel between Chamim and Suprapto at Barek, so that these brethren are now in harmony again. When we reached Gondang it was midnight and the village was asleep. Here took place my first farewell. Our party was packed into the Mayflower; Lukas and Sumali stood alone in the deserted street. I jumped out and told them I would not be back in Gondang before we left for England. We shook hands and commended one another to the Lord. These two are spiritual children of Rufus. Lukas, stout, stocky, ardent, a determined Christian, reclaimed for Christ after defecting from childhood faith into Islam, altogether renewed and now doctor-evangelist, the only immediate medical help for many thousands of people; Sumali, utterly Javanese, tall, thin, known everywhere as head of the village, a most sincere and genuine man, sharing Lukas' dogged faithfulness, an absolutely new trophy of God's grace. These two are neighbours and I think that they are set to go a long way. The old school-house, in which the basic work was done in 1957, has had to be demolished as a result of the earthquake nine months ago, but the living witness to Christ is bursting out everywhere and cannot be shaken down. It was my twenty-first visit to Gondang and I can only thank God upon every remembrance of the place.

Next morning two men from Kedok came to see me, brothers. They urged me to go there again and actually said, "Our people are glad to have a white man come among them," which is certainly not a common sentiment. One of them added, "My wife had a dream in which she saw lava pouring down the mountain, carrying people away. A man who looked like Pa David was calling them into an iron house where they were safe." Tilosa is preparing these two for baptism. So the work of the Lord goes on "while men sleep".

Truly "the kingdom of God cometh not with observation". Before they left they said, "We always thought this house was a school," alluding to the many children by whom we are being besieged again these days.

While Jess was with Susilo's daughters I attended the civil wedding of a soldier of twenty with a girl of seventeen, both from Celebes. It was conducted with cheerful informality by Rufus in a large hall set with well-separated chairs for fifty soldiers and about a dozen of our East Java Church company. All the men present were "Christians" from Celebes, temporarily stationed here. Rufus read the laws, questioned the couple, pronounced them man and wife while we all stood, and rapped his table vigorously with a chairman's mallet to settle the matter. Then he handed over to Tilosa. Happily everything was for once in Indonesian, since these soldier boys know less Javanese than I do, and mightily did I enjoy Tilosa's message. Linking Matthew 19:1-6 with Ephesians 5:22-31 he gave as Scriptural, rich and captivating a talk on matrimony as I have ever heard. He is a remarkable young man, most attractive in his strength of character, clarity of thought, and bounding vitality. Then he proceeded to a further matter, the preparation of parents for the baptism of their children next Sunday! Do we ever have such a ceremony in England? In front of all the soldiers he rounded on one papa and said, "Why are you going to have your child baptised?" Three times he asked this and three times found the answer to be inadequate. So then he explained that it is because of sin, because we are descendants of Adam and Eve, that we need Christ and His baptism, and he dwelt at length on Acts 2: 38-39 in proof. At the end he asked me to lead in prayer and I was glad he did so, for in a secular hall and in the presence of members of the armed forces it represented a signal victory for Christ and for our oneness in Him. I had only gone at all at his insistence. This excellent afternoon ended when I drove Rufus, Mrs Rufus, and four of their children back to Ringit, sensing again the privilege of being associated with this simple, grand family. As we drew up at their humble abode we saw what is now a familiar sight there—the figure of Nasur already making himself at home. Abandoning his notion of accompanying me to England he has most sensibly made friends with Rufus' boys and spends a lot of his spare time at Ringit now.

On Sunday morning, *June 14th*, the Sabrang church was packed well beyond capacity with 120 people drawn from various villages and including twenty soldiers from Celebes. Passers-by on the main road stopped to stare at such a large crowd assembled around the door. Tilosa led the proceedings, which lasted for over three hours. After I had preached on John 7: 37-39 he baptised the children of eight Christian families living in Sabrang. For the most part these families have been little touched by the work of the Holy Spirit and remain rather aloof from those who have. The parents sat at the front throughout the meeting, grandmothers producing the babies at the right moment. They all derived from Christian villages and the baptism of their children is a reflection of Tilosa's determination to have the churches under his care properly organised; if families bear the Christian name then he maintains that their children ought to be baptised.

Once the baptisms were over Tilosa conducted the religious part of the wedding of the couple from Celebes. The bride, who was only seventeen (though she would have passed as twenty-seven) came forward and first of all he baptised her! He is remarkably "apt to teach" and took his time over the ceremony, mixing in strong exhortations and warning her, "This is only a beginning." It was a stiff ordeal for the girl, standing alone for so long.

Her wedding followed. The bridegroom looked very immature to my eyes, but it was a grand occasion and they could hardly have had a better start. Although Rufus was away preaching near the south coast it was a heart-warming reunion of scattered Christian forces and I was particularly glad to see Prak, the sailor from Gerbo, there; regular meetings are now held in his home and Tilosa has devoted much attention to the place. Susilo was also absent, marching twelve young men from Triwung up to a newly responsive area on the Great Volcano. The guerrilla leader operates best on his own. The work that Rufus and he launched can sail without them now!

The Young People's Fellowship has become entirely independent of us. There were thirty-three at its thirty-second meeting. The

x

teacher Wagini is in charge and she runs it delightfully. The progress she has made in knowledge of the Lord since the night when she sat late in our house to hear jazz from Australia is amazing. Subir is to be treasurer of the Young People's Fellowship, as he is now back from his three months' spell of duty in the mountains. He had been on duty all Saturday night, but was present at the baptisms and the wedding, ran the Pentecostal Sunday School at 3 p.m., attended the Young People's Fellowship at 5, and only retired to bed at 8 p.m. At the same hour Rufus and I were at Kedok. I must admit that the meeting was rather disappointing to me as there were only twenty present and fifteen of them were believers from Barek, so that I had to drop my planned talk and give a Bible exposition. Rufus, however, felt that it was a useful time. Headmaster Suprapto of Barek led, and it was no small victory that Chamim attended and that Suprapto asked him to lead us in prayer. The farmer whose visit to Dr Darmo sparked off the remarkable developments in Srengat was also present.

Jess has been on the run lately in our struggle to get exit and re-entry permits and paid three visits to Surabaja. Results up to date are fair and we crawl towards our goal, which is to clear Sabrang on July 13th. On one occasion when she was standing in a crowded train an elderly Javanese gentleman called out, "Now which of you young men is going to give that lady his seat?"

On *June 16th*, while Jess was seeing the police in the city two elderly Javanese ladies from Barek appeared on the verandah. They were among the first to turn to Christ after Rufus came to Ringit in 1956 and have been steadfast in faith and good works ever since. Knowing that our time was getting short they came to see us. It was really fun for me to entertain two old ladies who had not many teeth and were continually lapsing into Javanese. They gave us a present of eggs; I gave them tea and biscuits while we chatted about the gospel and prayed together. That night I went to the cottage meeting and expounded the story of the Gadarene demoniac to twenty people. It was a splendid opportunity as most of them were the parents whose children were baptised the previous Sunday, that is to say Christian-village Christians, who set such a lukewarm example to newer believers. Not one of them was present, however, at the forty-ninth Weekly Bible School the following evening. At its close, having as usual taken Mawardi and his girls home to the market at Ringit, I called on Rufus at 10 p.m. He was wearing a dark blue, polo-neck sweater. He told me that Dr Darmo of Srengat, where the eighty-nine were baptised on May 31st, had been over to beseech him and me to go again next Sunday as interest in the way of salvation was still spreading in the town. "I belive we can have a thousand souls this year," said the doctor, which is perhaps unlikely but may stand as typical of his outlook on the work of the Lord. I took the opportunity of asking Rufus whether he thought our Sabrang district was unusually ready for the gospel or whether there would be the same response anywhere if the church took the message of salvation to the people in a friendly, but aggressive way. After pausing for a few moments his reply was, "I don't think there is anything unusual about this district and I believe there would be just the same response anywhere in East Java."

On Sunday, *June 21st*, at 8 a.m., I set off for Srengat in the Mayflower with Mrs Rufus and Beth Anstis, an Australian member of the C.I.M. who is spending her holiday with us. We were away for eleven hours and it was in every sense a glorious day. I have never seen the Great Volcano so clear before and for the first time I realised that for thousands of feet below the crater its steep sides are lava-covered and all trees obliterated. Rufus and Tilosa had preceded us on Saturday night. Mother Pardi's farm was well filled with sixty-five people when the time for the morning service came. To their broad pulpit they have now added a notice board announcing the order of service and the hymns, and the men, instead of being packed behind the women, are suitably settled on benches the other side of the aisle, as is the universal custom in the East. Strictly speaking I was the preacher, but I soon realised that it would be wiser to lie low and let my chance come in due course. Tilosa led and preached forcefully himself on Genesis 7:16, "And the Lord shut him in", using the flood and the ark as an illustration of salvation and linking it up with 2 Peter 3 and Matthew 24:36-39. It was very well done and most interesting, although in the enjoyment of detail he tends to lose sight of his main point at times.

The service over, photographs were taken by Rufus and then we all streamed down the main road (a splendid sight!) and up a precipitous path through land loaded with coffee, coconuts, jackfruit, and all rich and lovely things, with the peak of the Great Volcano close ahead. At 2500 feet we came to a substantial farm with a great carpet of coffee beans laid out to dry on the threshing-floor. There had been a Christian wedding the previous day and the celebrations were now continued. While Tilosa and the church leaders conferred in a back room, Rufus led the company in singing and then called on me to speak. A meal followed and then more photographs were taken by Rufus and others, including one of the tall, tapering, toothless church grand-father who (amidst uproarious hilarity) was made to link arms with his wife. The joyfulness and comradeship of these Srengat believers are perfectly delightful. Rufus and I then walked with Dr Darmo to his home and clinic at the market, where we observed that we were but twenty yards from the café in which Jess, Rupert, Mawardi, Rufus, and I had had tea and given out tracts twenty months ago! The doctor told us that the previous night he met a 5-foot tiger at his back door playing with his colt; he stood quietly by the well and watched it at a range of two yards. We then went together to several homes, but it is not easy for me to have close fellowship with the Srengat believers, as even Dr Darmo has but a smattering of Indonesian and many of them cannot speak a word of it.

Mother Pardi, the Lydia of Srengat, is a remarkable character, full of cackle and fun, noisy and large hearted. Her only child is a daughter recently married and living close by, but she did not turn to the Lord when the Spirit began to work in Srengat in February. However, on *May 30th* Mawardi, Rekso, and others arrived a day ahead of the eighty-nine baptisms, along with Rufus. They had a meeting in Mother Pardi's home and at 2 a.m. on the 31st of the month Rufus retired to bed. Mawardi and Rekso, who had no special part to play next day, held forth till dawn and among their audience was this daughter and her husband. By break of day they had come to the point of desiring to join with the others in confessing Christ. They were baptised with the rest a few hours after this decision. I do not know whether Tilosa was aware of it and I very much doubt whether he would have approved if he had been. Obviously risks are taken on such occasions, but Rufus seems to hold to the view that a greater risk is taken if Muslims are held off at a time when they are ready to identify themselves with the Christian church. In this manner, rightly or wrongly, the whole family stood together in their new allegiance. When at last we escaped from Srengat, Mother Pardi filled the boot of the Mayflower with fruit and vegetables and thrust ten rupiah notes into the hands of each of Rufus' children.

Thank God the little car went well and we were back at Sabrang before the Young People's Fellowship on our verandah had broken up. Immediately there began to burst upon us what was to prove virtually the concluding episode of these tumultuous years. Dr Suharta of Trawas came over from the hospital to say that his wife had just given birth to Siamese twins, which had died. She was very ill and he was standing by her, so we took a meal across to him late at night and towards midnight Jess drove some of his family home to Gerbo, taking Loti for company on the way back. Dr Suharta has never seemed to me to be a very bright or instructed Christian but it was good to hear the Doctor's testimony to the faithful way in which he had cared for his wife in the crisis. It appears he stood by her bed the whole of the first night before going back to his clinic at Trawas at dawn. Knowing that he was now about to stand up for the second night running we were so bold as to march into the hospital carrying a mattress which we laid beside her bed so that he might at least have some chance of rest. Next morning she was so much better that the hospital staff suggested he need not return in the evening but could sleep himself out at home.

And then the end began to draw very near, so far as we were concerned. It has been decided that we rent this house during our furlough as that will be cheaper than moving our furniture and belongings to the city, and it will also give us a base to which we can return next year. Arrangements for the meetings hitherto held at No. 122 pose quite a problem for Tilosa. At best they must move to the Sabrang church a mile away, but there are some, such as Riti, who will not want to go as far as that and there are others who do not want to enter a church at all. We are standing back and leaving all decisions to Tilosa.

Towards midnight on *June 25th-26th* we were awakened by hammering on our front door and the news that Mrs Suharta was sinking fast. I was asked to help in getting hold of Dr Suharta from Trawas, thirty miles away through the wild, tangled country south of the Great Volcano. Leaving Loti to keep an ear open for Rupert in case he woke, Jess spent the rest of the night at the hospital, while I piloted the Mayflower round the innumerable hairpins and steep ascents on the silent, moonlit mountain road past Ringit, Barek, Kedok, Gerbo, and Segaran. A young male nurse from the hospital came with me as I did not want to be alone in such remote parts at dead of night. Actually we missed Dr Suharta. As we turned into Trawas a policeman stood in the road flashing a red light; a phone message had warned him that I was coming. He told me that the doctor had already gone in a jeep but that other members of the family would like a lift with me. On the way back we were halted again by the police at the check-point in Gerbo, but everybody seemed to know of the affair and hurriedly passed us through.

The whole of the next day was taken up with this matter as the Doctor struggled to save her, stripped to his singlet in the heat. About noon he asked me to interpret to the husband for him. We sat in the living-room at the hospital and I marvelled at Dr Suharta's courageous bearing as the Doctor told him he thought his wife might still have a fifty-fifty chance. The Mayflower went back and forth all day long, with either Jess or myself at the wheel, collecting Christians to pray and helping many relatives to get from or to buses. With Loti and Yeny we ran a continuous buffet service from our home to the lawns of the hospital around the private ward where Mrs Suharta lay unconscious. Twenty or thirty relatives and Christians were constantly in or near the room and there were repeated periods of prayer. One of the relatives gave his blood to try to hold her. The quietness, sympathy and patience of those who kept vigil were really impressive. In fact it was to me yet another example of the reality of the faith of the Christian villages, from one of which the Suharta family derives. At long last Tilosa and Rufus arrived from journeys to distant places. The event grew to be one of the main experiences we have shared with our Javanese friends. As I write these words Dr Suharta, his wife's brother, and one of his little boys are asleep in my office. We have beds rigged up all over the house for those who can snatch a little rest. Mrs Suharta has had nine other children, of whom six are living. She married at eleven, so her exalted age is only thirty.

For the second night of acute danger six men and six women settled down at the hospital to watch by her bed. I wondered whether so many would have been found to do so in our own country. We provided drinks and coats against the chill night air. Jess was with them, indeed in sixty hours she had only two hours' sleep. I stayed with Rupert, but there were again comings and goings at our home throughout the night. She died at 7 a.m. Her husband, their children, and several other relatives, came straight over to our verandah and rested in easy chairs, as Susilo and his wife had done years before when their child died. We truly admired them; the husband kept saying, "She is with the Lord. She is all right."

In this climate funerals must follow at once. They moved the body to her husband's parents' home in a big village five miles outside the city. We took Dr Suharta and his children and then returned there again at 2 p.m. for the ceremony. We had to park the car on the main road and walk for a mile down a lane continuously packed with houses several rows deep, with repeated, equally congested turnings off it. On arrival we found the house full and the coffin covered with flowers. We were unable to get in, so stood outside with many others. The company was a mixed Christian and Muslim one; the spokesman for the family in his address at the end was gracious enough to thank us for our help. We did not go to the graveside but ferried visitors back to Sabrang. Barely had we straightened up our house when Dr Suharta, his children, and other relatives came on to the verandah. I snatched a meal, which they had already had, and then drove them to Trawas, thirty miles each way in the darkness and the pouring rain. They were very brave and the children thrilled with delight as their house came in sight. I drove home carefully in the deluge; strangely enough it was the very first time that I had ever been alone in the car far out in the country at night.

Next morning I preached for the fifteenth and last time in the Sabrang church, speaking from Acts 20:32, "And now, brethren, I commend you to God and to the word of His grace, which is able to build you up and to give you an inheritance among all them which are sanctified." There were forty-eight present, the majority new believers. Meanwhile the Doctor went straight into another struggle almost as acute as that for Mrs Suharta and through a window I observed him and Jeannette masked and in action in the operating theatre. The combination of hospital and church is ideal and an ever-increasing circle of people have to thank God upon every remembrance of the Doctor.

And I have not mentioned the very latest recruit to the forces of Christ in Sabrang—Lantip, the young teacher at whose wedding reception I spoke years ago in Karangan. He was brought up a Muslim and sent to teach in the school at Karangan, where he fell in love with a Christian girl and turned Christian in order to marry her. In his case at least a genuine spiritual experience was involved in this procedure and he has thrown himself gleefully into all church activities here, especially among young people, which has greatly strengthened the hands of Wagini. In the Sabrang church this morning it was Lantip who conducted the choir, and he did it in the most professional manner.

We now learn that Lukas, the doctor at Gondang, married a second wife in the years before he turned to Christ. It was for his sake that Tilosa was absent during the Suharta crisis, acting as middleman to arrange a separation. He excels in such practical matters and there are plenty of them to be handled when many Christians have but recently come out of such great darkness. One of the new believers at Srengat said to me, "I had four marriages and four divorces last year alone."

June 28th. The thirty-fifth, and so far as we are concerned, the last Young People's Fellowship was attended by thirty people on our verandah and led by Nasur—a delightful touch. The speaker was Lantip, the ex-Muslim teacher, and he expounded Ephesians 2:10, "We are His workmanship, created in Christ Jesus unto good works which God hath before ordained that we should walk in them." When he had finished, Nasur, in his comical way, sat down with determination, laid an Indonesian and a Javanese New Testament on the table and announced, "By way of experiment I will now preach a little myself." Lantip has already drawn back into Christian fellowship the son of Natmina, a teacher who was baptised by Rufus some years ago, but has rarely associated with Christians recently, being shy to attend without a suitable companion. At night I preached at the hospital to forty-five people, most of them strangers and Muslims.

Next morning Susilo appeared. We have seen little of him in recent months but he seems to have lost nothing of his zeal. A Chinese patient from the hospital dropped in and Susilo spoke to him about Christ so easily and attractively. It appears that after Mrs Suharta's funeral, when most of us escaped home to recover, Susilo, who only arrived just before she died, stayed on to comfort and witness to her relatives, many of them Muslims. He also showed me a letter from a teacher in a distant town, a son of Daddy Tain. Apparently this man listened to gramophone records on our verandah once and also bought a hymnbook and a New Testament. He has recently been baptised.

For the last Children's Meeting in our house we had forty boys and girls with us. Tilosa came too, for there has been some difficulty over the future of this meeting, which is attended chiefly by children from Muslim homes. His plan is to hold it at 8 a.m. on Sundays in the Sabrang church. Having had the children with us for years we know them much better than he does, so we pointed out that most of them attend the Sunday School in the hospital at exactly that time, and also that the death of Kardjo's child just after leaving the Sabrang church has made such a deep impression that no Muslim family would permit their children to enter the church, and that his plan would be likely to kill the meeting. However, he is a man who knows his own mind, and he insisted that it is time the Sabrang church had its own Sunday School, held on Sunday and in its own hands, irrespective of what the Salvation Army hospital might do. He said he could not be responsible for those who were unwilling to come to the church. Jess besought him to consider the souls of these children who have long been accustomed to choruses and Bible stories. Her remarks were not easy for him to receive but later he said to me, "You know, it was hard at the time, but it took my mind back to the text I used at my induction, 1 Corinthians 2:2, 'I determined not to know anything among you, save Jesus Christ, and Him crucified', and indeed to 1 Corinthians 9:16, 'Woe is unto me if I preach not the gospel'." What will be done once we have gone I really do not know. Rufus thinks above all of the good of souls. Tilosa's special mission is the right ordering of the Church, thus his duty to "Christians" is uppermost in his mind. In spite of the splendid singing of the children, he remained on the verandah and never actually saw what was taking place.

I was very glad that he and I were together that same evening for my last visit to Segaran, where the meeting was held in the home of a local official hard by the market. Tilosa spoke on Romans 3:23, I on the Gadarene demoniac, and Rufus on John 10:9-10. There were fifty people present, seated at long tables, almost every one of them new believers during the past fifteen months. The singing was vigorous and it was refreshing to notice many New Testaments on the tables; a few years ago only hymnbooks would have been visible. Wirojo sat by me and we had a long talk together when refreshments were served. He told me that his wife, with whose response to Susilo's message the whole movement of the Spirit of God in Segaran began, is Madurese, both her parents having been born on the island. Towards midnight we broke up, singing "God be with you till we meet again," everyone shaking hands with us as the song was repeated. Outside wags tied old tin cans to the Mayflower's bumpers and when these had been removed we sped swiftly home through the silent countryside.

Then on Wednesday, *July 1st*, we came to the fifty-first and last Weekly Bible School to be held on our verandah, seventeen months exactly from the day we began it. It was the longest of all these gatherings, attended by forty-five adults and ten children, a glorious assembly of the Sabrang-Ringit forces. I finished off the Epistle of Paul to the Colossians in the earlier half of the evening and we concluded with Nehemiah building the walls of Jerusalem in spite of every discouragement. By the time the last guest had departed four and a half hours had passed. This was the last meeting held in our home.

Nasur borrowed our gramophone for two days and his strongly Muslim family has been drinking in the gospel off twenty-nine different records.

After that the disposal and packing of our belongings became a primary claim upon our time, till on Sunday, *July 5th*, we drove to Paru Christian village with Rufus. I led and preached at the morning service, attended by about 300 souls. It was my first formal sermon there and the only time that a Christian village pulpit has ever been entirely surrendered to me. Four different choirs sang. There was no Bible apparent in the whole congregation except for those of Rufus, Jess, and myself. At the end we sat for a long time with the church leaders, and were glad to do so, since formerly none of us were welcome in Paru. By going there we deliberately avoided the Young People's Fellowship at Sabrang. Now that this and other gatherings have been committed to different hands we feel that we should stand back and leave them free to make what changes they wish. And it is inevitable that there will be big changes, not necessarily of a kind which we should consider beneficial. Some things will be done in a more Javanese way, and if some are not done at all we need not therefore regret having done them! At such a time one inevitably asks oneself, Is a man's work to be judged by what happens to it after he leaves? Partly perhaps, but I am persuaded that it is not entirely so. Paul knew that wolves would follow his own labours at Ephesus and even that some, whom he had had three years to influence, would "draw away disciples after them". That was all part of the battle for the souls of men, not proof of his incompetence or of the wrongness of his methods.

Then we decided that it was time we moved away altogether, chiefly to pursue more effectively our exit and re-entry visas in the city and in Surabaja, so we set Thursday, July 9th, as zero hour, instead of July 13th, thus avoiding another Sunday in Sabrang. Rufus wanted me to go to Srengat once more with him, but we felt that the time for long trips and late nights was over. Thus our last expedition together was the one to Paru.

Right to the end Loti, Yeny, and Man served us most cheerfully and unstintingly. On *July 6th* there was the usual Sabrang-Ringit cottage meeting, held this time in the home of Subir the policeman with no less than seventy present. Subir remains a most faithful and attractive witness for Christ. Tilosa led and spoke, giving good measure. I sat by Mawardi, who diligently looked up in his New Testament every verse that Tilosa mentioned. Best of all, Mr and Mrs Kardjo were there. He appeared suddenly at night at our home, looking happy and cheerful after a strenuous spell of guard duty at a remote plantation which was being constantly raided by six armed men. In the end Kardjo and his companions got them and then he asked for leave to return to Sabrang, knowing that our departure was imminent. This seemed to me evidence of his genuine desire to be the Lord's in spite of all that has happened, for had he wished to avoid us and other Christians he had a perfect alibi on the plantation.

On *July 7th* we kept our doors closed and packed and sorted day and night. *July 8th* was our last full day in Sabrang and I can remember little about it except the evening when a Valedictory Meeting was held for us in the Sabrang church. I think there were 160 people crammed into the tiny place, Mrs Rekso's bedroom, representing the believers from Sabrang, Ringit, Triwung, Barek, Gerbo, Gondang, and Segaran. Of course distance cut out many others, including all at Srengat, but with this exception the company was a grand epitome of our years here, for 90 per cent of them were close friends, each face a reminder of events in the past and of the marvellous grace of God. Lantip, the new teacher, was master of ceremonies. How little one dreamed of such a thing on the day when I spoke at his wedding reception down at Karangan! Tilosa and Suwarso sat at a side-table. Jess, Rupert, and I were at a central table and we prevailed upon Rufus to sit with us and cover our embarrassment. Tilosa preached first, followed by me. My text was Acts 14:22, "Confirming the souls of the disciples and exhorting them to continue in the faith and that we must through much tribulation enter into the kingdom of God". Various representatives of the churches had their say and finally Rufus preached on "Your feet shod with the preparation of the gospel of peace". Presentations were made and Jess expressed our thanks. Of course we could not control what folk said and there was an element of courteous back-patting in which the whole movement towards Christ was credited to us, and Rufus was entirely overlooked (not for the first time!). Yet glory was given to God and we were deeply moved at the warmth of love and Christian fellowship which pervaded all. Especially in these days of racial ill-will it was a demonstration of the uniting power of faith in Christ. At the end we both stood at the door and, not without feeling, shook hands with every soul. The Samaritan woman, in a typically independent gesture, bowed low and kissed my hand. Wirojo, Lukas, Sumali, Susilo, Subir, Kardjo, Wagini, Mawardi, and all our closest associates parted with us there. Finally, towards midnight, I stood in the road alone with Tilosa and Rufus, and then we also had to part. We were up most of the night and got away at 8 a.m. on *July 9th*, twenty-nine months after our arrival, Loti, Yeny, Mother Daro, and Man standing in a small and rather tearful group to bid us farewell. We moved slowly through Sabrang, jumping out of the car repeatedly to shake hands with people. Then we got away to Lakar, where we met Hasan the Madurese on the road, and so to the city.

All then depended on getting our exit and re-entry permits, so I went straight on to Surabaja and back, spending four hours in taxis. Next day we all went there and came within a hair's breadth of success in this long-drawn-out business. I stayed in the city overnight at Mrs Tan's and succeeded in securing them next morning. By this time Jess had a touch of malaria, so I drove back to Sabrang alone to put the final touches to closing up our house. It was dark before every last detail was finished, and I decided to slip round to Ringit for a final visit to Rufus. Happily he and Mrs Rufus and all their children were at home and there were no guests with them. We sat together for half an hour reviewing all the Lord's goodness to us and the wonderful works of God which we had had the immense privilege of witnessing together. Rufus prayed for fully fifteen minutes at the end and told me that after our furlough he hoped it would be possible for us to work together again, as he felt we could do more for Christ in that way than by functioning separately. And so at last I escaped into the darkness of the night. I decided to meet no one else, but drove quietly through Ringit and

Sabrang and then northwards to where the lights of the city were once again illuminating the evening sky. And so unto Him that is able to keep His children from falling and to present them faultless before the presence of His glory with exceeding joy, to the only wise God, our Saviour, be glory and majesty, dominion and power, both now and ever, Amen.

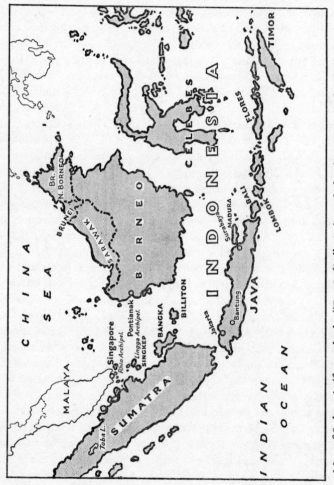

Map of Indonesia (formerly the "East Indies"), indicated, for the most part, by shaded areas.

DRAMATIS PERSONAE

Rufus	A Christian minister	Sabrang
Budi	A young man	Karangan
Tilosa	A young man, later a Christian minister	Karangan
Mawardi	A pensioned factory worker	Ringit
Rekso	A village wise man	Ringit
Chamim	A farmer	Barek
Susilo	A government official	Triwung
Sutikno	A Christian minister	Madura
Mother Daro	A landowner	Sabrang
Man	Her servant	Sabrang
Yeny	A girl, our servant	Sabrang
Mrs. Rakes	A widow	Sabrang
Pooh	A small boy	Sabrang
Riti	His older sister	Sabrang
Misli	His second sister	Sabrang
Suharta	A doctor	Trawas
Tias	A headmaster	Gondang
Lukas	A doctor	Gondang
Loti	A widow, our servant	Sabrang
Suwarso	A headmaster	Sabrang
Hasan	An engineer	Lakar
Sri	A mad woman	Sabrang
Wagini	A girl, a school-teacher	Sabrang
Hastari	A farmer	Triwung
Daddy Tain	His father	Triwung
Samari	A schoolboy	Sabrang
Muljono	Head of a village	Kabat
Suprapto	A headmaster	Barek
Lantip	A young school-master	Karangan
Akas	A business man	Surabaja
Sugiono	A farmer	Barek
Wirojo	A village secretary	Segaran

Wen	A Christian minister	Kabat
Sumantri	A man from outside Java	Segaran
Sudjono	A farmer	Tulen
Natmina	A housewife	Sabrang
Faral	A Christian minister	The city
Rubani	A Christian minister	The city
Rifai	An elderly man	Near Sabrang
Daddy Ren	A village wise man	Segaran
Sumali	Ex-head of a village	Gondang
Sardjonan	A man from West Java	Sabrang
Subir	A policeman	Sabrang
Kardjo	A policeman	Sabrang
Nasur	A salesman	Sabrang
Sari	An old widow	Sabrang
Prak	A retired sailor	Gerbo
Darmo	A doctor	Srengat
Mother Pardi	A farmer's wife	Srengat